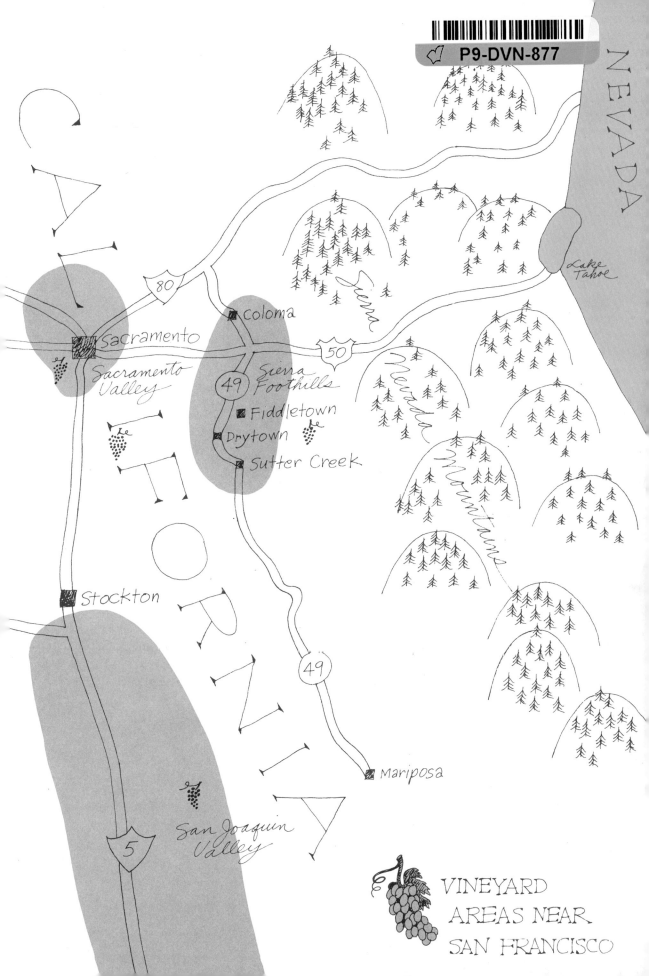

NEVADA

Lake Tahoe

80

coloma

Sacramento

50

Sacramento Valley

49

Sierra Foothills

Fiddletown

Drytown

Sutter Creek

Sierra

Nevada

Mountains

Stockton

49

Mariposa

5

San Joaquin Valley

CALIFORNIA

VINEYARD
AREAS NEAR
SAN FRANCISCO

SAN FRANCISCO
ENCORE

Other Books by The Junior League of San Francisco

SAN FRANCISCO A LA CARTE: *A Cookbook*
HERE TODAY: *San Francisco's Architectural Heritage*

SAN FRANCISCO

The Junior League

DOUBLEDAY
NEW YORK   LONDON   TORONTO   SYDNEY   AUCKLAND

ENCORE A COOKBOOK

of San Francisco

Illustrations by Earl Thollander

As the Junior League of San Francisco celebrates its seventy-five years of community service in this year, 1986, we also celebrate the release of our newest cookbook, *San Francisco Encore.*

Founded in 1911, the purpose of our organization is to train women to be effective community volunteers. Our founding purpose has withstood the test of time and is as valid today as it was seventy-five years ago. As the San Francisco Bay area population has grown and diversified, our Junior League community program has also responded to reflect the needs of people. The Junior League truly acts as a bridge to the community— funding projects in the areas of health, welfare, the arts, the environment, women's issues, and technical assistance for other agencies.

Although the Junior League of San Francisco is supported not only by individuals, but by corporations, foundations, and the general community, we realize that quality programs succeed only with adequate funding. We are continuously seeking new ways of raising funds, and our new cookbook, *San Francisco Encore,* will help our organization maintain a vital community program.

The Junior League of San Francisco

Published by DOUBLEDAY, a division of Bantam Doubleday Dell Publishing Group, Inc., 666 Fifth Avenue, New York, New York 10103.

DOUBLEDAY and the portrayal of an anchor with a dolphin are trademarks of Doubleday, a division of Bantam Doubleday Dell Publishing Group, Inc.

DESIGN BY M. FRANKLIN-PLYMPTON

Library of Congress Cataloging-in-Publication Data
San Francisco encore.
Includes index.
1. Cookery, American—California style. 2. San Francisco (Calif.)—Social life and customs. I. Junior League of San Francisco.
TX715.S182   1986   641.5   85-31107
ISBN 0-385-19237-1

Acknowledgments

The Junior League of San Francisco, Inc., would like to thank those whose diligence and commitment have made this book possible: members and friends who donated recipes; the test kitchen participants whose thoroughness, time, and talents have assured the quality of this book; the sustainers who helped and supported us in this endeavor; the writers; and the many people whose assistance, advice, and support were so vital.

| CHAIRMAN: | Janice Herwick | 1983–1985 |
| | Nancy Clock | 1985–1986 |

EDITORS IN CHIEF: Janice Herwick
Elaine Printz

EDITORS: Madeline Camisa
Nancy Clock

RECIPE RESEARCH
AND DEVELOPMENT: Janice Herwick
Elaine Printz

RECIPE COORDINATOR: Nancee Rubinstein

TESTERS: Mary Ann Athearn
Margaret Barton
Laurie Benson
Usha Burns
Elizabeth Cannon
Linda Castle
Margot Cookson
Letitia Devlin
Kristi Filter
Yvonne Fortier
Barbara Gloger
Marjorie Helfet
Marcella Howard
Lander Hynes
Karen Irvin

CONTENTS

HOW TO USE THIS BOOK

Whenever the name of a recipe is followed by a †, the recipe is included elsewhere in the book; consult Index for page numbers.

SAN FRANCISCO
ENCORE

THE BASICS

Napa Valley

Just as basic stocks and sauces provide a basis upon which many fine recipes are built, any discussion of the California wine country must begin with the Napa Valley. Napa Valley is at the heart of California's wine tradition. Rich in history, high in wine production and number of wineries, its fame lies also in the excellence of its fine varietal wines (those wines named for the variety of wine grapes from which they were made).

As one enters Napa Valley at its southern end, the wide, flat valley stretches several miles from side to side. Driving north through the valley, the visitor is immediately impressed with the prominent role that viticulture plays, as vineyards stretch as far as the eye can see. Traveling up Highway 29, the famous Wine Way running up the western side of the valley, one comes to a string of famous wineries that offer daily wine tours and wine-tasting. On the eastern side, the picturesque Silverado Trail winds from one end of the valley to the other, where another dozen wineries with colorful names can be found. The Silverado Trail was named after Robert Louis Stevenson's novel, *The Silverado Squatters.* Stevenson's descriptions of life in the 1860s in Napa Valley include a chapter on Napa wine: and today large roadside signs on Highway 29 quote: "The wine is bottled poetry."

Napa Valley is a popular weekend destination for San Franciscans the year round, as it is a mere hours drive from the city. A graceful valley with rounded hills running along the western and eastern edges, Napa Valley has its southern edge, the city of Napa, which is the county seat and a predominate business center. North of Napa, the vineyards begin in earnest, and a string of colorful towns—Yountville, Oakville, Rutherford, St. Helena, and Calistoga—parallel railroad tracks which once served as the chief means of transportation for city dwellers bound for the warm climate and restorative baths. Today, the visitor can find splendidly restored Victorians and old brick wineries converted into shops, restaurants, and inns for year-round visits. The relatively flat terrain of the valley floor is especially inviting for cyclists.

Of all California's wine-growing regions, Napa Valley offers the greatest choice of wineries, restaurants, shops, and historical sites—all within easy reach. In the chapters that follow, we encourage you to explore and enjoy the wide variety of recipes offered and to sample, as well, the wide spectrum of California wines available from all of the wine-growing regions of the San Francisco Bay area.

BEEF STOCK

MAKES ABOUT 2 QUARTS
PREPARATION TIME 10 MINUTES
COOKING TIME 6 HOURS
REFRIGERATION TIME 8 HOURS

Beef stock is made in much the same way as chicken stock. However, the bones and vegetables are browned before starting, resulting in a rich brown stock. Always start your stocks with cold water and never add salt.

2 tablespoons oil
3 pounds beef bones
3 pounds veal bones or chicken bones
1 large onion stuck with 4 whole cloves
1 leek, washed, trimmed, and coarsely chopped
2 carrots, peeled and chopped
2 celery stalks, peeled and chopped
6 fresh parsley sprigs
6 quarts water
1 bay leaf
1 teaspoon whole black peppercorns
1/2 teaspoon thyme

Preheat oven to 400 degrees. Place the oil in the bottom of a shallow roasting pan. Add the bones, onion, leek, carrots, celery, and parsley. Bake in the oven until nicely browned, about 20 to 30 minutes. Transfer to a large stock pot.

Pour 1 cup of the water into the roasting pan. Bring to a boil over high heat, scraping the brown bits that cling to the bottom of the pan. Pour the entire contents of the pan into the stock pot. Add the remaining water, bay leaf, peppercorns, and thyme. Bring to a slow boil over low heat, skimming off and discarding the foam and scum as they rise to the top. Simmer the stock for 6 hours. Follow the straining and cooling procedure described for the chicken stock.

CHICKEN STOCK

MAKES ABOUT 2 QUARTS
PREPARATION TIME 10 MINUTES
COOKING TIME 6 HOURS
REFRIGERATION TIME 8 HOURS

Although the cooking of stocks takes many hours, the procedure requires little supervision. The finished stocks may be refrigerated for 3 or 4 days or frozen for up to 6 months. Canned broths cannot be considered an acceptable substitute for the homemade varieties.

3 pounds chicken bones, wings, necks, and backs
3 pounds veal bones
6 quarts cold water
2 onions, peeled and coarsely chopped
2 carrots, peeled and coarsely chopped
2 celery stalks, peeled and coarsely chopped
5 fresh parsley sprigs
1/2 teaspoon dried thyme
1 bay leaf
1 teaspoon whole black peppercorns

Combine the bones and water in a large stock pot. Bring slowly to a boil, skimming off and discarding the foam and scum as they rise to the surface. Reduce the heat and simmer, uncovered, for 30 minutes. Add the remaining ingredients. Stir, partially cover and simmer for 5 to 6 hours, skimming as necessary.

With a slotted spoon, pick out and discard the bones. Strain the stock through a sieve lined with a double thickness of dampened cheesecloth. Discard the vegetables. Let the stock cool to room temperature. Refrigerate, uncovered, until thoroughly chilled and the surface has a layer of solidified fat. Before using, carefully lift off and discard the fat.

FISH STOCK

MAKES 2 QUARTS
PREPARATION TIME 10 MINUTES
COOKING TIME 1 HOUR

This stock can be cooled to room temperature, poured into a container and frozen.

2 pounds white fish trimmings, heads, tails, and bones
2 quarts water
1 cup dry white wine
1 shallot, coarsely chopped
1 onion, coarsely chopped
1 carrot, coarsely chopped
1 celery stalk, coarsely chopped
1 bay leaf
1/2 teaspoon dried thyme
5 whole black peppercorns

Place the fish trimmings, water, and wine in a stock pot. Bring slowly to a boil, skimming off the foam and scum as they rise to the surface. Add the remaining ingredients. Reduce heat to low. Partially cover pan and simmer for 1 hour.

With a slotted spoon, lift out and discard the fish bones and vegetables. Strain the stock through a strainer lined with a double thickness of dampened cheesecloth.

BROWN SAUCE (SAUCE ESPAGNOLE)

MAKES 3 TO 4 CUPS
PREPARATION TIME 10 MINUTES
COOKING TIME 1 1/2 HOURS

This is a basic brown sauce that serves as a base for many other sauces.

4 tablespoons butter
1 small onion, finely chopped
1 stalk celery, peeled and finely chopped
1 carrot, peeled and finely chopped
3 tablespoons flour
1 tomato, peeled, seeded, and finely chopped
2 tablespoons tomato purée
3 cups beef stock
1/4 cup dry sherry
1 bay leaf
Fresh parsley sprigs
Salt
Freshly ground pepper

In a saucepan, melt the butter. Add the onion, celery, and carrot. Cook until soft and lightly browned, about 5 minutes. Stir in the flour and cook for 2 minutes. Add tomato, tomato purée, beef stock, sherry, bay leaf, and parsley. Simmer, uncovered, for 1 1/2 hours. Put the sauce through a food mill or strainer. Season to taste with salt and pepper. The sauce may be used at once or cooled to room temperature. Brown Sauce can be frozen for several months.

SAUCE BORDELAISE

MAKES 2 1/2 CUPS
PREPARATION TIME 10 MINUTES
COOKING TIME 30 MINUTES

A red-wine sauce with shallots and beef marrow. You can leave out the marrow, if desired. Good over beef.

2 ounces beef marrow
1 cup red wine
1/2 cup finely chopped shallots
1/8 teaspoon dried thyme
1 cup Brown Sauce†

2 tablespoons chopped fresh parsley
Salt
Freshly ground pepper

Dice the beef marrow and place in a small bowl. Pour over enough boiling water to cover completely. Let stand for 1 minute. Drain and pat dry with paper towels. Set aside.

In a saucepan, combine the wine, shallots, and thyme. Bring to a boil over high heat. Cook briskly until the mixture has reduced to 1/2 cup. Add the Brown Sauce and simmer over low heat for 20 minutes. Just before serving, stir the diced marrow and parsley into the sauce. Season to taste with salt and pepper.

MADEIRA SAUCE

MAKES 2 CUPS
PREPARATION TIME 10 MINUTES
COOKING TIME 10 MINUTES

1/2 **pound fresh mushrooms,**
  thinly sliced
4 **tablespoons butter**

2 **cups Brown Sauce†**
1/2 **cup Madeira wine**
1 **tablespoon brandy**

Over high heat, sauté the mushrooms in the butter until golden. Add Brown Sauce and boil to reduce slightly. Stir in the Madeira and brandy. Heat to the boiling point. Lower heat and simmer for 5 minutes. Taste and adjust seasonings.

HUNTER'S SAUCE

MAKES 3 CUPS
PREPARATION TIME 15 MINUTES
COOKING TIME 10 MINUTES

Particularly good over chicken and lamb, especially when cooked in pastry.

4 **tablespoons butter**
2 **tablespoons oil**
1/4 **pound fresh mushrooms,**
  sliced
2 **teaspoons chopped shallots**

2 **tomatoes, peeled, seeded, and**
  chopped
2 **cups dry white wine**
1 **cup Brown Sauce†**
Fresh chopped parsley

In a skillet, heat the butter and oil. Add the mushrooms and sauté over high heat. Stir in the shallots, tomatoes, and wine. Cook until reduced by half. Stir in Brown Sauce. Cook for 5 minutes. Taste and adjust seasonings. Just before serving, stir in parsley.

TOMATO SAUCE

MAKES 4 CUPS
PREPARATION TIME 10 MINUTES
COOKING TIME 45 MINUTES

1/2 cup olive oil
1/2 cup finely chopped onion
1/4 cup finely chopped celery
1/4 cup finely chopped carrot
3 cups canned Italian plum
   tomatoes puréed with their
   juices, and strained

1 teaspoon salt
1/4 teaspoon sugar
Freshly ground pepper

Heat the oil in a large saucepan. Add the onion and sauté until soft but not browned. Stir in celery and carrot and sauté for an additional minute. Add the tomatoes, salt, sugar, and pepper to taste. Simmer, uncovered for 40 to 45 minutes. Purée through a food mill, if desired.

FRESH TOMATO SAUCE

MAKES 2 CUPS
PREPARATION TIME 10 MINUTES
COOKING TIME 10 MINUTES

Good over fish, vegetable pâtés, or pasta salads.

3 tablespoons butter
6 large fresh ripe tomatoes,
   peeled, seeded, and chopped

Salt
Freshly ground pepper

Heat the butter in a saucepan or skillet. Stir in the tomatoes and heat for 1 minute. Immediately remove from heat and cover. Let stand for 10 minutes. Season to taste with salt and pepper. Serve at room temperature or cold.

MARINARA SAUCE

MAKES 4 CUPS
PREPARATION TIME 10 MINUTES
COOKING TIME 45 MINUTES

3 tablespoons olive oil
3 cloves garlic, chopped
1 onion, chopped
1 carrot, peeled and chopped
1 28-ounce can Italian plum
    tomatoes, chopped

4 fresh tomatoes, diced
1 teaspoon salt
1 teaspoon dried oregano
1/2 teaspoon dried thyme
1/2 teaspoon dried basil
Freshly ground pepper

Heat the olive oil in a saucepan. Add the garlic, onion, and carrot; sauté until soft, about 10 minutes. Add the tomatoes and simmer for 10 minutes. Stir in the remaining ingredients. Simmer, uncovered, for an additional 30 minutes. The sauce should be nicely thickened. If not, cook longer.

SPICY TOMATO SAUCE

MAKES 4 CUPS
PREPARATION TIME 25 MINUTES
COOKING TIME 40 MINUTES

4 tablespoons olive oil
2 cloves chopped garlic
1/2 cup finely chopped onion
1/2 cup finely chopped green
    bell pepper
6 tomatoes, peeled, seeded, and
    chopped
3 tablespoons tomato paste

1/2 cup chicken stock
2 teaspoons freshly ground
    pepper
1 teaspoon salt
1/2 teaspoon dried oregano
1/2 teaspoon red pepper flakes
Dash of Tabasco sauce
1/2 cup chopped fresh parsley

Heat the olive oil in a large saucepan. Add the garlic, onion, and bell pepper. Sauté until softened, about 10 minutes. Stir in all the remaining ingredients, except the parsley. Cover and simmer for 45 minutes. Purée in a food processor. Return to the saucepan and reduce if too thin. Stir in parsley just before serving.

BEURRE BLANC

MAKES 1 CUP
PREPARATION TIME 10 MINUTES
COOKING TIME 5 MINUTES

This delicate wine-butter sauce will separate if it gets too hot. Delicious on grilled fish or steak.

1/2 cup dry white wine
1/2 cup white wine vinegar
2 shallots, finely chopped
8 ounces (2 sticks) unsalted
  butter, softened

2 tablespoons chopped fresh
  parsley
Salt
White pepper

In a saucepan, simmer white wine, vinegar, and shallots until reduced to 2 tablespoons. Remove from the heat and cool slightly. Over a very low flame, whisk in the softened butter, bit by bit. Remove from the heat and continue whisking for an additional minute. The sauce should be thick and creamy. Stir in the parsley, salt, and pepper to taste.

BÉARNAISE SAUCE

MAKES ABOUT 1 CUP
PREPARATION TIME 5 MINUTES
COOKING TIME 10 MINUTES

1/4 cup dry white wine
1/4 cup white wine vinegar
2 tablespoons minced shallots
1 teaspoon dried tarragon
1 teaspoon dried chervil
Freshly ground pepper
3 egg yolks

8 ounces (2 sticks) unsalted
  butter, softened
1 tablespoon fresh minced
  tarragon
1 tablespoon fresh minced
  parsley

In a saucepan, combine the wine, vinegar, shallots, dried herbs, and pepper. Cook over low heat until the liquid has reduced by half. Strain and cool.

    Beat the egg yolks until thick. Beat in the vinegar mixture. Place in a double boiler set over hot water. Whisk in the butter bit by bit, until nicely thickened. Stir in the fresh herbs.

BÉCHAMEL SAUCE

MAKES 2 CUPS
PREPARATION TIME 5 MINUTES
COOKING TIME 5 MINUTES

4 tablespoons butter
4 tablespoons flour
2 cups milk, room temperature

Salt
White pepper
Pinch of nutmeg

In a saucepan, melt the butter. Add the flour and cook over low heat for 1 minute without browning. Gradually add the milk, stirring constantly. Bring to a boil and simmer gently until the sauce has thickened. Season to taste with salt, pepper, and a few grindings of fresh nutmeg.

MAYONNAISE

MAKES ABOUT 2 CUPS
PREPARATION TIME 5 MINUTES

Have all ingredients at room temperature. The mayonnaise will keep at least 5 days under refrigeration.

2 egg yolks
1 tablespoon lemon juice
1 teaspoon Dijon mustard

1/2 teaspoon salt
Dash of white pepper
1 cup vegetable or olive oil

In a bowl, combine the egg yolks, half the lemon juice, Dijon mustard, salt, and pepper. Beat vigorously with a wire whisk. Add 1/4 cup of the oil, drop by drop, whisking constantly. Add the remaining lemon juice. Finish whisking in the oil in a steady stream. Taste and adjust seasonings, if necessary. Transfer to a storage container. Cover and refrigerate until ready to use.

The mayonnaise can also be made in a food processor. Combine the yolks, half of the lemon juice, mustard, salt, and pepper in the bowl of the processor fitted with a steel blade. Process for 1 minute. With the machine running, add the oil in a slow steady stream. When all of the oil has been added, turn off machine and scrape down the sides of the bowl. Add the remaining lemon juice and process another 10 seconds. Taste and correct seasonings.

PESTO SAUCE

MAKES 3 CUPS
PREPARATION TIME 10 MINUTES

Make a batch of Pesto Sauce when fresh basil is abundant and freeze for use during the winter months.

2 cups fresh basil leaves
1/2 cup olive oil
2 tablespoons pine nuts
2 cloves garlic

1 teaspoon salt
1/2 cup freshly grated Parmesan cheese
2 tablespoons butter, softened

In a food processor or blender combine the basil, olive oil, pine nuts, garlic, and salt. Mix, stopping from time to time to scrape down the bowl, until well blended. Transfer to a bowl. Beat in the cheese by hand, incorporating evenly. Beat in the butter. If you plan to freeze the Pesto, it is best not to add the Parmesan cheese and butter until ready to use.

BASIL GARLIC BUTTER

MAKES 6 TO 8 SLICES
PREPARATION TIME 10 MINUTES
REFRIGERATION TIME 1 HOUR

Compound butters—creamed and chilled—are used to enhance the flavor of grilled fish or meat. They can also be used as a spread on canapés or bread. Compound butters can be frozen for up to one month.

1 cup fresh basil leaves
4 cloves garlic
8 ounces (2 sticks) softened butter

White pepper

In a food processor, combine the basil and garlic. Process until minced. Add the butter and pepper; process until well blended. On a piece of plastic wrap, shape the butter into a log two inches thick. Chill until firm, at least 1 hour. To serve, cut into slices.

HOLLANDAISE SAUCE

MAKES 2 CUPS
PREPARATION TIME 10 MINUTES
COOKING TIME 5 MINUTES

4 egg yolks
8 ounces (2 sticks) unsalted
  butter, softened

Lemon juice
Salt
White pepper

In a saucepan, beat the egg yolks with 2 tablespoons of the butter. Over low heat, whisk in the butter, piece by piece. Heat until nicely thickened. Season to taste with the lemon juice, salt, and white pepper.

CREAM CHEESE PASTRY

MAKES ABOUT 1 POUND
PREPARATION TIME 10 MINUTES
REFRIGERATION TIME 3 HOURS

8 ounces (2 sticks) butter
8 ounces cream cheese

1/2 teaspoon salt
2 cups flour

Combine butter, cream cheese, and salt in a bowl. Beat until well blended and smooth. Add flour gradually and beat again until smooth. Form into a ball. Cover and chill for several hours. Remove from the refrigerator for 10 minutes before rolling.

CRÊPES

MAKES ABOUT 12
PREPARATION TIME 1 HOUR
COOKING TIME 10 MINUTES

3 eggs
1 1/2 cups milk
1 cup flour

Pinch of salt
2 tablespoons butter, melted

Place all the ingredients in a blender or processor. Process until well mixed. Pour into a pitcher or bowl. Let stand for 1 hour.

CRÈME FRAÎCHE

MAKES ABOUT 2 CUPS
PREPARATION TIME 5 MINUTES
REFRIGERATION TIME 4 HOURS

Crème Fraîche is an approximation of the heavy cream of France. It is wonderful used in sauces as well as sweetened and spooned over fresh fruits. Crème Fraîche can be substituted for heavy cream in most recipes.

1 cup heavy cream
1/2 cup sour cream

In a small saucepan combine the heavy cream and sour cream. Put over a very low flame and heat, stirring constantly, until just warm. Immediately remove from heat and pour into a glass jar. Chill, uncovered, in the refrigerator for several hours. It will keep refrigerated, in a closed jar, for up to 1 week.

APPETIZERS

Carneros

 The Carneros district, situated at the southernmost end of Napa County, is considered a separate area because of its distinct climate and grape-growing conditions. Bordering on the north shore of San Francisco Bay, the Carneros district is named for Carneros (sheep in Spanish) Creek, which runs south from the Mayacamas Mountains into San Francisco Bay. Five wineries are located here, and many Napa Valley wineries have extensive vineyards in this district. The mild coastal breezes cool these bayside vineyards and provide ideal growing conditions for the white varietals that cannot tolerate warmer climates.

The Carneros district's white varietals, such as Chardonnay, Riesling, and Sauvingon Blanc, are handsome accompaniments to the appetizers that follow. Carneros is also a prime growing region for the Chardonnay and Pinot Noir grapes that are used in some of Napa Valley's best sparkling wines, another excellent choice to accompany these California-style appetizers.

LAYERED MEXICAN DELIGHT

SERVES 8 TO 10
PREPARATION TIME 15 MINUTES

Sprinkle some bottled picante sauce over this cheesy appetizer for a hotter taste.

2 avocados
2 teaspoons lemon juice
1 package taco seasoning mix
1 cup sour cream
2 tablespoons mayonnaise
4 ounces Cheddar cheese, shredded

4 ounces Jack cheese, shredded
2 tomatoes, diced
6 ounces black olives, chopped
4 green onions, chopped
Picante sauce
Tortilla chips

Purée the avocados together with the lemon juice in a food processor or blender until smooth. Spread evenly onto a 10- to 12-inch flat plate. Blend the taco seasoning into the sour cream and mayonnaise. Spread over the avocado mixture. Layer the remaining ingredients over the sour cream mixture, making sure that each layer is even and ending with the green onions on top. Sprinkle with the picante sauce and place the tortilla chips around the edges of the plate.

ROTOLO AL FORNO

MAKES 24 TO 26 SLICES
PREPARATION TIME 10 MINUTES
COOKING TIME 25 TO 30 MINUTES

These swirled meat rolls are so versatile you can serve them at a football feast, a child's party, or as part of a buffet.

1 loaf frozen bread dough
Flour for kneading
1/4 pound salami, thinly sliced
1/4 pound mortadella, thinly sliced
1/4 pound ham, thinly sliced

1/3 pound Swiss cheese, thinly sliced
1/3 pound provolone cheese, thinly sliced
1 egg yolk, beaten

Thaw the bread and let it rise, covered, in a warm spot for 1 hour. Punch down and knead with a small amount of flour.

Preheat oven to 375 degrees. On a floured surface, roll dough out into a rectangle 12 × 16. Tear the meat into bite-size pieces and sprinkle over the bread. Tear the cheese into pieces and layer over the meat. Starting at the long end, roll up tightly, jelly-roll style. Pinch the ends together tightly and brush with a beaten egg yolk. Place on a cookie sheet and let rest for 20 minutes.

Bake for 25 to 30 minutes, or until nicely browned. Let rest for a few minutes before slicing. Slice thinly and arrange on a serving tray.

POTATO SKINS

MAKES 24
PREPARATION TIME 20 MINUTES
COOKING TIME 1 HOUR 15 MINUTES

Potato skins can be deep-fried or baked. The baked version can be prepared in advance and reheated, at 400 degrees for 8 minutes, just prior to serving.

POTATO SKINS
6 large russet potatoes
4 tablespoons (1/2 stick) melted butter

Fried crumbled bacon
Grated Cheddar or Jack cheese

Preheat oven to 450 degrees. Scrub the potatoes and pierce each one with a fork. Bake until tender, about 1 hour. Let stand until cool enough to handle. Cut in half lengthwise and scoop out flesh, leaving 1/8-inch-thick shells. Reserve the flesh for another use. Cut the skins into quarters.

Turn up oven to 500 degrees. Brush insides of skins with the melted butter. Place cut side up on baking sheet and sprinkle each with a little salt. Bake for 12 minutes or until lightly browned and crisp.

SALSA DIP
1 cup tomato sauce
4 ounces canned diced green chilies

1/4 cup chopped green onions, including some tops
Sour cream

Prepare the salsa by combining the tomato sauce, green chilies, and green onions. To serve: top the baked skins with some of the crumbled bacon and grated cheese. Run under the broiler until the cheese melts. Arrange on a serving platter with the salsa in the center. Pass the sour cream in a separate bowl.

CARAWAY CHEESE STICKS

MAKES 3 DOZEN
PREPARATION TIME 10 MINUTES
REFRIGERATION TIME 2 HOURS
COOKING TIME 10 MINUTES

Serve in crystal highball glasses for a touch of elegance.

1 cup flour
4 ounces (1 stick) butter, cut into pieces
1/4 teaspoon salt
2 ounces Cheddar cheese, grated
1 tablespoon caraway seeds

1 teaspoon dry mustard
Pinch of paprika
Pinch of cayenne
Dash red pepper sauce
2 to 3 tablespoons milk
1 ounce Parmesan cheese, grated

Place flour, butter, and salt in a bowl and mix until crumbly. Add the Cheddar cheese, caraway seeds, mustard, paprika, cayenne pepper, and red pepper sauce to the bowl and mix together. Add the milk and knead until the mixture forms a ball. Wrap and refrigerate for 2 hours.

Preheat oven to 375 degrees. Roll the dough out to 1/4-inch thickness on a floured surface. Cut into 5 × 1/2-inch strips. Place on a cookie sheet and sprinkle with the Parmesan cheese. Bake for 10 to 12 minutes or until nicely browned.

SHRIMP-STUFFED MUSHROOMS

MAKES APPROXIMATELY 28
PREPARATION TIME 20 MINUTES
COOKING TIME 15 MINUTES

1 pound fresh mushrooms, (about 28 to 30)
6 ounces cream cheese
2 tablespoons lemon juice
2 tablespoons chopped parsley

2 tablespoons chopped onion
3 tablespoons mayonnaise
1/4 teaspoon dried dill
Pinch of pepper
3/4 pound tiny shrimp

Preheat oven to 375 degrees. Wash and dry mushrooms. Remove and discard stems. Combine remaining ingredients and stuff mushrooms. Bake for 12 to 15 minutes. Serve warm.

CAVIAR SOUFFLÉ ROLL

MAKES 32 SLICES
PREPARATION TIME 1 HOUR
REFRIGERATION TIME 2 HOURS
COOKING TIME 20 TO 30 MINUTES

You will find yourself serving this soufflé roll frequently because it is so unusual and delicious. It may also be served as a first course for eight.

SOUFFLÉ ROLL

Butter and flour to coat pan
1/4 cup flour
1 cup milk
2 egg yolks
3/4 teaspoon salt
White pepper and nutmeg to taste
3 egg whites, room temperature

Preheat oven to 375 degrees. Line a 15 1/2 × 10 1/2-inch jelly-roll pan with foil or parchment paper. Spread generously with butter, then coat with flour.

In a pan make a thick paste with the flour and 1/4 cup of the milk. Stir in the remaining milk and cook over moderate heat, stirring constantly, until the mixture thickens. Remove from the heat and vigorously beat in the egg yolks and add the seasonings. Whip the egg whites until stiff and fold into the milk mixture. Spread evenly into the prepared pan and bake for 20 to 25 minutes.

Remove from the oven and cover with a dampened tea towel. Invert and remove the paper. Cover with a clean sheet of paper and then roll the soufflé, starting at the long end, in the towel. Refrigerate until chilled.

FILLING

6 ounces cream cheese, softened
2 tablespoons sour cream
2 tablespoons chopped green onion tops
1/2 teaspoon lemon juice
2 tablespoons lumpfish caviar
Fresh parsley

Mix the cream cheese, sour cream, green onion tops, and lemon juice together. Rinse and dry the caviar with paper towels and fold into the cream-cheese mixture. Remove the chilled roll from the refrigerator and unroll. Spread evenly with the cream-cheese mixture. Roll up tightly and wrap in plastic. Chill for several hours before serving. Slice with a serrated knife into 1/4-inch slices and serve on a platter garnished with fresh parsley.

MANGO CHUTNEY MOLD

SERVES 10 TO 12
PREPARATION TIME 10 MINUTES
REFRIGERATION TIME OVERNIGHT

This nutty cheese mold is covered with a canopy of mango chutney for easy, do-ahead cocktail fare.

12 ounces cream cheese
3 tablespoons mayonnaise
3 tablespoons chopped peanuts
3 tablespoons chopped raisins
3 slices fried bacon, chopped
2 teaspoons chopped green
  onions

1 1/2 teaspoons curry powder
1/2 cup shredded coconut
1 cup mango chutney, chopped

Assorted crackers

Combine the cream cheese with the mayonnaise, peanuts, raisins, and bacon in a processor or blender. Mix in the green onions and curry powder. Pour into a lightly oiled 3 to 4 cup mold and chill overnight. Remove from the mold and cover with the coconut and chutney. Serve with crackers.

SPICED MELON BALLS

SERVES 8 TO 10
PREPARATION TIME 10 MINUTES
MARINATING TIME 2 HOURS

This simple melon cooler tastes as good as it looks. Pile it in a crystal bowl or vase and garnish with lime slices. It can also be served in tall stemmed goblets as a first course.

1 medium Crenshaw or
  honeydew melon
1 large cantaloupe
2 tablespoons lime juice
2 tablespoons honey

1/4 teaspoon ground coriander
1/4 teaspoon nutmeg
Fresh mint leaves
Lime slices

Cut melons in halves; scoop out and discard seeds. Cut the fruit into balls, using a melon-ball cutter. Mix together the lime juice, honey, coriander, and nutmeg. Pour over the melon balls and toss until well coated. Cover and chill at least 2 hours. Spoon into a serving bowl and garnish with fresh mint leaves and lime slices. Serve with toothpicks.

CURRIED MUSHROOM AND CASHEW PÂTÉ

MAKES 2 CUPS

PREPARATION TIME 10 MINUTES

A simple variation on the traditional terrine.

4 tablespoons butter
1 pound mushrooms, chopped
1/2 cup minced onion
2 cloves garlic, pressed
1 1/2 teaspoons curry powder
1/2 to 1 teaspoon salt
1/4 teaspoon ground coriander

1/4 teaspoon ground cumin
1 cup roasted cashews
2 tablespoons oil
Chopped fresh parsley

Wheat crackers

In the butter, sauté the mushrooms, onion, garlic, curry powder, salt, coriander, and cumin. Cook until the mixture is fairly dry.

Chop the cashews finely in a food processor or blender and slowly add the oil to make a paste. Add the mushroom mixture and continue mixing until smooth. Taste and add more salt if necessary. Place in a serving bowl and sprinkle with chopped parsley. Serve at room temperature with wheat crackers.

PARMESAN PESTO DIP

MAKES 3 CUPS

PREPARATION TIME 10 MINUTES

REFRIGERATION TIME 2 HOURS

Water chestnuts may be substituted for the watercress for a nice crunchy texture.

1 1/2 cups sour cream
1 cup freshly grated Parmesan
  cheese
1 tablespoon oil
1/2 cup mayonnaise
2 tablespoons lemon juice
1 tablespoon finely chopped
  onion

1/2 cup coarsely chopped
  watercress
4 tablespoons Pesto Sauce†
1 teaspoon Worcestershire
  sauce
Salt to taste
Pepper to taste
Fresh vegetables for dipping

Combine all the ingredients. Season with salt and pepper. Refrigerate at least 2 hours. Serve chilled, surrounded by fresh vegetables.

SPINACH DIP

MAKES 3 1/2 CUPS
PREPARATION TIME 10 MINUTES

Arrange an attractive vegetable basket to serve with this easy-to-prepare dip.

10 ounces frozen chopped
   spinach, thawed
2 cups sour cream
1 cup mayonnaise
1/2 cup packaged dry leek soup
   mix

1/2 cup chopped parsley
1/2 cup chopped green onions
1 teaspoon dry dill
1 teaspoon dry Italian salad
   dressing mix

With your hands, squeeze the spinach dry. Combine with the remaining ingredients in a food processor or blender and process until blended. Refrigerate until ready to serve.

OLIVE WHIRLIGIGS

MAKES 2 DOZEN
PREPARATION TIME 10 MINUTES
REFRIGERATION TIME 1 1/2 HOURS
COOKING TIME 10 TO 20 MINUTES

Buttery, cheese-flavored pastry is rolled in green olives, sliced, and baked for a delightful, cocktail "nosh."

4 ounces Cheddar cheese,
   grated
3 tablespoons butter, softened
Dash of Tabasco sauce

1/2 cup sifted flour
1/2 cup chopped, pimento-
   stuffed green olives

Blend cheese, butter, and Tabasco sauce together. Stir in flour and gather into a ball. Cover and refrigerate for 30 minutes.

Roll chilled dough out to a 6 × 10-inch rectangle between 2 sheets of wax paper. Remove the top sheet of wax paper and sprinkle the dough with the chopped olives. Beginning with the long end, roll up as for a jelly roll, lifting the wax paper with each turn. Seal the edge well, wrap in wax paper and twist the ends so that the dough is tightly rolled. Chill 1 hour.

Preheat oven to 400 degrees. Cut roll into 1/4-inch slices. Bake 2 inches apart on ungreased cookie sheet until edges are lightly browned, about 10 to 20 minutes. Serve hot.

BAKED SPRING ROLLS

MAKES 30
PREPARATION TIME 45 MINUTES
COOKING TIME 15 MINUTES

Scrumptious spring rolls without deep frying. Because these freeze well, they can be made in advance.

1 tablespoon minced fresh
   ginger
1 teaspoon minced garlic
2 tablespoons sesame oil
1 tablespoon vegetable oil
2 cups fresh bean sprouts
12 ounces raw shrimp, chopped
8 ounces water chestnuts,
   minced
1/4 pound Canadian bacon,
   minced

1/2 cup minced green onion
1 medium carrot, grated
4 teaspoons soy sauce
2 teaspoons cornstarch mixed
   with 2 tablespoons water
15 phyllo pastry sheets
8 ounces (2 sticks) melted
   unsalted butter
Sesame seeds

Preheat oven to 375 degrees. Stir-fry the ginger and garlic in the hot oils for 30 seconds. Add the sprouts, shrimp, water chestnuts, bacon, green onion, and carrot; stir-fry for 2 minutes. Add soy sauce and the cornstarch mixture and stir until slightly thickened. Remove from heat and cool.

Cut the phyllo sheets in half crosswise to form rectangles. Fold in the short end of each rectangle to form a square. Cover each remaining rectangle with a damp towel. Brush the square lightly with some of the melted butter. Turn the square so that the corner points toward you. Place 1 tablespoon of filling in the corner and fold over to enclose. Fold over again. Fold the left and right corner flaps towards the center. Roll from the bottom to form a neat package. Place seam side down on a baking sheet. Repeat with remaining phyllo and filling. They can be prepared ahead to this point. Refrigerate or freeze until ready to use.

Brush the packages lightly with the remaining butter and sprinkle with sesame seeds. Bake for 10 to 15 minutes or until nicely browned. Serve immediately.

SHRIMP CHEESE STACKS

SERVES 10 TO 12
PREPARATION TIME 15 MINUTES

Layers of peppered cream cheese and spicy sauces are topped with shrimp for a zesty appetizer.

8 ounces softened cream
   cheese
1 tablespoon Worcestershire
   sauce
1/4 teaspoon grated lemon peel
1/2 tablespoon lemon juice
1/2 cup thinly sliced green
   onions

1/8 teaspoon hot pepper sauce
3/4 cup tomato-based chili
   sauce, drained
1/2 tablespoon horseradish
1/2 pound cooked tiny shrimp

Assorted crackers

Beat together the cream cheese, Worcestershire, lemon peel, lemon juice, green onions, and hot pepper sauce until smooth. Spread evenly on a 10- to 12-inch serving platter. Cover and chill. To serve: mix the chili sauce and horseradish, blending well. Spread evenly over the cheese and top with the bay shrimp. Serve with assorted crackers.

HERBED PUFFS

MAKES 3 DOZEN
PREPARATION TIME 20 MINUTES
COOKING TIME 20 TO 25 MINUTES

These tasty cheese puffs freeze well and can be reheated. For variety, fill them with pimento-stuffed olives after baking by slitting the sides and inserting olives.

2/3 cup water
1/3 cup plus 2 tablespoons milk
4 ounces (1 stick) butter,
   softened
1 teaspoon salt
1/2 teaspoon nutmeg
1/4 teaspoon pepper

1 cup flour
5 eggs
4 ounces Gruyère cheese,
   grated
2 green onions, minced
1 tablespoon minced parsley
1 teaspoon dried dill

Preheat oven to 400 degrees. Butter 2 baking sheets. Combine the water, milk, butter, salt, nutmeg, and pepper in a saucepan. Bring to a boil. Remove from heat and immediately pour in the flour all at once. Using a wooden spoon, stir rapidly until all of the flour is incorporated and the mixture leaves the sides of the pan. Return to a low heat and cook for an additional minute.

Beat in 4 of the eggs, one at a time, until the mixture is thick and smooth. Add the cheese, onions, parsley, and dill; mix thoroughly.

Spoon the batter into 1 1/2-inch mounds onto the prepared baking sheets. Beat together the remaining egg and a pinch of salt and brush over the tops of the puffs. Bake 20 to 25 minutes or until nicely browned. Remove from the baking sheets and cool on wire racks.

CURRIED MUSHROOM TURNOVERS

MAKES 4 DOZEN
PREPARATION TIME 15 MINUTES
REFRIGERATION TIME 2 HOURS
COOKING TIME 35 MINUTES

These may be frozen after baking. Allow to cool and transfer to an airtight container. To serve, just reheat for 15 minutes.

3/4 **pound finely chopped mushrooms**
1/2 **cup finely chopped onion**
2 **tablespoons butter**
1 **teaspoon curry powder**
1 **teaspoon lemon juice**
1 **tablespoon flour**

1/2 **teaspoon salt**
3 **tablespoons sour cream**
1 **recipe Cream Cheese Pastry†, chilled**
1 **egg yolk beaten with 2 tablespoons milk**

Preheat oven to 350 degrees. Sauté the mushrooms and onion in the butter over high heat for 5 minutes. Sprinkle with the curry, lemon juice, flour, and salt. Stir and simmer 2 minutes. Add the sour cream and cook, stirring until smooth and thickened. Cool before using.

Remove the dough from the refrigerator 10 minutes before rolling. Divide in half and roll each half in a 9 × 6-inch rectangle. Fold in thirds and roll; fold in thirds again and roll dough to 1/8-inch thickness. Cut into 2 1/2-inch rounds. Put a scant teaspoon of filling in the center of each round. Moisten the edges with water and fold in half. Press the edges with the floured tines of a fork to seal.

Place the turnovers on an ungreased baking sheet. Brush with the egg-yolk mixture and chill for 1/2 hour. Bake for 25 to 30 minutes or until nicely browned. Serve warm or cold.

SESAME-SHRIMP BALLS

MAKES 18 TO 20
PREPARATION TIME 15 MINUTES
REFRIGERATION TIME 8 HOURS

These cold appetizers are popular with large crowds as part of a party buffet.

8 ounces cream cheese
2 tablespoons lemon juice
1/2 pound cooked shrimp
2 tablespoons minced onion

1/4 teaspoon Tabasco sauce
1/4 teaspoon dry dill
Salt to taste
Toasted sesame seeds

Mix all the ingredients, except the sesame seeds, in a food processor just until blended (do not overprocess). Shape into small balls, about 1 inch in diameter, and roll in the toasted sesame seeds. Refrigerate at least 8 hours or overnight.

ONION CHEESE RING

SERVES 8 TO 10
PREPARATION TIME 20 MINUTES
COOKING TIME 20 MINUTES

Pass this ring on a serving tray and let your guests pull it apart.

2 1/2 cups sifted flour
3 teaspoons baking powder
1/2 teaspoon salt
4 ounces (1 stick) butter, cut
　into pieces

1/2 pound Cheddar cheese,
　shredded
1/2 cup coarsely chopped onion
3/4 cup milk
1 egg, slightly beaten

Preheat oven to 450 degrees. Sift flour, baking powder, and salt into a bowl. Cut in the butter until crumbly. Stir in 4 ounces of the cheese and onions; mix well. Pour the milk and egg, all at once, into the flour mixture. Stir until just moistened.

Drop dough by heaping tablespoons onto a greased baking sheet, forming a complete circle. (This will make a circle approximately 14 inches in diameter. If desired, make two smaller circles.) Each tablespoon of dough should barely touch the other. Sprinkle with the remaining cheese. Bake for 15 to 20 minutes, or until the bread is golden.

BRIE EN CROÛTE

SERVES 8 TO 10
PREPARATION TIME 15 MINUTES
COOKING TIME 15 TO 30 MINUTES

Any size wheel of Brie works beautifully. You can prepare a small wheel for an intimate gathering or a six-pound wheel for a large crowd. It is easy to make and it looks gorgeous!

1/2 **cup pine nuts**	**A 1- to 2-pound wheel of Brie**
2 **tablespoons melted butter**	1/2 **cup melted butter**
1/2 **pound phyllo dough**	

Preheat oven to 400 degrees. Sauté the pine nuts in the 2 tablespoons butter until nicely browned. Drain on paper towels. Brush 2 layers of the phyllo with some of the remaining butter. Place the wheel of Brie in the center. Place the pine nuts on the top of the cheese and gently press in. Enclose the entire wheel in the dough. Brush 2 more layers of phyllo with butter. Place the wheel in the center, seam side down, and enclose. Repeat this process until all the dough has been used. Place on a baking tray and refrigerate for 10 minutes.

   Brush the top with butter and bake for 15 to 20 minutes (depending on the size of the cheese used) or until golden brown. Transfer to a serving platter and let cool at least 30 minutes. Serve at room temperature.

TAPENADE

MAKES 3 CUPS
PREPARATION TIME 15 MINUTES

In France, this piquant sauce is considered the poor man's caviar. Spread on crackers or sliced baguettes, or use to dip vegetables.

1 **2-ounce can anchovies, drained**	1 **cup pitted black olives**
3 **tablespoons milk**	3/4 **cup olive oil**
2 **6** 1/2**-ounce cans tuna in oil, drained**	1/3 **cup Cognac or brandy**
	2 **tablespoons capers**
	1 **clove garlic**

Soak the anchovies in the milk for 10 minutes. Rinse and pat dry. Combine all the ingredients in a food processor or blender and mix until smooth.

ZUCCHINI AND CHEESE MELTS

MAKES 3 DOZEN
PREPARATION TIME 25 MINUTES
COOKING TIME 2 TO 3 MINUTES

3 medium zucchini, shredded
4 tablespoons butter or oil
9 green onions, finely sliced
2 small cloves garlic, minced
1/4 teaspoon dried basil
1/4 teaspoon oregano

Salt to taste
Pepper to taste
3/4 cup Jack cheese, shredded
French baguette or buffet rye
  slices

Pat the excess water from the zucchini. Sauté the zucchini for a few minutes in the melted butter or oil with 6 of the sliced onions and the garlic. Add the basil, oregano, salt, and pepper to taste. Remove from heat while zucchini is still green and slightly crisp. Cool and refrigerate.

To serve: toss the zucchini mixture with the shredded cheese and the remaining onions. Spread on French baguette or buffet rye slices that have been toasted on one side. Put under the broiler until hot and bubbly.

ARTICHOKE LEAVES WITH SHRIMP

SERVES 6 TO 8
PREPARATION TIME 10 MINUTES
COOKING TIME 30 MINUTES

2 large artichokes
Juice of 1 lemon
1/2 teaspoon salt
1 cup sour cream
1/2 cup mayonnaise
1/4 cup parsley

1 teaspoon Beau Monde
  seasoning
3 teaspoons minced green
  onion
1 teaspoon dried dillweed
1/2 pound tiny cooked shrimp

Cook artichokes in water with the lemon juice and salt until tender. Cool. Tear off the solid large leaves and set aside. Save the heart and bottom for another use.

Combine the remaining ingredients, except the shrimp, and blend. Do not overmix. Place a teaspoon of the dip on the end of each leaf. Place a shrimp on top. Arrange on a serving platter.

PARMESAN CHEESE PUFF ROUNDS

MAKES 5 DOZEN
PREPARATION TIME 5 MINUTES
REFRIGERATION TIME 1 HOUR
COOKING TIME 2 TO 3 MINUTES

You may want to store a batch of these in the freezer. Simply place the baking tray with the prepared rounds in the freezer. When frozen, transfer to plastic bags. When ready to use, thaw 15 minutes before broiling.

8 ounces cream cheese, softened
3 tablespoons mayonnaise
3 finely chopped green onions, including some of the tops
3 drops Tabasco sauce
2/3 cup Parmesan cheese
Thin-sliced white bread
Butter

In a food processor or blender, mix the cream cheese, mayonnaise, onions, and Tabasco. Transfer to a bowl, stir in 1/2 cup of the Parmesan cheese, and chill until ready to serve.

Cut out sixty 1 1/2-inch bread rounds and butter one side only. Place on a tray and broil until browned. Turn over and lightly brown the unbuttered side and spread with the cheese mixture, forming a point in the middle. Dip in the remaining Parmesan cheese. Place on a baking sheet and broil until puffy and light brown.

CANDIED WALNUTS

MAKES 5 CUPS
PREPARATION TIME 10 MINUTES

1 1/2 cups sugar
1/2 cup water
2 teaspoons cinnamon
1/2 teaspoon nutmeg
1/4 teaspoon ground cloves
1 teaspoon white corn syrup
1/4 teaspoon salt
5 cups walnut halves

In a large saucepan, bring all the ingredients, except the nuts, to a soft boil. Add the walnuts and stir just until creamy. Quickly pour out onto wax paper and separate with a fork. Let cool. Store in an airtight container. Keeps for up to 1 month.

PARMESAN TWISTS

MAKES 2 DOZEN
PREPARATION TIME 1 HOUR 15 MINUTES
REFRIGERATION TIME 1 HOUR
COOKING TIME 15 MINUTES

Light and delicate, a terrific accompaniment to soup or salad.

1 recipe Cream Cheese Pastry†
1 cup grated Parmesan cheese
1 egg yolk beaten with 2 tablespoons of milk

Divide the cream-cheese dough in half and roll each half in a rectangle 1/4 inch thick. Sprinkle with 1/3 of the cheese and press lightly into the dough with a rolling pin. Fold the dough into thirds and roll again. Sprinkle with another 1/3 of the cheese, press with the rolling pin, and fold again. Roll into an 8 × 5-inch rectangle and brush with the egg-yolk mixture. Sprinkle with the remaining cheese. Cut crosswise into strips 3/4 inch wide. Twist the strips into spirals, put on an ungreased baking sheet, and brush the ends with the remaining egg yolk. Chill 1 hour.

Preheat oven to 350 degrees. Bake for 15 to 20 minutes or until nicely browned. Serve warm or cold.

OPEN-FACED BISCUITS

MAKES 3 DOZEN
PREPARATION TIME 20 MINUTES
COOKING TIME 20 MINUTES

BISCUITS

2 cups flour	**1 cup heavy cream**
1 tablespoon baking powder	**1 tablespoon cold water**
1/4 teaspoon salt	**2 tablespoons milk**
2 tablespoons unsalted butter	

Preheat oven to 425 degrees. Sift together the flour, baking powder, and salt. Cut in the butter until the mixture is crumbly. Add the heavy cream and form a soft dough. If necessary, add 1 tablespoon of cold water to pull together. Roll dough to a thickness of 3/4 inch on a floured surface. Prick all over with a fork and cut into 1 1/2-inch rounds. Arrange on a greased baking sheet and brush with milk. Bake for 12 to 15 minutes until puffed and golden. Transfer to racks to cool.

TOPPING

1 **pound cooked shrimp or smoked ham**	1/4 **cup minced parsley**
1 **cup mayonnaise**	1 1/2 **tablespoons Dijon mustard**
1/2 **cup minced green onions**	1 **tablespoon tomato paste**
	Dash of Tabasco sauce

Preheat oven to 400 degrees. Coarsely chop the shrimp or ham in a food processor. Add the remaining ingredients and mix well. To serve: halve the biscuits and arrange, cut side up, on baking sheet. Spoon or pipe shrimp or ham mixture onto biscuit halves. Bake in the oven for 5 to 7 minutes.

QUESADILLAS

MAKES 24
PREPARATION TIME 15 MINUTES
COOKING TIME 15 TO 20 MINUTES

South-of-the-border's answer to a toasted cheese sandwich. Accompany these puffy wedges with a spicy salsa and sour cream.

2 **tablespoons oil**	3 **tablespoons roasted, peeled, and chopped green chili peppers**
1 **clove garlic, pressed**	
1/2 **cup chopped green bell pepper**	1/4 **teaspoon salt**
1 **4-ounce can chopped green chilies**	12 **ounces Jack cheese, grated**
	12 **flour tortillas**
1 1/2 **cups canned tomatoes, drained**	**Oil for frying**

Heat the oil and lightly sauté the garlic. Add the green pepper and sauté an additional 5 minutes. Stir in the canned chilies, tomatoes, chili peppers, and salt. Simmer for 15 minutes.

Sprinkle the cheese in the center of 6 tortillas. Top with 2 tablespoons of the sauce. Cover with the remaining tortillas, pressing down gently. Secure with toothpicks, if necessary.

Heat enough oil to cover the bottom of a large skillet. Add one quesadilla and fry on one side until crisp. Turn and fry other side. Drain well on paper towels. Place in a warm oven while frying the remaining quesadillas. Cut into quarters and arrange on a serving dish.

SHEPHERD'S BREAD FONDUE

SERVES 12 TO 14
PREPARATION TIME 10 MINUTES
COOKING TIME 35 MINUTES

Chunks of crab in a sherried cheese sauce make a stunning presentation in a hollowed-out round loaf of bread.

8 green onions, chopped	1/2 teaspoon horseradish
1/2 cup chopped parsley	2 teaspoons lemon juice
6 tablespoons butter	Salt to taste
2 tablespoons flour	Red pepper to taste
1 cup half-and-half	1/2 pound crab meat
4 ounces cream cheese	4 ounces toasted sliced
6 ounces Swiss cheese, grated	almonds
1 tablespoon sherry	1 round loaf bread, unsliced
1 tablespoon Worcestershire sauce	

Preheat oven to 375 degrees. Sauté the onions and parsley in the butter. Stir in the flour and continue cooking for an additional minute. Slowly blend in the half-and-half and stir until thickened. Add the remaining ingredients, except the crab, almonds and bread. Mix well. Fold in crab.

Slice the top off of the loaf and save. Remove the soft inside of the bread. Fill the cavity of the bread with the crab mixture and sprinkle with the toasted almonds. Replace the top and wrap the loaf in foil. Bake for 30 minutes or until hot. Serve with Italian breadsticks or toasted rounds of French bread.

THREE CHEESES IN PUFF PASTRY

SERVES 8 TO 10
PREPARATION TIME 20 MINUTES
COOKING TIME 20 MINUTES

2 tablespoons butter	1/4 cup crumbled goat cheese
2 tablespoons flour	1/4 cup crumbled Gorgonzola
1/2 cup milk	cheese
Pinch of fresh nutmeg	1 sheet frozen puff pastry
1/2 cup grated Gruyère cheese	1 egg, beaten

Preheat oven to 475 degrees. Melt the butter in a small saucepan. Add the flour and cook for 2 minutes without browning. Slowly add the milk, stirring constantly. Cook until thickened and smooth, stirring constantly (the sauce will be very thick). Stir in the nutmeg. Let cool.

Combine all the cheeses. Add the sauce and mix well. Roll out the pastry as thin as possible. Cut out two circles: one 6 inches, one 7 inches. Place the 6-inch circle on a baking tray. Place the cheese mixture in the center and spread out slightly. Moisten the edges with water. Place other pastry circle over cheese and press to seal the edges. Use the pastry scraps to decorate the top, if desired. Brush with egg, being careful not to get egg on the baking sheet.

Bake for 10 minutes. Reduce oven temperature to 375 and continue baking until brown and flaky. Transfer to wire rack to cool.

BLACK FOREST HAM ROLLS

MAKES 32
PREPARATION TIME 10 MINUTES
FREEZER TIME 30 MINUTES

These rolls may be wrapped and frozen for up to 4 weeks. Serve on thinly sliced baguette bread or on crackers with a dash of prepared mustard.

8 ounces cream cheese, softened
2 tablespoons mayonnaise
1 tablespoon chopped fresh chives
1 tablespoon finely chopped dill pickle
1 teaspoon Worcestershire sauce
1/4 teaspoon soy sauce

3 dashes Tabasco
1/4 teaspoon dry mustard
1/4 teaspoon prepared mustard
Pinch of salt
Pinch of freshly ground pepper
8 slices Black Forest ham

French baguette slices or crackers (optional)

Mix well all the ingredients except the ham and the bread slices. Dry the ham on paper towels. Spread a heaping tablespoon of the mixture on each slice of ham and spread evenly. Roll lengthwise. Place in the freezer for about 30 minutes, or until the rolls are hard enough to slice. Cut into 1/2-inch rounds. Serve the rounds on toothpicks or on bread slices with a little prepared mustard.

SPINACH BALLS

MAKES 4 DOZEN
PREPARATION TIME 20 MINUTES
COOKING TIME 20 MINUTES

2 10-ounce packages frozen chopped spinach
2 cups crumbled stuffing mix
3/4 cup chopped onion
4 eggs, beaten
3/4 cup (1 1/2 sticks) melted butter

3/4 cup grated Parmesan cheese
1/2 teaspoon garlic powder
1/4 teaspoon thyme
1/4 teaspoon freshly grated pepper
Cherry tomatoes

Preheat oven to 350 degrees. Thaw the spinach. Squeeze as dry as possible. Mix with the remaining ingredients, reserving 1/4 cup of the cheese. Roll into balls the size of walnuts. Roll in the remaining Parmesan cheese. Bake for 20 minutes. Serve on a platter garnished with cherry tomatoes. Pass with toothpicks.

If freezing for later use, do not roll in the remaining cheese. Place on a cookie sheet and freeze until firm. Place in plastic bags in the freezer. When ready to use, thaw for 10 minutes. Roll in the Parmesan cheese and bake.

HOT ARTICHOKE DIP

MAKES 3 CUPS
PREPARATION TIME 5 MINUTES
COOKING TIME 30 MINUTES

1 8 1/2-ounce can artichokes, packed in water
1 7 1/2-ounce can chopped green chilies

1 cup grated Parmesan cheese
1 cup mayonnaise

Preheat oven to 350 degrees. Combine all of the ingredients. Place in an ovenproof serving dish. Bake for 30 minutes. Let rest for 10 to 15 minutes before serving. Serve with tortillas or crackers.

DEVILED EGGS WITH BACON

MAKES 12
PREPARATION TIME 10 MINUTES
COOKING TIME 10 MINUTES

6 large hard-cooked eggs,
  shelled
1/4 cup minced celery
2 1/2 tablespoons minced
  shallot
1 teaspoon Dijon-style mustard
3/4 teaspoon vinegar

Salt
Cayenne
2 tablespoons mayonnaise
2 tablespoons cooked, finely
  chopped bacon
Chopped fresh parsley

Slice the eggs in half lengthwise. Carefully separate yolks from whites, keeping the whites clean. Place the yolks in a bowl. Cover the egg whites loosely with dampened paper towels. Mash the yolks with a fork until crumbly. Fold in the celery, shallot, mustard, and vinegar. Salt and pepper to taste.

When ready to fill egg whites, blend mayonnaise into filling. The mixture should be creamy. Add more mayonnaise if necessary. Fill each egg white with the yolk filling, mounding it attractively. Top with a pinch of the bacon. Sprinkle with the parsley. Serve at room temperature or slightly chilled.

CURRIED STUFFED EGGS

MAKES 24
PREPARATION TIME 10 MINUTES

12 hard-cooked eggs, shelled
4 teaspoons fresh lemon juice
1 tablespoon curry powder
1 tablespoon minced green
  onion

2 teaspoons soy sauce
Mayonnaise to moisten
Chutney

Halve eggs lengthwise and remove yolks. Put yolks through a sieve. Add the lemon juice, curry powder, onion, and soy sauce. Moisten with the mayonnaise. Fill the shells. Garnish each stuffed egg with a small piece of chutney.

ZUCCHINI MADELEINES

MAKES 3 DOZEN
PREPARATION TIME 30 MINUTES
COOKING TIME 25 MINUTES

Turning this cheesy vegetable mélange onto fluted madeleine cookie molds is sheer brilliance.

4 1/2 cups shredded zucchini
1 cup freshly grated Parmesan
  cheese
1 small onion, finely chopped
1/2 clove garlic, finely chopped
5 eggs, well beaten

1/3 cup olive oil
2 tablespoons vegetable oil
1/2 teaspoon freshly grated
  pepper
1 cup Bisquick

Preheat oven to 350 degrees. Salt and drain the zucchini for 1/2 hour. Squeeze dry. Mix all the ingredients together. Bisquick should be added last. Grease and flour madeleine molds. Fill with the zucchini mixture. Bake for 20 to 25 minutes or until puffed and brown.

SHRIMP PUFFS

MAKES 3 DOZEN
PREPARATION TIME 15 MINUTES
COOKING TIME 25 MINUTES

PUFFS
4 ounces (1 stick) butter
1 cup water
1/4 teaspoon salt

1 cup flour
4 eggs

Preheat oven to 375 degrees. Melt butter in water and salt. Bring to a boil and add flour, all at once. Mix well and continue stirring until a ball is formed. Remove from the heat. Add the eggs, one at a time, beating vigorously after each until mixture is smooth and shiny. Drop onto greased baking sheets by the teaspoonful. Bake for 25 minutes or until puffed and browned. Let cool. Split tops and set aside.

FILLING

2 1/2 cups minced cooked
   shrimp
1/2 cup minced green onions
1/2 cup minced water chestnuts
2 teaspoons Dijon mustard

1/2 cup mayonnaise
4 teaspoons lemon juice
2 teaspoons Worcestershire
1/2 teaspoon each salt and basil
Freshly ground black pepper

Combine the filling ingredients and mix well. Taste and adjust seasonings. Just prior to serving, spoon some of the filling into the puffs and replace tops and arrange on a serving platter.

MUSHROOMS PARMESANO

MAKES 24
PREPARATION TIME 15 MINUTES
COOKING TIME 20 MINUTES

24 fresh medium mushrooms
2 tablespoons butter
1 medium onion, finely
   chopped
1/2 pound spicy pork sausage
1 small clove garlic, minced
1/2 cup finely crushed buttery
   crackers

3 tablespoons grated Parmesan
   cheese
1 tablespoon chopped fresh
   parsley
1/2 teaspoon salt
1/4 teaspoon dried oregano
Freshly ground pepper
1/3 cup chicken stock

Preheat oven to 325 degrees. Wash mushrooms and remove stems. Melt the butter in a skillet. Briefly sauté the mushrooms. Using a slotted spoon, transfer to a bowl. Add the onion, sausage, and garlic. Cook until tender but not brown. Add the remaining ingredients. Spoon the stuffing into the mushroom caps, rounding the tops.

    Place the stuffed mushrooms in a shallow baking pan with about 1/4 inch of water covering the bottom. Bake for 15 minutes or until heated through.

CHICKEN DRUMETTES

MAKES 30
PREPARATION TIME 10 MINUTES
MARINATING TIME OVERNIGHT
COOKING TIME 30 TO 40 MINUTES

30 chicken drumettes or wings
Peel of 1 orange
3 shallots, minced
1 10-ounce jar red currant jelly
2 tablespoons red wine vinegar
1 tablespoon honey

1 tablespoon dry mustard
2 teaspoons ground ginger
1 teaspoon salt
1/4 teaspoon freshly ground
   pepper

Place drumettes or wings in a shallow baking dish just large enough to hold chicken in a single layer. (A jelly-roll pan works well as long as the legs fill it.) Combine the remaining ingredients in a food processor or blender. Mix thoroughly. Pour sauce over the chicken and let marinate overnight, turning occasionally.

Preheat oven to 375 degrees. Bake until browned and nicely glazed with the sauce, about 40 minutes. Turn the drumettes over while baking and brush with the sauce. Continue baking another 10 minutes. Watch carefully while baking to prevent burning and sticking to the pan. Immediately transfer to a serving platter. Serve warm or at room temperature.

CHUTNEYED CHICKEN LIVER PÂTÉ

MAKES 2 1/2 CUPS
PREPARATION TIME 1 HOUR
COOKING TIME 10 MINUTES

1 pound chicken livers
1 1/2 cups milk
8 ounces (2 sticks) butter
1 teaspoon sage
1/2 teaspoon salt
1/4 teaspoon freshly ground
   pepper

6 shallots, finely chopped
2 hard-cooked eggs
1 tablespoon chutney
1 tablespoon brandy
4 strips crisp bacon, crumbled

Melba toast rounds

Wash the chicken livers. Soak in the milk for 30 minutes. Drain and dry on paper towels. Melt 4 ounces of the butter in a sauté pan. Add the livers, sage, salt, pepper, and shallots and sauté, turning the livers occasionally, for 6 minutes. Cool and then drain.

In a food processor, chop the cooled livers with the eggs and chutney. Add the remaining butter and brandy and continue mixing until smooth. Taste and correct seasonings. Pour into a shallow serving bowl or mold and chill. Just before serving, sprinkle with the bacon. Pass with melba toast rounds and additional chutney to spoon on top.

PÂTÉ DE CAMPAGNE

MAKES 1 LOAF
PREPARATION TIME 20 MINUTES
REFRIGERATION TIME OVERNIGHT
COOKING TIME 1 1/2 TO 2 HOURS

This lovely mold will keep at least a week under refrigeration.

1 onion, finely chopped	1 1/2 teaspoons salt
2 tablespoons butter	1/2 teaspoon dried thyme
2 tablespoons brandy	1/2 teaspoon freshly ground
2 tablespoons Madeira wine	pepper
3/4 pound ground veal	1/4 teaspoon allspice
3/4 pound ground pork	Pork fatback or bacon
2 cloves garlic, finely chopped	6 ounces veal, pork, or ham
1/3 cup chopped toasted filberts	strips
2 eggs	1 bay leaf

Preheat oven to 350 degrees. Sauté the onions in butter until soft. Add brandy and Madeira and evaporate the liquid. Remove from the pan and combine with the remaining ingredients except the fatback, meat strips, and bay leaf. Cook a teaspoon of the mixture and taste and adjust for seasonings.

Line a pâté mold or loaf pan with the fatback or bacon. Add 1/2 of the pâté mixture. Smooth out and place the meat strips down the length of the pâté. Cover with the remaining pâté. Place the bay leaf on top and fold over the bacon or fat back to enclose. Cover pan with foil. Bake in a water bath for 1 1/2 to 2 hours. Remove from the water bath. Cover with foil and place something heavy (a brick works nicely) on top of the pâté in the pan to weigh it down. Refrigerate, weighted, overnight. Remove bay leaf and bacon or fatback before serving.

CAVIAR ÉLÉGANT

SERVES 10 TO 12
PREPARATION TIME 30 MINUTES
REFRIGERATION TIME OVERNIGHT

1 package unflavored gelatin
¹/₄ cup cold water
4 hard-cooked eggs, chopped
8 tablespoons mayonnaise
¹/₄ cup chopped fresh parsley
2 green onions, chopped
Hot pepper sauce
Salt
Freshly ground white pepper
1 avocado, puréed

1 avocado, diced
1 large shallot, minced
2 tablespoons fresh lemon juice
Freshly ground black pepper
1 cup sour cream
¹/₄ cup minced onion
4 ounces black caviar

Thinly sliced pumpernickel
   bread

Line a springform pan with foil. Lightly oil bottom and sides. Soften gelatin in the water. Heat to liquefy. Combine the eggs, 6 tablespoons of the mayonnaise, parsley, green onions, a dash of hot pepper sauce, salt, and white pepper to taste. Add 1 tablespoon of the gelatin and fold together gently. Taste and adjust seasonings. Spread into the prepared dish and smooth top.

Combine the avocados, shallot, lemon juice, the remaining 2 tablespoons of the mayonnaise, ¹/₄ teaspoon hot pepper sauce, salt, and black pepper with 1 tablespoon of the gelatin. Taste and adjust seasonings. Gently spread over the egg mixture. Smooth the top.

Mix the sour cream and minced onion with the remaining gelatin. Spread over the avocado layer. Cover with plastic wrap and refrigerate overnight.

Just prior to serving, remove mold from springform pan. Transfer to a serving platter. Spread caviar over the top. Serve with the pumpernickel bread.

SMOKED SALMON ÉCLAIRS WITH CAVIAR

MAKES 48
PREPARATION TIME 1 HOUR
COOKING TIME 20 MINUTES

These luscious stuffed éclairs will be a tour de force with any black caviar.

ÉCLAIRS

1 cup water
5 tablespoons butter, cut into pieces
1 teaspoon dry mustard
1/4 teaspoon salt
1/8 teaspoon cayenne
1 cup flour

4 eggs, room temperature
1/4 pound smoked salmon, minced
1/4 cup freshly grated Parmesan cheese
1 egg beaten with 1 teaspoon cream

Preheat oven to 425 degrees. Bring water, butter, mustard, salt, and cayenne to a boil until butter melts. Remove from heat and add the flour all at once. Mix until dough forms a ball and leaves the sides of the pan. Cool slightly.

Using an electric mixer or wooden spoon, beat the eggs into the dough, one at a time. Beat until smooth and shiny. Fold in the smoked salmon and Parmesan cheese.

Spoon dough into a pastry bag. Pipe onto buttered cookie sheets in 2-inch lengths. Brush lightly with the egg-cream glaze, being careful not to let it run onto the cookie sheets. Bake until puffed and nicely browned, about 25 minutes.

To dry out the insides of the éclairs, cut a slit into the side of each one. Place on a wire rack to cool completely before filling.

FILLING

8 ounces whipped cream cheese
1/4 pound smoked salmon

1/2 cup sour cream
4 ounces black caviar
Chopped fresh dill

Slice the éclairs horizontally into halves. Spread a thick layer of cream cheese on the bottom of each éclair and lay a piece of salmon on top. Spread a thin layer of sour cream over the salmon and top with a dab of caviar. Sprinkle with the fresh dill. Return the tops. Serve immediately.

WON TONS

MAKES 4 DOZEN
PREPARATION TIME 25 MINUTES
COOKING TIME 5 MINUTES

1/2 pound ground pork
1/4 pound tiny cooked shrimp, chopped
1/4 cup finely chopped water chestnuts
1/4 cup finely chopped green onion
1/2 teaspoon finely chopped fresh ginger
1 to 2 cloves garlic, minced

Few drops of sesame oil
3 to 4 reconstituted Chinese mushrooms, finely chopped
1/2 tablespoon saki or sherry
Dash of salt
1 teaspoon cornstarch
1 to 2 tablespoons soy sauce
1 package won ton wrappers
Oil for frying

Mix well all the ingredients, except the won ton wrappers. Place 1/2 teaspoon of filling in the center of each wrapper. Moisten the edges with water and fold to form a triangle. Fold the top triangle to meet the fold. Overlap the two corners and press together firmly.

Heat the oil in a wok or skillet. Add the won tons, a few at a time, and fry until browned. Serve warm with hot mustard or a sweet-and-sour sauce.

DUCK LIVER PÂTÉ WITH PISTACHIO NUTS

MAKES 1 POUND
PREPARATION TIME 40 MINUTES
MARINATING TIME 1 HOUR
REFRIGERATION TIME 4 HOURS

Serve this unusual pistachio-studded terrine with a Chardonnay.

3/4 pound duck livers
1/2 cup milk
1/4 cup Cognac
8 ounces (2 sticks) unsalted butter
1/2 cup chopped onion
1 small green apple, peeled, cored, and chopped

2 tablespoons sherry
2 tablespoons heavy cream
1/2 teaspoon salt
1/2 teaspoon fresh lemon juice
1/2 cup chopped shelled pistachio nuts

Place the livers in a bowl with the milk and Cognac. Soak for 1 hour. Melt 4 tablespoons of the butter in a large skillet. Add the onion and sauté until browned. Add the apple and cook an additional 4 minutes. Transfer to a food processor using a slotted spoon.

Drain the livers. Sauté in the butter remaining in the pan until just pink, about 10 minutes. Add to the mixture in the processor. Add the sherry to the skillet and cook, scraping up any brown bits clinging to the bottom. Add to the processor together with the heavy cream. Purée until smooth. Let cool.

With machine running, add remaining butter to the liver, blending well. Mix in salt, lemon juice and pistachio nuts. Spoon into a serving bowl or ramekin, smoothing the top. Refrigerate at least 4 hours or overnight.

HERBED LIVER PÂTÉ WITH ASPIC

MAKES 4 CUPS
PREPARATION TIME 30 MINUTES
REFRIGERATION TIME 3 HOURS

Rosemary, one of the most fragrant herbs, imparts a subtle flavor which is both sweet and savory.

3 tablespoons butter
2 small white onions, chopped
1 1/2 tablespoons dried rosemary, crumbled
1 1/2 teaspoons freshly ground pepper
2 teaspoons ground dried thyme
1 teaspoon salt
1 teaspoon dried basil, crumbled

1/2 teaspoon freshly grated nutmeg
1 1/4 pounds chicken livers
12 ounces (3 sticks) unsalted butter
2 hard-cooked eggs
2 tablespoons Cognac
2 tablespoons dry sherry
1 tablespoon chopped fresh parsley
Port Aspic (recipe follows)

Melt the 3 tablespoons of butter in a large skillet. Add the onions, rosemary, pepper, thyme, salt, basil, and nutmeg. Sauté until the onion is soft, about 10 minutes. Trim, wash, and dry the chicken livers. Add to the skillet and sauté until nicely browned, about 5 to 10 minutes. Remove from heat and let cool.

Mix the remaining butter in a food processor until fluffy. Add the liver mixture, eggs, Cognac, sherry, and parsley. Purée until smooth. Transfer to a glass serving bowl. Cover with the aspic and chill until firm, about 3 hours or overnight.

PORT ASPIC
1 cup rich beef broth
1 envelope unflavored gelatin
2 tablespoons port

Heat 1/2 cup of the broth until hot. Add gelatin and stir until dissolved. Add the remaining broth and port. Spoon half of the aspic over the prepared pâté. Chill until set. Add the remaining aspic and chill until set.

FIRST COURSES

Livermore Valley

The Livermore Valley, across the Bay from San Francisco to the south and east, is a sunny interior valley with oak-studded rolling hills and a rural feeling. It is reached via Highway 580 through populous Alameda County. This winegrowing region includes five wineries, two of which share a common early founding date: 1883. Production of sacramental and drugstore prescription wines helped these and many California wineries to survive the Prohibition era, and now a fourth generation carries on the family tradition of producing fine varietal wines.

Livermore Valley's gravelly, often rocky, soil, combined with the effects of moderating breezes from nearby San Francisco Bay, has helped this region to become famous for its white varietals, including Sauvignon Blanc, Semillion, Johannisberg Riesling, and Chardonnay. The unique growing conditions of this soil—which some say resembles that of Graves or certain sections of the Rhone Valley in France—have led to the belief that Livermore Valley produces some of California's superior white wines.

White wines in Livermore date back to the 1880s, when Charles Wetmore brought cuttings of Semillon, Sauvignon Blanc, and Muscadelle Bordelais from Château d'Yquem in Sauternes and planted them in Livermore.

A Livermore Valley white varietal wine, such as Semillon or Sauvignon Blanc, would be a pleasant complement to many of the first courses that follow.

ARAM SANDWICHES

MAKES ABOUT 27 SANDWICHES
PREPARATION TIME 1 HOUR

To keep these easy rolled sandwich slices fresh for a picnic, wrap individually in plastic.

1 package Armenian cracker bread (3 crackers)
12 ounces cream cheese, room temperature
Dillweed
1 large head leaf lettuce, washed and dried
3 medium tomatoes, thinly sliced
1 to 2 English cucumbers, thinly sliced
1 1/4 pounds thinly sliced roast beef
Salt
Pepper

Rinse the cracker bread with warm water. Wrap in a damp towel for 10 to 30 minutes, until pliable but not soggy.

Put the light side of 1 cracker bread up. Spread with 4 ounces of the cream cheese. Sprinkle with the dillweed. Layer with some lettuce, 1/3 of the tomatoes, 1/3 of the cucumbers, and 1/3 of the roast beef. Salt and pepper to taste. Repeat with the other pieces of cracker bread.

Roll up jelly-roll style. Wrap in plastic until ready to use. Using a serrated knife, slice off the ends. Slice the remainder of the roll into pieces approximately 3/4 to 1 inch thick.

TOASTY CRAB ROLLS

SERVES 4
PREPARATION TIME 10 MINUTES
COOKING TIME 10 MINUTES

4 French sandwich rolls
4 tablespoons (1/2 stick) melted butter
3/4 pound fresh crab meat
1 cup shredded Gruyère cheese
2 green onions, chopped
1/4 cup mayonnaise
2 tablespoons sour cream
Lemon juice
Salt
Freshly ground pepper
Ground nutmeg

Preheat oven to 400 degrees. Split rolls in half lengthwise. Brush with the butter. Toast lightly. Combine the crab, cheese, onions, mayonnaise, and sour cream. Season to taste with the lemon juice, salt, pepper, and nutmeg. Spoon the crab mixture onto half of the split toasted rolls. Place on a baking sheet. Bake for 5 to 10 minutes or until hot. Serve with the other half of the roll on the side.

STUFFED JAPANESE EGGPLANT

SERVES 12
PREPARATION TIME 30 MINUTES
COOKING TIME 4 HOURS

A variation of the classic Middle Eastern baked eggplant. This dish should be served very cold.

12 tiny eggplants, Japanese or Italian	8 ounces white raisins
Salt	4 ounces olives, sliced
8 ounces slivered almonds	3 teaspoons dried thyme
2 tablespoons butter	Freshly ground pepper
6 yellow onions, finely chopped	1 28-ounce can Italian plum tomatoes
2 cloves of garlic, minced	1 cup olive oil

Preheat the oven to 300 degrees. Remove the tops from the eggplants. Make a deep slit in each lengthwise, being careful not to cut through. Sprinkle the insides with salt and turn upside down on paper towels. Let drain for 15 minutes. Squeeze firmly over the sink to drain out as much moisture as possible.

Sauté the almonds in the butter. Drain on paper towels. In a large bowl, combine the onions, garlic, raisins, half the olives, half the almonds, the thyme, and the pepper. Drain the tomatoes, reserving the juice, and mash with a fork. Place the eggplants in a single layer in an ovenproof baking dish. Put a tablespoon of the tomatoes in each eggplant. Fill the slits with the vegetable mixture. Spoon the remaining tomatoes and juice around the eggplants. Sprinkle with the remaining olives and almonds. Pour the olive oil into the side of the dish. Baste the eggplants with some of the oil. Bake for 3 to 4 hours, basting every thirty minutes. The eggplants are cooked when they are very soft and collapse. Drain off the oil and cool to room temperature. Cover and store in the refrigerator for up to 4 days.

HOT STUFFED CLAMS

SERVES 6
PREPARATION TIME 15 MINUTES
COOKING TIME 3 TO 4 MINUTES

Be sure to serve with plenty of French bread for dipping in the escargot-like sauce. The clams can be prepared in advance and refrigerated until time to broil them.

24 clams, washed and scrubbed
1/4 cup water
4 tablespoons (1/2 stick) butter
1 large garlic clove, minced

2 tablespoons minced fresh parsley
3 tablespoons fine bread crumbs

Place the clams in a large pan with the water. Cover and steam just until their shells open. Remove the whole clams from their shells, saving half of the shells.

Preheat the broiler. Combine the butter, garlic, parsley, and bread crumbs. Place each clam back on the half shell. Spread with a teaspoon of the butter mixture. Place on a baking sheet. Place under the broiler and broil until lightly browned, about 3 to 4 minutes.

SANDWICH NIÇOISE

SERVES 6
PREPARATION TIME 20 MINUTES

This Mediterranean Niçoise salad stuffed into French rolls makes a hearty lunch.

6 French sandwich rolls, 5 to 6 inches long
3 to 4 tablespoons red wine vinegar
1 clove garlic, minced
3/4 cup olive oil
Salt
Freshly ground pepper
1 6 1/2-ounce can tuna, drained
1 green bell pepper, sliced into thin strips

1 large tomato, thinly sliced
2 hard-cooked eggs, thinly sliced
10 Greek black olives, quartered
1 2-ounce can anchovy fillets, drained and chopped
1 tablespoon drained capers
2 to 3 tablespoons chopped fresh basil
2 1/2 cups torn romaine lettuce

Split rolls in half lengthwise and pull out some of the bready center. In a small bowl, beat together the vinegar, garlic, oil, salt, and pepper to taste. Brush the hollowed rolls with some of the dressing. In a medium bowl, combine the remaining ingredients. Toss with the remaining dressing. Toss in lettuce just prior to serving. Fill the rolls with the mixture.

SZECHUAN SAUSAGE IN PITA POCKETS

SERVES 10 TO 12
PREPARATION TIME 30 MINUTES
COOKING TIME 15 MINUTES
REFRIGERATION TIME 1 HOUR

1 1/2 **pounds hot link sausages**
1 1/2 **pounds lean ground pork**
1 **medium eggplant, cubed**
3 **tablespoons peanut oil**
2 **baskets cherry tomatoes, halved**
2 **large red bell peppers, chopped**
1 **large onion, finely chopped**
3/4 **cup chopped green onions**
1/2 **pound mozzarella or Jack cheese, cubed**

4 **tablespoons minced garlic**
2 **tablespoons minced ginger root**
2 **tablespoons soy sauce**
2 **teaspoons sugar**
1 to 2 **tablespoons Chinese chili paste with garlic**
1/2 **cup chopped fresh cilantro**
2 **packages pita bread**
1 **head red leaf lettuce**

Sauté the link sausages until cooked, puncturing the skin to allow the grease to escape. Drain on paper towels. When cool, slice thinly. Sauté the pork until nicely browned, separating with a fork to prevent clumping. Drain well. Set aside with the sausages. Sauté the eggplant in the oil until soft. Drain and set aside.

In a large bowl, combine the tomatoes, red peppers, onion, green onions, and cheese. Mix in the eggplant, sausages, and pork. In a separate bowl, combine the garlic, ginger root, soy sauce, sugar, and chili paste. Add to the other ingredients and mix well. Refrigerate until chilled.

Just prior to serving, mix in cilantro. Warm the pita bread. Cut into halves. Fill the pita pockets with the sausage mixture. Cover a large serving platter with lettuce leaves. Arrange the filled pockets on the leaves. Serve immediately.

TORTINO DI SEMOLINO E FUNGHI

SERVES 6 TO 8
PREPARATION TIME 20 MINUTES
COOKING TIME 1 HOUR

Semolina—a coarse, granular durum wheat flour, is used in this Italian mushroom torte.

TORTINO

Butter

Bread crumbs

1 1/3 cups of milk

2/3 cup semolina flour

2 egg yolks

Pinch of freshly grated nutmeg

4 tablespoons (1/2 stick) butter

1/4 cup freshly grated Parmesan
  cheese

Preheat oven to 375 degrees. Butter a 9-inch springform pan. Sprinkle the bottom and sides with dry bread crumbs. Shake out the excess. In a large saucepan, bring the milk to a boil. Slowly add the semolina flour, stirring constantly so it does not become lumpy. Cook for 10 to 15 minutes, stirring occasionally with a wooden spoon to prevent sticking. Remove from the heat and stir in egg yolks, nutmeg, butter, and the cheese. Pour into the prepared tin. Wet a wooden spoon in cold water. Press the center of the tortino toward the sides, leaving a bowl-shaped indentation. Sprinkle with bread crumbs. Bake for 30 minutes.

FILLING

6 tablespoons butter

2 tablespoons olive oil

1 pound fresh mushrooms,
  sliced

2 cloves garlic, minced

1/2 cup, plus 2 tablespoons
  minced fresh parsley

Salt

Freshly ground pepper

Pinch of dried thyme

1/4 cup freshly grated Parmesan
  cheese

While tortino is in the oven, prepare the filling. Heat the butter and oil in a large skillet. Sauté the mushrooms for 3 to 4 minutes over a high heat. Add the garlic and all but 2 tablespoons of the parsley. Sauté an additional minute. Season to taste with salt, pepper, and a pinch of thyme.

ASSEMBLY

Remove the tortino from the mold and place on a serving platter. Gently reheat the mushrooms and toss with the Parmesan cheese. Place in the center of the tortino. Sprinkle with the remaining parsley and serve immediately.

SWEET AND SOUR AVOCADO

SERVES 4
PREPARATION TIME 10 MINUTES
COOKING TIME 5 MINUTES

2 avocados
4 ounces (1 stick) butter
4 tablespoons sugar
4 tablespoons ketchup
4 tablespoons vinegar

4 teaspoons soy sauce
4 slices bacon, cooked and
   chopped
Butter lettuce

Peel the avocados and slice into halves. In a saucepan, combine the butter, sugar, ketchup, vinegar, and soy sauce. Bring to a gentle simmer and cook until the sugar dissolves.

Place the avocado halves on a bed of butter lettuce leaves. Sprinkle with the crumbled bacon and spoon over the warm sauce.

MUSSELS IN ORANGE-BASIL SAUCE

SERVES 6
PREPARATION TIME 15 MINUTES
REFRIGERATION TIME 4 HOURS
COOKING TIME 5 MINUTES

This excellent dressing is equally delicious with prawns.

2/3 cup freshly squeezed orange
   juice
1/2 cup chopped fresh basil
   leaves
Salt
Freshly ground pepper

3/4 cup olive oil
36 large mussels
2/3 cup dry white wine
Fresh basil leaves
1 orange, cut into thin slices,
   then quartered

Combine the orange juice, basil, salt, and pepper. Slowly whisk in the olive oil. Refrigerate 4 hours or overnight. Remove from the refrigerator 1 hour before using.

Scrub and debeard the mussels. Place together with the wine in a deep pot. Cover and heat to boiling. Steam, stirring once or twice, until the mussels open. Remove to a bowl. Remove the top shells. Arrange the mussels six to a plate. Whisk dressing and spoon generously over the mussels. Garnish the plates with the basil leaves and orange quarters.

MOZZARELLA MARINARA

SERVES 6
PREPARATION TIME 10 MINUTES
REFRIGERATION TIME 30 MINUTES
COOKING TIME 10 MINUTES

The cheese can be prepared at least 3 to 4 hours in advance and refrigerated until frying.

12 ounces mozzarella cheese
2 eggs, beaten with a little
  water
3/4 cup flour

3/4 cup bread crumbs
1 tablespoon Parmesan cheese
Oil for frying
Marinara Sauce†

Slice the mozzarella cheese into 1-ounce pieces. Dip into the beaten egg, then into the flour. Dip into the beaten egg again and finally into the bread crumbs which have been mixed with the Parmesan cheese. Chill at least 30 minutes. Fry in 1/2 inch hot oil until nicely browned on both sides. Drain on paper towels. Spoon 3 tablespoons of Marinara Sauce onto each plate and place two pieces of the fried cheese over it. Top with a little more of the sauce.

MARINATED SNAPPER AND MUSSEL SALAD

SERVES 6 TO 8
PREPARATION TIME 20 MINUTES
COOKING TIME 20 MINUTES
MARINATING TIME 12 HOURS

24 mussels
1 onion, finely chopped
3 shallots, finely chopped
1/2 teaspoon peppercorns
Sprig of fresh parsley
1/2 cup white wine
2 tablespoons olive oil
1 clove garlic, crushed
1 pound fresh red snapper
  fillets
1/2 cup olive oil
1/4 cup lemon juice
1 red onion, finely chopped

2 tablespoons chopped fresh
  parsley
1 teaspoon freshly grated
  orange peel
1/2 teaspoon each cumin and
  paprika
1/4 teaspoon each coriander,
  cardamom, and ginger
1/8 teaspoon each cinnamon,
  ground cloves, and nutmeg
Fresh tomatoes, peeled, seeded,
  and cut into wedges

Scrub the mussels well to remove all dirt. Put them in a sauté pan together with the chopped onion, 2/3 of the shallots, peppercorns, parsley, and wine. Cover and steam until the mussels open. Remove the mussels from their shells and place in a glass or porcelain bowl. Strain the cooking juices left in the pan. Return to the pan and reduce to 2 tablespoons. Pour over the mussels. Heat the 2 tablespoons of oil and the garlic. Add the snapper fillets. Steam quickly, 2 to 3 minutes, covered. Cut into bite-size pieces. Add to the mussels.

Make a dressing with the remaining ingredients, including the shallots. Whisk together well and pour over the warm fish. Let marinate at least 12 hours. Serve cold, accompanied by the tomato wedges.

ARTICHOKE BOTTOMS WITH SALMON PURÉE

SERVES 8
PREPARATION TIME 15 MINUTES
COOKING TIME 30 MINUTES

When shopping for artichokes, look for plump chokes with green, fresh-looking petals; the buds should be tightly closed. For a more professional look, fill a pastry bag with the salmon purée and pipe onto the artichoke bottoms.

8 large artichokes	**Freshly ground pepper to taste**
Handful of finely chopped fresh chives	**1/2 pound fresh salmon, poached**
1/2 cup olive oil	**Mayonnaise**
1/4 cup vinegar	**1 tablespoon fresh lemon juice**
1 to 2 tablespoons Dijon mustard	**1/2 teaspoon dried dill**
Pinch of salt	**Paprika**
Pinch of sugar	**4 tablespoons drained capers**
	4 pitted black olives

Steam the artichokes until tender. Drain and remove the bottoms. In a small bowl, mix together the chives, olive oil, vinegar, mustard, salt, sugar, and pepper. Pour over the warm artichoke bottoms and let marinate for 15 minutes.

Purée the salmon in a food processor or blender and add just enough mayonnaise to bind it together. Add lemon juice, dill, salt, and pepper to taste. Chill until firm.

Drain the artichoke bottoms and fill with the salmon purée. Sprinkle lightly with paprika. Make a circle with the capers. Top with half a black olive. Chill again. Serve cold.

CALIFORNIA CALZONE

SERVES 8
PREPARATION TIME 1 ½ HOURS
COOKING TIME 30 MINUTES

Inside these uniquely shaped crusty pizza sandwiches, you will find the distinctive flavor of tangy goat cheese.

1 recipe Pizza Dough†
Olive oil
4 tomatoes, peeled, seeded, and sliced
4 ounces prosciutto, chopped
10 ounces chèvre cheese, crumbled

8 ounces Jack cheese, grated
¼ cup chopped fresh parsley
4 cloves garlic, minced
1 teaspoon dried thyme

Preheat oven to 450 degrees. Divide the dough into 8 pieces. Roll out into round shapes approximately ¼-inch thick. Brush lightly with olive oil. Arrange the tomato slices on half the dough. Sprinkle with the remaining ingredients, leaving a ½-inch border. Fold the top half of the dough over, pressing the edges together with the tines of a fork to seal. Brush with olive oil and cut two small slits on top. Place on a cookie sheet. Bake for approximately 20 to 30 minutes, or until puffed and nicely browned.

AMARETTO PRAWNS

SERVES 4
PREPARATION TIME 30 MINUTES
COOKING TIME 10 MINUTES

This rich and sweet dish is ideal in small portions as a first course to a candlelit dinner.

16 large prawns
2 tablespoons butter
¾ teaspoon finely grated lemon peel
½ teaspoon finely grated orange peel
2 tablespoons freshly squeezed lemon juice

2 tablespoons freshly squeezed orange juice
3 tablespoons brandy
2 teaspoons Amaretto liqueur
¾ cup heavy cream
Salt
White pepper

Shell prawns, leaving tails intact, and devein. Melt butter in a large skillet. Add prawns and cook for 4 to 5 minutes. Remove from the pan and set aside. Mix together the lemon and orange peel, lemon and orange juice, brandy, and Amaretto and bring to a boil in the pan. Add heavy cream and continue cooking until slightly reduced and thick enough to coat the prawns. Return the prawns to the pan and cook until heated. Season to taste with salt and pepper. Arrange the prawns, four to a plate, in a circular fashion with the tails pointing in. Mask with the sauce. Serve immediately.

PON-PON CHICKEN

SERVES 4 TO 6
PREPARATION TIME 10 MINUTES
COOKING TIME 20 MINUTES

This dish can be served either as a first course or as a light luncheon entree.

1 frying chicken, about 2 1/2 pounds, or 2 whole chicken breasts
1 1/2 tablespoons sesame paste
1 tablespoon soy sauce
1 teaspoon chili oil
1 teaspoon each sugar, sesame oil, rice vinegar, bean sauce

1 teaspoon minced green onion
1 teaspoon minced ginger root
1/2 teaspoon minced garlic
1/8 teaspoon crushed pepper flakes
4 ounces water chestnuts, sliced
Lettuce leaves
Fresh cilantro sprigs

Steam the chicken or chicken breasts until tender, about 20 to 30 minutes. Remove from heat and let stand until cool. Combine the remaining ingredients, except the water chestnuts, lettuce leaves, and cilantro. Mix well and refrigerate until ready to use. Remove the meat off the chicken and cut into strips.

Mix the sauce thoroughly again and pour over the shredded chicken and water chestnuts. Toss until evenly coated with the sauce. Cover the bottom of a serving platter with lettuce leaves. Arrange chicken strips on top of the lettuce. Garnish with cilantro sprigs, if desired.

HERB-STUFFED PRAWNS

SERVES 6
PREPARATION TIME 20 MINUTES
COOKING TIME 5 MINUTES

18 large prawns
1 large onion, chopped
2 tablespoons butter
2 tablespoons chopped fresh
  parsley
1 teaspoon dried tarragon
1 teaspoon dried chervil
2 cups fresh bread crumbs

2 eggs
1/4 cup heavy cream
Salt
Pepper
Flour
Dried bread crumbs
8 ounces (2 sticks) butter
2 tablespoons lemon juice

Preheat oven to 450 degrees. Shell prawns, leaving tails intact. Sauté the onion in the butter until soft. Add the parsley, tarragon, and chervil. Combine with the fresh bread crumbs, 1 beaten egg, and the cream. Season to taste with salt and pepper.

Split the prawns down the back. Place a spoonful of the filling down the middle. Dip the stuffed prawns first in the flour, then in 1 beaten egg, and lastly in the dried bread crumbs. Place on a greased cookie sheet. Melt 4 ounces of the butter with 1 tablespoon of the lemon juice. Brush the prawns and bake for 5 minutes. Melt the remaining butter and lemon juice. Pass separately.

GREEN CRÊPES

MAKES 12
PREPARATION TIME 1 HOUR
COOKING TIME 45 MINUTES

CRÊPE BATTER
4 eggs
1 cup milk
1 cup flour
5 ounces spinach, washed,
  cooked, and squeezed dry

1/4 teaspoon freshly grated
  nutmeg

Put all ingredients in food processor or blender. Mix until puréed and well blended. Transfer to a bowl and let rest for 30 minutes while making the filling. Follow directions for making Basic Crêpes†. Makes 12 crêpes.

CRÊPE FILLING

10 ounces fresh spinach,
   washed, cooked, and drained
1 cup grated Swiss cheese
1 small clove garlic, pressed
4 egg yolks
1/2 cup chopped fresh parsley
1/2 teaspoon freshly grated
   nutmeg

Salt
Freshly ground pepper
1/2 pound thinly sliced
   prosciutto
Tomato Sauce†

Preheat oven to 350 degrees. Finely chop the spinach. Mix with the cheese, garlic, egg yolks, parsley, and nutmeg. Season to taste with salt and pepper.

ASSEMBLY

Spread out the crêpes and cover with the prosciutto. Place a little of the spinach filling over the ham. Roll up the crêpe. Place seam side down, in a greased baking dish. Cover with foil. Bake for 15 minutes or until thoroughly heated. Place on individual plates. Spoon over the warmed Tomato Sauce. Serve immediately.

PECAN-STUFFED MUSHROOMS

SERVES 6
PREPARATION TIME 30 MINUTES
COOKING TIME 20 MINUTES

A festive holiday starter.

12 large mushroom caps
1 cup chopped pecans
4 tablespoons softened butter
3 tablespoons chopped fresh
   parsley
1/4 teaspoon chopped garlic

1/4 teaspoon dried thyme
1/4 teaspoon salt
Twist of freshly ground pepper
1/2 cup heavy cream
1/4 cup bourbon

Preheat oven to 375 degrees. Arrange the mushroom caps in a baking dish. Mix together the remaining ingredients, except the heavy cream and bourbon. Stuff into the caps. Combine the heavy cream and bourbon. Spoon over each cap. Bake for 10 minutes, covered. Remove the cover, baste with the sauce, and continue baking for an additional 10 minutes, uncovered. To serve: spoon some of the sauce onto a plate. Place two of the stuffed mushroom caps on top.

HAWAIIAN BAKED PAPAYA

SERVES 6
PREPARATION TIME 10 MINUTES
COOKING TIME 10 MINUTES

3 papayas, cut in half
3/4 cup cream cheese
3/4 cup cottage cheese
2 tablespoons chopped chutney
1/8 to 1/4 teaspoon curry
   powder

1/2 cup thinly sliced water
   chestnuts
1 tablespoon white raisins
1 tablespoon sugar
1 tablespoon cinnamon
2 tablespoons melted butter

Preheat oven to 450 degrees. Remove the seeds from the papayas. Slice a little piece from the bottoms so the papayas will sit flat. Place on a baking sheet. Combine the cheeses, chutney, and curry powder. Beat until smooth. Fold in the water chestnuts and raisins. Fill each papaya with some of the filling. Mix sugar and cinnamon together. Sprinkle over the top. Drizzle with the butter. Bake for 10 minutes. Serve immediately.

SPINACH PÂTÉ

SERVES 8
PREPARATION TIME 30 MINUTES
COOKING TIME 45 MINUTES

3 pounds fresh spinach,
   stemmed and washed
1 tablespoon butter
1/2 cup finely chopped onion
1/4 pound fresh mushrooms,
   finely chopped
1 clove garlic, minced
3 tablespoons dry white wine
1 teaspoon dried thyme
3 eggs
1/2 cup milk

1/2 cup bread crumbs
1/4 cup freshly grated Parmesan
   cheese
1/4 cup chopped fresh parsley
1 tablespoon lemon juice
1 teaspoon oregano
1/2 teaspoon salt
1/2 teaspoon freshly grated
   pepper
Pinch of freshly grated nutmeg
Tomato Sauce†

Preheat oven to 350 degrees. Place the spinach in a large pot with just the water that clings to it. Cook until just wilted. Drain and rinse under cold water. Squeeze out all the water. Chop until almost puréed.

Heat the butter in a skillet. Sauté the onion until soft. Add the mushrooms, garlic, wine, and thyme. Cook until the mushrooms are tender and all the liquid evaporates. Transfer to a bowl with the spinach. Whip the eggs with the milk. Stir into the spinach mixture, together with the remaining ingredients. Taste and adjust seasonings.

Butter a loaf pan or terrine. Line with buttered parchment or wax paper. Spoon the mixture into the prepared mold and smooth the top. Cover with foil. Bake for 45 minutes or until firm. Remove from oven and cool before unmolding. Serve garnished with Tomato Sauce.

BLUE CHEESE AND ARTICHOKE FLAN

SERVES 10 TO 12
PREPARATION TIME 30 MINUTES
COOKING TIME 35 MINUTES

To serve as an appetizer, bake in a square dish and cut into pieces. This can be made several hours in advance and brought to room temperature just before serving.

Butter
4 tablespoons fine dry bread
   crumbs
16 ounces cream cheese
1 1/3 cups sour cream
1 ounce crumbled blue cheese
3 tablespoons butter
3 eggs
2 tablespoons chopped fresh
   parsley
Pinch each of dried thyme and
   marjoram
Salt
Freshly ground black pepper
1 cup cooked artichoke hearts,
   quartered
4 cooked artichoke hearts

Preheat the oven to 375 degrees. Butter a 10-inch pie plate. Coat evenly with bread crumbs, shaking out the excess. Refrigerate until set.

Combine the cream cheese, 2/3 of a cup of the sour cream, blue cheese, and butter in an electric mixer or food processor. Blend well. Stir in the eggs, herbs, and seasonings. Fold in the quartered artichoke hearts. Spread evenly into the prepared plate. Bake until puffed and lightly browned, about 30 to 35 minutes. Let cool.

Spread the top of the cooled flan with the remaining sour cream. Cut the artichoke hearts in half. Arrange evenly over the top. Cut into wedges. Serve at room temperature.

ASPARAGUS TORTE

SERVES 8
PREPARATION TIME 25 MINUTES
COOKING TIME 25 MINUTES

The bread, used as the torte shell, must be very thinly sliced. Excellent for brunch when served in au gratin dishes.

3 pounds fresh asparagus, peeled
Loaf of white bread, thinly sliced
Softened butter
10 ounces Gruyère cheese, thinly sliced
1/2 pound prosciutto, thinly sliced and cubed

Salt
Freshly ground pepper
Freshly ground nutmeg
4 egg yolks
2/3 cup heavy cream
1/4 cup freshly grated Parmesan cheese

Preheat oven to 375 degrees. Cut the asparagus spears all the same length. Place in a skillet and cover with boiling water. Cook until tender. Drain under cold water and dry. Remove the crusts from the bread. Spread the slices with butter. Place, buttered side down, in a 10-inch round pizza pan. It may be necessary to cut some of the bread slices to fit the pan. The bottom of the pan should be completely covered. Layer half of the Gruyère over the bread slices. Arrange the asparagus in a spoke fashion, with the tips pointing in, over the cheese. Top with the remaining Gruyère and prosciutto. Sprinkle with a little salt, pepper, and nutmeg. Beat the egg yolks with the cream and pour over the torte. Sprinkle with the Parmesan cheese. Place on a cookie sheet and bake for 25 minutes, or until golden brown. Cut into wedges and serve immediately.

FRIED CAMEMBERT CRÊPES

SERVES 6
PREPARATION TIME 15 MINUTES
COOKING TIME 10 MINUTES

12 Crêpes†
12 ounces Camembert cheese
Flour
2 eggs, beaten with a little water

Fine bread crumbs
Oil for frying

Remove the rind from the cheese. Cut cheese into small pieces. Place in a food processor or mixer and beat until smooth. Flour hands and shape the cheese into a roll. Cut into 12 pieces. Place a piece of the cheese in the middle of each crêpe. Fold in the sides and roll up.

Dip the rolled crêpes first in the flour and then in the egg. Roll in the bread crumbs. Heat oil in a deep fryer or pan. Drop in the crêpes and fry until golden brown. Serve immediately.

BEUREK

SERVES 10 TO 12
PREPARATION TIME 30 MINUTES
COOKING TIME 35 MINUTES

While rolling a phyllo sheet for these Turkish cheese rolls, keep the other pastry sheets in a plastic bag in the refrigerator. Any favorite purée recipe will make a fine filling. Just remember to add an egg or bread crumbs to firm it up while baking.

1 pound Jack cheese, grated
2 1/2 pounds frozen spinach, thawed and drained
1 pound ricotta cheese
1 1/2 pounds cooked shrimp
1 egg
1 bunch green onions, finely chopped

1 bunch parsley, chopped
1/2 teaspoon oregano
Salt
Freshly ground pepper
1 pound phyllo dough
1 cup (2 sticks) melted butter
Sour cream
Fresh parsley

Preheat oven to 350 degrees. Combine all of the ingredients, except the phyllo dough, butter, sour cream, and parsley; mix well. Taste and correct for seasonings. Set aside.

Remove phyllo from package. Cut in half down the width. Take a half a sheet at a time and spread with a little butter. Place another half a sheet on top of it and spread with more butter. At the nearest end, place 1/2 cup of filling. Cover with another sheet of phyllo and brush lightly with butter. Take 1/2 inch on either side and fold over to make a tube. Roll the tube. Place on a cookie sheet seam side down. Keep prepared rolls covered while repeating the rolling process until all of the filling is gone. Place rolls 1 inch apart on the cookie sheet. Bake for about 35 to 40 minutes, or until golden brown. Serve immediately with a dollop of sour cream. Garnish with fresh parsley.

CHINESE-STYLE MUSHROOMS

SERVES 6
PREPARATION TIME 30 MINUTES
COOKING TIME 20 MINUTES

Serve on a bed of watercress as an elegant first course to a Chinese dinner.

24 large fresh mushrooms
1/2 pound lean ground pork
8 water chestnuts, minced
1 clove of garlic, minced
1 tablespoon soy sauce
1 tablespoon sherry

1/2 teaspoon sugar
1 teaspoon cornstarch
1/4 teaspoon salt
Oil for frying
1/2 cup beef or chicken stock
1 tablespoon oyster sauce

Clean the mushroom caps and remove the stems. Mince the stems. Combine with the ground pork, water chestnuts, and garlic. Add soy sauce, sherry, sugar, cornstarch, and salt. Mix well. Spoon 1 tablespoon of the filling into each mushroom cap.

Heat a little oil in a large skillet. Place the mushrooms in the pan with the filled side up. Brown for a minute. Add stock, cover and simmer for 15 minutes. Uncover and add oyster sauce to the pan. Baste each mushroom with a little of the sauce. Serve hot.

MINCED CHICKEN ON LETTUCE LEAVES

SERVES 4
PREPARATION TIME 20 MINUTES
COOKING TIME 15 MINUTES

Oil for deep frying
1/4 pound rice-stick noodles
Iceberg lettuce
1/4 cup peanut oil
1/2 pound chicken, skinned, boned, and finely chopped
3 green onions, finely chopped
8 dried Chinese mushrooms, rehydrated and minced
1 cup water chestnuts, minced
3 tablespoons minced smoked ham

1 to 2 teaspoons grated ginger root
1 tablespoon sherry
1 tablespoon oyster sauce
1 tablespoon soy sauce
1 tablespoon cornstarch, dissolved in 2 tablespoons of water
1 teaspoon sesame oil
1/2 teaspoon sugar
Pinch of white pepper

Heat oil in a deep fryer to 375 degrees or until a test noodle puffs without turning brown. Separate noodles and fry a little at a time until puffed. Drain on paper towels. Crush slightly and arrange on a platter.

Remove the outer cup-shaped leaves from lettuce one by one. Arrange around the noodles on the platter.

Heat the peanut oil in a wok or skillet. Add the chicken and green onions and stir-fry briefly. Add the mushrooms, water chestnuts, ham, and ginger root. Continue to stir-fry for 2 minutes. Mix the remaining ingredients together. Add to the chicken and stir-fry for 1 minute. Spoon over the fried noodles. Serve immediately.

SPINACH ROLL

SERVES 8
PREPARATION TIME 30 MINUTES
COOKING TIME 30 MINUTES

SPINACH ROLL

Oil	1 cup milk
3 tablespoons dry bread crumbs	Salt
	Pepper
1 cup chopped fresh spinach	Freshly grated nutmeg
3 tablespoons butter	4 egg yolks
4 tablespoons flour	4 egg whites

Preheat the oven to 375 degrees. Brush a jelly-roll pan with oil. Line with parchment paper. Brush the top of the paper with oil. Sprinkle with the bread crumbs. Cook the spinach. Drain and when cool enough to handle, squeeze as dry as possible. Set aside until needed.

Melt the butter in a saucepan. Add the flour and cook for 2 minutes without browning. Gradually stir in the milk. Bring to a boil and continue cooking for 3 minutes, stirring constantly. Remove from the heat and season with the salt, pepper, and nutmeg. Stir in the spinach. Let cool slightly, then beat in the egg yolks one at a time. Whip the egg whites until stiff. Gently fold into the spinach mixture. Spread evenly over the bottom of the pan. Bake for 15 to 20 minutes, or until nicely browned. Prepare the filling while the roll is baking.

FILLING

4 ounces (1 stick) butter	1 to 2 tablespoons
2 pounds of mushrooms, thinly sliced	Worcestershire sauce
	2 cups sour cream

Melt the butter in a sauté pan. Add the mushrooms, a few at a time, and sauté over a high heat. When the mushrooms have browned, stir in the Worcestershire sauce. Cook an additional 2 to 3 minutes. Season to taste with salt and pepper. Add the sour cream. Cook until most of the liquid evaporates and the cream thickens.

ASSEMBLY

Remove the roll from the oven. Turn out onto a sheet of wax paper. Carefully pull away the parchment paper. Brush lightly with a little melted butter. Spread the mushroom mixture evenly over the top. Roll up jelly-roll fashion, starting at the long end. Slice and serve hot.

SOUPS

Mendocino

Mendocino County, the northernmost of the Bay Area wine-growing regions, features some of California's most beautiful, rugged coastline and thick redwood forests. The area lies north of Sonoma County and extends from the Pacific Ocean to Lake County on its eastern borders.

Mendocino County has a rich and colorful past. The name Mendocino was first applied to Cape Mendocino in 1542 by Juan Rodriguez Cabrillo in honor of Antonio de Mendoza, the first Viceroy of Spain. In 1852, the redwood forests and their potential for logging were discovered, and a party set sail from San Francisco and built a sawmill on a point at the northwest edge of Mendocino Bay. Even though treacherous fogs and winter storms claimed many sailing vessels off its coast, the town grew and prospered as a lumber and fishing town until around 1937. Today, Mendocino has a large population of artists, and many of its unique nineteenth-century New England-style architectural treasures have been restored, some converted into bed and breakfast inns. Mendocino is a popular and romantic weekend getaway for San Francisco city dwellers. Many remember the movies, *Summer of 42* and *Same Time, Next Year,* which were filmed in and around the town.

In Mendocino County's north coast terrain, like other Bay Area wine-growing regions, hills alternate with valleys, but the hills are steeper, the valleys narrower, and the towns and population smaller. Its warm, inland, valley regions provide the right climate for growing Mendocino County's premium varietal grapes. Despite their exposure to the cool coastal fogs and breezes the steeper hills surrounding Mendocino's interior valleys provide enough warmth for most varietals. The town of Ukiah serves as the hub of a wheel from which Mendocino's five valleys fan out in all directions: Ukiah Valley, McDowell Valley, Redwood Valley, Potter Valley, and Anderson Valley.

Whether one sips a hearty, steaming soup in rugged old Mendocino on a foggy winter night, or enjoys a cool, chilled soup on a hot summer day in one of the areas interior valleys, Mendocino and soups go well together. Coupled with a Mendocino wine, they are a sublime duo.

SHRIMP GAZPACHO

SERVES 6
PREPARATION TIME 30 MINUTES
REFRIGERATION TIME 8 HOURS

On a warm summer night, this classic soup is refreshing. It can be prepared well in advance for easy entertaining as a first course or as a luncheon entree.

1 quart bottle clamato juice
1/4 cup peeled, seeded, and finely chopped cucumber
1/3 cup thinly sliced green onions
2 tablespoons olive oil
2 tablespoons red wine vinegar
1 tablespoon sugar
1 cup tomato juice
1 clove garlic, crushed

1/2 teaspoon Tabasco sauce
2 tablespoons lemon juice
1/2 to 3/4 pound tiny cooked shrimp
Salt and pepper to taste
1 avocado
4 ounces cream cheese, well chilled
Fresh chives

Place all the ingredients, except shrimp, avocado, cream cheese, and chives in a bowl and mix well. Add the shrimp. Taste and add salt and pepper as necessary. Chill well (at least 8 hours). When ready to serve, finely chop the avocado and cream cheese. Ladle the soup into bowls and top with the avocado and cream cheese pieces. Garnish with freshly chopped chives.

CHEDDAR CHEESE SOUP

SERVES 8
PREPARATION TIME 15 MINUTES
COOKING TIME 30 MINUTES

3 large onions, chopped
1 green pepper, seeded and chopped
2 celery stalks, chopped
6 tablespoons butter
4 tablespoons flour
4 to 4 1/2 cups chicken stock

Juice of 1 lemon
1 1/2 pounds Cheddar cheese, grated
2 cups half-and-half
1/4 teaspoon salt
1/8 teaspoon white pepper
Chopped fresh parsley

Sauté the onions, green pepper, and celery in the butter for 5 minutes or until softened. Stir in the flour and cook for 3 minutes. Add 4 cups of the chicken stock, the lemon juice, and the cheese. Cook an additional 15 minutes.

Put through a food mill or food processor. Return to a clean pot and add the half-and-half. Reheat and season with salt and pepper. Thin with the remaining stock if too thick. Garnish each serving with the chopped parsley.

MEXICAN BLACK BEAN SOUP CON SALSA

SERVES 8 TO 10
PREPARATION TIME 30 MINUTES
COOKING TIME 3 HOURS

Serrano peppers are firm, dark green, and only about 1 1/2 inches long. Fiery hot, they may be blanched and frozen. This zesty soup has a hearty dose of chili and an accent of fresh cilantro. Serve with crusty French bread and a Petite Sirah.

SOUP

1 pound dried black beans	2 chili pequins, crumbled
1 ham hock	1 tomato, peeled and chopped
2 tablespoons oil	1/2 teaspoon oregano
1 onion, chopped	Salt to taste
2 to 3 cloves garlic	Pepper to taste

Rinse the beans well and place, together with the ham hock, in a saucepan. Cover with cold water, bring to a boil, and simmer, uncovered, until tender (about 2 to 3 hours). Remove ham hock and save for another use.

Heat the oil in a skillet and sauté the onion for 2 to 3 minutes. Add the garlic and cook for an additional minute, without browning. Add the remaining ingredients and sauté for an additional 5 minutes, stirring occasionally. Add to the bean mixture and simmer for 20 minutes. Purée, a little at a time, in a blender or food processor. Add salt and pepper to taste. If soup becomes too thick when reheated, thin with a little chicken or beef stock.

SALSA

3 tomatoes, peeled and seeded	1 serrano (or jalapeño) chili,
1/3 onion	seeded
1/2 cup fresh cilantro	1 clove garlic
Juice of 1 lime	Sour cream for garnish

To prepare Salsa, finely chop all of the ingredients. To serve: ladle soup into serving bowls and garnish with some of the Salsa and a dollop of sour cream on each serving.

SHALLOT AND TARRAGON CREAM SOUP

SERVES 6
PREPARATION TIME 15 MINUTES
COOKING TIME 50 MINUTES

This is a very elegant soup, served hot or cold. Be a purist—use only shallots for a mild onion flavor.

6 cups chicken stock
8 large shallots, thinly sliced
2 sprigs fresh tarragon (or 1/2 teaspoon dried)
2 stalks celery with leaves, chopped

Salt to taste
White pepper to taste
4 egg yolks
1 cup heavy cream
Chopped fresh chives
Paprika

Bring the chicken stock, shallots, tarragon, and celery to a boil in a saucepan. Lower the heat, cover and simmer for 45 minutes. Pass through a food mill or strainer and season to taste with the salt and pepper. Cool slightly. Whip the egg yolks with the cream and add to the soup, whisking constantly. Slowly reheat, stirring constantly, until slightly thickened. Be careful not to boil or the soup will curdle. Serve hot, garnished with the freshly chopped chives and a dash of paprika.

CREAM OF TURKEY AND WILD RICE SOUP

SERVES 6 TO 8
PREPARATION TIME 15 MINUTES
COOKING TIME 35 MINUTES

An excellent way to use up leftover turkey. The addition of wild rice perfectly complements this festive dish.

6 tablespoons butter
4 tablespoons flour
2 cups half-and-half
3 cups turkey broth
1 cup chopped cooked turkey
1/2 cup chopped onion

1/2 cup sliced celery
1 1/2 cups cooked wild rice
Salt
Pepper
Thinly sliced blanched carrots

Melt the butter in a saucepan. Blend in flour and cook for two minutes without browning. Slowly add the half-and-half and 1 cup of the broth, whisking constantly. Bring to a boil and cook for a few minutes. Add the remaining broth, turkey, onion, celery, and the wild rice. Season with the salt and pepper and simmer for 30 minutes. Garnish with the carrots.

HOT AND SOUR SOUP

SERVES 6 TO 8
PREPARATION TIME 45 MINUTES
COOKING TIME 25 MINUTES

This spicy-hot soup is seasoned with sherry and ginger for a delicate flavor. Slashes of mushroom and shredded pork make it a most satisfying meal in itself.

4 dried Chinese mushrooms
3 pieces wood or tree ears
4 cups chicken stock
1/4 cup sherry
6 green onions, chopped
2 tablespoons chopped fresh ginger
3 tablespoons sesame seed oil
1/2 cup bamboo shoots, shredded
1/4 pound boneless pork, cut into thin strips
1/2 teaspoon salt
1 tablespoon soy sauce
1 piece of bean curd, 4 × 4, shredded
1/4 teaspoon white pepper
3 tablespoons wine vinegar
2 tablespoons cornstarch, mixed with 1 tablespoon water
1 egg, lightly beaten
1 green onion, finely chopped (include green top)
1 teaspoon chili oil (optional for a hotter soup)

Soak the mushrooms and wood ears in 1/2 cup of warm water for 30 minutes. Drain and cut into thin strips.

In a saucepan, combine the stock, sherry, green onions, ginger, and 1 tablespoon of the sesame seed oil. Bring to a boil, simmer over low heat for 20 minutes, and strain.

Return to the pan. Add the mushrooms, wood ears, bamboo shoots, pork, salt, and soy sauce. Bring to a boil, immediately reduce heat to low, cover pan, and simmer for three minutes. Drop in the bean curd and add the pepper and vinegar. Bring to a boil again. Stir the cornstarch mixture and pour into the soup, stirring until the soup thickens. Slowly pour in the beaten egg, stirring all the while. Remove the soup from the heat, stir in the remaining sesame seed oil, and sprinkle the top with the green onion. For a hotter soup, add the chili oil.

MEDITERRANEAN FISHERMAN'S SOUP WITH HOT PEPPER SAUCE

SERVES 6 TO 8
PREPARATION TIME 30 MINUTES
COOKING TIME 1 HOUR 10 MINUTES

Here is a simple fish chowder enriched by the Rouille, a garlic and pepper sauce. Marvelous as a main course.

2 cups thinly sliced onions
1 cup thinly sliced leeks
3/4 cup olive oil
2 cups dry white wine
6 cups water
2 pounds fish bones and
   trimmings
6 cups canned tomatoes,
   chopped
1 clove finely chopped garlic
1 piece fresh orange peel
1 teaspoon dried thyme

2 parsley sprigs
1 bay leaf
1/2 teaspoon saffron
Pinch of salt
Freshly ground black pepper
8 slices dried French bread,
   rubbed with garlic
1/2 cup freshly grated Parmesan
   cheese
Basil Rouille or Bell Pepper
   Rouille (recipes follow)

In a large saucepan, cook the onions and leeks in the oil over low heat, stirring frequently, for 5 minutes. Add the wine, water, fish bones and trimmings, tomatoes, garlic, orange peel, herbs, and seasonings. Cook uncovered over moderate heat for 1 hour. Pass through a food mill or strainer, pressing against the back with a wooden spoon. Return to the pot and reheat.

Toast the French bread. To serve: ladle the soup into bowls, place a slice of bread on top and sprinkle with some of the cheese. Spoon a tablespoon of one of the following Rouille sauces on top.

BASIL ROUILLE
2 small dried red chilies
1 small bunch basil leaves
2 to 3 cloves of garlic
1/4 teaspoon salt
1/8 teaspoon pepper
1 thick slice of French bread,
   soaked in water and squeezed
   dry

1 red bell pepper, broiled,
   skinned, and seeded
1/2 cup olive oil

In a food processor or blender, crush the dried chilies. Add the basil, garlic, salt, and pepper and blend to a paste. Add bread and the red pepper and continue blending until puréed. Add the oil slowly and blend until the mixture is thick.

BELL PEPPER ROUILLE

2 small green bell peppers, seeded and chopped
1 dry chili pepper (optional)
1 cup water
2 pimentos, drained and dried

4 cloves of garlic
6 tablespoons olive oil
1 to 3 tablespoons fine bread crumbs
Hot pepper sauce

Simmer the green peppers and the chili pepper in the water for 10 minutes. Drain and pat dry. In a food processor or blender, mash the peppers, pimentos, and garlic to a smooth paste. Slowly beat in the olive oil and add enough bread crumbs to thicken the sauce. Taste and season with a few drops of hot pepper sauce if the chili pepper has been omitted.

PORTUGUESE VEGETABLE SOUP

SERVES 8
PREPARATION TIME 15 MINUTES
COOKING TIME 2 HOURS

An unusual and spicy vegetable soup. You can substitute Italian or pork sausage if linguica is unavailable.

1 to 1 1/2 pounds ham hocks
12 ounces linguica sausage, diced
3 medium potatoes, diced
3 celery stalks, including leaves, chopped
2 medium carrots, diced
1 green bell pepper, seeded, deveined and chopped

1/2 bunch parsley, chopped
2 15-ounce cans kidney beans, rinsed and drained
1 15-ounce can tomato sauce
1 bay leaf
1/2 to 1 teaspoon hot pepper sauce, or to taste
1/4 teaspoon salt
1 teaspoon pepper

Combine ham hocks and sausage in large saucepan. Sauté over medium high heat for 5 minutes. Add the remaining ingredients together with water to cover, about 6 cups. Bring to a boil, skimming foam from the surface. Reduce heat and simmer 2 hours. Remove the ham hocks and bay leaf from the soup. Remove the meat from the bone, cut into bite-size pieces, and return to the soup. Ladle into bowls and serve hot.

RED PEPPER SOUP

SERVES 6
PREPARATION TIME 30 MINUTES
COOKING TIME 45 MINUTES

Roasted red peppers give this unusual soup the smoky flavor of Mayan cooking.

6 large red peppers
3 carrots, peeled
4 shallots, peeled
1 pear, peeled
1 clove garlic, peeled
2 tablespoons olive oil
4 tablespoons butter

4 cups chicken stock
1/2 teaspoon crushed dried red
  pepper
Pinch of cayenne pepper
Salt and pepper to taste
Fresh tarragon or parsley

Roast two of the red peppers directly over a gas flame or under the broiler. Roast until completely charred and remove the skin under cold running water. Remove the seeds, drain on paper towels, and set aside until needed. Thinly slice the remaining peppers, carrots, shallots, pear, and garlic.

Sauté the sliced vegetables and pear in the oil and butter until tender, about 10 minutes. Add the stock, dried red pepper, cayenne pepper, and a dash of salt and black pepper. Bring to a boil and simmer, covered, for 30 minutes.

Purée the soup in a blender or food processor, adding one of the roasted red peppers. Pour the puréed soup back into the pan and reheat. Julienne the remaining red pepper and add to the soup. Garnish with fresh tarragon or parsley.

CREAM OF BROCCOLI SOUP

SERVES 6
PREPARATION TIME 20 MINUTES
COOKING TIME 30 MINUTES

4 tablespoons butter
1 medium onion, chopped
3 tablespoons flour
3 cups chicken stock
1 1/2 pounds fresh broccoli

2 cups milk
1/2 teaspoon salt
1/2 teaspoon pepper
Grated Parmesan or Swiss
  cheese for garnish

Melt the butter in a saucepan over medium heat. Add the onion and sauté for 10 minutes or until golden. Stir in the flour and cook for an additional minute. Gradually add the stock and the broccoli. Bring to a boil, stirring frequently. Cover and simmer for 15 minutes, or until the broccoli is tender.

Purée in a blender or food processor. Return to the saucepan. Add the milk and salt and pepper. Reheat, stirring occasionally. Ladle into ovenproof bowls and sprinkle with the cheese. Run under a preheated broiler until the cheese is nicely browned.

CREAM OF CHESTNUT SOUP

SERVES 8

PREPARATION TIME 30 MINUTES

COOKING TIME 2 1/2 HOURS

A perfect soup for a Christmas or holiday dinner.

1 1/2 **pounds fresh chestnuts or** 1 **pound canned**	2 **cups dry white wine**
1 **veal knuckle**	1 **tablespoon salt**
3 **carrots, peeled and chopped**	2 **garlic cloves (wrapped in cheesecloth)**
3 **celery stalks, chopped**	1 **cup heavy cream**
3 **medium onions, chopped**	2 **tablespoons brandy**
3 **tablespoons butter**	**Freshly ground black pepper**
9 **cups water**	**Fresh chopped parsley**

If using fresh chestnuts, make a deep crisscross gash on the flat side of each nut. Cover with boiling water and simmer for 20 minutes. Drain the chestnuts and, while still warm, remove the shells and skins. Set aside.

Wash the veal knuckle. Pat dry and set aside. In a large stock pot, cook the carrots, celery, and onions in the butter for 10 minutes without browning. Place the veal knuckle on top and add the water, wine, and salt. Cover the pot and simmer for 2 hours.

Let the stock cool. Remove the veal knuckle and meat; skim the fat from the surface with paper towels. Strain the stock, reserving the vegetables. Return the vegetables to the pot along with 6 cups of the broth, the peeled chestnuts, and the garlic. Cover and simmer the broth for 20 minutes. Remove the garlic and purée the mixture in a food mill or processor, a little at a time, until smooth. Return to the pot. Add the cream and brandy. Bring the soup to a simmer and add salt and pepper to taste. If the soup is too thick, add a little veal stock. Serve hot, sprinkled with the parsley.

CHICKEN-CHEESE CHOWDER

SERVES 6
PREPARATION TIME 15 MINUTES
COOKING TIME 10 MINUTES

A colorful, tangy soup with an intriguing trio of cheese, carrots, and chicken for its main flavors.

1 cup shredded carrots
1/4 cup chopped onion
4 tablespoons butter
4 tablespoons flour
2 cups milk
2 cups chicken stock
2 cups diced cooked chicken
2 tablespoons dry white wine

1/2 teaspoon Worcestershire
sauce
1/2 teaspoon celery seed
Salt
Freshly ground black pepper
2 cups grated sharp Cheddar
cheese
Fresh chives

In a large saucepan, simmer carrots and onion in butter until soft but not brown. Blend in flour and cook for 1 minute, stirring constantly. Slowly pour in the milk and chicken stock and stir until thickened. Let simmer for 5 minutes.

Add the cooked chicken, wine, Worcestershire sauce, and celery seed to the stock. Add salt and pepper to taste. Add the cheese and stir until just melted. Do not let it boil. Serve garnished with chopped chives.

SPINACH SOUP

SERVES 4 TO 6
PREPARATION TIME 20 MINUTES
COOKING TIME 10 MINUTES

A pure delight.

2 pounds fresh spinach
1 cup beef or chicken broth
4 tablespoons butter
4 tablespoons flour
1 1/4 cups half-and-half
1 clove pressed garlic
6 ounces finely grated Gruyère
cheese

Salt to taste
Freshly grated black pepper
Freshly grated nutmeg, or sour
cream
1 lemon, thinly sliced

Wash the spinach, remove the stems, and cook with just the water that clings to the leaves, until tender. Drain and squeeze out as much moisture as possible. Purée in a food processor or blender together with the broth. Set aside.

Melt the butter in a saucepan, add the flour, and cook for 2 minutes without letting it brown. Slowly add the puréed mixture together with the half-and-half, garlic, and cheese. Blend and adjust seasonings, adding salt and pepper as needed. Serve with a sprinkling of freshly grated nutmeg or a dollop of sour cream and a piece of thinly sliced lemon floating on top.

MUSHROOM BISQUE WITH A GARNISH OF FRESH MUSHROOMS

SERVES 6 TO 8
PREPARATION TIME 15 MINUTES
COOKING TIME 30 MINUTES

The texture of the barely heated raw mushrooms in this creamy soup will delight your senses.

4 ounces (1 stick) butter
2 cups (approximately 2 bunches) thinly sliced green onion
3 tablespoons flour
5 cups chicken stock

3/4 pound fresh mushrooms
1 cup heavy cream
1/4 cup dry sherry
Freshly ground black pepper
Salt

Melt the butter in a large saucepan. Stir in the green onions; cover and simmer over low heat for 20 minutes. Be careful not to let the onions brown. Stir in the flour and cook for 1 minute. Pour in the stock and bring to a boil. Finely chop 1/2 pound of the mushrooms and add to the stock. Reduce to a simmer and cook, partially covered, for 10 minutes. Purée in a food mill or blender, return to the pot, and stir in the cream and sherry. Taste and correct for seasoning.

Thinly slice the remaining mushrooms. Place the sliced mushrooms on the bottom of a large tureen or individual serving bowls and pour the hot soup over them. Serve at once.

SOUPE DE TOMATES EN CROÛTE

SERVES 6–8
PREPARATION TIME 30 MINUTES
COOKING TIME 2 HOURS
REFRIGERATION TIME 1 HOUR

When served at the Domaine Chandon Winery in the Napa Valley, this spectacular pièce de résistance *turns diners' heads. Though it looks more like a dessert than a soup, it's hearty enough to serve as a luncheon main course along with a green salad and a chilled bottle of brut sparkling wine.*

SOUP

1 pound yellow onions, chopped
2 tablespoons butter
2 pounds fresh tomatoes, quartered
6 cloves garlic, peeled

1 bay leaf
Pinch of thyme
1 cup of heavy cream
Salt to taste
White pepper to taste

Cook onions in butter until soft. Add tomatoes, garlic, bay leaf, and thyme. Cook slowly, uncovered, for 1 1/2 hours. Remove bay leaf. Run through a blender or food processor and strain. Add the cream and salt and pepper to taste.

CROÛTE

1 package of frozen puff pastry
1 egg for wash
1 carrot, julienned and blanched

Green of leek, julienned and blanched

Roll out the puff pastry to about 3/16-inch thick. Make an egg wash with the egg beaten with a little water. Brush the pastry surface with a little of the egg wash. Cut circles of pastry about 2 inches larger in diameter than the oven-proof soup crocks in which the soup will be served.

ASSEMBLY

Preheat oven to 450 degrees. Cool the soup slightly. Place it in the crocks with the thinly julienned carrots and leeks for garnish. Lay a circle of puff pastry (egg-wash side down) on top of the crock and stretch it tight and down the sides. Refrigerate the crocks for 1 hour. Remove from the refrigerator, brush the top with the remaining egg wash and bake for 20 minutes. Serve immediately.

SOUPE DE POISSON

SERVES 8
PREPARATION TIME 40 MINUTES
COOKING TIME 35 MINUTES

This complex-textured French soup is ideal for formal entertaining. Brimming with chunks of fresh fish in a rich broth flavored with a hint of Pernod and finished with a garlic-paprika sauce, it is a culinary achievement that will bring praise from your guests. Serve it with a Sauvignon Blanc.

1 pound white fish
1/2 pound shrimp
1 pound scallops
12 mussels, well scrubbed
1/4 cup olive oil
3/4 cup finely chopped celery
2 cups finely chopped onions
2 cups finely chopped leeks
1 cup seeded, finely chopped
   green pepper
1/2 teaspoon salt

1/2 teaspoon crushed fennel
1/4 teaspoon black pepper
1/4 teaspoon cayenne pepper
1/2 cup dry white wine
3 cups canned tomatoes,
   puréed
4 cups fish stock
1 tablespoon Pernod
16 croutons
1 cup Sauce Rouille (recipe
   follows)

Cut the fish into bite-size pieces. Shell and devein the shrimp. Cut the scallops into quarters (if large). Scrub the mussels. Set the fish and shellfish aside.

Heat the oil in a large saucepan. Add the celery, onions, leeks, and green pepper. Cook until soft (about 5 minutes). Add salt, fennel, black pepper, cayenne pepper, wine, and tomatoes. Stir and cook for 5 minutes. Add the fish stock and simmer for an additional 20 minutes.

Add the fish and cook for 2 additional minutes. Add the shrimp, scallops, and mussels. Stir often and continue cooking until the mussels open, about 3 minutes. Stir in the Pernod. Serve with the croutons and Sauce Rouille on the side.

SAUCE ROUILLE
2 teaspoons finely chopped
   garlic
1/2 teaspoon paprika
1 egg yolk

Juice of half a lemon
Salt and pepper to taste
1 cup olive oil

In a food processor or blender, crush the garlic and paprika to make a paste. Add the egg yolk, lemon juice, salt and pepper and beat rapidly. Gradually, start adding the oil by drops until emulsified. Continue beating until all the oil is added and the sauce is thickened and smooth.

GREEN FENNEL SOUP

SERVES 8 TO 10
PREPARATION TIME 20 MINUTES
COOKING TIME 35 MINUTES

A fine vegetable, fennel becomes very sweet upon cooking and imparts an interesting flavor to this soup.

1/2 pound fennel bulb
4 tablespoons butter
1 medium onion, chopped
   (approximately 1 cup)
8 cups chicken stock
1/2 bunch parsley, tied together
1 pound spinach, washed,
   stemmed, and chopped

1/2 cup quick-cooking oats
1/2 teaspoon dried tarragon
1/2 teaspoon dried basil
1 cup half-and-half
Salt and freshly ground
   pepper to taste
Fresh parsley

Peel the fennel bulb and cut into thin slices. Melt the butter in a saucepan, add the fennel and onion, and cook for 10 minutes. Add the chicken stock and the tied parsley leaves. Bring to a boil. Reduce the heat; cover and simmer until fennel is tender, about 10 to 15 minutes. Add the spinach and cook an additional 5 minutes.

Remove the parsley and purée the remaining mixture in batches until smooth. Return to the saucepan and bring to a simmer. Blend in the oats, tarragon, and basil, stirring rapidly to prevent lumps. Add the half-and-half with salt and pepper to taste. Mix well and simmer for 2 minutes without boiling. Garnish with minced parsley.

CHEESY VEGETABLE BISQUE

SERVES 6
PREPARATION TIME 15 MINUTES
COOKING TIME 30 MINUTES

A very rich, flavorful soup that would taste delicious on a chilly autumn day.

1 cup sliced leeks
1 cup sliced mushrooms
3 tablespoons butter
3 tablespoons flour
3 cups chicken stock

1 1/2 cups broccoli flowerets
1 cup half-and-half
1 cup shredded Jarlsberg
   cheese

In a large saucepan, sauté the leeks and mushrooms in the butter for 10 minutes without letting them brown. Add the flour and cook for another minute. Slowly blend in the chicken stock, stirring constantly, and cook until thickened and smooth. Add the broccoli pieces; reduce heat to low and simmer for 20 minutes. Stir in half-and-half and cheese and mix until blended. Simmer until heated through and cheese is melted. Do not let soup come to a boil.

SOUPE AU PISTOU

SERVES 6 TO 8
PREPARATION TIME 20 MINUTES
COOKING TIME 35 MINUTES

This is a wonderful Mediterranean vegetable soup with a tomato-basil pesto sauce stirred into it.

8 cups beef or chicken stock	**8 ounces cooked kidney beans**
1 1/4 cups diced carrots	**4 ounces thin noodles, broken**
1 1/4 cups diced onions	**into pieces**
1 1/4 cups diced potatoes	**Salt and pepper to taste**
1 cup diced green beans	**Pistou (recipe follows)**
1 cup diced zucchini	

Pour the stock into a soup pot and bring to a boil. Add the carrots and onions; simmer for 20 minutes. Add the remaining ingredients, except the Pistou, and cook for an additional 15 minutes, or until the vegetables are tender. Season to taste with salt and pepper. Stir the Pistou into the soup just before serving.

PISTOU

2 large garlic cloves, crushed	**1/2 cup Parmesan cheese**
4 tablespoons tomato paste	**4 tablespoons olive oil**
3 tablespoons chopped fresh	
basil	

In a food processor or blender, combine all the ingredients except the olive oil, and mix until they form a paste. Blend in the oil drop by drop, beating well after each addition.

TORTILLA SOUP

SERVES 6
PREPARATION TIME 10 MINUTES
COOKING TIME 15 MINUTES

Ideal for casual dining. Chorizo—a highly seasoned pork sausage—is a main staple in Mexican cooking and is often homemade with lean pork.

6 cups chicken stock	Oil for frying
1 finely chopped onion	1 1/2 cups cooked chicken,
2 tablespoons oil	shredded
1 cup tomato sauce	2 avocados, cut into bite-size
1 sprig fresh mint	pieces
8 ounces chorizo sausage	6 tablespoons chopped cilantro
6 corn tortillas, cut into strips	4 ounces Jack cheese

Heat the chicken stock in a saucepan. In a skillet, sauté the chopped onion in the oil until soft but not browned. Add to the broth together with the tomato sauce and mint. Simmer for 10 minutes. Remove the mint.

Remove the chorizo from its casing and fry until dry and crumbly. Drain on paper towels. Fry the tortillas in a little oil until crisp. Drain on paper towels.

In each soup bowl, place some crisp tortilla strips, 1/4 cup chicken, and some avocado pieces. Pour on the hot soup. Sprinkle with the chorizo and cilantro. Top with some grated Jack cheese.

CREAM OF ASPARAGUS SOUP

SERVES 6 TO 8
PREPARATION TIME 15 MINUTES
COOKING TIME 30 MINUTES

A hint of saffron adds a subtle complexity to this unusual asparagus soup.

2 pounds fresh asparagus	6 cups chicken stock
4 tablespoons (1/2 stick) butter	2 egg yolks
4 large shallots, finely chopped	1 cup half-and-half
6 tablespoons flour	White pepper to taste
1/4 teaspoon saffron	

Cut off the tips of the asparagus, drop in boiling water for 30 seconds, drain, and set aside. Cut the remaining stalks into ½-inch lengths. Melt half of the butter and sauté the stalks and shallots for 5 minutes. Set aside.

In another pot, melt the remaining butter and stir in the flour. Cook for 1 to 2 minutes without browning. Add the saffron, stock, and sautéed asparagus stalks. Simmer for 15 minutes or until tender. Pass through a food mill or strainer. Cool slightly.

Whisk the egg yolks and half-and-half together. Slowly add to the puréed soup, whisking constantly. Cook over low heat for 5 minutes. Season to taste with the white pepper. Serve garnished with the reserved asparagus tips.

CAULIFLOWER-EDAM SOUP

SERVES 8
PREPARATION TIME 30 MINUTES
COOKING TIME 30 MINUTES

3 cups chicken stock
1 medium boiling potato, peeled and chopped
1 medium onion, chopped
3 tablespoons butter
3 tablespoons flour
1 ¼ pounds (2 cups) cauliflower, trimmed and diced
¼ pound prosciutto, diced

2 tablespoons chopped fresh chives
Salt
Pinch cayenne
1 cup heavy cream
2 tablespoons dry white wine
2 egg yolks, beaten
1 cup shredded Edam cheese
1 tablespoon chopped fresh chives

In a saucepan, combine 1 ½ cups of the stock, the potato, and the onion. Bring to a boil. Reduce heat, cover, and simmer until potato is soft, about 10 minutes. Transfer to a food processor or blender and purée until smooth. In a saucepan, melt the butter. Stir in the flour and cook for 3 minutes without browning. Gradually blend in the remaining stock, potato purée, cauliflower, prosciutto, chives, salt, and cayenne. Bring to a simmer. Reduce heat to low, cover, and cook for 10 minutes, stirring occasionally.

Beat cream and wine into the egg yolks. Whisk some of the soup into the egg mixture. Stir the egg mixture back into the soup. Reserve 2 tablespoons of the cheese for garnish. Add the remaining cheese to the soup and cook until cheese melts. Do not allow soup to come to a boil. Ladle into soup bowls. Garnish with the remaining cheese and chives. Serve immediately.

POTAGE CRÉCY

SERVES 6
PREPARATION TIME 15 MINUTES
COOKING TIME 35 MINUTES

Delicately seasoned with herbs and spices, this beautiful carrot soup would be an elegant opener to an important dinner.

1 cup sliced carrots	1 teaspoon sugar
3 tablespoons butter	1/2 teaspoon nutmeg
1/2 cup finely chopped onion	1/3 cup uncooked white rice
4 cups chicken stock	1/2 cup half-and-half
1 bay leaf	Pinch of white pepper
1/2 teaspoon salt	
1 teaspoon dry basil	Fresh croutons

Sauté the sliced carrots in the butter for 5 minutes without browning. Add the onion and sauté for 3 minutes more. Add the chicken stock, bay leaf, salt, basil, sugar, nutmeg, and rice. Cover and simmer for 30 minutes. Remove the bay leaf and purée in a food processor or food mill. Add the half-and-half and the pepper. Taste and correct for seasonings. Reheat and serve with fresh croutons.

MINESTRONE DI PASTA E CARCIOFI

SERVES 8
PREPARATION TIME 15 MINUTES
COOKING TIME 20 MINUTES

An unusual rendition of the famed Italian soup with the addition of pancetta. If it is unavailable, blanched bacon may be substituted.

6 slices pancetta, diced	3/4 to 1 cup orzo or other small pasta
2 onions, thinly sliced	2 stalks celery, chopped
2 cloves garlic, minced	Salt
2 tablespoons olive oil	Freshly ground pepper
1 cup peeled, seeded, and chopped tomatoes	4 to 6 artichoke hearts
1 cup chopped parsley	1 cup Parmesan cheese
6 to 7 cups chicken stock	

Sauté the pancetta, onions, and garlic in the oil until pancetta is crisp. Add the tomatoes and parsley; simmer for 10 minutes. Pour in the chicken stock; bring to a boil. Add the pasta and celery. Cook until the pasta is tender, about 10 minutes. Season to taste with salt and pepper.

Cut the artichoke hearts into thin wedges. Just before serving, stir in the artichoke hearts and the cheese. Serve hot.

CRAB CHOWDER

SERVES 8 TO 10
PREPARATION TIME 1 HOUR
COOKING TIME 1 HOUR

8 cups bottled clam juice
1 cup dry sherry
1/2 cup brandy
1/4 cup minced shallots
1 tablespoon minced garlic
8 fresh parsley sprigs
4 bay leaves
4 medium potatoes, peeled and diced
3 slices bacon, diced
2 ounces salt pork without rind, diced

2 cups finely chopped onion
1 1/2 cups finely chopped celery
1 tablespoon dried thyme
1/4 cup flour
2 cups heavy cream
Salt
White pepper
Hot pepper sauce
3/4 pound crab meat
Chopped fresh parsley

Heat the clam juice, sherry, brandy, shallots, garlic, parsley, and bay leaves in a large saucepan. Bring to a boil, reduce heat, and let simmer, uncovered, for 15 minutes. Strain through a fine meshed sieve and keep warm. Boil the potatoes in salted water until tender, about 5 minutes. Drain and set aside.

In a large saucepan, cook the bacon and salt pork until crisp. Add the onion and celery and sauté until soft, about 10 minutes. Add the thyme. Stir in flour and cook for 3 minutes without browning, stirring constantly.

Slowly, stir the clam broth into the vegetables until smooth. Bring to a boil. Reduce heat to low and simmer, uncovered, for 30 minutes, skimming the surface occasionally. Stir in the potatoes and heavy cream and heat to boiling. Season to taste with the salt, white pepper, and red pepper sauce.

Just before serving, stir in the crab meat. Heat until the crab is hot. Ladle the chowder into bowls. Garnish with the chopped parsley.

AUTUMN ROOT SOUP

SERVES 6 TO 8
PREPARATION TIME 25 MINUTES
COOKING TIME 35 MINUTES

This richly satisfying vegetable soup freezes well.

6 cups chicken stock
3 medium carrots, peeled and chopped
2 medium parsnips, peeled and chopped
1 medium celery root, peeled and chopped

1 medium onion, chopped
1/2 teaspoon grated nutmeg
Salt
Freshly ground pepper
1/2 cup sour cream
2 tablespoons fresh dill

Bring the stock to a boil. Add the carrots, parsnips, celery root, and onion; bring back to a boil. Reduce the heat, cover, and simmer until tender, about 30 minutes. Purée in a food processor or blender; strain and return to the pot. Season with nutmeg, salt, and pepper. Warm, and garnish each serving with a dollop of sour cream and the dill.

TOMATO ORANGE SOUP

SERVES 6 TO 8
PREPARATION TIME 20 MINUTES
COOKING TIME 65 MINUTES

This velvety soup is best served in small portions as a subtle beginning to a romantic evening.

1 28-ounce can whole tomatoes, drained
1 medium carrot, peeled and thinly sliced
1 medium onion, thinly sliced
1 lemon, thinly sliced
1 orange, peeled and thinly sliced
6 peppercorns

1 bay leaf
1 cup fresh orange juice
4 cups chicken stock
1/4 teaspoon salt
3 tablespoons butter
3 tablespoons flour
Pinch of sugar
3/4 cup lightly whipped cream
Orange slices

In a large stainless steel saucepan, place the tomatoes, carrots, onion, lemon and orange slices, peppercorns, bay leaf, orange juice, chicken stock, and salt. Bring to a boil and simmer, uncovered, for 1 hour. Strain through a food mill or sieve.

Rinse the pan and add the butter. Melt over low heat. Stir in the flour and cook for 1 minute without browning. Return the soup to the pot. Bring to a boil and simmer for 5 minutes, or until thickened. Add the sugar and serve hot. Garnish with the whipped cream and orange slices.

CREAM OF PISTACHIO SOUP

SERVES 6 TO 8
PREPARATION TIME 30 MINUTES
COOKING TIME 40 MINUTES

4 slices bacon, cut into pieces
1/2 cup finely chopped celery
1/2 cup finely chopped onion
1 clove garlic, minced
1 bay leaf
1/2 cup dry sherry
6 cups chicken stock

1/4 cup white rice
1 1/2 cups shelled, unsalted
   pistachio nuts
1/4 cup chopped fresh parsley
1 cup heavy cream
White pepper

Sauté bacon until crisp and brown. Remove from pan with a slotted spoon and drain on paper towels. Add the celery, onion, and garlic to the pan. Cook for 5 minutes. Remove from the pan with a slotted spoon. Drain on paper towels.

Combine the bacon and vegetables in a large pot. Add the bay leaf and sherry. Bring to a boil, reduce heat, and cook until all the wine evaporates. Stir in the chicken stock and rice. Bring to a boil, reduce the heat, and simmer for 30 minutes, or until the rice is soft. Discard the bay leaf.

Finely grind the pistachio nuts in a food processor. Remove 1/4 cup of the nuts and set aside. Add the broth and parsley to the remaining nuts in the processor. This may be done in batches. Purée until smooth. Return to the pot and stir in the cream. Season with pepper. Serve hot. Garnish with the reserved pistachio nuts.

SPINACH AND CLAM SOUP

SERVES 6 TO 8
PREPARATION TIME 20 MINUTES
COOKING TIME 20 MINUTES

1 small onion, diced
5 strips of bacon, diced
1 clove garlic, minced
4 ounces (1 stick) butter
2 tablespoons flour
4 cups chicken stock
1 10-ounce package frozen
spinach, thawed and
squeezed dry

2 6 1/2-ounce cans of clams,
drained
1 cup heavy cream
Salt and pepper

Sauté the onion, bacon, and garlic in a skillet until lightly browned. Remove with a slotted spoon and set aside.

Melt the butter in a saucepan. Add the flour and cook for 2 minutes, stirring constantly. Slowly add the stock and bring to a boil. Add the onion and bacon mixture together with the spinach and clams. Bring to a boil, stirring occasionally. Pour in the heavy cream, heat thoroughly, and season to taste with salt and pepper.

ICED CANTALOUPE COCONUT SOUP

SERVES 4 TO 6
PREPARATION TIME 15 MINUTES
REFRIGERATION TIME 1 HOUR

2 ripe cantaloupes, halved and
seeded
4 tablespoons dry white wine
1/2 cup canned unsweetened
coconut milk
1/2 cup heavy cream
Grated zest of 1 lime
4 tablespoons fresh lime juice

1 teaspoon salt
1/2 teaspoon white pepper
1/4 teaspoon nutmeg
2 tablespoons orange juice
4 slices Black Forest ham,
julienned
4 tablespoons shredded
coconut

Peel the skin from the cantaloupes and cut the flesh into small pieces, discarding the seeds. Purée in a food processor or blender until very smooth. Place the purée in a bowl. Stir in the wine, coconut milk, heavy cream, lime zest and juice, salt, pepper, nutmeg, and orange juice. Blend well. Taste and correct seasonings. Chill for at least 1 hour. When ready to serve, sprinkle with the ham and shredded coconut.

MEXICAN ALBONDIGAS SOUP

SERVES 8
PREPARATION TIME 20 MINUTES
COOKING TIME 30 MINUTES

Serve this soup with warmed and rolled flour tortillas.

3/4 **pound ground beef**
6 **to 8 cups chicken stock**
3 **tablespoons bread crumbs**
1 **egg**
2 **tablespoons chopped fresh parsley**
1/2 **teaspoon crushed oregano**
Oil for frying
1 **red chili pepper, seeds removed**

1 **medium onion, finely chopped**
4 **carrots, peeled and grated**
1/3 **cup rice**
1 **cup tomato sauce†**
1/3 **cup chopped fresh cilantro**
1/2 **pound shredded spinach**

Lime wedges

Combine the ground beef, 1/4 cup of the stock, bread crumbs, egg, parsley, and oregano. Shape into 1-inch balls. Heat a skillet with oil and lightly brown the meatballs. Drain on paper towels.

Place the remaining stock, chili pepper, onion, carrots, rice, tomato sauce, and cilantro into a soup pot. Bring to a boil and reduce to a simmer. Add the meat balls and cook for 20 minutes. Add the spinach. Heat until hot. Ladle into bowls. Pass the lime wedges.

SALADS

Santa Cruz Mountains

Hidden in the steep foothills and valleys of the Santa Cruz Mountains to the south of San Francisco are some of California's least-known yet extraordinary wine regions. Where the peninsula ends, the Santa Cruz Mountains rise steeply to three thousand feet in elevation and form a massive range running south to Monterey Bay.

In the Napa Valley vineyards stretch as far as the eye can see, but here the vineyards are hidden in geographic pockets carefully selected for their climate and soil conditions. They are not easily reached, being accessible only from Highway 280 running south from San Francisco to San Jose, or from the steeply winding Highway 17, leading from San Jose to the ocean town of Santa Cruz. These wineries produce small quantities but their wines show a big, rich quality which some commentators attribute to the mountain-grown grapes or hillside vineyards. It is said that when vines are "stressed" by the extra difficulty of growing on a hillside, with its variation in sunlight, soil, and moisture, they actually produce superior wine.

These smaller wineries that dot the Santa Cruz Mountains and nearby foothills create a more rigorous wine-tasting expedition than those in more accessible locations. But it is well worth the trip, for like a crisp salad in a spiced dressing, these wineries in the mountain air provide wines of unusual excellence—perfect accompaniments to the salads that follow.

ASPARAGUS WITH DILL AND MUSTARD SAUCE

SERVES 6 TO 8
PREPARATION TIME 10 MINUTES
COOKING TIME 5 MINUTES

Prepare this salad in the spring when asparagus is plentiful.

2 pounds fresh asparagus
1 cup Crème Fraîche† or
    yogurt
1/4 cup mayonnaise
4 tablespoons Dijon mustard
2 tablespoons chopped fresh
    dill

2 tablespoons chopped fresh
    chives
1/2 teaspoon salt
Freshly ground pepper

Peel the asparagus and cut so that they are uniform in length. Blanch in boiling salted water until firm but tender. Drain immediately and run under cold water. Place in a bowl of ice water and set aside until needed.

To make the sauce, combine the remaining ingredients in a bowl. Whisk until well blended.

Drain the asparagus and pat dry with paper towels. Arrange on a serving platter or individual plates. Cover with the sauce and refrigerate until ready to serve.

ARTICHOKE WITH FRESH HERB SAUCE

SERVES 6
PREPARATION TIME 20 MINUTES
COOKING TIME 30 MINUTES
REFRIGERATION TIME 1 HOUR

The fine quality of the vinaigrette makes this dish a success.

ARTICHOKES
6 large artichokes
Juice of 1 large lemon

1 clove of garlic, crushed
2 teaspoons of salt

Wash the artichokes and trim 1/2 inch from the top. Remove the stem and snip the tips of the leaves with scissors. Stand the artichokes upright in a saucepan and cover with boiling water. Add the lemon juice, garlic, and salt.

Cover and simmer for 30 minutes or until the outside leaves pull off easily. Drain upside down until cool. Gently spread the leaves apart and remove the choke. Refrigerate until chilled.

HERB SAUCE

1/2 cup raspberry vinegar
3/4 cup olive oil
1 clove of garlic, crushed
2 teaspoons grated onion
1 tablespoon fresh tarragon
1 tablespoon fresh chervil

1 1/2 teaspoons salt
1/2 teaspoon sugar
1/4 teaspoon dry mustard
Freshly ground black pepper
Red leaf lettuce

Combine the ingredients and whisk until blended. Let stand at room temperature until ready to serve. To serve: Place the artichoke on a piece of leaf lettuce and fill the center with some of the sauce.

SHRIMP RÉMOULADE

SERVES 4 TO 6
PREPARATION TIME 15 MINUTES
REFRIGERATION TIME 1 HOUR

Rémoulade, a piquant sauce, is combined with shrimp in this classic Cajun-Creole salad. Create your own Cajun magic by serving this dish with Blackened Red Snapper and a crisp Fumé Blanc.

1 bunch green onions
2 stalks peeled celery
2 sprigs fresh parsley
3 tablespoons Creole mustard
4 teaspoons paprika
1 teaspoon salt
1/2 teaspoon black pepper
1/4 teaspoon cayenne
6 tablespoons white vinegar

5 teaspoons fresh lemon juice
1 teaspoon fresh basil or 1/2 teaspoon dried
3/4 cup olive oil
1 pound raw small or medium shrimp, cooked
1 head romaine lettuce, coarsely chopped

Chop the green onions, celery, and parsley in a blender or processor almost to a purée. Transfer to a bowl and add the mustard, paprika, salt, pepper, cayenne, vinegar, lemon juice, and basil. Blend well and slowly beat in the olive oil. Pour over the shrimp and refrigerate until chilled.

To serve, place some of the lettuce on a salad plate. Top with some of the shrimp mixture.

NAPA BEAN SALAD

SERVES 6 TO 8
PREPARATION TIME 15 MINUTES
COOKING TIME 5 MINUTES

The varied colors and textures of this salad add to its appeal.

1 1/2 pounds green beans
1 small red onion, finely
   chopped
3/4 cup black Greek olives,
   pitted and quartered
8 ounces chèvre, crumbled

3 tablespoons vinegar
1/3 cup olive oil
1 clove of garlic, pressed
1/4 teaspoon cayenne
1/2 teaspoon salt

Trim the green beans and cut into strips. Blanch in boiling salted water until crisp but tender. Immediately immerse into cold water. Place the onion, olives, and cheese in a bowl. Add the cooled beans.

Mix the remaining ingredients until thoroughly blended. Pour over the salad and mix gently, being careful not to break up the cheese. Let stand at room temperature until ready to serve.

RAW BROCCOLI SALAD

SERVES 6 TO 8
PREPARATION TIME 10 MINUTES
REFRIGERATION TIME 30 MINUTES

1 bunch fresh broccoli
1/3 cup salad oil
1 teaspoon salt
1/2 teaspoon freshly ground
   black pepper
2 tablespoons lemon juice

4 ripe tomatoes, peeled, seeded
   and chopped
1/3 cup sour cream
1 tablespoon Dijon mustard
Lettuce cups

Rinse the broccoli. Cut the broccoli flowers at the ends of the stems. Coarsely chop the flowerets. Place in a bowl and add the salad oil, salt, pepper, and lemon juice. Mix well and chill for 30 minutes.

Mix tomatoes and broccoli. Blend the sour cream and the mustard together. Toss with the broccoli and tomatoes, mixing well. Serve on lettuce cups.

CURRIED PEA SALAD WITH CASHEWS

SERVES 4 TO 6
PREPARATION TIME 15 MINUTES

This is a delightfully light and crunchy salad.

10 ounces frozen baby peas
5 green onions, chopped
1/2 cup chopped celery
3 slices cooked bacon, chopped
2/3 cup sour cream
1 1/4 teaspoons curry powder

1 teaspoon salt
1/2 teaspoon freshly ground
   pepper
1/2 cup roasted cashews
Lettuce leaves

Defrost the peas and drain in a colander. Mix together the peas, onions, celery, and bacon. Combine the sour cream, curry powder, salt, and pepper. Adjust the seasonings to taste. Mix with the vegetables just until coated. Fold in the cashews just before serving. Serve on lettuce leaves.

TOMATO ASPIC

SERVES 6
PREPARATION TIME 15 MINUTES
REFRIGERATION TIME 4 HOURS

This low-calorie aspic imparts both a sweet and tangy flavor.

2 tablespoons gelatin
1/2 cup cold water
2 cups tomato juice
1/2 cup vinegar
1/2 cup sugar

1 teaspoon salt
Pinch of cayenne
1 tablespoon grated onion
1 tablespoon horseradish
1 tablespoon lemon juice

Dissolve the gelatin in the water for 5 minutes. Simmer the tomato juice, vinegar, sugar, salt, and cayenne for 5 minutes. Remove from the heat and add the gelatin mixture. Stir until completely dissolved. Add the onion, horseradish, and lemon juice. Pour into a lightly oiled mold. Refrigerate until set, at least 4 hours. When firm, unmold onto a serving platter.

FIRE AND ICE TOMATOES

SERVES 6 TO 8
PREPARATION TIME 20 MINUTES
REFRIGERATION TIME 24 HOURS

This unusual marinated salad is best when tomatoes are at their peak.

6 large tomatoes	1 1/2 teaspoons celery salt
1 large green pepper	1 1/2 teaspoons mustard seed
1 red onion	1/2 teaspoon salt
3/4 cup vinegar	1/2 teaspoon freshly ground
1/4 cup cold water	black pepper
4 1/2 teaspoons sugar	Pinch of red pepper

Peel and quarter the tomatoes. Slice the green pepper into strips. Peel and slice the red onion into rings. Place in a bowl. Place the remaining ingredients in a saucepan. Boil for 2 minutes. Pour the hot marinade mixture over the tomatoes. Refrigerate for 24 hours. Serve cold.

ELEVEN-LAYER SALAD

SERVES 6 TO 8
PREPARATION TIME 30 MINUTES
REFRIGERATION TIME 6 HOURS

Be sure to serve in a glass bowl because the beauty of this salad is in the layering.

SALAD

1 head iceberg lettuce, shredded	1 teaspoon dill
1 cup chopped fresh parsley	1 cup sliced radishes
4 hard-cooked eggs, chopped	3/4 pound sharp Cheddar cheese, shredded
1 large red pepper, sliced	1/2 pound crisply cooked bacon, chopped
4 carrots, shredded	1 red onion, sliced
1 cup olives, sliced	
3/4 pound cooked green beans, sliced	

Have ready a 3-quart glass bowl or soufflé dish. Arrange the lettuce on the bottom. Sprinkle with all but 2 tablespoons of the parsley, making sure it comes to the edges of the bowl. Continue layering with the eggs, red pepper, carrots, olives, green beans, dill, radishes, Cheddar cheese, and bacon. Finish with a layer of the sliced red onion.

DRESSING

2 cups mayonnaise
1/2 cup chopped parsley
1/2 cup sour cream

2 tablespoons sugar
1 teaspoon dried basil
1 teaspoon dried dill

Whisk together the dressing ingredients. Spoon 1/2 of the dressing over the salad and spread evenly. Sprinkle with the reserved parsley. Cover tightly and refrigerate from 6 to 12 hours. Serve with the additional sauce on the side.

EGGPLANT SALAD

SERVES 6 TO 8
PREPARATION TIME 40 MINUTES
COOKING TIME 30 MINUTES

Serve this Moroccan salad warm or cold.

2 eggplant, diced
2 zucchini, diced
4 cloves of garlic, chopped
1 cup oil
2 teaspoons paprika
2 tablespoons cumin
2 teaspoons pepper
1 teaspoon salt
Cayenne to taste

2 green peppers, diced
2 green, hot chili peppers
  skinned and diced
4 tomatoes, skinned and diced
3 tablespoons white vinegar
Leaf lettuce

Cracker bread

In a large sauté pan, cook the eggplant, zucchini, garlic, oil, and spices in enough water just to cover, for 30 minutes. Add the peppers and tomatoes and continue to cook, uncovered, until all of the liquid evaporates. Mash the ingredients slowly while cooking. Let cool. Add vinegar and adjust seasonings if necessary. Arrange the lettuce leaves on a serving platter. Spoon the salad into the middle and serve with the cracker bread.

SWISS CHEESE SALAD

SERVES 8
PREPARATION TIME 20 MINUTES

Shred the Swiss cheese and omit the mortadella to serve as part of an antipasto or deli sandwich.

1 pound Swiss cheese, cubed
8 ounces mortadella, cubed
1/2 cup chopped sweet pickles
1/3 cup olive oil
2 tablespoons grainy mustard

1 tablespoon vinegar
1/2 teaspoon freshly ground
    black pepper
1/4 teaspoon salt
1 bunch salad greens

Place the cheese and mortadella in a bowl and add the rest of the ingredients, excepting the salad greens. Toss together well to coat the cheese.

Place the greens on individual salad plates or on a large platter. Arrange the cheese on top.

CASHEW-ORANGE CHICKEN SALAD

SERVES 4
PREPARATION TIME 30 MINUTES
COOKING TIME 20 MINUTES

A delicately flavored chicken salad.

1 cup orange juice
1/4 cup fresh cilantro or parsley
1/4 cup vegetable oil
1 tablespoon red wine vinegar
1 tablespoon Dijon mustard
1 teaspoon grated orange rind
1 teaspoon sugar
1 teaspoon salt
Freshly ground black pepper
6 poached chicken breast
    halves

3 celery stalks cut into strips
2 cups shredded romaine or
    iceberg lettuce
3 green onions, including tops
    sliced
1 large red bell pepper, cut
    into strips
3/4 cup salted cashews
1 11-ounce can mandarin
    oranges

Place the orange juice in a pan, bring to a boil, and reduce to 1/2 cup. Let cool. Combine the orange juice, cilantro, oil, vinegar, mustard, orange rind, sugar, salt, and black pepper in a food processor or blender. Mix for 20 seconds.

Cut the chicken into 1/2-inch slices. Transfer to a large bowl. Add the celery, lettuce, green onions, red bell pepper, and cashews. Pour over the dressing and toss gently. Mound the salad on glass plates and surround with the mandarin orange slices. Sprinkle with additional chopped cashews if desired.

PAPAYA-SHRIMP SALAD

SERVES 6 TO 8
PREPARATION TIME 30 MINUTES
COOKING TIME 5 MINUTES
REFRIGERATION TIME 1 HOUR

This lovely tropical salad may be served as a first course or light luncheon entree.

2/3 cup vegetable oil	2 pounds raw medium shrimp
3 tablespoons vinegar	1 lemon, sliced
1 tablespoon orange juice	1 bay leaf
1 egg	6 whole peppercorns
1 clove peeled garlic	1 1/2 teaspoons salt
2 sprigs of parsley	2 avocados
1 teaspoon salt	2 papayas
1/4 teaspoon white pepper	1 roasted red pepper, peeled
1/4 teaspoon sugar	1 head Boston lettuce

Place the oil, vinegar, orange juice, egg, garlic, parsley, salt, pepper, and sugar in a food processor or blender. Mix for 30 seconds, or until well blended.

Drop the shrimp, lemon, bay leaf, peppercorns, and salt into a pot of boiling water. Let the water return to the boil and continue cooking for 1 minute. Drain and rinse under cold water. Peel and devein.

Peel and pit the avocados. Cut into 1/2-inch slices. Peel and remove the seeds from the papayas. Cut into 1/2-inch slices. Remove the stems and seeds from the red pepper. Cut into 1/2-inch slices.

Place the shrimp, avocado, papaya, and peppers in a bowl. Pour over the dressing and toss gently to coat. Chill 1 hour. Wash and dry the lettuce leaves. Arrange several leaves on each salad plate. Divide the shrimp mixture evenly among the plates. Spoon any remaining dressing over the top.

COLD SCALLOPS WITH CUMIN VINAIGRETTE

SERVES 6 TO 8
PREPARATION TIME 10 MINUTES
REFRIGERATION TIME 2 HOURS

For easy entertaining, make this first-course salad early in the day and chill.

2 pounds tiny scallops
2/3 cup sliced green onions,
  with tops
1/3 cup olive oil
1/4 cup vegetable oil
1/4 cup red wine vinegar
2 tablespoons minced shallots
1 to 2 teaspoons ground cumin

1/2 teaspoon sugar
1 teaspoon salt
1/4 teaspoon white pepper
Pinch of cayenne pepper
4 tomatoes, peeled and seeded
2 cups shredded lettuce
Fresh parsley

Wash the scallops and drop into rapidly boiling water for 30 seconds. Drain and refresh under cold water. Place in a bowl together with the green onions.

Whisk together the remaining ingredients, except the tomatoes, lettuce and parsley, until well blended. Pour over the scallops and onions. Refrigerate at least 2 hours.

Before serving, slice the tomatoes into strips. Place a bed of shredded lettuce leaves on each salad plate. Remove the scallop mixture from the bowl with a slotted spoon and place in the center of the lettuce. Spread the tomato slices around the scallop mixture. Sprinkle with some of the cumin vinaigrette and chopped parsley.

CURRIED TUNA SALAD

SERVES 6
PREPARATION TIME 30 MINUTES

An updated version of the classic tuna salad.

TUNA SALAD
1/2 cup chopped tart apples
3 stalks peeled, chopped celery
6 green onions, sliced
1/2 cup sliced, toasted almonds
2 tablespoons currants

2 tablespoons minced red
  onion
2 7-ounce cans of tuna, packed
  in water and drained

Place all the ingredients except the tuna in a bowl and mix well. Place the tuna in a strainer and press lightly to remove as much water as possible without mashing it. Add to the other ingredients in the bowl.

CURRIED MAYONNAISE

2 egg yolks	**1 teaspoon lemon juice**
1/4 cup curry powder	**1/2 teaspoon salt**
2 tablespoons chutney	**1/4 teaspoon pepper**
1 tablespoon vinegar	**1 to 1 1/2 cups vegetable oil**

Place all the ingredients, except the oil, in a food processor or blender. Purée until smooth. Add the oil slowly until thickened.

ASSEMBLY

Add just enough Curried Mayonnaise to the tuna mixture to coat it nicely. Stir well and chill until ready to serve.

POTATO AND FETA CHEESE SALAD

SERVES 4
PREPARATION TIME 15 MINUTES
COOKING TIME 10 MINUTES

Bring new style to your summer entertaining with this deliciously different potato salad, which keeps—covered and chilled—overnight.

1/2 pound boiling potatoes	**1/2 teaspoon dried oregano**
1/4 cup lemon juice	**1/2 cup olive oil**
1/2 cup diced pimento	**Salt and pepper**
1/2 cup pitted black olives	**4 ounces feta cheese**
4 green onions, chopped	

Quarter the potatoes lengthwise. Set them in a steamer over boiling water, cover and steam until just tender, about 10 minutes. When cool enough to handle, cut potatoes into slices. Toss with 2 tablespoons of the lemon juice. Add the pimento, the olives, and the green onions. In a small bowl, whisk together the remaining lemon juice and oregano. Add the oil slowly, in a stream, and whisk until the dressing is emulsified. Pour over the salad and toss until the potatoes are well coated. Season to taste with salt and pepper. Crumble the feta cheese and toss in just before serving. Serve at room temperature.

WARM POTATO SALAD

SERVES 6
PREPARATION TIME 10 MINUTES
COOKING TIME 20 MINUTES

2 pounds red potatoes
6 strips of bacon, diced
3/4 cup finely chopped green
onion
1 teaspoon salt

1/4 cup cider vinegar
1/4 cup olive oil
1 tablespoon sugar
2 teaspoons prepared mustard
4 tablespoons chopped parsley

Bring a pot of water to a boil. Add the whole red potatoes and cook until tender, about 8 to 10 minutes. Do not overcook. Drain the water from the pot and return the potatoes. Let them sit until cool. Slice.

Fry the bacon until crisp. Pour off any fat in the skillet. Add the onion and salt, and sauté briefly. Add the vinegar, olive oil, sugar, and mustard to the skillet. Bring to a boil. Pour over the potatoes and mix. Sprinkle with the parsley. Serve immediately.

INSALATA DI MARE

SERVES 8
PREPARATION TIME 45 MINUTES
COOKING TIME 10 MINUTES
MARINATING TIME 4 HOURS

This authentic Italian seafood salad is well worth the cost of the ingredients.

2 tablespoons vinegar
1 teaspoon salt
1 bay leaf
4 black peppercorns
1/2 pound shrimp, peeled and
deveined
1/2 pound squid, peeled and cut
into rings
1/3 pound large scallops
12 mussels, scrubbed
12 clams, scrubbed
2 ounces black olives, sliced

2 ounces green olives, sliced
1 charred red pepper, skinned
and sliced
1 bay leaf
3 cloves crushed garlic
1/2 cup lemon juice
1/3 cup olive oil
3 teaspoons vinegar
2 teaspoons dry mustard
1/4 teaspoon cayenne
1 teaspoon salt

Bring to a boil 6 cups of water, together with the vinegar, salt, bay leaf, and peppercorns. Drop in the shrimp and cook 1 to 2 minutes or until pink. Remove from the water with a slotted spoon. Add the squid and cook for 1 minute. Remove with a slotted spoon. Add the scallops and cook for another minute. Drain and cut into quarters. Set all the fish aside to cool.

Place the mussels and clams in a large skillet. Cover and cook over a high heat until their shells open. Detach from their shells and set aside with the other fish to cool.

Place the seafood in a serving bowl and add the olives, sliced pepper, bay leaf, and garlic. In another bowl combine the lemon juice, olive oil, vinegar, mustard, cayenne, and salt. Mix well and pour over the fish. Let stand for 4 to 5 hours. Remove the garlic and bay leaf just before serving.

BRAZILIAN SHRIMP SALAD

SERVES 6

PREPARATION TIME 30 MINUTES

REFRIGERATION TIME 1 HOUR

Cilantro, also known as Chinese parsley, is spicy yet refreshing. It is used often in Chinese dishes and Mexican salsa.

- 1 **pound medium shrimp, cooked**
- 1 **cup celery, julienned**
- 1 **cup green pepper, julienned**
- 1 **cup blanched carrots, julienned**
- 1/2 **cup chopped fresh cilantro**
- 3/4 **cup vegetable oil**
- 3 **tablespoons lime juice**
- 3 **teaspoons sugar**
- 3/4 **teaspoon grated lime peel**
- 1/4 **teaspoon crushed red pepper**
- 3/4 **teaspoon ground cumin**
- 2 **bunches torn spinach leaves**
- 3 **bananas, sliced**
- 3/4 **cup chopped unsalted peanuts**
- 1/2 **cup shredded coconut**

Combine the shrimp, celery, green pepper, carrots, and cilantro in a bowl. In another bowl, whisk together the oil, lime juice, sugar, lime peel, red pepper, and cumin. Pour over the shrimp mixture and toss together well. Cover and chill.

Arrange the spinach leaves on salad plates. Place some of the shrimp mixture on the spinach. Arrange the banana slices around the shrimp and sprinkle with the peanuts and shredded coconut. Spoon over any remaining dressing.

VEGETABLE PRIMAVERA

SERVES 6 TO 8
PREPARATION TIME 20 MINUTES
COOKING TIME 10 MINUTES

This colorful vegetable salad is harmonious with picnic fare and casual suppers. Serve either warm or cold.

3/4 cup pitted black olives
1 10-ounce package frozen
     artichoke hearts
2 green bell peppers
2 red bell peppers
1 large red onion
1 pound small fresh
     mushrooms

1/3 cup olive oil
3 tablespoons vinegar
3 cloves minced garlic
2 teaspoons dried oregano
1/2 teaspoon salt
1/2 teaspoon pepper

Drain the olives. If they are large, cut in half. Defrost and drain the artichokes. Cut into bite-size pieces. Place in a bowl and set aside until needed.

Remove the stems and seeds from the green and red peppers and cut into bite-size pieces. Cut onion into bite-size pieces. Clean the mushrooms and trim the stem ends.

Heat 4 tablespoons of the oil in a sauté pan until hot. Combine the green and red peppers, onion, and mushrooms with the remaining oil, vinegar, garlic, and seasonings. Add to the hot oil and cook over high heat, stirring constantly, for 2 minutes or until the vegetables are just tender. Add to the olives and artichokes.

FRESH MUSHROOM SALAD

SERVES 10
PREPARATION TIME 30 MINUTES
MARINATING TIME 1 HOUR

A refreshing summer salad well worth the time it takes to prepare.

1 pound mushrooms
2/3 cup vegetable oil
1/2 cup olive oil
1/3 cup wine vinegar
1 teaspoon salt

1/2 teaspoon tarragon
1/4 teaspoon nutmeg
4 cups spinach leaves
6 cups butter lettuce

Wash, dry, and thinly slice the mushrooms. Mix together the oils, vinegar, and seasonings. Pour over the mushrooms. Cover and let stand for one hour. (Do not let it marinate longer than 2 hours or the mushrooms will turn dark.)

Remove the stems from the spinach. Wash, dry, and tear into pieces. Wash and dry the butter lettuce. Break into pieces. Combine the mushrooms, dressing, and greens in a salad bowl and toss lightly.

CANLIS' SPECIAL SALAD

SERVES 6 TO 8

PREPARATION TIME 15 MINUTES

A slight twist on the ever-popular Caesar salad, this one originated at Canlis' Restaurant in Honolulu. It uses Romano cheese and bacon instead of Parmesan and anchovy.

2 heads romaine lettuce
2 peeled tomatoes
2 tablespoons olive oil
Salt
1 clove garlic
1/4 cup chopped green onion

1/2 cup freshly grated Romano cheese
1 pound cooked bacon, finely chopped
1/4 cup croutons

Slice the romaine into 1-inch strips. Cut the tomatoes into eighths. Pour the olive oil into a large wooden bowl, sprinkle with salt, and rub firmly with the garlic. Remove the garlic and in the bowl first place the tomatoes, then the romaine. Add the green onion, cheese, and bacon.

DRESSING

Juice of 1 lemon
1 teaspoon fresh chopped mint
1/2 teaspoon ground black pepper

1/4 teaspoon dried oregano
1 coddled egg
1/2 cup olive oil

Into a small bowl, pour the lemon juice and seasonings. Add the coddled egg and whip vigorously. Add olive oil slowly, whipping constantly.

When ready to serve, pour Dressing over the salad. Add croutons last. Toss generously.

CHICKEN AND GRAPE SALAD

SERVES 8
PREPARATION TIME 15 MINUTES

This is especially colorful when served in a papaya or cantaloupe half.

SALAD

5 cups diced cooked chicken
1 cup chopped celery
3 cups seedless grapes

1/2 cup mayonnaise
1/2 cup sour cream
Lettuce leaves

Mix the chicken, celery, and grapes with the mayonnaise and sour cream. Arrange the lettuce leaves on salad plates. Place a spoonful of the chicken mixture in the center of the lettuce.

CRANBERRY FRENCH DRESSING

1/2 cup whole jellied cranberry
  sauce
1/2 cup oil
1/4 cup vinegar

1 teaspoon sugar
1 teaspoon salt
1/2 teaspoon paprika
1/4 teaspoon dry mustard

Blend the ingredients until well mixed. Spoon over the chicken. Pass additional dressing.

SEASHELL PASTA SALAD

SERVES 6 TO 8
PREPARATION TIME 10 MINUTES
COOKING TIME 5 MINUTES
REFRIGERATION TIME 2 HOURS

The best mozzarella comes from the water buffaloes of Italy. Unfortunately, it does not travel well, so we must substitute the cow's-milk form found in most specialty cheese shops. The better the quality of the cheese, the better the result.

1 pound fresh ripe tomatoes
4 cloves garlic
30 large fresh basil leaves
1/2 cup olive oil
1 teaspoon salt

1 teaspoon pepper
1 pound small shell pasta
1/2 pound mozzarella
6 ounces pitted black olives

Finely chop the tomatoes and garlic in a food processor or blender. Transfer to a bowl. Tear the basil leaves into pieces and add to the bowl together with the oil, salt, and pepper. Mix all the ingredients together. Cover and refrigerate for at least 2 hours.

Bring a large pot of salted water to a boil. Cook the pasta until al dente (about 8 to 10 minutes). Drain and place in a serving bowl. Slice the mozzarella into strips. Cut the olives into quarters. Add to the pasta. Pour on the refrigerated sauce, mixing well. Serve at room temperature.

INDONESIAN RICE SALAD

SERVES 6 TO 8
PREPARATION TIME 30 MINUTES
REFRIGERATION TIME 1 HOUR

An unusual salad that can double as a great vegetarian dish.

SALAD

- 2 cups cooked brown rice
- 1/2 cup raisins
- 2 green onions, chopped
- 1/4 cup toasted sesame seeds
- 1/2 cup thinly sliced water chestnuts
- 1 cup fresh bean sprouts
- 1/4 cup toasted cashews
- 1 green pepper, chopped
- 1 stalk celery, chopped
- Freshly chopped parsley
- Salt to taste
- Pepper to taste
- Leaf lettuce

Place all of the ingredients for the salad except the lettuce leaves in a large serving bowl. Season to taste with salt and pepper.

DRESSING

- 2/3 cup orange juice
- 1/3 cup vegetable oil
- Juice of 1 lemon
- 3 to 4 tablespoons soy sauce
- 2 tablespoons dry sherry
- 1 clove minced garlic
- 1 teaspoon freshly grated ginger root

Mix dressing ingredients together. Toss salad with dressing. Chill until ready to serve. Arrange lettuce leaves on a serving platter and using a slotted spoon place the salad in the center.

MARINATED COLESLAW

SERVES 8 TO 10
PREPARATION TIME 15 MINUTES
REFRIGERATION TIME 12 HOURS

This raw cabbage salad will keep for a week if it is stirred occasionally.

1 cup vegetable oil
1/3 cup sugar
3/4 cup apple cider vinegar
1 head green cabbage, shredded
3 large carrots, coarsely grated
1 small red onion, thinly sliced

1/4 cup raisins
1/4 cup chopped fresh parsley
1/4 cup chopped fresh basil
1 tablespoon dry mustard
1 teaspoon celery seed
1/2 teaspoon salt

Bring the oil, sugar, and vinegar to a boil. Combine the remaining ingredients. Add the dressing and mix well. Cover and chill overnight.

FUSILLI SALAD

SERVES 6 TO 8
PREPARATION TIME 10 MINUTES
COOKING TIME 5 TO 10 MINUTES

Easy to prepare, this pasta salad is a pleasant respite from the usual picnic or barbecue fare.

1 pound fusilli
1 cup olive oil
1/3 cup white vinegar
1 green bell pepper, cut into strips
1 red pepper, cut into strips
1/2 cup freshly grated Parmesan cheese

2 cloves minced garlic
1/4 cup chopped parsley
2 tablespoons fresh basil
1 1/2 to 2 teaspoons salt
1 teaspoon pepper

Cook the pasta in boiling salted water until al dente. Immediately rinse under cold water to stop the cooking. Transfer to a bowl and toss with the oil and vinegar. Add the remaining ingredients and mix together well. Taste and correct for salt and pepper. Allow to marinate at room temperature for several hours before serving.

TURKEY AND WILD RICE SALAD

SERVES 8 TO 10
PREPARATION TIME 20 MINUTES
COOKING TIME 45 MINUTES

This hearty salad is perfect for using up leftover turkey.

2 1/2 cups water
2 teaspoons salt
3/4 cup brown rice
1/2 cup wild rice
1/2 cup peanut oil
1/4 cup tarragon vinegar
4 tablespoons Dijon mustard

1 teaspoon dried tarragon
1 teaspoon black pepper
8 cups cooked cut-up turkey
2 cups cooked peas
3/4 cup sliced green onions
3/4 cup sliced almonds, toasted
1/2 cup chopped red pepper

Bring the water to a boil in a saucepan. Add the salt and rice. Return to the boil and reduce heat. Cover and simmer until water is absorbed, about 45 minutes.

Whisk the oil, vinegar, mustard, tarragon, and pepper in a serving bowl. Stir in the turkey, peas, onions, all but 2 tablespoons of the almonds, the red pepper, and the cooked rice. Sprinkle with the reserved almonds. Serve warm or at room temperature.

ORANGE SALAD

SERVES 4 TO 6
PREPARATION TIME 20 MINUTES
REFRIGERATION TIME 30 MINUTES

The acid from the oranges gives a delightful tang to this salad.

1 head romaine lettuce
2 oranges
1/2 cup sliced radishes
1/4 cup olive oil
2 tablespoons orange juice

2 teaspoons lemon juice
1/2 teaspoon pepper
1/2 teaspoon salt
Pinch of cardamom

Wash and chill the lettuce. Reserve until later. Peel the oranges, making sure to remove all of the white. Slice into sections. Mix together with the remaining ingredients and chill.

To serve, add the lettuce to the other ingredients and mix together. Serve immediately.

ORIENTAL CHICKEN SALAD

SERVES 8
PREPARATION TIME 20 MINUTES

SALAD

4 whole chicken breasts,
  cooked
3 red bell peppers
1/2 pound snow peas, blanched

3 carrots, blanched
1 cup water chestnuts
3 bunches green onions
3 stalks of celery

Slice the chicken breasts into bite-size pieces. Slice on the diagonal the red peppers, snow peas, carrots, water chestnuts, green onions, and celery. Place into a serving bowl with the chicken.

DRESSING

1 cup soy sauce
1/2 cup Mirin wine
2 cloves minced garlic
2 tablespoons minced fresh
  ginger

1 teaspoon red pepper flakes
1 teaspoon sesame seed oil
1 tablespoon sesame seeds

Whisk the soy sauce, wine, garlic, ginger, red pepper, and sesame seed oil together until blended. Toss with the chicken and vegetables. Sprinkle the sesame seeds over the top.

BAKED GOAT CHEESE SALAD

SERVES 4
PREPARATION TIME 10 MINUTES
COOKING TIME 5 MINUTES

Goat cheese, also called chèvre—the French word for goat—is one of California's newest food rages. It has a distinctive earthy, nutty flavor—subtle when young, bold and intense when aged.

2 heads butter lettuce
4 2-inch rounds of goat cheese
3/4 cup dry bread crumbs
1/2 cup olive oil
1/4 cup walnut oil

3 tablespoons vinegar
Salt to taste
Pepper to taste
3/4 cup walnut pieces

Preheat oven to 400 degrees. Wash and dry the lettuce. Tear into pieces. Dip the goat-cheese rounds into the bread crumbs and pat lightly. Place on a lightly oiled baking sheet. Bake for 5 minutes or until nicely browned.

Prepare the vinaigrette by whisking together the olive oil, walnut oil, and vinegar. Season to taste with salt and pepper. Toss the lettuce with enough of the dressing to coat the leaves lightly. Arrange on salad plates and place the warm cheese in the center of the lettuce leaves. Sprinkle the walnut pieces around the cheese.

SMOKED TURKEY, APPLE, AND WALNUT SALAD

SERVES 6

PREPARATION TIME 20 MINUTES

REFRIGERATION TIME 4 HOURS

- **2 pounds smoked turkey, cut into strips**
- **3 tart green apples, cored and diced**
- **6 celery stalks, sliced**
- **6 cups chopped watercress**
- **Lemon Dressing (recipe follows)**
- **Salt and pepper**
- **Romaine lettuce leaves**
- **1 cup toasted, chopped walnuts**
- **Watercress sprigs**

Toss the turkey pieces, apples, celery, and chopped watercress in a bowl. Pour on Lemon Dressing and toss again. Season to taste with salt and pepper. Cover and refrigerate for no more than 4 hours.

Line a serving platter with the lettuce leaves. Mound the salad in the center. Sprinkle with the chopped walnuts. Garnish with watercress sprigs.

LEMON DRESSING
- **5 teaspoons fresh lemon juice**
- **4 teaspoons Dijon mustard**
- **1 egg yolk**
- **1/4 teaspoon salt**
- **1/4 teaspoon pepper**
- **1/2 cup olive oil**
- **1/2 cup vegetable oil**

Combine the lemon juice with the mustard, egg yolk, salt, and pepper. Whip until thickened. Add the oils slowly, until thickened.

FRUITY WILD RICE

SERVES 6 TO 8

PREPARATION TIME 20 MINUTES

A sensational holiday dish.

1/2 cup raisins
1/2 cup dried apricots, chopped
3/4 cup cooked wild rice
3/4 cup cooked white rice
3/4 cup red seedless grapes, cut in halves
3/4 cup toasted walnuts coarsely chopped
4 green onions, chopped
1/3 cup chopped chives

4 tablespoons chopped parsley
Juice of 1 small lemon
5 tablespoons olive oil
2 teaspoons honey
2 teaspoons chopped fresh mint
Salt to taste
Pepper to taste
Chopped parsley

Place the raisins and dried apricots in a bowl. Cover with boiling water and let sit until softened and plump. Drain well and transfer to a salad bowl. Add the cooked rice, grapes, walnuts, onions, chives, and parsley. Mix together.

In a small bowl, whisk together the lemon juice, olive oil, honey, and mint. Add to the rice mixture and toss gently. Salt and pepper to taste. Garnish with chopped parsley.

ORANGE AND JÍCAMA SALAD

SERVES 4

PREPARATION TIME 20 MINUTES

REFRIGERATION TIME 4 HOURS

Jícama is a sweet, crunchy root vegetable of Mexican origin. Serve this picture perfect salad with the flauta tart for a real Mexican fiesta.

1 pound jícama
1/2 cup orange juice
2 tablespoons chopped cilantro

1/2 teaspoon salt
2 large oranges
Fresh cilantro leaves

Peel and dice the jícama. In a small bowl, combine with the orange juice, cilantro, and salt. Chill for at least 4 hours.

Peel and thinly slice the oranges. Transfer the jícama with a slotted spoon to a serving platter. Arrange the orange slices around the jícama. Garnish the edge of the platter with sprigs of fresh cilantro leaves.

AVOCADO, PAPAYA, AND HEARTS OF PALM SALAD

SERVES 4 TO 6
PREPARATION TIME 25 MINUTES
REFRIGERATION TIME 2 HOURS

1 papaya
1 large avocado
1 14-ounce can hearts of palm
2 tomatoes
Juice of 1 lemon

1/4 teaspoon each of salt,
   coriander, ground allspice,
   and white pepper
1 1/2 cups watercress leaves

Peel and seed the papaya. Cut into 1-inch cubes. Peel the avocado and cut into 1-inch cubes. Drain the hearts of palm and cut into 1/4-inch slices. Peel, seed, and cube the tomatoes. Place together in a glass bowl. Mix the lemon juice, salt, coriander, allspice, and white pepper. Pour over the ingredients in the bowl and toss gently. Add the watercress and toss again. Chill the salad for at least 2 hours before serving.

CAPRICE SPINACH SALAD

SERVES 6
PREPARATION TIME 15 MINUTES

This spinach salad is served at the Caprice Restaurant in Tiburon. For a fresh taste, you may want to try orange slices in place of the mandarin oranges.

3 bunches fresh spinach,
   washed and torn into bite-
   size pieces
1 avocado, peeled and cut into
   bite-size pieces

1/3 cup mandarin orange
   segments
1/3 cup fresh sliced mushrooms
1/4 cup fresh bacon bits
Dressing (recipe follows)

Toss ingredients thoroughly with Dressing.

DRESSING

5 ounces olive oil
2 ounces apple cider vinegar
2 tablespoons chopped onions
2 tablespoons sugar
1/2 teaspoon celery salt

1/2 teaspoon ground mustard
   powder
1/2 teaspoon paprika
1/2 teaspoon salt
1/2 teaspoon black pepper

Combine ingredients until well blended.

SAUSALITO RICE SALAD

SERVES 10 TO 12
PREPARATION TIME 45 MINUTES
COOKING TIME 15 MINUTES
REFRIGERATION TIME 12 HOURS

4 cups chicken stock
1/4 teaspoon saffron powder
1 teaspoon salt
1 1/2 cups rice
1/2 pound ham, diced
1 cup chopped green onions
1 cup chopped fresh parsley
1/2 cup cooked tiny peas
1/2 cup shredded carrots, blanched
1/2 cup diced red pepper

1/2 cup diced green pepper
1/2 cup chopped fresh basil
1/2 cup sliced olives
1/4 cup toasted pine nuts
4 tablespoons capers
Salt
Freshly ground pepper
1 cup diced Italian Fontina cheese
4 to 5 tablespoons olive oil
2 tablespoons vinegar

Bring the chicken stock, saffron, and salt to a boil. Stir in the rice and cook for 15 minutes. Drain well. Transfer to a large serving bowl. Toss with the remaining ingredients, except the cheese, oil, and vinegar. Let cool to room temperature. Add the Fontina cheese, cover and refrigerate overnight. Four hours before serving, toss with the oil and vinegar. Taste and adjust seasonings if necessary. Serve at room temperature.

UNION STREET SALAD

SERVES 8 TO 10
PREPARATION TIME 40 MINUTES

4 whole chicken breasts, poached
2 bunches spinach
1 pound Chinese pea pods, blanched
1 bunch green onions (including some of the tops), chopped
4 ounces thinly sliced mushrooms

1 cup thinly sliced water chestnuts
1/2 pound cooked crumbled bacon
3/4 cup toasted sliced almonds
Curry Dressing (recipe follows)
4 sliced hard-cooked eggs
Cherry tomatoes

Cut the chicken breasts into 2-inch chunks. Stem spinach, wash, and dry well. Place in a serving bowl together with all the remaining ingredients, except the eggs and tomatoes. Just before serving toss with the Curry Dressing. Garnish with the sliced egg and cherry tomatoes.

CURRY DRESSING

2 cups sour cream	**2 cloves garlic, pressed**
1/4 cup toasted sesame seeds	**1/2 teaspoon pepper**
3 tablespoons fresh lemon juice	**1/4 teaspoon salt**
2 teaspoons curry powder	

Combine all of the ingredients. Mix together well.

ORANGE-LACED CAULIFLOWER SALAD

SERVES 8
PREPARATION TIME 15 MINUTES
MARINATING TIME 2 HOURS
COOKING TIME 5 MINUTES

The attractive combination of cauliflower, oranges, and carrots is impressive.

1 small head cauliflower	**1 teaspoon dried basil**
Boiling salted water	**1 teaspoon cracked black**
2 carrots, julienned	**pepper**
1/2 cup olive oil	**1/2 teaspoon salt**
1/2 cup tarragon vinegar	**1/2 cup sliced green onions**
1 teaspoon freshly grated	**2 heads mixed salad greens,**
orange peel	**torn into bite-size pieces**
1/4 cup fresh orange juice	

Break the cauliflower into flowerets. Slice into bite-size pieces. Cook in the water until just tender but still crisp. Drain and run under cold water. Blanch the carrots until just tender but still crisp. Drain and run under cold water. Place in a bowl with the cauliflower. Combine oil, vinegar, orange peel and juice, basil, pepper, and salt. Pour over cauliflower and carrots. Toss lightly with the onions. Cover and marinate for 2 to 3 hours. Toss with the salad greens just before serving.

CAESAR SALAD

SERVES 8

PREPARATION TIME 10 MINUTES

2 pounds romaine lettuce

3 eggs

3 to 4 cloves of garlic

2 ounces canned anchovies
with their oil

2 tablespoons chopped fresh
parsley

2 teaspoons dry mustard

2/3 cup olive oil

Juice of 2 small lemons

1/4 cup vinegar

Dash of Tabasco

Freshly ground pepper

1/2 cup Parmesan cheese

1 cup homemade croutons

Wash and dry the lettuce leaves. Cut into 2-inch pieces. Place in a salad bowl
and set aside.

Place the eggs in a pan of boiling water. Immediately remove the pan from
the heat and cover. Let stand for 1 minute. Remove the eggs from their
shells. Place in a blender or processor. Add the remaining ingredients except
the Parmesan cheese and croutons. Blend for 1 minute. If not using right
away, pour into a covered glass jar and refrigerate. The dressing can be
stored for up to 3 weeks.

Pour 1/2 cup of the dressing over the lettuce leaves. Sprinkle with the
Parmesan cheese and croutons. Toss until mixed. Serve immediately.

SPINACH SALAD WITH CHUTNEY

SERVES 4 TO 6

PREPARATION TIME 10 MINUTES

1 large or 2 small bunches
fresh spinach

6 to 10 sliced fresh mushrooms

1 8-ounce can water chestnuts,
sliced

6 to 10 slices cooked bacon,
crumbled

1/2 cup shredded Gruyère
cheese

1/4 cup thinly sliced red onion

Chutney Dressing (recipe
follows)

Wash the spinach and remove the stems. Dry the spinach leaves well. Combine with the remaining ingredients, except the dressing. Toss with Chutney Dressing just before serving.

CHUTNEY DRESSING

1/4 cup wine vinegar
4 tablespoons finely chopped fruit chutney, with liquid

1 clove garlic, minced
2 tablespoons Dijon mustard
2 tablespoons sugar

Mix together well.

ROMAINE AND PINE NUT SALAD

SERVES 6 TO 8
PREPARATION TIME 20 MINUTES

1 1/2 pounds romaine lettuce leaves, washed
1/4 pound endive, washed
1/4 cup pine nuts
1 tablespoon butter
1/4 cup fresh squeezed lemon juice
2 tablespoons Parmesan cheese

1 small clove garlic, peeled and cut in half
1/4 teaspoon dried oregano
3/4 cup olive oil
1/4 cup peanut oil
Salt
Freshly ground pepper

Tear the lettuce into bite-size pieces. Slice the endive. In a small skillet, lightly sauté the pine nuts in the butter. Drain on paper towels.

Whisk together the lemon juice, cheese, garlic, and oregano. Combine the oils and add to the lemon-juice mixture in a thin stream, whisking constantly. Whisk until well combined. Season to taste with salt and pepper. Remove garlic before using. Toss salad with dressing. Sprinkle with pine nuts.

PARMESAN VINAIGRETTE DRESSING

MAKES 2 CUPS
PREPARATION TIME 10 MINUTES

1 cup vegetable oil
1/2 cup vinegar
1 clove crushed garlic
2 tablespoons freshly grated
   Parmesan cheese

2 teaspoons Dijon mustard
2 teaspoons salt
3/4 teaspoon freshly ground
   pepper
1/4 teaspoon sugar

Combine all of the ingredients in a jar with a tight-fitting lid. Shake vigorously until well blended. Refrigerate for at least 1 hour before serving. Will keep for 2 weeks in the refrigerator.

HERBED VINAIGRETTE

MAKES 1 1/2 CUPS
PREPARATION TIME 5 MINUTES

1 egg
1 cup vegetable oil
1/4 cup white wine vinegar
1 clove garlic, minced
2 tablespoons minced fresh
   parsley

2 tablespoons minced fresh dill
   or thyme
1 teaspoon dried basil
Pinch of sugar
Salt
Freshly ground pepper

Beat egg until light and creamy. Gradually whisk in the oil. Add the remaining ingredients. Salt and pepper to taste.

ROQUEFORT TARRAGON DRESSING

MAKES ABOUT 2 CUPS
PREPARATION TIME 5 MINUTES

This dressing is particularly good over crisp bibb or butter lettuce.

1 cup olive oil
1/4 cup rice vinegar
1 clove garlic, pressed
1 1/2 teaspoons dried tarragon

1/2 teaspoon Dijon mustard
2 ounces crumbled Roquefort
   cheese

Whisk together the olive oil, vinegar, garlic, tarragon, and mustard until well blended. Stir in the Roquefort cheese. Refrigerate until ready to use.

ORANGE THYME VINAIGRETTE

MAKES 1 1/2 CUPS
PREPARATION TIME 5 MINUTES

1 egg
1 cup vegetable oil
1/4 cup wine vinegar
2 tablespoons orange juice
  concentrate
1 tablespoon grated orange
  rind

1 clove garlic, pressed
1 teaspoon dried thyme
Salt
Freshly ground pepper

Beat the egg until light and creamy. Gradually whisk in oil. Add the remaining ingredients. Taste and correct seasonings.

DIJON MUSTARD VINAIGRETTE

MAKES 2 CUPS
PREPARATION TIME 5 MINUTES

1 hard-cooked egg, chopped
1 egg yolk
3 tablespoons Dijon mustard
1 tablespoon finely chopped
  onion
2 teaspoons finely chopped
  shallot
2 teaspoons chopped fresh
  parsley

1 teaspoon chopped fresh basil
1 clove of garlic, minced
1/2 teaspoon salt
Pinch of sugar
Freshly ground pepper
3 tablespoons white wine
3 tablespoons white wine
  vinegar
1 cup olive oil

Combine all the ingredients except the wine, vinegar, and oil in a bowl. Whisk in the wine and vinegar. Whisk in the oil in a slow steady stream. Place in a covered jar until ready to use.

SWEET ONION DRESSING

MAKES 1 CUP

PREPARATION TIME 10 MINUTES

This dressing will keep for up to 1 week in the refrigerator. It is especially tasty on romaine or spinach salads. It may also be used on an avocado-citrus fruit salad.

1/2 cup vegetable oil
1/4 cup vinegar
1/2 teaspoon celery seed
1 small onion, grated

1/2 teaspoon prepared mustard
1/2 teaspoon salt
1 1/2 to 2 tablespoons sugar

Combine all of the ingredients in a jar with a tight-fitting lid. Shake vigorously until well blended. Let flavors blend at room temperature for a few hours. Shake jar briskly before serving.

CREAMY TARRAGON DRESSING

MAKES 1 CUP

PREPARATION TIME 10 MINUTES

A member of the sunflower family, chopped fresh tarragon has a slight licorice flavor and is a wonderful addition to homemade dressing or sprinkled on fresh greens.

2/3 cup mayonnaise
2 teaspoons prepared mustard
1 teaspoon lemon juice
1/2 teaspoon dried tarragon, crushed
2 tablespoons finely chopped dill pickle

1 tablespoon finely chopped parsley
1 tablespoon finely chopped green onion
1 tablespoon finely chopped capers

Blend the mayonnaise, mustard, lemon juice, and tarragon. Stir in the dill pickle, parsley, green onion, and capers. Cover and refrigerate several hours to blend flavors.

CREAMY GARLIC VINAIGRETTE

MAKES 1 1/2 CUPS
PREPARATION TIME 5 MINUTES

4 cloves garlic
2 green onions
1 teaspoon chopped parsley
2 1/2 tablespoons lemon juice
2 tablespoons raspberry
  vinegar

1/2 tablespoon Dijon mustard
1/2 teaspoon sugar
2 twists of the pepper mill
3/4 cup vegetable oil
1/4 cup olive oil

In a food processor, combine all the ingredients except the oils. Process until well blended. With the machine running, slowly add the oils. Store in a covered jar in the refrigerator.

ANGEL ISLAND SALAD DRESSING

MAKES 2 CUPS
PREPARATION TIME 10 MINUTES

An excellent dressing with salad greens.

1 cup mayonnaise
2 tablespoons prepared
  mustard
4 tablespoons ketchup
3 to 4 tablespoons wine vinegar
1 to 2 cloves garlic, grated
1 teaspoon paprika

1/2 teaspoon salt
1/4 teaspoon freshly grated
  pepper
2 tablespoons chopped fresh
  parsley
2 hard-cooked eggs, finely
  chopped

Combine all ingredients, except parsley and egg, in a food processor or blender. Mix well and fold in remaining ingredients. Chill.

EGGS AND
CHEESE

Sonoma

The town of Sonoma is rich in California history. Sonoma's plaza, an eight-acre square, is a national historic landmark, surrounded by ten historic buildings. These include the Sonoma Mission, founded on July 4, 1823, by Father Jose Altamura as Mission San Francisco Solano de Sonoma. It is the last and northernmost of California's twenty-one missions and is open to visitors. It was in this famous plaza that the Bear Flag was first hoisted in 1846, declaring California an independent republic free of Mexican rule. The Sonoma Barracks, next door to the Mission, was the headquarters of the Bear Flag Party. On the day the flag was raised Sonoma Mission's wine grapes had been in cultivation for thirty years.

One illustrious individual was responsible for Sonoma's ascendency as a wine producing area. Hungarian Colonel Agoston Haraszthy was a self-proclaimed Colonel and a flamboyant figure in California history. Born in 1812 in Hungary to an aristocratic family, Haraszthy left there for San Diego, where he first tried grape-growing. He then tried his hand at growing grapes at Crystal Springs, near San Mateo, and later on an estate near Mission Dolores, San Francisco. Finding the climates there too moist and foggy for growing wine grapes, Haraszthy purchased a 500-acre estate on the slopes of the Mayacamas Mountains, which he named Buena Vista (Spanish for beautiful view). This is the name of the winery located there today, just a few blocks from Sonoma Plaza.

Haraszthy was convinced that California's climate, soils, and growing season were ideal for cultivating wine grapes, and he produced the first report of its kind on California viticulture, *Report on Grapes and Wine in California.* In 1861, Haraszthy traveled to Europe to collect cuttings that could be grown in California. He imported 100,000 cuttings of nearly 140 varieties of wine grapes. Some credit Haraszthy, now called the Father of California Viticulture, with importing the Zinfandel varietal, a grape whose origin is uncertain and is now found only in California.

In Haraszthy's day, Sonoma Valley was Northern California's largest-producing wine district, with 1,100,000 vines in production, second only to Los Angeles, which had 1,200,000 vines. In the 1860s, Sonoma surpassed the Napa Valley both in acreage and number of wineries. However, in the twentieth century, the impact of Prohibition took its toll, and Sonoma has not yet regained its pre-Prohibition position of leadership.

Today, Old Town Sonoma is noted for its cheeses, including Sonoma Jack and Cheddar. Goat cheeses, notably the California chèvres, are also produced locally. Whether Sonoma cheeses are used in the Mexican Brunch Eggs or Savory Quiche, one can envision this romantic old California plaza, with its Spanish mission, cheese factories, and wineries close by.

BREAKFAST SAUSAGE PUDDING

SERVES 8
PREPARATION TIME 20 MINUTES
REFRIGERATION TIME 24 HOURS
COOKING TIME 1 HOUR

2 to 3 tablespoons softened butter

12 slices white bread, crusts removed

1/2 pound fresh mushrooms, sliced

2 cups thinly sliced yellow onion

4 ounces (1 stick) butter

1 1/2 pounds mild Italian sausage

1 pound Cheddar cheese, grated

5 eggs

2 1/2 cups milk

3 teaspoons Dijon mustard

1 teaspoon nutmeg

1 teaspoon dry mustard

2 tablespoons chopped fresh parsley

Butter bread with the softened butter. Set aside. Sauté the mushrooms and onions in the 4 ounces butter over medium heat until soft, about 5 to 10 minutes. Cook the sausage and cut into bite-size pieces.

In a greased 13 × 9-inch casserole, layer half the bread, mushroom mixture, sausage, and cheese. Repeat, ending with the cheese. Mix all the remaining ingredients, except the parsley. Pour over the casserole. Cover and refrigerate overnight.

Preheat oven to 350 degrees. Sprinkle with the parsley. Bake, uncovered, for 1 hour or until bubbly. Serve immediately.

CONFETTI EGGS

SERVES 6
PREPARATION TIME 10 MINUTES
COOKING TIME 25 TO 30 MINUTES

12 eggs, slightly beaten
2 large tomatoes, peeled, seeded, and diced
2 cups diced salami

3/4 cup diced green pepper
3/4 cup chopped green onion
1 teaspoon salt
1/4 teaspoon pepper

Preheat oven to 350 degrees. Combine all ingredients. Pour into a buttered 9 × 13-inch pan. Bake for 25 to 30 minutes or until set. Cut into squares. Serve immediately.

CANADIAN BACON PUFF

SERVES 6 TO 8
PREPARATION TIME 15 MINUTES
REFRIGERATION TIME 12 HOURS
COOKING TIME 1 HOUR

Canadian bacon is very lean. For a delicious flavor, use a home-cured variety, if possible, in this easy brunch or luncheon dish.

Butter
16 pieces white bread, crusts removed
8 ounces Cheddar cheese
8 slices Canadian bacon

6 eggs, beaten
4 cups milk
2 teaspoons salt
1/4 teaspoon white pepper
Currant jelly

Butter the bread slices. Generously butter a 9 × 13-inch baking dish. Arrange 8 slices of the bread in the dish. Cut the cheese into 8 slices. Place a piece of cheese over each slice of bread. Place a slice of Canadian bacon over the cheese. Top with the remaining bread slices. Combine eggs, milk, salt, and white pepper and mix well. Pour over the bread. Cover and refrigerate overnight.

Preheat oven to 350 degrees. Place the baking dish in a water bath. Bake for approximately one hour, or until puffed and brown. Cut into 8 squares. Serve with a dollop of jelly on each piece.

CREAMY EGGS WITH LOX AND ONIONS

SERVES 4 TO 6
PREPARATION TIME 10 MINUTES
COOKING TIME 10 MINUTES

12 eggs
1/4 cup heavy cream
2 tablespoons chopped fresh
   parsley
1/2 teaspoon salt

Freshly ground pepper
4 ounces smoked salmon, cut
   into 1/2-inch pieces
6 tablespoons butter
1 cup finely chopped onion

Whisk together the eggs, cream, parsley, salt, and pepper to taste. Stir in the smoked salmon. Melt 4 tablespoons of the butter in a skillet. Sauté the onion until softened but not browned. Add the remaining butter to the skillet. Pour in the egg mixture. Cook over a low heat, stirring constantly, until eggs are just set.

MEXICAN BRUNCH EGGS

SERVES 6
PREPARATION TIME 10 MINUTES
COOKING TIME 30 MINUTES

The sauce can be prepared a day in advance. Reheat and slip the eggs in just before serving.

4 slices bacon, diced
1 onion, minced
2 cloves garlic, minced
1 1-pound 12-ounce can Italian
   tomatoes
2 to 3 tablespoons chopped
   fresh green chilies
1/2 teaspoon salt

1/2 teaspoon dried oregano
   leaves
6 eggs
1 1/2 cups cubed Jack cheese
1/4 cup chopped fresh cilantro
Guacamole (optional)
Flour tortillas (optional)

In a 10-inch frying pan, cook bacon until crisp. Remove from pan with slotted spoon and drain. Add onion and garlic to bacon drippings in the pan. Cook until onion is soft. Stir in tomatoes, chilies, salt, and oregano. Bring to a boil, stirring constantly. Continue boiling until sauce thickens, about 15 minutes.

Reduce heat to low. Crack eggs and slowly slip into sauce, one at a time. Sprinkle cheese and bacon over the top. Cover and simmer until eggs are set, about 5 to 7 minutes. Sprinkle with the cilantro. Serve with guacamole and warmed flour tortillas on the side of the plate, if desired.

BLINTZ SOUFFLÉ

SERVES 8

PREPARATION TIME 20 MINUTES

COOKING TIME 1 HOUR

This blintz can be made in advance. Cover and refrigerate for up to 8 hours.

6 eggs
1 1/2 cups sour cream
1/2 cup orange juice
1/3 cup sugar
8 ounces (2 sticks) butter
2 teaspoons baking powder
2 cups flour

8 ounces cream cheese
2 cups small-curd cottage cheese
2 egg yolks
1 tablespoon sugar
1 teaspoon vanilla
Cherry Sauce (recipe follows)

Preheat oven to 350 degrees. In a food processor or blender, mix eggs, sour cream, orange juice, sugar, butter, and baking powder. Add the flour and continue mixing until blended. Pour 1/2 of the batter into a 9 × 13 casserole.

Dice the cream cheese. Mix with the cottage cheese, egg yolks, sugar, and vanilla. Drop by spoonfuls evenly over the batter in the dish. Gently pour the remaining batter over all. Bake until puffed in the center and golden brown, about 55 minutes. Serve immediately with Cherry Sauce.

CHERRY SAUCE
3 cups pitted sweet cherries
1/2 cup water
1/4 cup sugar

2 teaspoons lemon juice
2 teaspoons cornstarch

In a saucepan, combine all of the ingredients. Bring to a boil over medium heat, stirring constantly, until the sauce is thick and clear. Serve warm, or cooled.

PUFFED CINNAMON-APPLE PANCAKE

SERVES 6 TO 8
PREPARATION TIME 10 MINUTES
COOKING TIME 25 MINUTES

Cinnamon and tart apples make this breakfast opener extra delicious.

8 tablespoons butter
1/4 cup sugar
2 teaspoons ground cinnamon
2 large green apples, peeled,
   cored, and thinly sliced

4 eggs
1 cup flour
1 cup plus 2 tablespoons milk
1 teaspoon vanilla
Powdered sugar

Preheat oven to 425 degrees. In a skillet, melt butter over medium-high heat. Stir in the sugar and cinnamon. Add the apples. Cook, stirring, until apples are translucent, about 5 minutes. Place the pan in the oven while you prepare the batter.

Beat the eggs. Add the flour and milk. Beat until smooth. Pour the batter evenly over the apples in the pan. Bake, uncovered, until pancake is puffy and golden, about 15 minutes. Sift powdered sugar over the pancake. Cut into wedges. Serve immediately.

FRESH STRAWBERRY PANCAKE

SERVES 6 TO 8
PREPARATION TIME 10 MINUTES
COOKING TIME 30 MINUTES

Absolutely spectacular for a weekend breakfast. An orange-flavored liqueur can be substituted for the orange juice.

6 eggs
1 cup milk
1/4 cup orange juice
1 cup flour
1/2 cup sugar
1/4 teaspoon salt

4 ounces (1 stick) butter
1 basket fresh strawberries,
   sliced
Sugar to taste
2 tablespoons orange juice
Powdered sugar

Preheat oven to 425 degrees. With a mixer or by hand, mix eggs, milk, orange juice, flour, sugar, and salt until well blended. Place butter in a 9 × 13-inch baking dish. Heat in the oven until bubbly but not brown. Pour the batter over the sizzling butter. Bake for 20 minutes or until puffed and brown.

While pancake is baking, heat the strawberries in a small saucepan until hot. Add enough sugar to sweeten. Stir in orange juice and cook until slightly thickened. Remove pancake from the oven. Sprinkle with powdered sugar. Serve immediately with the warm strawberries. The pancake falls quickly after it is out of the oven.

BANANA SURPRISE PANCAKES

MAKES 30 TO 35 PANCAKES
PREPARATION TIME 10 MINUTES
COOKING TIME 15 MINUTES

A delightful breakfast treat. Inside these rich puffy pancakes is a hidden banana slice which provides a delectable surprise.

1 cup cottage cheese	1 cup sifted flour
1 cup sour cream	1 teaspoon baking powder
2 1/2 tablespoons honey	2 medium firm bananas, cut
1/2 teaspoon vanilla	diagonally into 1/4-inch slices
Dash of salt	Flour
4 eggs at room temperature	Vegetable oil or butter

Blend the cottage cheese, sour cream, honey, vanilla, and salt in processor or blender until smooth. Add the eggs, one at a time. Sift together the flour and baking powder. Slowly stir egg mixture into flour. Stir out the lumps but do not overmix.

Lightly dust banana slices with flour. Brush a griddle with oil or butter. Drop batter by tablespoons onto the griddle. Top each with a banana slice. Spoon more batter on top of each banana slice, to cover. Cook until bubbles form on top surface. Flip over and cook on other side until golden brown. Serve with warmed maple syrup.

COTTAGE CHEESE PANCAKES

MAKES 10 TO 12
PREPARATION TIME 15 MINUTES
COOKING TIME 10 MINUTES

6 eggs, separated
3 tablespoons sugar
2/3 cup small-curd cottage
   cheese

6 tablespoons flour
3 to 4 tablespoons butter
Powdered sugar
Strawberry preserves

Beat the egg whites until foamy. Add the sugar and continue beating until stiff but not dry. In a large bowl, beat the egg yolks. Add the cottage cheese; blend well. Blend in flour until smooth. Fold in the egg whites.

Melt some of the butter in a large skillet or griddle over medium high heat. Drop batter by tablespoons onto the skillet. Cook until the underneath side is brown. Flip the pancakes over and continue cooking until the second side is brown. Repeat with the remaining batter, adding more butter to the skillet as necessary. Sprinkle with powdered sugar. Serve immediately with the warmed preserves.

STACKED WHOLE GRAIN HOT CAKES

MAKES ABOUT 24 LARGE
PREPARATION TIME 45 MINUTES
COOKING TIME 15 MINUTES

1/3 cup old-fashioned rolled
   oats
3/4 cup whole wheat flour
1/3 cup yellow corn meal
1/3 cup white flour
2 teaspoons baking powder
1 teaspoon baking soda

1 teaspoon salt
6 tablespoons butter, melted
2 cups buttermilk
2 eggs, lightly beaten
3 tablespoons maple syrup
Blueberry Sauce†

In a blender or food processor, grind the oats into a coarse powder. Transfer to a large bowl and stir in the remaining dry ingredients. In another bowl, combine the butter, buttermilk, eggs, and maple syrup. Add to the dry mixture and blend well. Let stand for 30 minutes.

Heat a griddle or skillet. Brush with butter. Pour some of the batter onto the griddle. Cook until the underside is brown and the top is bubbly. Flip over and cook other side. Transfer to a platter to keep warm while preparing the rest of the hot cakes. Serve with warmed Blueberry Sauce.

WALNUT ORANGE PANCAKES

MAKES 12 TO 15
PREPARATION TIME 10 MINUTES
COOKING TIME 10 MINUTES

A change-of-pace pancake. Keeping in mind compatibility of taste, try different flavors of honey for more variety.

2 eggs	1 3/4 cups buttermilk baking
1 cup orange juice	mix (Bisquick)
1 tablespoon grated orange	1/2 cup ground walnuts
rind	1 orange, peeled and thinly
3 tablespoons honey	sliced

In a food processor or blender, combine the eggs, orange juice, orange rind, and honey. Mix until well blended. Transfer to a bowl and add the buttermilk baking mix and walnuts. Beat until just blended.

Pour approximately 1/4 cup batter onto a greased griddle. Cook until golden brown on underneath side and the top has a bubbly surface. Turn and continue cooking until underneath side is nicely browned. Serve with fresh orange slices.

JELLY-ROLL PANCAKE

SERVES 4
PREPARATION TIME 10 MINUTES
COOKING TIME 20 MINUTES

1 tablespoon vegetable oil	1 cup milk
6 eggs	3 ounces cream cheese,
1 teaspoon salt	softened
2 tablespoons sugar	1/2 cup raspberry jam
2/3 cup flour	Sifted powdered sugar

Pour oil in a jelly-roll pan. Place in the oven while oven is heating to 450 degrees. Beat the eggs with the salt until light. Blend the sugar with the flour. Add to the eggs and beat until batter is smooth. Stir in milk and mix thoroughly. Remove pan from the oven and pour in the batter.

Bake for 15 minutes, or until puffy and brown. Immediately spread with the cream cheese and jam. Roll up jelly-roll fashion. Sprinkle with the powdered sugar. Serve immediately.

FRENCH TOAST AMANDINE

SERVES 8
PREPARATION TIME 40 MINUTES
COOKING TIME 5 MINUTES

6 eggs
1 cup half-and-half
1 tablespoon dark brown sugar
1 1/2 teaspoons almond extract
1/2 teaspoon freshly grated
   nutmeg

A 1-pound loaf French bread,
   cut into 16 slices
4 to 6 tablespoons butter
1/2 cup sliced, toasted almonds
Powdered sugar
Syrup

In a medium bowl, beat eggs and half-and-half. Add brown sugar, almond extract, and nutmeg. Mix well. Dip bread slices into the egg mixture, one at a time, until well coated. In a shallow dish or pan, place the coated slices in a single layer. Pour the remaining batter over the slices. Let bread soak at least 30 minutes or up to 2 hours.

    Melt some of the butter in a large skillet. Add bread and cook until lightly browned on both sides, adding more butter as necessary. Top with almonds and sifted powdered sugar. Serve immediately. Pass syrup.

ORANGE FRENCH TOAST

SERVES 4 TO 6
PREPARATION TIME 5 MINUTES
REFRIGERATION TIME 12 HOURS
COOKING TIME 5 MINUTES

Great for overnight houseguests. Garnish with sliced oranges, raspberries, or strawberries.

6 eggs
Grated rind of 1 orange
2/3 cup orange juice
1/3 cup Grand Marnier
1/3 cup milk
3 tablespoons sugar

1/4 teaspoon vanilla
1/4 teaspoon salt
8 3/4-inch slices of French
   bread
Butter for frying

Beat the eggs and add all the remaining ingredients, except the bread. Mix well. Coat the bread slices with the batter. Place in a single layer in a dish.

Pour the remaining batter over the bread layer. Cover and refrigerate over-night, turning occasionally.

Melt butter in a large skillet over medium-high heat. Add the French toast, a few pieces at a time, and sauté until nicely browned. Serve immediately.

SPINACH CRÊPES

SERVES 4
PREPARATION TIME 30 MINUTES
COOKING TIME 30 MINUTES

A nice brunch or luncheon dish.

1 10-ounce package frozen chopped spinach	1/4 teaspoon salt
1 cup chopped onion	1/4 teaspoon freshly grated nutmeg
2 tablespoons butter	8 Crêpes†
1 cup grated Swiss cheese	Sauce (recipe follows)
2 teaspoons Dijon mustard	

Preheat oven to 350 degrees. Thaw spinach and squeeze as dry as possible with your hands. Sauté the onion in the butter until soft, about 5 to 10 minutes. Add spinach and cook until moisture evaporates. Stir in cheese, mustard, salt, and nutmeg. Mix well.

Place approximately 1/4 cup filling on each crêpe. Roll up. Place, seam side down, in a buttered baking dish. Cover with foil and bake until heated thoroughly, about 15 minutes.

SAUCE

2 tablespoons butter	1/2 cup half-and-half
2 tablespoons flour	2 teaspoons Dijon mustard
1 cup milk	1/2 pound ham, diced

While crêpes are heating, prepare the sauce. Melt the butter in a saucepan. Stir in the flour and cook for 2 minutes, without browning. Slowly add the milk and half-and-half, stirring constantly until thickened. Stir in the mustard. Fold in the ham. Serve the sauce over the crêpes.

CRUSTLESS SPINACH QUICHE

SERVES 6 TO 8
PREPARATION TIME 25 MINUTES
COOKING TIME 45 MINUTES

Also good as an appetizer. Bake in a rectangular pan and cut into bite-size pieces.

Butter
1 large shallot, chopped
1 large onion, chopped
2 tablespoons oil
1 10-ounce package frozen
   spinach, thawed

5 eggs
3/4 pound Muenster cheese,
   grated
1/4 teaspoon cayenne
Salt
Freshly ground pepper

Preheat oven to 350 degrees. Butter a 9-inch pie plate. Sauté the shallot and onion in the oil until soft, about 5 to 10 minutes. With hands, squeeze spinach as dry as possible. Add to shallot and onion. Cook until all moisture evaporates. Let cool.

    In a bowl, beat eggs. Add cheese and cayenne. Stir into onion-spinach mixture. Season to taste with salt and pepper. Turn into pie plate, spreading evenly. Bake for 40 to 45 minutes, or until top is nicely browned and quiche is firm.

COUNTRY SALMON PIE WITH PARMESAN CRUST

SERVES 8
PREPARATION TIME 30 MINUTES
COOKING TIME 1 1/2 HOURS

Serve as a first course, light entree, or luncheon dish. The Parmesan crust and dill are a refreshing change from your basic quiche.

1 pound fresh salmon, poached
1 large onion, diced
1 clove garlic, pressed
2 tablespoons butter
2 cups sour cream
4 eggs

1 1/2 cups shredded Gruyère
   cheese
1 teaspoon dried dill
1/4 teaspoon salt
Parmesan Crust, partially baked
   (recipe follows)

Break salmon into bite-size pieces. Sauté onion and garlic in butter until soft, about 5 to 10 minutes. Beat sour cream and eggs together until well blended. Stir salmon, onion, 1 cup of the Gruyère cheese, dill, and salt into the sour-cream mixture. Pour into Parmesan Crust. Top with the remaining 1/2 cup cheese. Bake for approximately 1 hour or until set. Cool in pan for 5 minutes before removing. Cut into wedges. Serve immediately.

PARMESAN CRUST

1 1/2 cups flour

1/2 cup freshly grated Parmesan cheese

3/4 cup vegetable shortening

3 to 4 tablespoons water

Preheat oven to 375 degrees. Combine flour and cheese. Cut in shortening until mixture is crumbly. Stir in the water. Form into a ball, adding more water as needed. Press into bottom and sides of a 9-inch springform pan. Bake for 15 to 20 minutes.

SAVORY QUICHE

SERVES 8

PREPARATION TIME 35 MINUTES

COOKING TIME 35 MINUTES

For a spicy rendition, add chopped chili peppers to the custard.

1/2 pound fresh mushrooms, coarsely chopped

3 tablespoons butter

1/2 cup finely chopped saltine crackers (14 halves)

1 bunch green onions, chopped

2 tablespoons butter

8 ounces shredded Jack cheese

1 cup sour cream

3 eggs

1/4 teaspoon cayenne

Paprika

Preheat oven to 375 degrees. Sauté the mushrooms in the butter until limp. Stir in the crackers. Pour into a buttered 10-inch pie pan. Press evenly into the bottom and on the sides. Sauté the onions in the butter until soft. Spread the onions over the crust. Sprinkle cheese over the onions. Beat sour cream, eggs, and cayenne until smooth. Pour over cheese. Sprinkle with the paprika. Bake for 25 minutes. Turn up oven to 400 degrees. Bake for 10 additional minutes. Let rest 5 minutes. Cut into wedges and serve immediately.

SPINACH AND SAUSAGE FRITTATA

SERVES 8
PREPARATION TIME 30 MINUTES
COOKING TIME 45 MINUTES

Serve warm or cool. Luxurious, too, for a country weekend picnic.

2 Italian sausages
1/4 cup olive oil
1 medium onion, chopped
1/2 pound mushrooms, sliced
1 10-ounce package frozen
  spinach, thawed
6 eggs
3/4 cup grated Parmesan cheese

2 cloves garlic, minced
1/2 teaspoon basil
1/4 teaspoon marjoram
Salt to taste
Pepper to taste
1/4 cup grated Parmesan cheese
1 cup grated mozzarella cheese

Preheat oven to 350 degrees. Remove the sausages from their casings and cook until browned. Crumble with a fork, remove with a slotted spoon, and drain on paper towels. Pour off any remaining fat in the pan. Add the olive oil to the pan and sauté the onion and mushrooms until soft. Squeeze the spinach dry, add to the pan, and sauté for another minute. Transfer to a bowl and let cool.

Butter a 9-inch square pan. Combine the eggs, the 3/4 cup Parmesan cheese, garlic, basil, marjoram, and salt and pepper. Mix well. Stir into the sausage-and-vegetable mixture. Pour into the prepared pan and sprinkle with the remaining cheeses. Bake for 20 to 25 minutes or until set. Cut into squares and serve on a colorful serving platter.

LEEK TART

SERVES 8
PREPARATION TIME 20 MINUTES
REFRIGERATION TIME 30 MINUTES
COOKING TIME 40 TO 50 MINUTES

PASTRY
1 cup flour
4 ounces (1 stick) unsalted
  butter

Pinch of salt
1/4 cup ice water

In a food processor or by hand, blend together the flour, butter and salt until crumbly. Pour the cold water into the flour and form into a ball. Cover and refrigerate for 30 minutes. Preheat oven to 400 degrees. Roll out to fit a 9-inch quiche pan. Bake blind for 10 minutes. Let cool before filling.

FILLING

2 bunches leeks, cleaned and thinly sliced (about 4 cups)	**3 eggs**
	²/₃ cup heavy cream
3 tablespoons butter	**Pinch nutmeg**
1 cup grated Gruyère or Jarlsberg cheese	**2 tablespoons butter**

Preheat oven to 375 degrees. Simmer leeks in the butter until soft, about 10 minutes. Spread the grated cheese over the pastry. Cover with the leeks. Beat the eggs together with the cream and nutmeg. Pour over the leeks. Dot with remaining butter and bake for 30 to 40 minutes, or until the tart is puffed and golden.

LAYERED SHRIMP CRÊPE

SERVES 4
PREPARATION TIME 45 MINUTES
COOKING TIME 35 MINUTES

Fun and easy do-ahead luncheon or light dinner dish.

8 ounces creamy garlic-herb cheese, room temperature	**3 tablespoons chopped fresh chives**
8 Crêpes†	**2 ¹/₂ cups shredded Jack cheese**
¹/₂ pound tiny cooked shrimp	

Preheat oven to 350 degrees. Spread approximately 2 tablespoons of the garlic-herb cheese over 1 crêpe. Place, cheese side up, on a buttered baking sheet or ovenproof serving plate.

Mix shrimp, chives, and 2 ¹/₄ cups of the Jack cheese. Sprinkle ¹/₂ cup of this mixture evenly over crêpe. Repeat layering with remaining crêpes, cheese, and shrimp mixture, ending with crêpe on top. Sprinkle with the remaining Jack cheese. Bake until heated throughout, 30 to 35 minutes. Cut into wedges. Serve immediately.

CABLE CAR QUICHE

SERVES 4 TO 6
PREPARATION TIME 30 MINUTES
COOKING TIME 50 MINUTES

3 eggs
1 1/2 cups milk
1/2 cup buttermilk baking mix
  (Bisquick)
1/3 cup melted butter

2 cups shredded Gruyère
  cheese
12 strips cooked bacon,
  crumbled
1/2 cup chopped onion

Preheat oven to 375 degrees. Combine the eggs, milk, baking mix, and butter. Mix well. Pour into a buttered 10-inch pie plate. Sprinkle with the cheese, bacon, and onion. Bake 50 minutes or until set. Serve immediately.

PASTA AND RICE

Sierra Foothills

Winding north and south through historic El Dorado, Amador, and Calaveras counties, Route 49 leads to most of the thirty-five Sierra Foothill wineries. This is one of California's oldest wine-growing regions, and its history is closely tied to the Gold Rush of 1849. These vineyards are nestled in the gentle, rolling hills and valleys at the western base of the Sierra Nevada. Both enjoy the warm inland climate, several hundred miles from coastal breezes, as well as the cooler nights.

The colorful history of the region is captured in the names of the local towns: Fiddletown, Dry Town, Sutter Creek, and Colma, the latter being the location of Sutter's Mill, where the first nugget of California gold was discovered. Today, historic Victorian residences have been turned into bed-and-breakfast inns, offering old-fashioned charm and rural hospitality. Deserted mines and shattered ghost towns provide fascinating glimpses into California's history, and one can rekindle the spirit of Gold Rush days by touring these old mine sites and museums filled with relics of that historic time.

Some who came seeking their fortune in gold turned to planting vineyards and orchards, at first to support the bustling mine population, but continuing on as the Gold Rush waned. By 1890, the winemaking industry was substantial, and, as in other wine-growing regions, wineries still bear the names of the Italian families who founded them. The D'Agostini Winery, established in 1856, is a state historical landmark whose original Zinfandel vines are still in production today.

This region is known for its intense red wines, particularly Zinfandels. Foothill wineries are also producing white Zinfandel, Zinfandel rose, and even late harvest sweet Zinfandel and Zinfandel port—relatively new, eye-opening and pleasant surprises. Similarly the new ways that pasta and rice are being prepared present new horizons on the culinary front. Try a bottle of Amador County Zinfandel and the Angel Hair Pasta with Chèvre or Cannelloni with Porcini Mushrooms. Buon Appetito!

EGG PASTA

PREPARATION TIME 15 TO 30 MINUTES

This is the basic pasta all'uovo that is used in preparing all homemade egg noodles. It requires approximately 3/4 cup all-purpose, unbleached flour for each large egg used. It is definitely much easier to make with a pasta machine. Commercial noodles can be substituted for homemade ones in all of our recipes. The servings given are for first-course portions. If you are preparing as an entree, you will need more.

4 SERVINGS	6 SERVINGS	8 SERVINGS
2 eggs	3 eggs	4 eggs
1 1/4 cups flour	2 1/4 cups flour	3 cups flour

Place the desired amount of flour on a work surface. Make a well in the center of the flour. Crack the eggs into the well and beat lightly with a fork. Add the flour gradually to the egg, drawing it from the inside of the well. When the eggs are no longer runny, tumble the rest of the flour over them, and mix with your palms and fingertips until well combined. Add as much of the flour as the mixture will absorb without becoming stiff and dry. Never exceed 1 cup flour per egg. It is possible that you may need more flour or not use the whole amount. When the mixture is blended and ready for kneading, put it into the pasta machine or knead by hand for 15 minutes. Hand-knead by pressing against the dough with the heel of your palm, folding it over, and turning it again and again. Roll out thinly and let stand for 10 to 15 minutes, or until dry enough to cut. Cut into desired shape by hand or machine. Use immediately or let dry.

You can also prepare the dough in a food processor. Place the flour in the bowl. With the machine running, add the eggs through the feed tube. Process until the dough forms a ball. Wrap the dough in plastic. Let it rest for 30 minutes before rolling.

PASTA VERDE

SERVES 3 TO 4
PREPARATION TIME 30 MINUTES

1/2 package frozen spinach	2 eggs
1/4 teaspoon salt	1 1/2 cups flour

Cook the frozen spinach with the salt for 5 minutes. Drain and cool. Squeeze as dry as possible with your hands. Purée, with the eggs, in a food processor. Place the flour on a work surface. Make a well in the center of the flour. Place the spinach-egg mixture in the center of the well. Add the flour gradually to the spinach-egg mixture, drawing from the inside of the well. It may be necessary to add more flour if the dough is too sticky. Incorporate as much flour as possible without the dough becoming stiff and dry. When the mixture is ready for kneading and rolling, proceed as though it were egg pasta.

PASTA ROSSA

PREPARATION TIME 35 MINUTES

This vegetable pasta is made from a purée of roasted red peppers. Pasta rossa (red pasta) can also be made with puréed beets by following the directions for spinach pasta. Substitute 5 ounces of beets for the spinach.

2 pounds red bell peppers
2 cups flour
2 eggs

Char the skins on the peppers until black. This can be done by placing directly over a gas flame or by baking in a 500-degree oven until skins are blackened on all sides. Under running water, peel off and discard skins, stems, and seeds. Purée peppers in a food processor or blender. In a small saucepan, cook the purée until reduced to 1/3 cup.

Mound the flour on a work surface. Make a well in the center. Add the purée and eggs. Add the flour gradually to the purée mixture, drawing from the inside of the well. Incorporate as much flour as possible without the mixture becoming stiff and dry. It is possible that you may need more flour or not use the whole amount. When the mixture is blended and ready for kneading, proceed as though it were egg pasta.

LEMON PASTA

MAKES 1 POUND
PREPARATION TIME 30 MINUTES

This pasta tastes best tossed in a butter-cream sauce.

2 1/2 to 3 cups flour
2 eggs
2 tablespoons minced lemon
zest

4 tablespoons strained lemon
juice
1/2 teaspoon salt
3 to 4 tablespoons water

Place the flour on a work surface. Make a well in the flour. Add the eggs, lemon zest, lemon juice, and salt. Using your hands, work the dough together. Add 1 to 2 tablespoons of water and keep working the dough until it forms a ball. If more water is needed, add to the dough.

Turn dough out onto a lightly floured board. Knead for 10 minutes, adding more flour if necessary. Cover and let rest for 15 minutes. Follow the directions for rolling out and shaping egg pasta.

SICILIAN SPAGHETTI

SERVES 8
PREPARATION TIME 45 MINUTES
COOKING TIME 30 MINUTES

3 pounds eggplant, peeled and
cubed
1 pound mild or hot Italian
sausage
1/2 cup olive oil
3 to 4 cloves garlic, minced
1 28-ounce can whole Italian
plum tomatoes
1 28-ounce can crushed Italian
plum tomatoes
3 red bell peppers, roasted,
peeled, and cut into strips

1 3 1/4-ounce can pitted black
olives
1/2 cup chopped fresh parsley
1/2 cup chopped fresh basil
1/4 cup capers
1/2 teaspoon dried red pepper
flakes
1 1/2 pounds spaghetti
Freshly grated Parmesan cheese

Sprinkle the eggplant with salt. Place in a colander to drain for 30 minutes. Rinse and dry between paper towels. Remove the casings from the sausage and crumble.

Heat 1 tablespoon of the oil in a large skillet. Sauté sausage and garlic until meat is browned. Remove with a slotted spoon and drain on paper towels. Pour off the grease in the pan. Add the remaining oil and sauté eggplant, stirring until just translucent. Stir in the tomatoes and simmer for 10 minutes. Add peppers, olives, parsley, basil, capers, and pepper flakes. Simmer, uncovered, for 10 minutes.

Bring a large pot of salted water to a boil. Add spaghetti and cook until tender but firm. Transfer to a serving bowl. Pour the sauce over the spaghetti. Toss to mix well. Sprinkle with Parmesan cheese. Serve immediately.

RIGATONI WITH SHRIMP AND FETA

SERVES 4
PREPARATION TIME 30 MINUTES
COOKING TIME 25 MINUTES

5 tablespoons olive oil
1 1/4 pounds medium shrimp (about 36), peeled and deveined
1/4 teaspoon red pepper flakes
1 small clove garlic, finely chopped
1/2 cup dry white wine
2 cups fresh tomatoes, peeled and cubed

1/3 cup chopped fresh basil
1 teaspoon dried crumbled oregano
Salt
Freshly ground pepper
6 ounces crumbled feta cheese
12 ounces rigatoni

Preheat oven to 400 degrees. Heat 3 tablespoons of the olive oil in a skillet. Sauté shrimp just until they turn pink. Stir in the red pepper flakes. Transfer shrimp and pan juices to a baking dish. Add the remaining oil to the skillet. Briefly sauté the garlic. Add the wine and cook for 2 minutes over high heat. Stir in the tomatoes, basil, oregano, and salt and pepper to taste. Simmer, uncovered, for 10 minutes. Sprinkle the feta cheese over the shrimp. Spoon the tomato sauce over all. Cover dish and bake for 10 minutes.

Cook the rigatoni in a large pot of boiling salted water until tender but still firm. Drain and transfer to a serving bowl. Add the shrimp-tomato mixture and gently mix with the rigatoni noodles. Serve immediately.

FETTUCCINE VERDE AL GORGONZOLA

SERVES 6
PREPARATION TIME 10 MINUTES
COOKING TIME 10 MINUTES

The rich, buttery flavor of the Gorgonzola cheese gives this sauce its unique flavor. Al dente literally means to the tooth. Pasta cooked in this manner is tender but still firm. To achieve this delicate balance, taste the pasta during cooking and check for doneness.

4 ounces imported Italian
  Gorgonzola cheese, crumbled
1/2 cup milk
3 tablespoons butter
1/4 cup heavy cream

3 Egg Pasta Verde† or 1 pound
  spinach fettuccine
1/3 cup freshly grated Parmesan
  cheese

In a small saucepan, combine cheese, milk, butter, and heavy cream. Place over low heat and stir until smooth. Continue cooking over low heat until sauce is hot and well blended.

Fill a large pot with water. Bring to a boil and add salt. Drop the pasta into the boiling water. Test every few seconds until cooked. Cook until tender but firm. Fresh pasta will cook in approximately 1 to 2 minutes. Dried pasta will take longer. Drain and toss with the cheese sauce. Sprinkle with the Parmesan cheese and toss gently. Serve immediately.

PASTA AI QUATTRO FORMAGGI

SERVES 4 TO 6
PREPARATION TIME 10 MINUTES
COOKING TIME 10 MINUTES

Use only genuine Italian Fontina and Gorgonzola cheeses, available at most cheese shops and delis.

4 tablespoons unsalted butter
1/4 pound Italian Fontina,
  cubed
1/4 pound Gorgonzola, cubed
1/4 pound Bel Paese, cubed

3/4 cup freshly grated Parmesan
  cheese
1 cup heavy cream
Freshly ground black pepper
1 pound tagliarini or linguini

Melt the butter in a saucepan. Add the Fontina, Gorgonzola, and Bel Paese cheeses, stirring constantly over a low heat until the cheese melts. Add 1/2 cup of the Parmesan cheese and the heavy cream. Continue stirring until you have a smooth sauce. Do not let the sauce boil at any time. Add pepper to taste.

Bring a large pot of salted water to the boil. Add the pasta and cook until tender but firm. Drain well and transfer to a serving bowl. Pour in the cheese sauce, stirring thoroughly until well mixed. Sprinkle with the remaining Parmesan cheese. Serve immediately.

PASTA PRIMAVERA

SERVES 4 TO 6
PREPARATION TIME 15 MINUTES
COOKING TIME 15 MINUTES

Primavera is Italian for springtime. Use any fresh vegetables to create a dish that will remind you of the beauty of Italy in the spring.

- 2 to 3 cloves garlic, minced
- 2 small carrots, julienned
- 1 small eggplant, peeled and julienned
- 1/2 pound mushrooms, julienned
- 3 tablespoons butter
- 2 small zucchini, shredded
- 2 ounces prosciutto, julienned
- 1 large tomato, peeled, seeded and cut into tiny wedges
- 1/2 cup heavy cream
- 1/2 cup chopped fresh basil
- Salt
- Freshly ground pepper
- 12 ounces spaghetti or fettuccine
- 1/2 cup freshly grated Parmesan cheese

Sauté garlic, carrots, eggplant, and mushrooms in the butter over high heat for 2 minutes. Stir in zucchini and prosciutto. Sauté one minute longer. Add tomato wedges and cream. Simmer for 5 minutes. Stir in the basil. Season to taste with salt and pepper.

Bring a large pot of salted water to a boil. Add pasta and cook until tender but firm. Drain and transfer to a serving bowl. Toss with the sauce. Sprinkle Parmesan cheese on top. Serve immediately.

ANGEL HAIR PASTA WITH CHÈVRE

SERVES 4 TO 6
PREPARATION TIME 10 MINUTES
COOKING TIME 15 MINUTES

Some consider angel hair (capelli d'angelo) to be the finest of all pastas. It is worthy of a truffle's company.

6 ounces chèvre, cut into pieces
1 cup heavy cream
4 tablespoons butter
3 ounces cooked ham, julienned

12 ounces angel hair pasta
2 tablespoons chopped fresh parsley
1 small can sliced truffles (optional)

In a saucepan, combine the chèvre, heavy cream, and butter. Stir over low heat until the cheese melts. Continue cooking until thickened slightly. Stir in the ham.

Bring a large pot of salted water to a boil. Add the pasta and cook until just tender but still firm, about 2 minutes for fresh and 4 minutes for dry. Drain and transfer to a serving bowl. Pour the sauce over the pasta. Sprinkle with the parsley. Toss gently to coat all the strands with sauce. Serve immediately, with the sliced truffles on top, if desired.

PASTA WITH SALMON AND SPRING VEGETABLES

SERVES 6
PREPARATION TIME 30 MINUTES
COOKING TIME 15 MINUTES

1/2 pound mushrooms, sliced
4 tablespoons butter
1/2 cup chopped green onion, including some top
2 cloves garlic, minced
3 tablespoons flour
1 cup chicken broth
1 cup milk
1/4 cup grated Parmesan cheese
Grated peel and juice of 1 small lemon

1/2 teaspoon dried basil
1/4 teaspoon dried oregano
1/8 teaspoon pepper
10 to 12 ounces spiral pasta, cooked and drained
1 pound poached salmon, cut into bite-size pieces
1 small zucchini, julienned and blanched
1 tomato, diced

In a large skillet, sauté the mushrooms in 2 tablespoons of the butter until soft. Remove from the skillet. Add the remaining 2 tablespoons butter and sauté the green onion and garlic. Stir in the flour. Cook for 1 minute without browning. Gradually, stir in the chicken broth and milk. Cook, stirring constantly, until smooth and thickened, about 2 to 3 minutes. Stir in the Parmesan cheese, lemon peel and juice, basil, oregano, and pepper. Cook for an additional few minutes. Add the cooked pasta and toss to mix. Gently stir in the mushrooms, salmon, zucchini, and tomato. Cook until heated. Arrange on a serving platter. Serve immediately.

FETTUCCINE WITH SCAMPI

SERVES 2
PREPARATION TIME 20 MINUTES
COOKING TIME 15 MINUTES

Scampi, available frozen at selected fish markets, are very expensive meaty shellfish that taste like baby lobster. But the famous Venetian scampi are so closely related to shrimp you can easily use large prawns as a substitute in this lovely pasta dish.

4 tablespoons (1/2 stick) butter
1 clove garlic, minced
1 tablespoon brandy
2 tablespoons white wine
2 teaspoons lemon juice
Pinch each of dried basil and oregano
6 scampi or large prawns, peeled, deveined, and sliced halfway through

4 fresh mushrooms, sliced
3 ounces chopped clams
3 ounces heavy cream
2 tablespoons brandy
1/2 pound fettuccine
1 green onion with green, cut into strips

In a food processor or blender, combine the butter, garlic, brandy, wine, lemon juice, basil, and oregano to make an herbed butter. Sauté the scampi in the butter until pink. Remove from pan and set aside. Add mushrooms, clams, cream, and brandy. Cook until reduced and thickened.

Bring a large pot of salted water to a boil. Add the fettuccine and cook until tender but firm. Drain and transfer to a heated platter. Toss with the herbed butter mixture. Return scampi to the pan and cook until heated through. Place scampi and sauce on the bed of noodles. Sprinkle with the green onions. Serve immediately.

FETTUCCINE CAPRICCIO

SERVES 8
PREPARATION TIME 10 MINUTES
COOKING TIME 30 MINUTES

1/3 pound pancetta, cubed
10 pitted black olives, halved
2 cups Tomato Sauce†
4 tablespoons (1/2 stick) butter
1 cup heavy cream
2 tablespoons chopped fresh
  parsley

Salt
Freshly ground black pepper
1 1/2 pounds fettuccine, green
  or white
3/4 cup freshly grated Parmesan
  cheese

In a large skillet, cook the pancetta and olives over medium heat until the pancetta is browned. Drain off all the fat. Add Tomato Sauce and butter. Simmer 5 minutes. Stir in cream, parsley, salt, and pepper. Cook for an additional 10 minutes.

Bring a large pot of salted water to a boil. Add the fettuccine and cook until tender but still firm. Drain and transfer to a serving bowl. Pour the sauce over the noodles and toss gently. Sprinkle with the Parmesan cheese and toss again. Serve immediately.

LINGUINI WITH CREAMY CLAM SAUCE

SERVES 4
PREPARATION TIME 20 MINUTES
COOKING TIME 15 MINUTES

24 clams, scrubbed
1/4 pound fresh mushrooms,
  sliced
1 clove garlic, chopped
2 tablespoons olive oil
2 tablespoons butter
1/4 cup dry sherry

1 cup heavy cream
2 tablespoons chopped fresh
  parsley
Salt
Freshly ground pepper
12 ounces linguini

Place the scrubbed clams in a heavy skillet. Do not add water. Cover and steam until shells open. Remove clams from shells and chop. Strain the clam liquid through a sieve and reserve.

Sauté the mushrooms and garlic in the oil and butter until soft. Add the sherry and boil for 1 minute. Stir in the reserved clam broth and the cream. Cook, stirring occasionally, until slightly thickened. Stir in the chopped clams, parsley, salt, and pepper. Heat through.

Bring a large pot of salted water to a boil. Add the linguini and cook until tender but firm. Drain and transfer to a warmed bowl. Toss in the creamy clam sauce. Serve immediately. If desired, garnish with the clam shells.

SPAGHETTI WITH RED CLAM SAUCE

SERVES 6 TO 8
PREPARATION TIME 12 MINUTES
COOKING TIME 40 MINUTES

Traditionally, cheese is not used with seafood pasta dishes in Italian cooking. If you feel compelled, you may add it to the dish just prior to serving.

- 2 to 3 cloves garlic, finely chopped
- 2 tablespoons butter
- 2 tablespoons olive oil
- 2 6 1/2-ounce cans chopped clams
- 1/2 cup dry white wine
- 1 28-ounce can Italian plum tomatoes, chopped
- 1/4 cup chopped fresh parsley
- 2 tablespoons chopped fresh basil
- 1/2 teaspoon dried oregano
- 1/2 teaspoon sugar
- 1/2 teaspoon salt
- 1/8 teaspoon red pepper flakes (optional)
- 1 pound spaghetti

Sauté garlic in butter and oil until golden. Drain the clam liquid from the clams, reserving clams. Add the liquid to the pan together with the wine. Boil for 1 minute. Stir in the tomatoes, parsley, basil, oregano, sugar, salt, and pepper flakes. Simmer, uncovered, for 30 minutes. Add clams and heat through.

Bring a large pot of salted water to a boil. Add the spaghetti and cook until tender but firm. Drain and transfer to a serving bowl. Pour the clam sauce over the spaghetti and toss to coat. Serve immediately.

PASTA ROLL WITH TOMATO CREAM SAUCE

SERVES 8 TO 10
PREPARATION TIME 1 1/2 HOURS
COOKING TIME 1 HOUR

A fabulous party dish well suited for a crowd. Don't let the preparation time scare you. It can be prepared 2 days in advance.

TOMATO CREAM SAUCE

1/2 cup minced onion
1/2 cup finely chopped carrot
1/2 cup finely chopped celery
4 ounces (1 stick) butter
1 28-ounce can Italian plum
  tomatoes, chopped

1/4 teaspoon sugar
3/4 to 1 cup heavy cream
Salt
Freshly ground pepper

In a saucepan, sauté the onion, carrot, and celery in the butter until soft but not brown. Add the tomatoes and sugar. Simmer, covered, for 1 hour, stirring occasionally. Purée in processor or food mill. Return to the saucepan and stir in the heavy cream. Season to taste with the salt and pepper.

PASTA ROLL

1 small onion, finely chopped
4 tablespoons butter
2 Italian sausages, skins
  removed
1 1/2 pounds fresh spinach,
  cooked, drained, and
  squeezed dry
1 cup ricotta cheese
1 cup freshly grated Parmesan
  cheese

1 egg yolk
1/4 teaspoon freshly grated
  nutmeg
Salt
Freshly ground pepper
5 to 6 pasta sheets, 5 inches
  wide and 16 inches long

Preheat oven to 375 degrees. Sauté the onion in the butter until soft. Add the sausage meat and cook until browned. (The sausages should be broken up into tiny pieces.) Finely chop the dry spinach. Stir into the pan with the meat. Cook for a minute. Remove pan from heat and let cool. Stir the ricotta, Parmesan cheese, egg yolk, nutmeg, salt, and pepper into the cooled mixture. Taste and correct seasonings.

Spread a layer of filling on top of each pasta sheet, leaving a 1-inch edge on ends and a 1/4-inch edge along the sides. Fold over 1 inch of pasta and continue to fold, jelly-roll fashion, until all of the sheet is rolled up. Wrap the roll tightly in cheesecloth and tie ends. You should have at least 5 rolls.

Bring a large pot of water to a boil. Carefully add the rolls and simmer gently for 20 minutes. Remove the rolls and unwrap while still hot. Let cool before slicing. (If making well in advance, wrap rolls in plastic and refrigerate until ready to serve.)

Spread a small amount of the sauce on the bottom of a baking dish. Slice rolls into 3/4-inch slices. Arrange the rolls in the baking dish. Cover and bake for 15 minutes, or until warmed. To serve, place the rolls on a serving dish or individual plates. Spoon some of the tomato cream sauce over the rolls. Pass additional sauce. Serve immediately.

LASAGNA WITH PESTO

SERVES 6
PREPARATION TIME 30 MINUTES
COOKING TIME 40 MINUTES

This dish is different from traditional lasagna because the noodles are filled and rolled. It can be prepared and assembled 1 day in advance.

1 pound ricotta cheese
1 1/2 cups freshly grated
   Parmesan cheese
1 cup shredded mozzarella
   cheese
1/2 cup minced fresh parsley
1/2 cup minced green onion
1/2 teaspoon minced garlic
1 egg yolk

1 teaspoon dried basil
1/2 teaspoon dried marjoram
Salt
Freshly ground pepper
3/4 pound lasagna, cooked,
   rinsed in cold water, and
   drained
Pesto Sauce†

Preheat oven to 350 degrees. Grease a shallow baking dish. Combine all the ingredients, except noodles and Pesto Sauce. Blend well. Taste and correct seasonings. Spread some of the filling over each lasagna noodle. Roll up jelly-roll fashion. Stand vertically in the baking dish in a single layer. Spoon Pesto Sauce over the top of each roll. Cover and bake for 30 to 40 minutes, or until bubbly and heated through. Serve immediately.

GREEN LASAGNA

SERVES 8
PREPARATION TIME 2 HOURS
COOKING TIME 20 MINUTES

A delicate lasagna. Never use more than 6 layers of pasta. The filling should be thin and subtle.

MEAT SAUCE

1 onion, chopped
2 tablespoons olive oil
1 clove garlic, minced
1 28-ounce can Italian tomatoes
chopped, with juice
2 tablespoons dried basil
1/2 teaspoon dried oregano

1 teaspoon sugar
3/4 pound ground beef,
crumbled, cooked, and
drained
Salt
Freshly ground pepper

To make Meat Sauce, sauté the onion in oil for 10 minutes without browning. Add the garlic and cook for 2 minutes. Stir in tomatoes and herbs. Bring to a boil and cook until some of the liquid evaporates, approximately 5 minutes. Add the sugar and meat. Season to taste with salt and pepper. Set aside until needed.

BÉCHAMEL SAUCE

6 tablespoons butter
4 tablespoons flour
3 cups warm milk

Salt
White pepper

For the Béchamel Sauce, melt the butter in a large saucepan. Stir in flour and cook for 2 minutes without browning. Slowly add the warm milk, stirring constantly until thickened and smooth. Cook until the consistency of thick cream. Season to taste with the salt and pepper.

PASTA VERDE†
1 1/3 cup freshly grated Parmesan cheese

Prepare the 2-egg Pasta Verde or buy commercially prepared noodles. If making your own, roll out into sheets the size of the baking dish you are using. Bring a large pot of salted water to a boil. Drop in the noodles, a few at a time, and cook until tender. Remove with tongs and immediately plunge into ice water to stop the cooking. Dry on towels.

ASSEMBLY

Preheat oven to 400 degrees. Grease a large baking dish. Spread a small amount of Tomato Sauce on the bottom. Make a layer of noodles. Cover with more of the Tomato Sauce and the Béchamel. Sprinkle with the Parmesan cheese. Continue layering, making no more than 6 layers and ending with a layer of noodles. Spread the top with Béchamel Sauce. Dot with butter and sprinkle with Parmesan cheese. Cover and bake for 15 minutes, or until bubbly and heated through. Let rest 5 minutes before cutting.

SEAFOOD SHELLS WITH SAFFRON SAUCE

SERVES 6
PREPARATION TIME 40 MINUTES
COOKING TIME 40 MINUTES

Saffron is made from the golden orange stigmas of the autumn crocus. The finest saffron comes from Spain.

SEAFOOD SHELLS

30 jumbo pasta shells
4 tablespoons butter
1/2 pound shrimp, peeled, deveined, and chopped
1/2 pound scallops, diced
1/2 pound bass, diced
2 tablespoons minced shallot
2 1/2 tablespoons flour
1 cup warm milk
3 teaspoons fresh lemon juice
1/2 teaspoon grated lemon zest
1/2 teaspoon salt
1/4 teaspoon freshly ground black pepper
Pinch of cayenne
3/4 pound fresh spinach leaves, cooked
1/2 cup heavy cream
Saffron Sauce (recipe follows)

Cook the pasta in a large pot of boiling salted water until tender, about 10 minutes. Drain and rinse under cold water to stop the cooking. Drain again. Reserve 20 to 24 of the best pasta shells and set aside.

Preheat oven to 350 degrees. Melt 2 tablespoons of the butter in a skillet. Sauté the shrimp until just pink, about 1 to 2 minutes. Transfer to a bowl with a slotted spoon. Add scallops and bass to skillet. Sauté until opaque, about 1 to 2 minutes. Using a slotted spoon, transfer to the bowl with the shrimp. Add the remaining butter to the skillet. Sauté the shallot until soft. Stir in the flour and cook for 1 minute, stirring constantly. Slowly whisk in the milk and cook until thickened and smooth. Pour in any liquid collected from the fish while sitting. Stir in lemon juice, zest, salt, pepper, and cayenne. Cook for a few minutes. Remove from heat and let cool.

With your hands, squeeze as much moisture as possible from the spinach. Chop finely. Toss spinach and seafood together. Add to the cooled sauce, tossing carefully to mix. Spoon approximately 2 tablespoons of the stuffing into each shell. Place the stuffed shells in a buttered baking dish. Pour the heavy cream into the bottom of the dish. Cover with foil. Bake 20 minutes or until shells are thoroughly heated. Prepare Saffron Sauce while shells are heating.

SAFFRON SAUCE

1/4 cup dry vermouth	Pinch of cayenne
1 tablespoon fresh lemon juice	1 to 1 1/4 cups heavy cream
2 teaspoons minced shallot	1/4 teaspoon salt
1/4 teaspoon powdered saffron	

Combine vermouth, lemon juice, shallot, saffron, and cayenne in a saucepan. Bring to a boil. Cook, stirring occasionally, until reduced to 1 tablespoon. Add 1 cup of the cream. Cook until reduced to 2/3 cup, about 10 minutes. Stir in the salt. If too thick, thin with the additional cream. Taste and correct seasonings.

When shells are heated, remove dish from oven. Add any cream remaining in the baking dish to the sauce. Stir until blended and heated through. Place 3 or 4 shells on individual plates. Spoon Saffron Sauce over the shells. Serve immediately.

GREEN GNOCCHI WITH CREAM SAUCE

SERVES 6
PREPARATION TIME 45 MINUTES
COOKING TIME 20 MINUTES

GNOCCHI

1 pound fresh spinach, washed, stems removed	1 egg, lightly beaten
2 tablespoons finely chopped onion	1/4 teaspoon fresh grated nutmeg
3 tablespoons butter	Salt
1 pound ricotta cheese	White pepper
1 cup freshly grated Parmesan cheese	3/4 to 1 cup flour

Cook the spinach with just the water that clings to it from cleaning. Cool. Squeeze as dry as possible with hands and chop finely. Sauté the spinach and onion in the butter until soft. Transfer to a bowl. Stir in ricotta, Parmesan, and egg. Mix well. Season with nutmeg, salt and pepper. (You can mix in processor before adding the flour.) Stir in flour. The mixture will be slightly sticky. Flour hands and shape mixture into small balls, no larger than 3/4 inch in diameter. Reflour hands whenever mixture begins to get sticky. Dry on a floured baking tray. To freeze: place in freezer on trays until firm. Transfer to plastic bags to store.

CREAM SAUCE
4 tablespoons butter
1 cup heavy cream
3/4 cup freshly grated Parmesan cheese

Simmer butter and cream in a saucepan over medium heat until thickened, about 20 to 30 minutes. Bring a large pot of salted water to a boil. Drop in the gnocchi. Let the water return to a boil and cook gnocchi until they float to the top. Remove with a slotted spoon and place in a warmed bowl. Add Cream Sauce and the Parmesan cheese. Gently toss to coat well. Serve immediately.

FETTUCCINE WITH SCALLOPS

SERVES 4
PREPARATION TIME 15 MINUTES
COOKING TIME 15 MINUTES

3 tablespoons butter
2 tablespoons olive oil
2 red bell peppers, cut into thin strips
2 cloves garlic, minced
Peel of 1 small lemon, cut into thin slices
1/2 teaspoon crushed, dried hot red pepper
3/4 cup chicken stock
1/4 cup fresh lemon juice
1 pound scallops, cut if large
3/4 cup chopped fresh parsley
12 ounces fettuccine

Heat the butter and oil in a skillet over medium-high heat. Add red bell peppers, garlic, lemon peel, and red pepper. Cook for 2 minutes. Add chicken stock and lemon juice. Reduce by half. Stir in scallops and cook for an additional 2 minutes. Sprinkle with the parsley.

Cook the fettuccine in a large pot of boiling salted water until tender but firm. Drain and place in a serving bowl. Pour the sauce over the pasta. Toss and serve immediately.

CANNELLONI WITH PORCINI MUSHROOMS

SERVES 6 TO 8
PREPARATION TIME 1 HOUR
COOKING TIME 1 HOUR

If you don't want to use store-bought cannelloni, you may make your own cannelloni skins by following the directions for basic egg dough. Roll out and cut into 6 × 6-inch squares. Just like lasagna noodles, they must be boiled before baking. Porcini mushrooms are the best-known Italian wild mushroom. Their incredible flavor is preserved and somewhat intensified by drying. Dried porcini are available in Italian markets and gourmet shops.

FILLING

1 ounce dry porcini mushrooms

1/4 cup finely chopped onion

2 tablespoons olive oil

1/2 pound lean ground beef

1/2 cup dry white wine

3 ounces prosciutto, chopped

1 28-ounce can Italian tomatoes, chopped

Soak the mushrooms in warm water for 30 minutes. Rinse and remove all the dirt. Squeeze dry and coarsely chop. Set aside.

Sauté the onion in the oil until soft. Add the ground beef and sauté over high heat until it loses its red color. Add the wine and cook until it evaporates. Stir in the prosciutto and chopped mushrooms. Cook briefly and add the tomatoes. Simmer for 45 minutes.

BÉCHAMEL SAUCE

4 tablespoons butter

3 tablespoons flour

2 cups warm milk

Salt

White pepper

Melt the butter in a saucepan. Add the flour and cook for 2 minutes without browning. Slowly stir in the warm milk and continue cooking until thickened and smooth. This sauce should have the consistency of a thick cream. Season to taste with salt and pepper.

PASTA SQUARES

Butter

1/3 cup freshly grated Parmesan cheese

Preheat oven to 400 degrees. Have 8 6 × 6-inch pasta squares ready. Butter the bottom of an ovenproof baking dish. Place some of the meat filling in the center of each pasta square and spread it out. Roll into a loose tube. Place, seam side down, in the dish. Spread Béchamel Sauce over the cannelloni, coating evenly. Over this, spoon a little of the meat sauce that you used as a filling. Sprinkle with freshly grated Parmesan cheese. Cover and bake for 15 minutes or until heated through. Let rest 5 minutes before serving.

PAGLIA E FIENO

SERVES 6
PREPARATION TIME 15 MINUTES
COOKING TIME 15 MINUTES

This dish is named for the color of its noodles—straw and hay. It often is made with tiny peas in the sauce. Cook the green and white noodles in separate pots.

1/4 cup minced onion	Salt
3 tablespoons butter	Freshly ground pepper
3/4 pound mushrooms, thinly sliced	8 ounces white fettuccine
	8 ounces green fettuccine
4 ounces prosciutto, cut into strips	3 tablespoons melted butter
	1/2 cup freshly grated Parmesan
1 cup heavy cream	cheese

Sauté the onion in the butter until softened. Add the mushrooms and cook over high heat for an additional minute. Add the prosciutto and sauté briefly. Stir in the heavy cream. Cook until the sauce thickens slightly, about 10 minutes. Season to taste with salt and pepper.

Bring 2 large pots of salted water to a boil. Add the noodles and cook until tender but firm. The green fettuccine will take slightly longer to cook, so you may want to start it a little earlier than the white noodles. Drain and transfer to a warmed serving bowl. Coat with the melted butter. Add the warmed sauce and sprinkle with the cheese. Toss to mix well. Serve immediately.

HUNAN NOODLES

SERVES 6 TO 8
PREPARATION TIME 15 MINUTES
COOKING TIME 5 MINUTES

You may add any other desired vegetables, such as bean sprouts or enoki mushrooms.

1 pound Chinese noodles
3 1/2 tablespoons sesame oil
3 1/2 tablespoons soy sauce
2 tablespoons rice wine vinegar
2 tablespoons sugar
1 tablespoon hot chili oil

1 teaspoon grated fresh ginger
   root
5 tablespoons sliced green
   onions
2/3 cup frozen peas, thawed
2/3 cup grated carrots

Cook noodles. Drain and toss with the sesame oil. Combine the soy sauce, vinegar, sugar, chili oil, and ginger. Mix well. Pour over the noodles and toss to coat well. Chill up to a day ahead. Two to 3 hours before serving, add the onions, peas, and carrots.

BOMBAY PILAF

SERVES 6 TO 8
PREPARATION TIME 5 MINUTES
COOKING TIME 25 MINUTES

An intriguing blend of textures and flavors. This seasoned rice dish is great with roast chicken.

3 cups chicken broth
1 1/2 cups long-grain white rice
3 tablespoons vegetable oil
1/2 cup golden raisins
1 1/2 tablespoons soy sauce
1/2 teaspoon curry powder

1/4 teaspoon turmeric
1/3 cup toasted, slivered
   almonds
2 tablespoons chopped fresh
   parsley

Bring chicken broth to a boil in a medium saucepan. In another saucepan, sauté rice in the oil until translucent. Stir in raisins, soy sauce, curry powder, and turmeric. Pour in the boiling broth. Cover and cook over a low heat for 20 minutes or until all liquid is absorbed and rice is tender. Gently fold in almonds. Sprinkle with the parsley.

BARLEY PILAF

SERVES 8
PREPARATION TIME 10 MINUTES
COOKING TIME 1 HOUR

1 3/4 cups pearl barley
8 tablespoons butter
2 onions, chopped
1/2 pound fresh mushrooms,
    thinly sliced
2 cups strong beef stock

Salt
Pepper
1/2 cup toasted macadamia nut
    bits
1/2 cup chopped fresh parsley

Preheat oven to 350 degrees. Sauté the barley until golden in 4 tablespoons of the butter. Spoon into a large buttered casserole. In the remaining butter, sauté the onions and mushrooms. Stir into the barley. Pour the stock over the mixture. Cover tightly and bake for 30 minutes. Uncover and bake an additional 20 minutes, stirring occasionally. Add more liquid if mixture becomes dry. Season to taste with salt and pepper. Stir in the macadamia nuts and parsley just before serving.

WILD RICE WITH PINE NUTS

SERVES 4 TO 6
PREPARATION TIME 10 MINUTES
COOKING TIME 50 MINUTES

3 slices bacon, cut into 1/8-inch
    strips
1/2 cup chopped onion
1 celery stalk, cut into 1/4-inch
    cubes
1 clove garlic

1 cup wild rice
3 cups of water
Salt
1/2 cup pine nuts
4 tablespoons butter

Sauté the bacon in a skillet until almost cooked. Add the onion, celery, and garlic. Cook for 3 minutes or until onion is soft. Add the rice and water. Season to taste with the salt. Cover and simmer over medium heat for 45 minutes, or until the rice has absorbed the water. Uncover and set aside to cool and dry. Discard the garlic.

Just prior to serving, sauté the pine nuts in the butter. Add to the rice. Toss to mix well. Cook until heated through.

BROWN RICE WITH PUMPKIN SEEDS

SERVES 4 TO 6
PREPARATION TIME 10 MINUTES
COOKING TIME 1 HOUR

The whimsical combination of long-cooking brown rice and pumpkin seeds creates an appropriate autumn side dish.

1 tablespoon butter
1 small onion, chopped
1 cup long-grain brown rice

2 cups chicken stock
1/2 to 3/4 cup shelled pumpkin
   seeds

Melt the butter in a medium saucepan. Sauté the onion until soft, about 2 to 3 minutes. Add rice and sauté for 3 minutes. Stir in chicken stock and bring to a boil. Reduce the heat and simmer, covered, for 45 minutes. Remove from heat and allow to steam another 15 minutes. Stir in the pumpkin seeds and serve.

BROWN RICE PILAF

SERVES 4 TO 6
PREPARATION TIME 15 MINUTES
COOKING TIME 40 MINUTES

2 cups brown rice
3 cups chicken stock
2 tablespoons butter
2 teaspoons salt
3 bay leaves
6 peppercorns
2 tablespoons vegetable oil
1 onion, sliced
2 celery stalks, thinly sliced on
   the diagonal

2 tablespoons currants
1 tablespoon finely chopped
   fresh ginger
1 1/2 teaspoons coriander
1/2 teaspoon cumin
Pepper
2 tablespoons soy sauce

In a large pot, place the rice, chicken stock, butter, salt, bay leaves, and peppercorns. Cover and bring to a boil over high heat. Reduce heat and simmer until liquid has been absorbed by the rice, about 25 to 35 minutes.

Heat the oil in a skillet. Add the onion and sauté for 3 minutes. Add celery, currants, ginger, coriander, cumin, and pepper to taste. Cook for an additional minute or two. Stir into the cooked rice. Add the soy sauce and mix well. Taste and adjust seasonings if necessary.

ORANGE RICE

SERVES 6
PREPARATION TIME 10 MINUTES
COOKING TIME 25 TO 30 MINUTES

Serve with lamb, chicken, or game birds.

4 tablespoons butter
1/2 cup chopped celery
1/4 cup chopped green onion
1 cup long-grain white rice
1 cup orange juice
1 cup water

1 teaspoon salt
1 orange, peeled with all white
  removed, and cubed
1/4 cup toasted slivered
  almonds

Melt the butter in a saucepan. Sauté celery and onion until soft, about 5 minutes. Stir in the rice and brown lightly, stirring constantly for 3 to 4 minutes. Add orange juice, water, and salt. Bring to a boil. Cover and reduce heat. Simmer for 25 to 30 minutes, or until rice is tender and liquid is absorbed. Gently fold in orange cubes and almonds.

CUMIN SEED RICE

SERVES 6 TO 8
PREPARATION TIME 15 MINUTES
COOKING TIME 30 MINUTES

This Spanish-style rice can really dress up a grilled entree.

1 green bell pepper, coarsely
  chopped
1 onion, chopped
2 stalks celery, chopped
2 tablespoons butter
1 1/2 tablespoons oil
1 1/2 cups rice

1 clove garlic, minced
1 to 1 1/2 cups tomatoes,
  peeled, seeded, and chopped
3 cups water
2 to 3 teaspoons cumin seed
1 1/2 teaspoons salt
Freshly ground pepper

Sauté the pepper, onion, and celery in the butter and oil. Add the rice and sauté until lightly browned. Stir in garlic and sauté for an additional minute. Add tomatoes, water, cumin seed, salt, and pepper. Bring to a boil. Cover and reduce heat. Simmer for 20 to 30 minutes, or until liquid is absorbed and rice is tender.

BAKED RICE WITH PEPPERS

SERVES 6 TO 8
PREPARATION TIME 20 MINUTES
COOKING TIME 40 MINUTES

A superb dish with a definite Mexican accent. For authentically fine Mexican cuisine, serve with Orange and Jícama Salad, a pork roast, and a chayote (squash) dish.

1 onion, chopped	1 red bell pepper, chopped
3 tablespoons butter	1 green bell pepper, chopped
1 cup long-grain white rice	1/2 cup chopped celery
2 cups chicken stock	1 1/2 cups sour cream
1 cup white wine	1/2 cup shredded Swiss cheese
1 to 2 hot green chili peppers, seeded and chopped	1/2 cup shredded Cheddar cheese

Preheat oven to 350 degrees. Sauté onion in butter until soft but not brown. Stir in rice and coat with the butter. Add stock, wine, and chili peppers. Bring to a boil and transfer to an ovenproof casserole. Cover and bake for 15 minutes, or until liquid is absorbed. Remove from oven.

Increase oven temperature to 400 degrees. Transfer rice to a bowl and add the bell peppers, celery, sour cream, and cheeses. Spoon into a lightly buttered baking dish. Bake, uncovered, for 20 minutes or until nicely browned.

ORIENTAL RICE

SERVES 6 TO 8
PREPARATION TIME 10 MINUTES
COOKING TIME 35 TO 45 MINUTES

3 cups chicken stock	3/4 cup frozen thawed peas
1 1/2 cups rice	1/3 cup shredded carrots
2 tablespoons peanut oil	2 cups fresh bean sprouts
2 eggs, lightly beaten	3 tablespoons soy sauce
1/2 cup chopped onion	Salt
3/4 cup chopped green onion	Freshly ground pepper
3/4 cup sliced celery	

Bring the stock to a boil. Stir in rice. Return to a boil. Cover and simmer for 25 to 30 minutes, or until rice is tender and liquid is absorbed.

Heat the oil in a wok or large skillet. Break eggs into the oil and scramble quickly with a fork until cooked and broken up in small pieces. Add onion and green onion and stir-fry for 2 minutes. Add the celery, peas, and carrots. Stir-fry for 2 minutes. Add bean sprouts and stir-fry for 1 minute. Stir in soy sauce and cooked rice. Season to taste with salt and pepper.

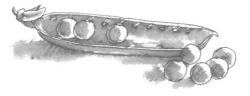

RICE PILAF

SERVES 8 TO 10
PREPARATION TIME 45 MINUTES
COOKING TIME 45 MINUTES

A fail-proof pilaf recipe from Chef Jenanyan at the Old Poodle Dog Restaurant in San Francisco. Blanched unsalted almonds, pine nuts, or any other garnish may be gently folded into the pilaf after it is cooked—before the final rest period.

8 ounces (2 sticks) unsalted
  butter, cut into pieces
4 cups chicken stock
5 to 6 grinds of fresh black
  pepper
3 tablespoons vegetable oil

1 1/2 cups loosely packed
  vermicelli, broken into 1-inch
  pieces
2 cups long-grain white rice
Salt
Freshly ground pepper

Place the butter, stock, and black pepper in a 4-quart saucepan. Place over medium heat, uncovered. In another casserole, heat the oil until hot but not smoking. Brown the vermicelli in the oil, stirring rapidly and constantly until golden. Do not burn. Immediately add the rice and continue stirring until most of the grains turn white in the center. (The vermicelli should be dark golden and the rice grains white in the center and slightly translucent.)

Boil the stock. Remove the rice mixture from the heat. Pour the boiling stock very slowly over the rice, keeping your face away from the casserole. Put the pilaf back on the lowest possible flame. Cover and do not disturb for 25 minutes. Partially remove the cover and cook another 10 minutes, or until the vermicelli has begun to curl. Remove from heat and let rest for 15 minutes. Season to taste with salt and pepper.

APPLE-ALMOND RICE

SERVES 4 TO 6
PREPARATION TIME 10 MINUTES
COOKING TIME 30 MINUTES

2 cups apple juice
1 tablespoon butter
1 teaspoon salt
1 cup long-grain white rice
1/2 cup almonds

3 tablespoons butter
1 tablespoon finely grated
    orange peel
Freshly ground pepper

Bring apple juice, butter, and salt to a boil. Stir in rice. Return to a boil. Cover, reduce heat, and simmer for 25 to 30 minutes, or until rice is tender and liquid is absorbed.

Sauté the almonds in the remaining butter until nicely browned. Gently fold into the rice together with the orange peel. Season to taste with salt and pepper.

VEGETABLES

Santa Clara Valley

 Once a bustling agricultural valley of fruit orchards and vegetable farms, Santa Clara Valley, with its central metropolis of San Jose, has enjoyed phenomenal commercial and industrial growth in recent years. Santa Clara Valley is now sometimes referred to as Silicon Valley because of its computer hardware industry, built on silicon micro-chips. Yet amid the suburban growth and industrial parks, one can still find evidence of the farmhouses, orchards, and wineries of olden days.

Because of its background as a fruit-growing area, some of Santa Clara Valley's wineries feature fruit wines, which can be sampled in tasting rooms located along Highway 101 just south of San Jose.

Many of these wineries reflect the names of the fine old Italian families who founded them. Third and fourth generations are carrying on the family wine-making traditions today.

South Santa Clara Valley is famous for its garlic fields. The delights of garlic are celebrated each August with Gilroy's Festival, when garlic is cooked in competitions, sampled in all types of food, and sold in the Festival marketplace in long braided chains. California produces 90 percent of America's garlic output, and most of it is within a ninety-mile radius of Gilroy, the self-proclaimed garlic capital of the world. A specialized type of garlic, grown in Santa Clara Valley as well as in Sonoma and Napa counties, is the elephant garlic. Its heads may grow as large as a baseball, with correspondingly large individual cloves, which are mild and sweet. Not surprisingly, most of this garlic goes to Bay Area restaurants. However, it can be found in some food specialty shops.

Santa Clara Valley's renowned garlic and stunning variety of still wines, champagnes, ports, sherries, and fruit wines make this Bay Area winegrowing region one of the most varied. Sample the Mushrooms in Garlic Butter, Country Style Tomatoes, or any of the other vegetable recipes with a rich Santa Clara Valley wine and think of the Italian forefathers who put this wine region on the map.

HERBED ASPARAGUS

SERVES 8
PREPARATION TIME 10 MINUTES
COOKING TIME 5 MINUTES

3 pounds fresh asparagus
10 fresh basil leaves
4 sprigs watercress
5 large mint leaves
Small handful of parsley
1 tablespoon chives

1/2 teaspoon salt
1/4 teaspoon freshly ground
  pepper
3 tablespoons fresh lemon juice
1/3 cup olive oil

Trim, wash, and peel the asparagus. Cook in boiling water until just tender. Drain and run under cold water to stop the cooking. Dry on paper towels. On a serving platter or individual plates, arrange with tips pointing toward the center.

Place all of the herbs in a processor or blender. Add the salt and pepper and process for a few seconds. Slowly add the lemon juice and oil while the machine is running. Spoon the sauce over the asparagus. Serve at room temperature.

INDIVIDUAL ASPARAGUS SOUFFLÉS

SERVES 6
PREPARATION TIME 10 MINUTES
COOKING TIME 30 MINUTES

Light and predictable soufflés that forgo traditional preparation.

Butter for soufflé dishes
6 teaspoons Parmesan cheese
1 pound fresh asparagus, tough
  ends trimmed
7 eggs
1/3 cup heavy cream
1/2 cup shredded Swiss cheese
1 teaspoon Dijon mustard

1/2 teaspoon salt
1/4 teaspoon freshly ground
  pepper
1/8 teaspoon ground nutmeg
8 ounces ricotta cheese

Sour cream

Preheat oven to 375 degrees. Butter six 2/3-cup-size soufflé dishes. Sprinkle

1 teaspoon of Parmesan cheese into each dish. Place on a rimmed baking sheet.

Cook the asparagus in boiling salted water until just tender, 5 to 10 minutes. Drain and rinse with cold water. Pat dry. Cut off and reserve 6 of the nicest tips. Cut the remaining spears into pieces.

In a processor or blender, combine the eggs, cream, Swiss cheese, mustard, salt, pepper, and nutmeg. Mix until smooth. With the machine running, add the asparagus pieces, a few at a time. Gradually add the ricotta cheese and continue mixing until smooth. Spoon into the prepared dishes.

Bake for 20 to 25 minutes or until a knife inserted in the center comes out clean. Top each with an asparagus tip. Serve immediately accompanied by a bowl of sour cream.

ASPARAGUS-ORANGE SPEARS

SERVES 6
PREPARATION TIME 15 MINUTES
COOKING TIME 15 MINUTES

You can enjoy this pungent green vegetable from early spring until fall. For best flavor, choose stalks with tight buds and the least amount of tough white ends.

1 1/2 **pounds asparagus**
3 **tablespoons butter**
1 **clove garlic, crushed**
2 **tablespoons grated orange peel**
1/4 **cup fresh squeezed orange juice**

Salt
Freshly ground pepper
1 **whole orange, peel and white part removed**

Trim the tough ends from the asparagus and peel. In a skillet large enough to hold the asparagus, bring to boiling enough water to cover. Lay the spears in the pan. Boil, uncovered, until tender, about 5 minutes. Drain and set aside.

In the same pan, melt the butter. Add the garlic and sauté briefly. Remove garlic. Add orange peel and juice to the pan. Return asparagus to pan and toss to coat with the peel. Cook over high heat until asparagus is hot and the liquid reduces to 3 tablespoons.

Lift out the asparagus and arrange on a serving platter. Spoon the reduced sauce over the spears. Sprinkle with salt and pepper. Thinly slice the orange. Cut each round in half. Place the orange slices around the outside edges of the platter. Serve immediately.

BROCCOLI IN ORANGE SHALLOT BUTTER

SERVES 6
PREPARATION TIME 10 MINUTES
COOKING TIME 20 MINUTES

In shopping for fresh broccoli, look for tight buds, gray-green leaves, and slender stems.

3 pounds broccoli
1/2 cup fresh orange juice
1/4 cup minced shallots
5 ounces (1 1/4 sticks) unsalted
    butter

2 tablespoons julienned
    orange peel
Salt
Freshly ground pepper

Cut broccoli flowerets into bite-size pieces. Cook in boiling salted water until tender but still firm, about 5 minutes. Drain and run under cold water. Pat dry.

Simmer orange juice in a large saucepan with the shallots until juice reduces to 2 tablespoons. Add the butter and orange peel and cook until butter has melted. Toss in the broccoli and cook until heated through. Season to taste with salt and pepper. Serve immediately.

SESAME BROCCOLI

SERVES 6
PREPARATION TIME 5 MINUTES
COOKING TIME 5 MINUTES

For best results, serve this broccoli dish at room temperature. To prevent discoloration, toss in marinade just before serving.

1 large bunch broccoli
1/2 cup toasted sesame seed
1/4 cup sake

1 tablespoon soy sauce
2 teaspoons sesame oil
2 teaspoons honey

Trim broccoli and cut into bite-size flowerets. Cook in boiling salted water until tender. Drain and run under cold water to stop the cooking. Let sit at room temperature.

Combine the remaining ingredients. Just prior to serving, toss the broccoli with the marinade and mix well.

CARROTS SAUTÉED WITH APRICOTS

SERVES 4 TO 6
PREPARATION TIME 10 MINUTES
COOKING TIME 20 MINUTES

Combined with the vinegar, the apricots give the carrots a sweet-and-sour flavor.

4 tablespoons butter
1 medium onion, thinly sliced
1 pound carrots, shredded
2 ounces dried apricots, thinly
  sliced

1/2 cup chicken or beef stock
1 to 2 tablespoons sherry wine
  vinegar
Salt
Freshly ground pepper

Melt the butter in a skillet. Add the onion and sauté until lightly browned, about 5 to 10 minutes. Add carrots and apricots and continue cooking for 2 more minutes. Stir in the stock, cover, and continue cooking until the carrots are just tender but still crisp, about 5 minutes. Uncover and quickly evaporate the liquid. Stir in the vinegar. Season to taste with salt and pepper.

CARROTS AND GRAPES

SERVES 6 TO 8
PREPARATION TIME 20 MINUTES
COOKING TIME 5 MINUTES

So colorful it should be served in a glass bowl, sprinkled with fresh mint or parsley.

2 cups orange juice
1/4 cup sugar
1/4 cup Gerwurtztraminer or
  Chenin Blanc wine
1 teaspoon cornstarch
  dissolved in 2 tablespoons
  water

Salt
Freshly ground pepper
1 1/2 pounds carrots, cut
  diagonally in 1/4-inch slices
  and cooked
1 cup seedless grapes, washed
  and drained

In a saucepan, bring orange juice, sugar, and wine to a boil. Reduce the heat slightly. Gradually stir in enough dissolved cornstarch to thicken the sauce. Cook for 1 minute, whisking constantly. Season to taste with salt and pepper. Stir in carrots and grapes. Continue cooking until heated through. Serve immediately.

ORANGE-GLAZED CARROTS

SERVES 4
PREPARATION TIME 10 MINUTES
COOKING TIME 15 MINUTES

2 cups diagonally sliced carrots
1/2 cup fresh orange juice
1/4 cup sherry
1 tablespoon brown sugar
2 teaspoons cornstarch

1 teaspoon grated fresh ginger
root
1/2 teaspoon grated orange peel
1/4 teaspoon salt
1 tablespoon butter

Cook the carrots in boiling water until just tender; drain. In a saucepan, combine the orange juice, sherry, brown sugar, cornstarch, ginger, orange peel, and salt. Cook, stirring, until thickened. Stir in the butter. Pour over the carrots. Toss to coat. Serve immediately.

MUSTARD-GLAZED BABY CARROTS

SERVES 6
PREPARATION TIME 10 MINUTES
COOKING TIME 20 MINUTES

Large carrots can be made to resemble baby carrots. Cut the carrots into approximate length desired. Carve away the edges with a paring knife or peeler, forming rounded edges.

2 pounds baby carrots, peeled
1/4 cup brown sugar
3 tablespoons butter

3 tablespoons Dijon mustard
1/4 cup chopped fresh parsley

Cook the shaped carrots in boiling salted water until tender, about 10 to 15 minutes; drain. In a saucepan, combine the sugar, butter and mustard. Cook until syrupy, about 3 minutes. Stir in the carrots and simmer for 5 minutes. Sprinkle with the parsley. Serve immediately.

CARROT PURÉE

SERVES 6
PREPARATION TIME 5 MINUTES
COOKING TIME 25 MINUTES

If desired, add 1 teaspoon ground ginger or dried dillweed to this purée.

2 pounds carrots, peeled and sliced
6 tablespoons butter

1/4 cup heavy cream
Salt
White pepper

Cook the carrots in boiling salted water until soft, about 20 minutes; drain. Purée in a food mill or processor until smooth. Return the purée to the pan. Stir in the butter and heavy cream. Season to taste with salt and pepper. Serve hot.

CARROT FRITTERS

MAKES 12 FRITTERS
PREPARATION TIME 5 MINUTES
COOKING TIME 5 TO 10 MINUTES

6 medium carrots, grated
2 eggs
1 tablespoon sugar
1/2 teaspoon salt

Pinch of freshly grated nutmeg (optional)
1/4 cup flour
4 to 6 tablespoons butter

Mix the carrots with the eggs, sugar, salt, and nutmeg. Blend in the flour to make a batter the consistency of a thick cream. Melt a little of the butter in a heavy skillet. Drop the batter by tablespoons into the hot butter. Press down slightly to flatten out. Fry for a few minutes on each side until nicely browned. Drain on paper towels. Repeat with the remaining butter and batter. Serve immediately.

CAULIFLOWER AND WATERCRESS PURÉE

SERVES 6
PREPARATION TIME 35 MINUTES
COOKING TIME 30 MINUTES

People who normally do not like cauliflower will love this dish.

1 head cauliflower	1/3 cup grated Swiss cheese
1 bunch watercress, stems removed	Salt
	White pepper
2 tablespoons butter	1/3 cup fresh bread crumbs
3 tablespoons flour	2 tablespoons butter
1 cup warm milk	2 tablespoons grated Swiss cheese
1/4 cup heavy cream (optional)	

Preheat oven to 375 degrees. Separate cauliflower into flowerets, discarding the tough stems. Drop into a large pot of boiling salted water. Boil, uncovered, for 5 minutes. Add the watercress leaves and continue boiling for another 5 to 10 minutes, or until the cauliflower is soft enough to purée. Drain well.

Melt the butter in a small saucepan. Add the flour and cook for 2 minutes without browning. Slowly add the milk and cook, stirring constantly, until smooth and thick. Purée the vegetables in a food processor or food mill. Add just enough of the prepared sauce to make it creamy. You may not need the entire amount. Stir in the heavy cream, if desired, and the cheese. Season to taste with salt and white pepper. Spread into an au gratin dish. Brown the bread crumbs in the melted butter. Sprinkle crumbs and cheese over top. Bake for 20 minutes.

GREEN BEANS WITH PECANS

SERVES 6 TO 8
PREPARATION TIME 15 MINUTES
COOKING TIME 5 TO 10 MINUTES

The contrast of green beans with pecans makes this dish decorative in itself. This could easily become a holiday favorite with roast beef, veal, or duck.

2 pounds fresh green beans   3 tablespoons minced parsley
3 tablespoons butter   Salt
4 tablespoons minced shallots   Freshly ground pepper
1 cup pecan halves

Clean and trim beans, leaving whole. Steam beans until just tender but still firm. Heat the butter in a skillet. Sauté shallots until softened, about 3 minutes. Add pecans and brown lightly. Stir in beans and parsley. Toss to coat and heat thoroughly. Season to taste with salt and pepper.

GREEN BEANS AND BACON

SERVES 4 TO 6
PREPARATION TIME 10 MINUTES
COOKING TIME 10 MINUTES

1 pound fresh green beans   Salt
4 slices bacon   Freshly ground black pepper
1 medium onion, chopped   Dash of Tabasco sauce
2 cups canned tomatoes,
   drained and chopped

Cook the beans in boiling water until tender, about 5 to 7 minutes. Drain and set aside.

Cook bacon until crisp. Drain on paper towels. Pour off all but 1 tablespoon of the bacon grease from the pan. Sauté the onion in the bacon grease until golden. Stir in the tomatoes and cook for an additional minute. Add the beans to the onion and tomatoes. Crumble bacon and toss with the beans. Season to taste with salt, pepper, and Tabasco. Serve immediately.

GREEN BEANS WITH TOMATO VINAIGRETTE

SERVES 6 TO 8
PREPARATION TIME 15 MINUTES

Serve with any of the grilled meats or fish.

2 pounds fresh green beans
2 ripe tomatoes, chopped
1 small yellow onion, chopped
2 shallots, chopped
1 small clove garlic, chopped

3/4 cup olive oil
1 tablespoon tarragon vinegar
Salt
Freshly ground pepper

String the beans and cut off ends, leaving beans long. Steam until just tender; drain.

Mix remaining ingredients and stir well. Toss with the green beans. Serve at room temperature.

GREEN BEANS WITH HOT BLACK BEAN SAUCE

SERVES 6
PREPARATION TIME 10 MINUTES
COOKING TIME 5 MINUTES

Fermented whole black beans are available at specialty food stores. Black bean paste can be substituted if whole beans are unavailable.

1 1/2 pounds tender green beans
1/4 cup vegetable oil
1 tablespoon fermented black beans
1 teaspoon minced fresh ginger
1/2 tablespoon minced garlic

2 tablespoons minced green onion
1 teaspoon cornstarch
1/2 cup chicken stock
1 tablespoon sesame oil
2 teaspoons soy sauce

Wash the beans and drain. Cut into 2-inch slices. Heat the oil in a wok or skillet until smoking. Add the beans and stir-fry until just tender. Add black beans, ginger, garlic, and green onion. Stir-fry for a few seconds. Dissolve the cornstarch in the chicken stock. Stir into the beans together with the sesame oil and soy sauce. Reduce heat. Cover and steam for 2 minutes. Serve immediately.

NORMANDY FRENCH BEANS

SERVES 6 TO 8
PREPARATION TIME 15 MINUTES
COOKING TIME 20 MINUTES

1 pound green beans, sliced
   into thin strips
6 tablespoons butter
1 medium onion, thinly sliced
   into rings

2 apples, peeled, cored, and
   coarsely chopped
1/3 cup sliced almonds

Steam the green beans until just tender. Drain and set aside. Melt the butter in a skillet. Add the onion slices and apples. Cook, stirring occasionally, until the onion is nicely browned and the apples are tender but still firm. Stir in the beans and almonds. Cook until the beans are heated through. Serve immediately.

GREEN BEANS PARMESAN

SERVES 8
PREPARATION TIME 20 MINUTES
COOKING TIME 15 MINUTES

1 onion, chopped
2 small green bell peppers,
   chopped
1 clove garlic, minced
1/4 cup olive oil
2 pounds fresh green beans,
   trimmed and cut into 2-inch
   pieces

1/4 cup water
2 teaspoons dried basil
1/4 teaspoon salt
1/4 teaspoon freshly ground
   pepper
2 ounces grated Parmesan
   cheese

Sauté the onion, bell peppers, and garlic in the olive oil for 5 minutes. Add the green beans, water, basil, salt, and pepper. Cook, covered, over medium heat until tender, approximately 10 minutes. Drain off any remaining liquid. Stir half of the cheese into the beans. Spoon into a serving dish. Sprinkle with the remaining cheese.

EGGPLANT ROLLATINE

SERVES 8
PREPARATION TIME 40 MINUTES
COOKING TIME 40 MINUTES

A fresh variation on the popular Neapolitan dish Eggplant Parmigiana. Baking, rather than sautéeing, makes for a lighter, less oily dish.

2 large eggplants, peeled
Salt for draining eggplant
Olive oil
1/2 cup grated mozzarella
    cheese
1/4 cup grated Parmesan cheese
1 tablespoon chopped fresh
    parsley
1 egg

2 cloves garlic, chopped
1/2 cup olive oil
2 cups canned Italian tomatoes,
    chopped
1 teaspoon oregano
Salt
1/2 teaspoon crushed red
    pepper flakes (optional)
8 teaspoons Parmesan cheese

Slice the eggplant lengthwise into 8 slices about 1/4-inch thick. Sprinkle with salt and allow to drain for 30 minutes. Rinse and pat dry.

Preheat oven to 400 degrees. Brush the eggplant slices with olive oil. Place on a greased baking sheet. Bake until nicely browned, about 15 minutes. Mix the cheeses, parsley, and egg together for the filling. Place 2 tablespoons of filling on each slice and roll lengthwise. Place in a baking dish.

Reduce oven temperature to 375 degrees. Brown the garlic in the olive oil. Add the tomatoes, oregano, salt to taste, and red pepper flakes, if desired. Simmer for 15 minutes or until slightly thickened. Spoon over the rolled eggplant. Sprinkle with the remaining Parmesan cheese. Bake for approximately 10 minutes or until heated through.

STUFFED FENNEL

SERVES 6
PREPARATION TIME 15 MINUTES
COOKING TIME 1 HOUR

The anise-flavored fennel can be prepared and stuffed a day before cooking.

6 fennel
1/2 cup grated Parmesan cheese
1/4 pound salami, chopped
Salt
Pepper

Freshly grated nutmeg
1 egg, beaten
1/4 cup bread crumbs
1/2 cup heavy cream
1/4 cup chopped fresh parsley

Wash and trim the fennel. With a small sharp knife, remove a good deal of the central portions of the fennel. Dry the scooped-out portions and chop finely. Set aside. Bring a large pot of salted water to a boil. Add the cleaned fennel and return to a boil. Cover and cook for 20 minutes. Drain well and cool.

Preheat oven to 375 degrees. In a bowl, combine the chopped fennel, Parmesan cheese, and half of the salami. Season to taste with salt, pepper, and nutmeg. Stuff the fennel, filling the cavities and mounding the excess mixture above the tops of the hollows. Brush the tops with the egg. Sprinkle with bread crumbs and again brush with the egg. Pour the heavy cream into a baking dish. Place the stuffed fennel on the cream. Distribute the remaining salami and chopped parsley around the cream. Bake until nicely browned and crusted, about 40 minutes. Serve hot with some of the sauce from the bottom of the baking dish spooned over.

MUSHROOM PIE

SERVES 6
PREPARATION TIME 30 MINUTES
COOKING TIME 30 MINUTES

1 medium onion, chopped
3 tablespoons butter
1 pound mushrooms,
  quartered, if large
1 1/2 tablespoons flour
1/2 cup half-and-half

1 tablespoon Cognac
1/2 teaspoon salt
1/4 teaspoon freshly ground
  pepper
Pastry for Double Crust 8-inch
  Pie†

Sauté onion in butter until soft. Wash and dry mushrooms. Trim stem end. Sauté with the onion for 5 minutes. Stir in flour and cook an additional minute. Add half-and-half and bring to the boil, stirring constantly. Add Cognac, salt, and pepper. Cool.

Preheat oven to 425 degrees. Prepare pastry. Roll out three fourths of the pastry and line an 8-inch pie plate. Fill with the cooled mushroom mixture. Roll out remaining dough and cut into 1/2-inch strips. Moisten edge of pastry with water. Arrange the strips over the top in a lattice fashion. Press the ends to the rim of the pastry and flute the edges. Bake on lower oven rack for 20 to 30 minutes or until crust is browned. Let rest for 5 minutes. Cut into wedges.

COUNTRY STYLE MUSHROOMS

SERVES 4 TO 6
PREPARATION TIME 10 MINUTES
COOKING TIME 10 MINUTES

6 slices bacon
2 pounds fresh mushrooms,
  cleaned and sliced
1 teaspoon lemon juice
1 small onion, finely chopped
1 clove of garlic, crushed

2 tablespoons dry bread
  crumbs
1/2 teaspoon salt
Freshly ground pepper
1 tablespoon chopped fresh
  parsley

Cook the bacon until crisp. Drain on paper towels; crumble. Pour off all but 4 tablespoons of the bacon grease. Sauté the mushrooms for 5 minutes over high heat. Sprinkle with the lemon juice. Stir in the onion, garlic, and bread crumbs. Sauté over high heat for an additional 3 to 5 minutes. Add the bacon, salt, pepper, and parsley. Toss to mix well. Serve hot.

MUSHROOMS IN GARLIC BUTTER

SERVES 6
PREPARATION TIME 20 MINUTES
COOKING TIME 10 MINUTES

Mushrooms are delicious both as a finger food or as a side dish. Use firm medium to large mushrooms that are relatively uniform. For effortless entertaining, prepare this dish hours ahead, but cover and refrigerate.

24 fresh mushrooms
6 tablespoons butter, softened
2 cloves garlic, minced
2 shallots, minced

1/2 cup minced fresh parsley
1/2 teaspoon fresh lemon juice
1/2 teaspoon salt
1/4 teaspoon pepper

Preheat oven to 400 degrees. Wipe the mushrooms with a damp cloth and remove the stems. Combine butter, garlic, shallots and parsley. Mix until well combined. Stir in the lemon juice, salt, and pepper. Fill each cap with some of the butter mixture. Bake for 10 minutes.

DILLED ONION SOUFFLÉ

SERVES 4
PREPARATION TIME 20 MINUTES
COOKING TIME 15 TO 18 MINUTES

Serve this low-calorie vegetable with grilled fish.

2 tablespoons butter
1 medium onion, minced
1/2 teaspoon dried dillweed
1/4 teaspoon salt
2 tablespoons flour

3/4 cup milk
3 eggs, separated
2 tablespoons grated Parmesan
cheese

Preheat the oven to 375 degrees. Lightly butter a 3- to 4-cup soufflé dish. In a saucepan, melt the butter. Add the onion and sauté until golden. Sprinkle on the dillweed, salt, and flour. Cook for an additional 2 minutes. Slowly pour in the milk, whisking constantly. Cook until thickened. Remove from the heat and beat in the egg yolks, one at a time.

Whip the egg whites until firm but not dry. Carefully fold into the onion mixture. Pour into the prepared mold. Sprinkle with the cheese. Bake for 15 to 18 minutes, or until puffed and browned. Serve immediately.

ONION PIE

SERVES 6 TO 8
PREPARATION TIME 10 MINUTES
COOKING TIME 50 MINUTES

1 cup chopped yellow onion
4 tablespoons butter
1 tablespoon olive oil
1/4 cup sugar
1 pound small white onions,
    peeled
1/4 to 1/2 cup chicken stock

2 whole eggs
3 egg yolks
1 cup half-and-half
1/8 teaspoon nutmeg
Salt
Freshly ground pepper
A 9-inch prebaked pie crust

Preheat oven to 375 degrees. Sauté the chopped onion in 2 tablespoons of the butter and oil until soft, about 10 minutes. In a saucepan, melt the remaining butter with sugar. Add white onions and toss to coat. Cook until lightly browned. Add stock and cook until tender, about 5 minutes. Drain and cut onions in half.

In a bowl, combine eggs, egg yolks, half-and-half, and seasonings. Spread the yellow onions on the bottom of the pastry shell. Arrange white onions on top, cut side down. Slowly pour in the custard mixture. Bake for 25 to 30 minutes, or until custard is set.

BAKED STUFFED ONIONS THREE WAYS

MAKES 6 STUFFED ONIONS
PREPARATION TIME 20 MINUTES
COOKING TIME 35 MINUTES

6 onions
Salt
3 tablespoons melted butter

Double Onion Filling or
Tomato Filling (recipes
follow)

Preheat oven to 350 degrees. Cut off the tops of 6 onions, leaving the skins on. With a small knife or melon ball cutter, hollow out the centers, leaving at least 3 outside layers. Be careful not to pierce through the bottoms. Reserve the hollowed-out centers if making the Double Onion Filling.

Bake the unfilled cases for 15 minutes. Remove from oven. Salt the insides. Spoon the desired filling into the shells. Place in a buttered baking dish. Brush with the melted butter. Bake for 15 to 20 minutes. Remove the skins before serving.

DOUBLE ONION FILLING

The centers of 6 onion cases, chopped
2 onions, chopped
6 tablespoons butter
1 tablespoon olive oil
1/2 cup chicken broth
3 tablespoons sherry wine
1 teaspoon sugar
Salt
Freshly ground white pepper

Sauté the onions in the butter and oil. Add the remaining ingredients. Cook mixture until all the liquid evaporates.

TOMATO FILLING

1 1/2 cups chopped onion
1 large clove garlic, chopped
4 tablespoons butter
2 tablespoons olive oil
1 28-ounce can Italian plum tomatoes, drained and chopped
1/2 cup beef broth
2 teaspoons chopped capers
1 teaspoon dried basil
1 teaspoon sugar
Salt
Freshly ground pepper

Sauté the onion and garlic in the butter and oil until translucent. Add the remaining ingredients and cook until all the liquid evaporates.

SPINACH FILLING

1 cup chopped onion
3/4 cup chopped mushrooms
1 small clove garlic, minced
4 tablespoons butter
1 pound fresh spinach, stemmed, washed, dried, and chopped
1/2 cup beef broth
Salt
Freshly ground pepper

Sauté the onion, mushrooms, and garlic in the butter for 5 minutes. Add the spinach. Cook until just wilted. Stir in the remaining ingredients. Cook until all the liquid evaporates.

SLICED ROASTED POTATOES

SERVES 6 TO 8
PREPARATION TIME 10 MINUTES
COOKING TIME 35 MINUTES

8 baking potatoes
4 tablespoons melted butter
Salt

Preheat oven to 450 degrees. Peel potatoes. Cut in halves and then into thirds. Blanch the potatoes in boiling salted water for 3 minutes. Pat dry. Arrange in a single layer in a buttered baking dish. Dribble with the melted butter. Sprinkle with salt. Bake for 15 minutes. Turn and bake an additional 15 minutes. Serve hot.

POTATOES WHIPPED WITH CHEESE

SERVES 6 TO 8
PREPARATION TIME 30 MINUTES
COOKING TIME 30 MINUTES

You can prepare the potatoes hours ahead and bake at the last minute.

3 pounds potatoes, cooked and whipped
4 ounces (1 stick) butter, cut into pieces
6 ounces cream cheese, cut into pieces
1 green bell pepper, chopped
1 small bunch green onions, sliced
1 small jar diced pimento with juice
1/2 cup grated Parmesan cheese
1/2 cup grated Cheddar cheese
1/4 teaspoon powdered saffron
Salt
Freshly ground pepper

Preheat oven to 375 degrees. While the potatoes are still hot, add all of the remaining ingredients. Season to taste with the salt and pepper. Whip until well blended. If the mixture seems too dry, add a bit of milk or cream. Transfer to a baking dish. Bake until hot, about 10 to 15 minutes.

POTATOES CALIFORNIA STYLE

SERVES 8
PREPARATION TIME 20 MINUTES
COOKING TIME 15 MINUTES

4 large white potatoes, cut
  lengthwise into strips
1/4 cup bacon drippings
1 medium onion, thinly sliced
1/4 cup chopped green bell
  pepper

1 large clove garlic, minced
1 large tomato, seeded and
  chopped
Salt
Freshly grated pepper

Sauté the potatoes in the bacon drippings over medium-high heat. When almost done, after about 10 minutes, add the remaining ingredients. Continue cooking over medium heat until the onion is soft. Serve immediately.

MUSTARD POTATOES

SERVES 4
PREPARATION TIME 15 MINUTES
COOKING TIME 25 MINUTES

After a quick sauté, the potato slices are tossed with Dijon mustard for an explosion of color and taste. Dijon is a rich and pungent mustard made from black mustard seeds, salt, wine, or vinegar, and spices; it contains no sugar.

2 garlic cloves, crushed
2 tablespoons butter
2 tablespoons olive oil
3 red potatoes, unpeeled and
  thinly sliced

1 yellow onion, thinly sliced
Salt
Freshly ground pepper
Paprika
2 tablespoons Dijon mustard

Sauté the garlic in butter and oil until soft. Add the potatoes and sauté until brown on both sides, one layer at a time. When done, transfer to a plate and set aside. Add the onion to the remaining oil and sauté until soft. Pour off the oil and return the potatoes to the pan with the onion. Season to taste with salt, pepper, and paprika. Add the mustard and toss carefully to coat all the potatoes. Serve immediately.

SERVES 4
PREPARATION TIME 10 MINUTES
COOKING TIME 30 MINUTES

3 medium potatoes, peeled
1 tablespoon vegetable oil

1 tablespoon water
Salt

Preheat oven to 475 degrees. Cut potatoes into strips. Stir oil and water in a bowl. Add potato strips and mix until well coated. Brush a shallow roasting pan with a little oil. Sprinkle pan with salt. Add potatoes in a single layer. Bake for 30 minutes, turning potatoes over after 15 minutes. Serve hot.

CHUTNEY-CHEESE POTATOES

SERVES 4
PREPARATION TIME 10 MINUTES
COOKING TIME 1 HOUR

4 baking potatoes
4 ounces Cheddar cheese,
  grated
2 teaspoons chutney

1 celery stalk, finely chopped
4 tablespoons (1/2 stick)
  softened butter

Preheat oven to 375 degrees. Bake the potatoes with their skins until tender, about 45 minutes. Let cool slightly. Remove a 1/2-inch slice from the top flat side of the potato. Scoop out the inside of each potato to within 1/4-inch of the shell. Do not pierce the skin. Place the potato flesh in a bowl. Place the potato skins in a shallow roasting pan.

Combine the potato flesh, cheese, chutney, celery, and butter. Beat with a wooden spoon until thoroughly mixed. Spoon the filling into the potato skins. Bake for 10 to 12 minutes, or until golden brown.

SNOW PEAS AND ALMONDS

SERVES 4
PREPARATION TIME 10 MINUTES
COOKING TIME 10 MINUTES

1/4 cup chopped green onion
  including some of the top
2 tablespoons peanut oil
1/2 pound fresh snow peas
1 cup fresh sliced mushrooms

2 teaspoons cornstarch
2/3 cup chicken stock
2 teaspoons soy sauce
2 tablespoons toasted slivered
  almonds

Sauté the onion in the oil until soft but not brown. Add the snow peas and mushrooms. Cook over high heat for 1 minute. Stir the cornstarch into the stock. Add to the peas together with the soy sauce. Cook, stirring, just until thickened and bubbly. Toss with the almonds. Serve immediately.

GARDEN FRESH PEAS WITH TOASTED PINE NUTS

SERVES 8
PREPARATION TIME 10 MINUTES
COOKING TIME 8 TO 10 MINUTES

1 cup chicken stock
4 green onions, sliced,
  including some of the top
1/2 teaspoon sugar
3 pounds fresh peas, shelled
3 tablespoons butter

1/2 cup pine nuts
1 tablespoon minced fresh
  rosemary
Salt
Freshly ground pepper
8 red cabbage leaves

In a large saucepan, bring stock, onions, and sugar to a simmer. Add the peas and simmer until tender, about 5 to 10 minutes. Drain and set aside.

Melt the butter in a skillet. Add the pine nuts and stir until lightly browned. Add the rosemary and cook for 1 minute. Add peas and onions. Stir until hot. Season to taste with salt and pepper. Arrange the cabbage leaves on dinner plates. Spoon the peas onto the leaves. Serve immediately.

PEAS À LA FRANÇAISE

SERVES 8 TO 10
PREPARATION TIME 15 MINUTES
COOKING TIME 10 MINUTES

3 10-ounce packages frozen
    tiny peas
24 tiny white boiling onions
4 tablespoons (1/2 stick) butter
1/4 cup boiling water
1 tablespoon sugar

1/4 teaspoon dried chervil
1/4 teaspoon dried thyme
1 teaspoon salt
Freshly ground black pepper
2 cups shredded lettuce

Thaw the peas and let drain. Peel the onions. If only large onions are available, remove 2 to 3 outside layers and pare down until tiny. Cook in a pot of boiling salted water for 5 minutes; drain.

Melt the butter in a large saucepan. Add the cooked onions, 1/4 cup of boiling water, sugar, chervil, thyme, salt, and pepper to taste. Add the peas. Toss to blend. Stir in the lettuce. Cover and cook until peas are tender, approximately 5 minutes.

SUMMER SQUASH STUFFED WITH PEAS

SERVES 8 TO 10
PREPARATION TIME 15 MINUTES
COOKING TIME 15 MINUTES

A dressy presentation for a summer vegetable.

10 small yellow summer squash
2 tablespoons melted butter
Salt
1/2 cup minced onion
4 tablespoons butter
2 cloves garlic, minced
2 1/2 cups frozen tiny peas,
    thawed

1/2 teaspoon dried crumbled
    tarragon
1/2 teaspoon salt
1/4 teaspoon white pepper
1 teaspoon fresh lemon juice

Preheat oven to 400 degrees. Peel narrow strips from squash to create a striped appearance. Trim the ends and cut into 2-inch lengths. Hollow out the centers from one end, using a melon baller and leaving a 1/2-inch base. Reserve the hollowed-out centers.

Cook the squash in a large pot of boiling salted water until barely tender, about 5 minutes. Rinse with cold water and drain. Brush with the melted butter and sprinkle with salt. Arrange standing up in a baking dish.

Sauté the onion in the remaining butter until soft, about 5 minutes. Add the reserved squash and garlic. Stir until the squash begins to soften. Add peas, tarragon, salt, and pepper. Cook for 2 minutes. Stir in lemon juice. Spoon mixture into the prepared cups. Bake until hot, 5 to 10 minutes.

YELLOW SQUASH CASSEROLE

SERVES 8 TO 10
PREPARATION TIME 30 MINUTES
COOKING TIME 45 MINUTES

A very tasty, satisfying combination. Served with mesquite-grilled fish and a spinach salad, it's lovely for summer dining.

2 pounds yellow crookneck squash, sliced	2 tablespoons butter
3 eggs, lightly beaten	1 teaspoon salt
1/2 cup heavy cream	1/2 teaspoon white pepper
2 tablespoons melted butter	1 1/2 cups shredded Cheddar cheese
1 1/2 cups thinly sliced celery	9 slices cooked bacon, crumbled
1 cup finely chopped onion	

Preheat oven to 350 degrees. Cook the squash in boiling salted water until tender. Drain well and mash. Transfer the squash to a large bowl and mix with the eggs, cream, and melted butter. Sauté the celery and onion in the remaining butter until transparent. Add to the squash together with the salt, pepper, and 3/4 cup of the cheese. Pour into a 9 × 13-inch pan. Sprinkle with the remaining cheese and top with the bacon. Bake for 45 minutes. Serve immediately.

YELLOW SQUASH CANOES

SERVES 8 TO 10
PREPARATION TIME 25 MINUTES
COOKING TIME 30 MINUTES

6 slices bacon
12 yellow squash
3 eggs, slightly beaten
1/2 cup heavy cream

1/2 teaspoon salt
1/2 teaspoon nutmeg
1/8 teaspoon freshly ground
   pepper

Preheat the oven to 350 degrees. Cook the bacon until crisp. Drain on paper towels; crumble. Reserve 2 tablespoons of the bacon fat.

Split the squash in half and discard the seeds. Hollow out the halves into a canoe shape. Chop the scooped-out flesh and sauté in the bacon fat for 5 minutes.

Blend the eggs with the cream. Add the salt, nutmeg, pepper, crumbled bacon, and sautéed squash flesh. Spoon some of the mixture into each canoe, filling to the edges. Place in a shallow baking dish. Add enough hot water to come up 1/2 inch from the bottom of the pan. Bake for 25 minutes or until set.

GENOA STYLE SPINACH

SERVES 4 TO 6
PREPARATION TIME 15 MINUTES
COOKING TIME 5 MINUTES

1/4 cup pine nuts
1/4 cup olive oil
2 pounds fresh spinach,
   stemmed, cooked, and
   drained
1/3 cup raisins plumped in
   white wine and drained

Salt
Freshly ground pepper
2 tablespoons chopped fresh
   parsley

Sauté the pine nuts in the olive oil until lightly browned. Stir in the spinach and raisins. Season to taste with salt and pepper. Cook over a low heat for 5 minutes. Sprinkle with the fresh parsley. Serve immediately.

DILLY TOMATOES

SERVES ANY NUMBER
PREPARATION TIME 5 MINUTES
COOKING TIME 10 MINUTES

Large fresh tomatoes
FOR EACH TOMATO HALF
1 tablespoon sherry
1/8 teaspoon dried dillweed

2 twists black pepper
1 tablespoon mayonnaise
1 tablespoon grated Cheddar cheese

Remove the core from each tomato. Slice the tomato in half. Place, cut side up, on a cookie sheet. Pierce several times with a fork. Sprinkle each half with the sherry, dillweed, and pepper. Broil for 5 to 6 minutes, or until just heated through. Top each half with a mixture of the mayonnaise and cheese. Return to the broiler and broil until bubbly and slightly browned. Serve immediately.

ROQUEFORT-STUFFED TOMATOES

SERVES 8
PREPARATION TIME 1 HOUR
COOKING TIME 15 MINUTES

Serve this extremely rich vegetable dish with a grilled entree.

8 small ripe tomatoes
1 1/4 pounds mushrooms, sliced
4 ounces (1 stick) butter
4 teaspoons flour
1 cup sour cream
3 ounces Roquefort cheese

2 tablespoons sherry
2 teaspoons chopped parsley
1/2 teaspoon fines herbes
1 tablespoon ground almonds
Paprika

Cut a slice from the top of the tomatoes. Scoop out centers with a small knife. Set upside down to drain for 45 minutes.

Preheat oven to 375 degrees. Sauté mushrooms in butter until soft and all the moisture evaporates. Stir in flour and cook for a minute. Blend in sour cream over low heat until thick and bubbly. Stir in the Roquefort and mix until smooth. Add sherry, parsley, and fines herbes and mix well. Stuff tomatoes with the filling. Sprinkle the tops with the almonds and paprika. Bake until hot and bubbly, about 15 minutes.

COUNTRY STYLE TOMATOES

SERVES 6
PREPARATION TIME 10 MINUTES
COOKING TIME 5 MINUTES

These herbed cheese tomato "sandwiches" are incredibly attractive and have an outstanding flavor.

8 ounces cream cheese,
    softened
1 clove garlic, minced
1/4 cup minced parsley
1 1/2 teaspoons chopped fresh
    basil leaves
1/4 teaspoon salt
4 large tomatoes, peeled

1/2 cup flour
1 egg beaten with 1 tablespoon
    milk
2/3 cup dry bread crumbs
3 tablespoons butter
3 tablespoons olive oil
Chopped fresh parsley

Whip the cream cheese, garlic, parsley, basil, and salt in a food processor or mixer. Cut tomatoes into 12 even slices, about 1/2 inch thick. Spread 6 slices with the cream-cheese mixture. Top with the remaining slices to make 6 sandwiches.

Dip in the flour, then in the egg mixture and finally into the bread crumbs. Fry in the butter and oil until nicely browned on both sides. Sprinkle with the parsley. Serve immediately.

SPINACH-STUFFED TOMATOES

SERVES 6
PREPARATION TIME 20 MINUTES
COOKING TIME 20 MINUTES

6 medium tomatoes
2 pounds fresh spinach or 2
    packages frozen
2 to 2 1/2 cups fresh bread
    crumbs
8 slices cooked bacon,
    crumbled

1/4 teaspoon freshly ground
    pepper
Salt
Sour cream

Preheat oven to 375 degrees. Cut a thin slice off the tips of the tomatoes. Scoop out the centers with a small curved knife. Turn upside down to drain. Remove the stems from the spinach and wash. Cook the spinach with just the water that clings to the leaves when washed. Drain well and chop fine. Combine spinach, bread crumbs (the amount you use will depend on how dry the spinach is), bacon, and pepper. Sprinkle the inside of the tomatoes with salt.

Stuff the tomatoes with the spinach mixture. Arrange in a greased baking dish. Bake, uncovered, until tomatoes are just tender but still hold their shape. Serve, topped with a dollop of sour cream.

TOMATO FLANS

SERVES 6
PREPARATION TIME 20 MINUTES
COOKING TIME 45 MINUTES

Butter for ramekins
3 cherry tomatoes
1 cup minced onion
2 tablespoons butter
1 tablespoon olive oil
1 pound fresh tomatoes,
   peeled, seeded, and chopped

4 eggs
1/2 cup heavy cream
1/4 cup grated Emmenthaler
   cheese
1/4 cup grated Parmesan cheese
Salt
Freshly ground pepper

Preheat the oven to 375 degrees. Generously butter six 1/2-cup ramekins. Cut the cherry tomatoes in halves. Place 1 tomato half cut side down in each ramekin.

Sauté the onion in the butter and oil until translucent, about 10 minutes. Add the chopped tomatoes and cook over high heat until all the liquid evaporates. Let cool slightly.

Beat eggs into the heavy cream. Stir in the cheeses and the tomato mixture. Season to taste with salt and pepper. Spoon mixture into the ramekins. Place in a baking pan. Add enough hot water to come halfway up the sides of the ramekins. Bake for 30 to 35 minutes, or until a tester inserted in the middle comes out clean. Let rest for 5 minutes. Run a knife around the inside of the ramekins to loosen the flans. Invert onto a plate. Serve immediately.

YAM-PECAN CASSEROLE

SERVES 10 TO 12
PREPARATION TIME 15 MINUTES
COOKING TIME 2 HOURS

3 1/2 pounds yams or sweet
   potatoes
4 to 6 tablespoons butter,
   melted
2 eggs, beaten
1/2 cup milk
1 cup dark brown sugar

4 tablespoons butter, softened
4 tablespoons flour
1 cup coarsely chopped pecans
1/4 teaspoon salt
1/4 teaspoon cinnamon
1/4 teaspoon nutmeg
1/2 teaspoon vanilla

Preheat oven to 350 degrees. Bake yams until tender when pierced, about 1 to 1 1/2 hours. Remove from oven and let cool. Increase oven temperature to 375 degrees. Scoop out the pulp from the yams. Place in a large bowl. Mash pulp until smooth. You should have 4 cups. Whisk melted butter and eggs into the yams. In a small saucepan, heat the milk. Stir the hot milk and 1/2 cup of the sugar into the yams. Blend thoroughly. Spread the mixture into a buttered 11 × 7 inch baking dish.

   Mix the remaining 1/2 cup sugar, butter, and flour until crumbly. Stir in the remaining ingredients. Sprinkle over the yam casserole. Bake until topping is crusty, about 30 minutes. Let cool for 5 minutes before serving.

ZUCCHINI-ONION PANCAKES

SERVES 8
PREPARATION TIME 25 MINUTES
COOKING TIME 20 MINUTES

Even non-lovers of zucchini will enjoy this.

1 large onion, thinly sliced
3 tablespoons butter
3 cups julienned zucchini
1/2 cup milk
3 eggs
1/3 cup flour
1/2 cup grated Parmesan cheese

1/8 teaspoon freshly grated
   nutmeg
Salt
Freshly ground pepper
Dash of cayenne
Oil or butter for frying
Grated Parmesan cheese

Sauté the onion in the butter until very tender but not brown, about 15 minutes. Add the zucchini and sauté until zucchini is almost tender, about 3 to 4 minutes. Transfer to a bowl and set aside to cool.

Blend milk, eggs, flour, Parmesan cheese, and nutmeg in blender or processor until smooth. Season to taste with salt, pepper, and cayenne. Combine with the vegetables in the bowl.

Heat the oil or butter on a griddle or heavy skillet over medium-high heat. Ladle a 3-inch pancake onto griddle. Cook until bottom is nicely browned, 2 to 3 minutes. Turn and brown other side. Repeat until all the batter is used, adding more oil or butter as necessary. Pass around extra Parmesan cheese to sprinkle on top.

ZUCCHINI AND GRITS CUSTARD

SERVES 4
PREPARATION TIME 20 MINUTES
COOKING TIME 20 TO 30 MINUTES

This unusual custard is a favorite of Chef Ogden at the Campton Place Hotel in San Francisco.

GRITS

1/4 cup uncooked grits
1 cup heavy cream
1/2 teaspoon kosher salt

1/4 teaspoon minced garlic
1/4 teaspoon white pepper

Preheat oven to 350 degrees. Simmer the grits with the heavy cream, salt, garlic, and pepper for 20 minutes.

ZUCCHINI

3/4 cup heavy cream
2 eggs
1 teaspoon kosher salt
1/4 teaspoon white pepper
1/8 teaspoon freshly ground nutmeg

2 tablespoons sweet butter
4 tablespoons grated Parmesan cheese
1/2 cup grated zucchini

Combine the heavy cream, eggs, salt, pepper, and nutmeg to form the custard mix. Butter 4 timbale molds. Place 2 tablespoons of the cooked grits, 1 tablespoon of the cheese, 2 tablespoons of the zucchini, and 2 ounces of the custard mix in each mold. Bake for 20 to 30 minutes, or until custard mix is set. Let cool for 5 minutes and remove from molds.

ZUCCHINI TIMBALES

SERVES 6
PREPARATION TIME 15 MINUTES
COOKING TIME 35 TO 40 MINUTES

Great at the end of summer when you're looking for one more way to serve home-grown zucchini.

Butter for greasing six 4 3/4-
ounce custard cups
2 tablespoons butter
1 large tomato, peeled, seeded,
and finely chopped
1/2 teaspoon crumbled dry basil
2 cups thinly sliced zucchini,
blanched and well drained

2 egg yolks
1 whole egg
1 cup heavy cream
Salt
Freshly ground pepper
Nutmeg

Preheat oven to 375 degrees. Generously butter the custard cups. Melt the 2 tablespoons of butter in a heavy saucepan. Add the tomato and cook for 5 minutes. Remove from heat and add basil. Combine tomato and zucchini. Divide evenly among the custard cups, filling each cup 3/4 full.

Combine yolks and whole egg and beat lightly. Gradually beat in cream. Season to taste with salt, pepper, and nutmeg. Pour the custard mixture over the vegetables. Place the cups in a shallow baking dish. Add enough hot water to come halfway up the sides. Bake until custard is set, about 30 to 35 minutes. Remove from water bath and let set for 5 minutes. Unmold onto plates. Serve immediately.

SWEET-AND-SOUR ZUCCHINI

SERVES 6
PREPARATION TIME 10 MINUTES
COOKING TIME 25 MINUTES

4 tablespoons butter
2 tablespoons vegetable oil
2 pounds zucchini, sliced
2 red onions, sliced
2 teaspoons red wine vinegar
2 teaspoons lemon juice

1 teaspoon salt
1/4 teaspoon freshly ground
pepper
1 clove of garlic, cut in half
2 tablespoons grated Parmesan
cheese

Preheat the oven to 350 degrees. Melt the butter and oil in a large skillet. Add the zucchini and sauté until lightly browned on both sides. Remove from the pan with a slotted spoon. Add the onions to the pan and cook until soft. Remove from the pan with a slotted spoon. To the pan, add the vinegar, lemon juice, salt, and pepper; stir to blend. Remove from the heat.

Rub the inside of a casserole with the garlic. Layer half of the zucchini in the casserole. Cover with the onions. Top with the remaining zucchini. Pour the vinegar mixture over the vegetables. Sprinkle with the grated cheese. Bake for 15 to 20 minutes.

ZUCCHINI BOATS

SERVES 4

PREPARATION TIME 10 MINUTES

COOKING TIME 30 MINUTES

4 medium zucchini
1/4 pound mushrooms, chopped
1/4 cup chopped shallots
3 tablespoons butter
1/4 teaspoon salt
2 tablespoons flour

1 teaspoon dried basil
1/4 teaspoon freshly grated pepper
1 cup shredded Gruyère cheese
3 tablespoons sour cream

Preheat oven to 350 degrees. Cook whole zucchini in boiling salted water for 5 minutes. Drain. Cut off ends and slice lengthwise. Scoop out the pulp, leaving a 1/4-inch shell.

Sauté the mushrooms and shallots in the butter for 5 minutes. Add salt and continue cooking until all the moisture evaporates. Stir in flour, basil, and pepper. Cook for 2 minutes. Cool slightly. Stir in cheese and sour cream. Spoon into zucchini boats. Bake for 15 minutes or until hot and bubbly. If desired, sprinkle with additional cheese and run under the broiler until nicely browned.

ZUCCHINI SOUFFLÉ

SERVES 2
PREPARATION TIME 10 MINUTES
COOKING TIME 40 MINUTES

1 cup chopped zucchini
2 tablespoons butter
1 tablespoon cornstarch
1/2 teaspoon crushed dried
   basil
1/8 teaspoon salt

Dash cayenne
1/2 cup milk
1/2 cup shredded Cheddar
   cheese
2 eggs, separated

Preheat oven to 350 degrees. Sauté the zucchini in the butter until tender. Stir in cornstarch, basil, salt, and cayenne. Add the milk, all at once. Cook over low heat, stirring constantly, until thick and bubbly. Stir in the cheese and cook until melted. Remove from the heat.

Beat the egg yolks until thick and lemon-colored. Stir into the zucchini mixture. Beat the egg whites until firm. Carefully fold into the zucchini mixture. Pour into an ungreased 3-cup soufflé dish with a greased collar. Bake for 30 minutes. Serve immediately.

ZUCCHINI CHEESE CASSEROLE

SERVES 6 TO 8
PREPARATION TIME 10 MINUTES
COOKING TIME 8 MINUTES

3 tablespoons butter
1 1/2 pounds zucchini, cut on
   the diagonal
1 onion, cut into small wedges
1 teaspoon minced garlic
1/2 teaspoon salt

1/2 teaspoon dried basil,
   crumbled
1/4 teaspoon freshly ground
   pepper
6 ounces Jack cheese, cubed

Melt the butter in a large skillet. Add the zucchini, onion, garlic, salt, basil, and pepper. Cover and cook over a medium heat, stirring occasionally, until tender crisp, about 5 minutes. Turn into a shallow baking dish. Sprinkle with the cheese. Run under the broiler until the cheese has melted.

ZUCCHINI BAKE

SERVES 8
PREPARATION TIME 15 MINUTES
COOKING TIME 30 MINUTES

1 1/4 pounds zucchini
4 eggs
1/4 cup flour
1/2 cup Parmesan cheese
3 tablespoons chopped fresh parsley
3 tablespoons chopped green onions

1 small clove garlic, chopped
1 1/4 teaspoons salt
3/4 teaspoon dried oregano
1/4 teaspoon freshly ground pepper
18 cherry tomatoes

Preheat oven to 350 degrees. Finely chop the zucchini. Beat the eggs and add flour, half the cheese, the parsley, onions, garlic, salt, oregano, and pepper. Stir in the zucchini. Pour the mixture into a 1 1/2-quart baking dish. Cut the tomatoes in half. Arrange the tomatoes, cut side up, over the zucchini. Sprinkle with the remaining cheese. Bake, uncovered, for 30 minutes or until hot and bubbly.

VEGETABLE CURRY

SERVES 6 TO 8
PREPARATION TIME 10 MINUTES
COOKING TIME 40 MINUTES

This curry dish can be made with almost any fresh vegetables. Cabbage, cauliflower, eggplant, or string beans work well. For a hotter curry, add the 1/4 teaspoon of cayenne.

1 medium onion, quartered
1/2 teaspoon chopped garlic
2 tablespoons oil
1 teaspoon cumin
3/4 teaspoon coriander
1/2 teaspoon ginger
1/2 teaspoon turmeric

1/8 to 1/4 teaspoon cayenne
1 potato, sliced and parboiled
1 head of cabbage or cauliflower, broken into pieces
1 cup fresh peas
Salt

Brown the onion and garlic in the oil together with the cumin, coriander, ginger, turmeric, and cayenne. Add the potato and cook for 15 minutes. Add the cabbage (or whatever vegetable you choose) and the peas. Cover and cook for 20 minutes. Salt to taste. Taste and correct seasonings.

MIXED VEGETABLE TART

SERVES 6 TO 8
PREPARATION TIME 1 HOUR
COOKING TIME 1 HOUR

This attractive vegetable tart is well worth the effort. It is so versatile that you can also use it as a first course or luncheon dish.

PASTRY

1 cup flour	1/4 teaspoon salt
4 ounces (1 stick) unsalted butter, cut into pieces	2 to 4 tablespoons ice water
	1 tablespoon Dijon mustard

Combine the flour, butter, and salt. Work mixture until butter is incorporated into flour. Add enough water to bring mixture together into a firm ball. Flatten slightly, cover and refrigerate for 10 minutes.

Preheat oven to 375 degrees. Flour a work surface. Roll out dough to a 12-inch circle. Transfer to a 9-inch tart pan. Shape to fit pan, trimming the edges. Prick the bottom. Line with parchment paper and weigh down with pie weights or beans. Bake 35 minutes. Remove weights and paper. Continue baking until nicely browned, about 5 minutes. Remove from oven and immediately brush bottom with mustard. Let cool.

FILLING

1 onion, thinly sliced	1 1/4 pounds broccoli, trimmed and blanched
4 tablespoons oil	1/2 pound Gruyère cheese, grated
3/4 pound zucchini, sliced	
2 large red bell peppers, charred	Butter to grease aluminum foil

Preheat oven to 375 degrees. Sauté the onion in half the oil until soft, about 5 to 7 minutes. Set aside. Sauté the zucchini in remaining oil until tender, about 5 to 7 minutes. Drain and set aside. Remove the skin, core, and seeds from the charred peppers, cut in halves. Cut the broccoli into small flowerets.

Sprinkle 1/2 cup of the cheese on the bottom of the tart. Cover with a layer of the zucchini. Top with 1/3 cup of cheese. Layer onions over cheese. Top with 1/3 cup of cheese. Place the peppers flat over the cheese. Sprinkle the remaining cheese over the peppers. Arrange broccoli flowerets around outside edges of tart, leaving a circle of red showing in the center. Cover loosely with buttered aluminum foil. Bake until heated through and cheese melts.

LAYERED VEGETABLE TIMBALES

MAKES 6
PREPARATION TIME 30 MINUTES
COOKING TIME 25 MINUTES

Butter to grease molds
1 pound broccoli
1 pound carrots, sliced
1 pound fresh spinach,
  stemmed and cleaned
1 carrot

2 mushrooms
6 tablespoons butter
Salt
Freshly ground pepper
4 eggs
2 tablespoons heavy cream

Preheat oven to 350 degrees. Butter six 1/2-cup molds. Line the bottoms with parchment paper. Butter the paper. Cook the broccoli, carrots, and spinach individually in large pots of boiling salted water, until very soft. Drain the vegetables. Cool under cold water.

Prepare the garnish for the timbales. Slice the carrot into thin rounds. Cut notches out of each round to form a flower. Cook the flowers in boiling water until tender. Drain and dry. Cut the mushrooms into strips. Decorate the bottoms of the molds with carrot flowers, using the mushroom pieces as stems.

Purée separately the broccoli, carrots, and spinach. Put each in a small saucepan with 2 tablespoons of the butter. Cook, stirring, until all the liquid evaporates. Season well with salt and pepper.

Whisk eggs and cream until well blended. Divide into three portions. Stir each portion into the three vegetable purées. Cook over low heat for another minute.

Fill 1/3 of each mold with spinach mixture. Add a layer of carrot, then a layer of broccoli. Cover the mold with buttered foil. Place in a baking dish. Fill the baking dish with hot water, to reach halfway up the molds. Bake for 20 to 25 minutes or until a tester inserted in the center comes out clean. Unmold onto a serving platter or individual plates.

FISH

Monterey County

The coastline of this fertile, agricultural region along the central coast of California is among the most beautiful of any in the world. The seventeen-mile drive, which threads through Pacific Grove between the seacoast towns of Carmel and Monterey, is justly famous worldwide. Monterey, a longtime bustling fishing port, was immortalized in John Steinbeck's *Cannery Row*. To the south, Carmel features wide, sandy beaches, and its quaint cottages house restaurants, shops, and inns. Here some of California's best seafood can be purchased.

Monterey County is the most southerly of the Bay Area's wine regions, whose grape-growing areas are located in the giant Salinas Valley. This hundred-mile long valley, long known for its salad bowl and vegetable crop production, became one of California's largest wine-grape regions in the 1960s. The Monterey vineyard boom resulted when urbanization of neighboring Santa Clara and Livermore valleys to the north pushed some of their biggest growers southward. Previously, it had been thought that this area was too cool for growing wine grapes, because of the strong cold winds and fog from Monterey Bay.

Unlike the wine-tasting in Napa Valley where wineries are located all in a row, Monterey County's wine-tasting involves more effort and more travel through the countryside. Some of the wineries have tasting rooms located in the towns of Carmel and Monterey, removed from the vineyards.

The artichoke is one of this area's famous crops. Castroville, a small coastal town close to Monterey, calls itself the artichoke capital of the world and it is true that this region produces virtually all of the nation's artichokes. This delectable vegetable is actually a flower bud related to the thistle. Each year, Castroville's nine thousand foggy, sandy acres produce over 73 million pounds of artichokes, which can be used in nearly every type of dish from soup to cake.

Whether you are enjoying an Artichoke with Fresh Herb Sauce or Poisson avec Artichauts, be sure to accompany it with one of Monterey's fine wines.

GRILLED SEA BASS WITH HERBED BUTTER

SERVES 6
PREPARATION TIME 10 MINUTES
MARINATING TIME 2 HOURS
COOKING TIME 10 MINUTES

2 1/2 pounds sea bass fillets or
  steaks, 6 ounces each
2 cloves crushed garlic
1/2 cup olive oil

Juice of 1 large lemon
Handful of fresh herbs
Herbed Butter (recipe follows)

Marinate the fish for 2 hours in the garlic, olive oil, lemon juice, and herbs.
  Remove the fish from the marinade and grill for 3 minutes, each side, over a medium fire or under the broiler. Season with a little salt and pepper. Serve immediately, topped with a spoonful of the Herbed Butter.

HERBED BUTTER

8 ounces (2 sticks) unsalted
  butter
1 shallot, chopped
1/2 cup parsley
1/2 cup chives

4–6 anchovy fillets
2 teaspoons capers
1 clove garlic, chopped
2 hard-cooked egg yolks

In a food processor or blender, cream together the butter and shallot. Coarsely chop the parsley, chives, and anchovies. Add to the butter and process a few seconds. Add the capers, garlic, and egg yolks and blend until a smooth paste is formed. Refrigerate until 15 minutes before serving time.

MOROCCAN SEA BASS

SERVES 4
PREPARATION TIME 10 MINUTES
COOKING TIME 15 MINUTES

This spicy dish is equally good when made with snapper or cod.

4 sea bass fillets, 6 ounces each
4 tablespoons butter
1/2 cup chopped onion
2 cloves minced garlic
2 teaspoons curry powder

1/2 cup dry white wine
3 tablespoons soy sauce
3 tablespoons chili sauce
1 teaspoon dry dillweed

Preheat oven to 450 degrees. Rinse the fillets and pat dry. Arrange on a piece of foil in a shallow roasting pan. Set aside.

Melt the butter in a small frying pan. Sauté the onion and garlic until the onion is limp. Stir in the curry powder and cook for a few minutes. Add the wine, soy sauce, chili sauce, and dillweed. Stir and cook until hot. Brush the fish generously with the sauce.

Bake the fish, uncovered, for about 15 minutes or until it flakes. Brush with the baste several times while cooking.

PESCADO EN SALSA VERDE

SERVES 8 TO 10
PREPARATION TIME 1 HOUR
COOKING TIME 25 MINUTES

Jalapeño chilies impart a pleasing "bite" to this delightful dish. After roasting, these hot peppers become very fragile. Use rubber gloves to remove charred skins. This spicy salsa is particularly good over rice pilaf.

- 1 **pound fresh long green chilies or 10 canned jalapeño chilies**
- 2 **pounds green bell peppers**
- 1 **large onion**
- 1 **cup fresh parsley**
- 1/2 **cup oil**
- 2 **large cloves garlic, minced**
- **Salt**
- **Freshly ground black pepper**
- **Juice of 1 large lemon**
- 1 **sea bass or 4 pounds sea bass fillets**
- 1 **tablespoon oil**

Place chilies and bell peppers under broiler or over gas flame. Cook until the skin blisters and blackens on all sides. Remove the blackened skins under cold, running water. Remove stems and seeds. Finely chop in a food processor or blender, together with the onion and parsley.

Heat the oil in a large frying pan and sauté the minced garlic. Add the chili mixture, salt and pepper to taste. Stir in half of the juice from the lemon. Simmer the sauce until the oil rises to the top.

Preheat the oven to 350 degrees. Place the fish in a large oiled pan. Sprinkle with the remaining juice of the lemon, salt and pepper. Bake the fillets, uncovered, for 20 minutes or until done. If using a whole fish, bake for 45 minutes to 1 hour.

Remove fish from pan and keep warm. Add the broth from the pan to the chili mixture and mix together well. Place the fish onto a serving platter and cover with some of the sauce. Pass additional sauce in a sauce boat. If using a whole fish, you may want to remove the bones first before masking with the sauce.

STEWED SEA BASS

SERVES 4
PREPARATION TIME 20 MINUTES
MARINATING TIME 30 MINUTES
COOKING TIME 25 MINUTES

This delicious, low-calorie dish is especially colorful when served over tomato or spinach pasta in large soup bowls.

2 pounds sea bass fillets
3 tablespoons fresh lime juice
4 tablespoons olive oil
1 green bell pepper, cut into
   1/4-inch slices
1 medium leek, white part only,
   cut into 1/4-inch slices
3 cloves garlic, minced
3 shallots, minced
1 onion, chopped
1/4-inch slice of fresh ginger,
   chopped

1/2 cup dry white wine
2 large tomatoes, peeled,
   seeded, and chopped
1/2 cup fish stock
1/2 teaspoon curry powder
1/2 teaspoon dried thyme
1/4 teaspoon cayenne
Bouquet garni
Fresh parsley sprigs

Wash fillets and pat dry. Cut into 2-inch pieces. Place in a small bowl. Sprinkle with the lime juice and let stand for 30 minutes, turning occasionally. Drain the fish on paper towels and pat dry.

Heat 2 tablespoons of the oil in a skillet. Add fish and sauté until nicely browned on both sides. Transfer to a plate and set aside.

Heat the remaining oil in a large pot. Add the green pepper, leek, garlic, shallots, onion, and ginger. Sauté until softened and lightly browned. Add the wine and cook for an additional minute. Add the tomatoes, stock, spices, and bouquet garni. Simmer for 5 minutes. Add the browned fish. Cover and simmer for 20 minutes. Remove the bouquet garni and serve, garnished with the parsley sprigs.

BAKED FISH RATATOUILLE

SERVES 8
PREPARATION TIME 20 MINUTES
COOKING TIME 1 HOUR 10 MINUTES

Chunks of tomatoes and eggplant simmered in wine make a delectable low-calorie sauce for your favorite white fish.

2 pounds fresh fish fillets, such as snapper, bass, or sole
Olive oil
Salt and pepper
Paprika

1/2 pound fresh mushrooms, sliced
Eggplant-Tomato Sauce (recipe follows)

Preheat the oven to 400 degrees. Place the fish in a shallow baking dish. Brush both sides with a little oil. Sprinkle with salt, pepper and paprika. Bake, uncovered, for 5 to 10 minutes. Add the mushrooms and spoon the Eggplant-Tomato Sauce over all. Cover, return to the oven and bake an additional 15 minutes. Uncover and bake 5 minutes more.

EGGPLANT-TOMATO SAUCE

16 ounces canned tomatoes
3/4 cup tomato juice cocktail
1 cup peeled and diced eggplant
1/2 cup chopped onion
1/2 cup chopped celery
1/4 cup dry white wine
1/2 cup seeded and chopped green pepper
2 tablespoons olive oil
2 tablespoons chopped parsley

1 tablespoon Worcestershire sauce
2 teaspoons sugar
1 teaspoon dried basil, crushed
1/4 teaspoon dried thyme, crushed
1/4 teaspoon dried oregano, crushed
2 tablespoons chopped fresh parsley

Combine all of the ingredients in a saucepan. Bring to a boil and reduce the heat slightly. Gently boil, uncovered, until thickened, about 40 minutes. Stir occasionally while cooking.

FILLET OF COD WITH MUSTARD CAPER SAUCE

SERVES 4
PREPARATION TIME 5 MINUTES
COOKING TIME 10 MINUTES

A lovely last-minute dish. The light sauce has a subtle hint of mustard.

4 cod fillets, 8 ounces each
Salt
Freshly ground black pepper
1/2 cup flour
6 tablespoons butter
1 small shallot, chopped

1/2 cup vermouth
1 1/2 tablespoons capers,
  drained
2 teaspoons Dijon mustard
1/2 cup heavy cream

Pat fillets dry with paper towels. Sprinkle lightly with salt and pepper. Dust the fillets in the flour. Melt 4 tablespoons of the butter in a large skillet. Add the fillets and fry for approximately 2 minutes per side, or until done. Remove to a serving dish and keep warm.

Pour off any remaining butter from the pan. Melt the remaining butter in the same pan. Sauté the shallot for 1 minute. Add the vermouth, capers, and mustard. Cook rapidly, scraping up any bits remaining on the bottom. Add the cream and continue to cook, stirring frequently, until the sauce thickens enough to lightly coat a spoon. Spoon the sauce over the fillets and serve immediately.

BROILED HALIBUT WITH SALMON BUTTER

SERVES 4
PREPARATION TIME 10 MINUTES
COOKING TIME 10 TO 14 MINUTES

SALMON BUTTER
4 ounces (1 stick) butter, room
  temperature
3 ounces smoked salmon, finely
  chopped

1 teaspoon lemon juice
1 teaspoon grated onion
1/2 teaspoon dried dill

Cream the butter until light and fluffy. Add the remaining ingredients, mixing well. Place on a piece of plastic wrap and form into a 2-inch cylinder.

Twist the ends of the plastic wrap together to form a tight roll. Refrigerate until firm, about 2 hours. When ready to serve, slice into 1/2-inch disks. Top each broiled fillet with a slice of the butter.

BROILED HALIBUT
4 8-ounce halibut fillets
Oil

Preheat the broiler. Pat the fish dry. Brush each side with a little oil. Broil, turning once, until just opaque and lightly browned. Transfer to a plate and top with the Salmon Butter.

OVEN-POACHED HALIBUT

SERVES 8
PREPARATION TIME 15 MINUTES
COOKING TIME 45 MINUTES

4 tablespoons butter　　　　　**Salt**
4 tablespoons flour　　　　　　**White pepper**
3 cups half-and-half　　　　　**1 cup dry white wine**
1/2 cup chopped fresh dill or 2　**3 tablespoons chopped shallots**
**　tablespoons dry**　　　　　　**8 halibut fillets**
1/3 cup capers　　　　　　　**Dill sprigs and lemon wedges**
1/4 cup caper juice

Preheat oven to 400 degrees. Melt the butter in a saucepan. Add the flour and cook until lightly browned, about 2 to 3 minutes. Remove from heat and cool slightly. Slowly whisk in the half-and-half. Return to the heat and bring to a boil, whisking occasionally, until sauce coats the back of a wooden spoon, about 20 minutes. Strain and stir in dill, capers, caper juice, salt and pepper to taste. Keep warm.

Place the wine and shallots in a baking dish large enough to hold the fillets in a single layer. Arrange the halibut on top. Cover with a piece of buttered parchment paper. Bake for 10 minutes or until done. Remove with a slotted spoon to a serving platter. Mask with the sauce. Garnish with dill sprigs and lemon wedges.

STEAMED MUSSELS WITH FRESH TOMATOES AND BASIL

SERVES 6
PREPARATION TIME 20 MINUTES
COOKING TIME 5 TO 10 MINUTES

6 dozen mussels
1/4 cup olive oil
2 cloves garlic, finely chopped
1/2 cup dry white wine
8 tomatoes, peeled, seeded and chopped

1 small bunch fresh basil leaves
Salt
Freshly ground pepper
3 tablespoons butter

Scrub the mussels well and set aside. Heat the oil in a sauté pan. Add the garlic and sauté until softened but not browned. Pour in the white wine and cook until almost all of the liquid evaporates. Add the tomatoes and continue cooking a minute longer. Tear the basil leaves into pieces and add to the tomatoes. Salt and pepper to taste. Remove from the heat.

In another sauté pan, place the cleaned mussels. Cover and steam until opened. Drain from their juice and arrange in warmed bowls in a circular fashion. Gently reheat the sauce and swirl in the butter. Spoon the sauce over the mussels, reserving some to place in the center of the bowl.

MONKFISH ARMORICA

SERVES 4
PREPARATION TIME 15 MINUTES
COOKING TIME 45 MINUTES

Armorica is the ancient name for Brittany, where this sauce was created for fresh seafood. The sauce can be prepared ahead; the monkfish added just before serving.

2 tablespoons butter
1 tablespoon olive oil
6 large shallots, minced
1 clove garlic, minced
1/4 teaspoon dried tarragon
3 tablespoons brandy
Cayenne to taste
3/4 cup dry white wine

1 cup fish stock
2 tablespoons tomato paste
1 cup peeled, seeded, and chopped tomatoes
1/2 cup heavy cream
Salt
Freshly ground pepper
1 1/2 pounds monkfish

Melt the butter and oil in a large skillet over medium heat. Add the shallots and garlic. Cook until softened, about 4 minutes. Stir in tarragon, brandy, and cayenne. Cook over high heat until liquid has completely evaporated. Pour in wine and reduce to 1/4 cup. Add fish stock and tomato paste. Cook to reduce slightly. You should have about 1 cup of liquid. Stir in the tomatoes, reduce the heat, cover, and simmer for 30 minutes.

Add the cream and cook uncovered, until reduced to a saucelike consistency, about 5 minutes. Season to taste with salt and pepper.

Cut the monkfish into 1/2-inch pieces. Add to the sauce and cook over a medium-high heat until the fish pieces turn opaque.

GRILLED BODEGA BAY OYSTERS

SERVES 3
PREPARATION TIME 15 MINUTES
COOKING TIME 2 MINUTES

This recipe gets its name from the thriving fishing port of Bodega Bay, famous as the film location of Hitchcock's The Birds. *Any fresh oysters will work beautifully in this dish.*

12 oysters	2 teaspoons molasses
2 tablespoons butter	6 dashes red pepper sauce
1/2 small onion, chopped	1 1/2 tablespoons
1/2 cup ketchup	Worcestershire sauce

Open the oysters. From each oyster shell, scoop out the body, being careful to keep it intact. Replace the body in the larger, deeper half shell. Set aside until needed.

Melt the butter in a saucepan. Add onions and cook 2 to 3 minutes. Add ketchup, molasses, red pepper sauce, and Worcestershire sauce. Simmer for 15 minutes.

Preheat a barbecue grill. Place a dollop of sauce on each oyster, making sure not to cover the body completely. Place the oyster shell on the grill. Cover the grill and cook, just until the edges of the oysters start to bubble. Serve hot.

PRAWNS IN HOT GARLIC SAUCE

SERVES 4
PREPARATION TIME 5 MINUTES
COOKING TIME 5 MINUTES

The chili paste with garlic is available at specialty food stores. Serve these spicy prawns with sautéed Chinese vegetables.

1 pound medium prawns
1 1/2 teaspoons cornstarch
1/4 teaspoon salt
Dash of pepper
1 1/2 teaspoons chili paste with garlic
1 1/2 tablespoons ketchup
1 1/4 tablespoons oyster sauce

1 tablespoon sugar
2 tablespoons white wine
1 1/2 tablespoons sesame oil
2 tablespoons oil
2 teaspoons finely chopped garlic
1 green onion, chopped

Shell and devein the prawns. Wash and pat dry. Add the cornstarch, salt, and pepper to the prawns and mix well. Set aside.

Mix the chili paste, ketchup, oyster sauce, sugar, white wine, and sesame oil. Heat a wok or skillet. Add the oil and garlic. Stir-fry for 30 seconds. Add the prawns and stir-fry for 2 minutes over high heat. Add the sauce and continue cooking for an additional minute. Remove to a serving platter and garnish with the green onion.

PRAWNS SAUTÉ PROVENÇAL

SERVES 6
PREPARATION TIME 10 MINUTES
COOKING TIME 10 MINUTES

2 pounds large prawns
1/3 cup olive oil
1 teaspoon finely chopped garlic
2 ounces white wine
4 whole green onions, sliced
4 tablespoons butter
2 teaspoons finely chopped fresh parsley

1 teaspoon finely chopped fresh basil
1/2 teaspoon lemon juice
2 drops Tabasco
1 teaspoon Worcestershire sauce
Pinch of dried oregano
1 large tomato, peeled and chopped

Peel the prawns, leaving on the tail, and butterfly. Wash and pat dry. Heat the oil in a large sauté pan. When the oil is very hot, add the prawns and sauté lightly, turning them with a fork so the oil will fry all sides. Remove prawns from pan and set aside. Add garlic and brown lightly. Pour in wine and simmer for 20 seconds. Add the remaining ingredients, except the tomatoes, and continue cooking for 2 more minutes. Add the chopped tomatoes and prawns. Mix well and cook for an additional minute. Serve immediately.

POACHED SALMON WITH RASPBERRY BEURRE BLANC

SERVES 6
PREPARATION TIME 20 MINUTES
COOKING TIME 20 MINUTES

Raspberry beurre blanc is a fruity butter sauce.

SALMON

2 cups dry white wine
1/2 cup water
2 stalks chopped celery
2 carrots, sliced
1 onion, sliced
4 peppercorns

2 parsley sprigs
1 bay leaf
1/4 teaspoon salt
6 pieces salmon fillets, 8
   ounces each

Combine the first nine ingredients in a large pan or fish poacher and bring to a simmer. Add the salmon fillets, cover, and poach over a medium-low heat for 8 to 10 minutes or until tender. Do not allow the poaching liquid to boil.

RASPBERRY BEURRE BLANC

1/2 cup raspberry vinegar
1/4 cup minced shallot
8 ounces (2 sticks) unsalted
   butter

2 tablespoons raspberry jam,
   strained

While the salmon is poaching, prepare the sauce. Combine the vinegar and shallot in a saucepan. Cook until reduced to 2 tablespoons. Remove from the heat. Cut the butter into small pieces. Whisk 3 or 4 pieces of the butter into the vinegar, one piece at a time. Return the pan to a low heat and continue whisking in the remaining butter. The sauce should have the consistency of a light mayonnaise. Whisk in the strained raspberry jam.

SAUMON TRUITE AU CAVIAR NOIR, BEURRE BLANC

SERVES 2
PREPARATION TIME 30 MINUTES
COOKING TIME 30 MINUTES

An original recipe from the late Chef Masataka Kobayashi's culinary legacy. His restaurant—Masa's, near San Francisco's Union Square—is a tribute to the celebrated artist's attention to visual detail. In this recipe, the pale meat of the coho salmon contrasts beautifully with the black caviar.

2 boned coho salmon (or trout if coho is not available)	4 tablespoons chopped chives
	2 chopped shallots
4 ounces salmon fillet	2 cups dry white wine
2 egg whites	2 cups fish stock (or one fish
2 tablespoons brandy	bouillon cube dissolved in 1
3 cups heavy cream	cup water)
Salt and pepper to taste	4 tablespoons butter
4 tablespoons black caviar	

Clean coho, trim fins from stomach area. Prepare the salmon mousse: Process the salmon fillet in a food processor until smooth. Add the egg whites and process a few more seconds. Add the brandy and 1 cup of the heavy cream and process just until mixed. Salt and pepper to taste. Chill until ready to use.

Lay open the coho and season lightly with salt and pepper. Place half of the caviar down the center of each fish. Sprinkle the chopped chives over the caviar. Place the salmon mousse into a pastry bag, fitted with a large tube, and pipe over the chives. Close the coho together. Form into an "S" shape on their sides and place into a medium sauté pan.

Preheat oven to 500 degrees. Add the chopped shallots, white wine, and fish stock to the pan with the fish. Bake in the oven for 20 minutes. Remove the coho from the pan and cover with foil to keep warm. Add the heavy cream to the remaining liquid and reduce by half. Add the butter, strain through a fine sieve, and season to taste with salt and pepper.

Remove the skin from the coho and place on plates. Spoon the sauce over the fish. Garnish with additional caviar if desired. Serve immediately.

STUFFED SALMON FLORENTINE

SERVES 6
PREPARATION TIME 35 MINUTES
REFRIGERATION TIME 2 HOURS
COOKING TIME 10 TO 12 MINUTES

Try to purchase a wide piece of the fillet; it will be easier to stuff.

8 tablespoons butter
2 tablespoons flour
3/4 cup milk
Salt
White pepper
2 tablespoons dry sherry
10 ounces fresh spinach
1 cup mushrooms, chopped
1/2 cup chopped yellow onion
4 green onions, chopped
1 teaspoon dried basil

1/2 teaspoon dried oregano
1/4 teaspoon dried thyme
1/2 cup Parmesan cheese
6 6-ounce salmon fillets
Lemon juice
1/2 cup bread crumbs
1/2 cup (1 stick) melted butter
1/2 cup white wine
1/4 cup water
Lemon wedges
Chopped fresh parsley

Heat 2 tablespoons of the butter in a saucepan. Add the flour and cook without browning for 4 to 5 minutes. Gradually add the milk, whisking constantly. Continue to stir until the sauce has thickened and is smooth. Season to taste with the salt and pepper. Stir in the sherry and set aside.

Wash the spinach well and blanch in boiling water until softened. Squeeze dry and chop. Melt the remaining 6 tablespoons of butter in a saucepan. Sauté the spinach for a minute. Add the mushrooms, onion, green onions, basil, oregano, and thyme. Sauté over a medium heat for 5 minutes. Stir in the Parmesan cheese and continue to cook until the cheese has melted. Combine with the white sauce. Taste and correct for seasoning. Place a piece of plastic wrap directly onto the sauce and refrigerate until set (about 2 to 4 hours).

Preheat the oven to 425 degrees. Cut a slit in the side of each salmon fillet, making a pocket. Leave 1/4 inch intact at each end. Carefully open each slit and place some of the filling into the pocket. If necessary, use a toothpick to close the slits. Squeeze a little fresh lemon juice over each fillet and place in a buttered shallow baking dish. Sprinkle with the bread crumbs and drizzle the butter evenly over all. Pour the wine and water into the bottom of the pan. Bake for 10 to 12 minutes or until flaky. Serve garnished with lemon wedges and chopped parsley.

SAUMON AU CHAMPAGNE

SERVES 6
PREPARATION TIME 15 MINUTES
COOKING TIME 20 MINUTES

Technically, only sparkling wine from the Champagne region of France is champagne, but in California the terms champagne and sparkling wine are used interchangeably.

6 salmon fillets	**Salt**
1 1/2 cups dry champagne	**Pepper**
Bay leaf	**Pinch of sugar**
4 peppercorns	**1 teaspoon cornstarch**
4 tablespoons butter	**1 1/2 cups heavy cream**
1/2 pound sliced mushrooms	
3 tomatoes, peeled, seeded and chopped	

Preheat oven to 375 degrees. Place the salmon fillets in a buttered shallow baking dish. Add the champagne, bay leaf, and peppercorns. Butter a piece of parchment or wax paper and place, buttered side down, directly over the salmon. Bake in the oven for 15 minutes or until done.

While salmon is baking, prepare the sauce. Melt the butter in a sauté pan. When the butter is very hot, add the mushrooms, a few at a time. Sauté over high heat until nicely browned. Add the tomatoes and continue cooking over high heat until all the liquid evaporates. Season with salt, pepper, and sugar. Set aside until needed.

Remove the fish from the oven and keep warm. Pour the poaching liquid into a sauté pan and reduce to 3 tablespoons. Add to the vegetable mixture. Mix the cornstarch into the heavy cream. Return the vegetable mixture to the heat and slowly stir in the heavy cream. Bring to a boil, reduce the heat slightly, and continue cooking until thickened. It should be thick enough to coat the fish nicely.

Arrange the salmon on a flameproof serving platter. Spoon some of the sauce over each fillet. Run under the broiler until the top is nicely browned.

COULIBIAC DE SAUMON

SERVES 8 TO 10
PREPARATION TIME 40 MINUTES
COOKING TIME 40 MINUTES

Coulibiac is the Russian version of English pasty and French pâte en croûte. *This is a delicate Russian creation with French overtones.*

PASTRY

6 ounces cream cheese   1 1/2 **cups flour**
6 ounces (1 1/2 sticks) butter   1/4 **teaspoon salt**

Mix together the cream cheese and butter. Sift the flour and salt. Add to the cream cheese and butter and work together until a dough is formed. Cut the dough into two pieces, one slightly larger than the other. Refrigerate at least 1 hour.

FILLING

1 1/2 **pounds poached salmon**   2 **cooked carrots, chopped**
Juice of 1 small lemon   2 **hard-cooked eggs, chopped**
2 **tablespoons capers**   1/4 **cup fresh chopped parsley**
2 **tablespoons butter**   1/4 **cup fresh chopped chives**
1 **teaspoon dried dill**   1 **egg yolk, beaten with 1**
1 1/2 **cups cooked rice**   **tablespoon water**
4 **tablespoons butter**   4 **tablespoons melted butter,**
1 1/2 **cups thinly sliced onions**   **mixed with 1 teaspoon curry**
Salt   **powder**
White pepper

Preheat oven to 400 degrees. Cool poached fish and break into pieces. Toss with the lemon juice and capers. In a separate bowl, stir the 2 tablespoons of butter and dill into the rice. Melt the 4 tablespoons of butter in a skillet. Sauté the onions until softened and golden.

Roll out the smaller piece of dough into a rectangle about 8 inches long. Place on a baking sheet. Spread the rice to within 1/2 inch of the edges. Season with salt and pepper. Cover with layers of salmon, onions, carrots, eggs, parsley, and chives, seasoning each layer. Roll out the remaining piece of dough large enough to cover filling. Brush the edges with water and pinch together with a fork. Brush the dough with the egg wash. Make a few slashes in the top to allow the steam to escape. Bake for 30 minutes or until nicely browned. Transfer to a serving platter and pour the butter into the slashes. Serve immediately.

COQUILLE ST. JACQUES
(BEURRE DE SAFFRON)

SERVES 6
PREPARATION TIME 15 MINUTES
COOKING TIME 10 TO 15 MINUTES

The California Culinary Academy, San Francisco's school for professional chefs, suggested this unusual presentation for scallops. It is delicious either as a first course or an entree.

2 pounds scallops
1/4 cup dry white vermouth
1/2 cup dry white wine
1/4 cup chopped shallots
1 cup heavy cream
Pinch of powdered saffron

1/2 pound (2 sticks) butter,
   softened
Salt
White pepper
Caviar (optional)

Wash scallops and pat dry. Heat the vermouth and white wine in a sauté pan. Add the scallops and sauté for 2 to 3 minutes. Do not overcook. Using a slotted spoon, remove from the pan and keep warm. Add the shallots to the sauté pan and reduce the remaining liquid to a thick glaze. It should look like thick marmalade. Add the cream and saffron and simmer until thickened. Whisk in the butter a piece at a time. Add salt and pepper to taste. Mix in the scallops. Serve on a plate garnished with a dollop of caviar, if desired.

SCALLOPS TRIFOLATI

SERVES 4
PREPARATION TIME 10 MINUTES
COOKING TIME 3 TO 5 MINUTES

Trifolare describes the Italian method of quickly sautéing vegetables, meat, or fish in olive oil, garlic, and parsley. To these basic flavors, other ingredients are often added. The success of this dish will depend, in part, on the freshness of the scallops.

1 pound fresh small scallops
4 tablespoons olive oil
2 teaspoons finely chopped
   garlic
2 tablespoons finely chopped
   parsley

Freshly ground black pepper
2 tablespoons chopped capers
4 tablespoons chopped roasted
   red bell peppers
3 tablespoons plain bread
   crumbs

Wash the scallops and pat dry. Place the olive oil in a sauté pan and heat. Add the garlic and parsley and sauté until lightly colored, being careful not to let the garlic brown. Stir in the scallops and add a few twists of the pepper mill. Cook over medium heat, stirring frequently, for 3 to 5 minutes.

Remove the pan from the heat and add the capers, red peppers, and 2 tablespoons of the bread crumbs. Mix thoroughly and divide into 4 scallop shells or au gratin dishes. Sprinkle with the remaining bread crumbs. Run under the broiler just until the tops of the shells are nicely browned. Serve immediately.

SPICY SCALLOPS AND MUSHROOMS

SERVES 4
PREPARATION TIME 20 MINUTES
COOKING TIME 30 MINUTES

2 tablespoons olive oil
1/3 cup finely chopped onion
2 to 3 cloves minced garlic
1 1/4 pounds scallops
2 tablespoons minced fresh
    parsley
1/2 teaspoon crumbled dried
    thyme
Pinch cayenne

Salt
Freshly ground pepper
2 cups sliced fresh mushrooms
2 tablespoons Cognac
3/4 cup dry white wine
1/2 cup tomato sauce
Bread crumbs
Butter

Preheat the oven to 450 degrees. Heat the oil in a large skillet over high heat. Add the onion and garlic and sauté until transparent. If using large scallops, cut in half. Add scallops and sauté for 2 minutes. Reduce the heat and sprinkle with the parsley, thyme, cayenne, salt, and pepper. Add mushrooms and cook for 5 minutes.

Heat Cognac in a small saucepan. Pour into the skillet and ignite, shaking the pan gently until the flame subsides. Transfer the scallops and mushrooms to a shallow baking dish, using a slotted spoon.

Add the wine and tomato sauce to the liquid remaining in the skillet. Bring to a boil. Reduce heat and simmer for 10 minutes. Pour over the scallops and mushrooms. Sprinkle with bread crumbs and dot with butter. Bake until top is golden brown, about 10 minutes. Serve immediately.

SCALLOP MOUSSE WITH SCALLOP SAUCE

SERVES 4
PREPARATION TIME 1 HOUR
COOKING TIME 1 HOUR

SCALLOP MOUSSE

16 mussels	2 large eggs
4 large shallots, chopped	2/3 cup minced fresh parsley
1/4 cup white wine	1 teaspoon salt
1/4 cup dry vermouth	1/2 teaspoon Tabasco sauce
1 slice white bread, crust removed	1/2 teaspoon freshly grated nutmeg
1 1/2 cups heavy cream	Scallop Sauce (recipe follows)
1 pound scallops	

Preheat oven to 250 degrees. Wash and scrub the mussels. Place shallots and wine in a large sauté pan. Add mussels, cover, and steam until shells open. Remove the mussels from their shells and set aside. Reserve 1/4 cup of the mussel liquid. Add the vermouth to the remaining liquid and cook until almost all the liquid evaporates.

Soak the bread in some of the heavy cream until soft. Place in a food processor together with the cooked shallots and the raw scallops. Process for about 5 seconds. Add the rest of the heavy cream and process a few seconds more. Add the reserved mussel liquid, eggs, parsley, salt, Tabasco, and nutmeg. Process 10 seconds.

Butter a large ring mold or smaller individual molds. Spoon half of the mousse mixture into the prepared molds. Tap mold lightly to remove any air bubbles. Arrange reserved mussels over the mousse. Cover with remaining mousse mixture and smooth top. Tap gently. Cover with a buttered piece of parchment. Bake for 15 minutes. Turn the heat down to 225 degrees and bake an additional 35 minutes. Remove from oven and let stand for 5 minutes. Unmold and serve with Scallop Sauce.

SCALLOP SAUCE

2 large shallots, chopped	1 teaspoon warm water
2 tablespoons butter	1/4 teaspoon dry mustard
2 tablespoons water	1/2 teaspoon salt
1/2 pound scallops, sliced	Pinch of white pepper
2 tablespoons vermouth	5 ounces (1 1/4 sticks) butter
1 large egg yolk	1/4 cup chopped fresh parsley

Cook the shallots in the 2 tablespoons of butter and 2 tablespoons of water until soft. Add the scallops and vermouth to the shallots and cook until the scallops turn opaque.

Whisk the egg yolk together with the teaspoon of warm water, dry mustard, salt, and pepper until thick. Heat the remaining butter until bubbling and add to the egg mixture slowly, whisking vigorously until the sauce thickens. Combine with the shallot and scallop mixture and heat gently. Stir in the parsley just before serving.

SCALLOPS WITH A RED PEPPER PURÉE

SERVES 6
PREPARATION TIME 10 MINUTES
COOKING TIME 1 HOUR 10 MINUTES

The Red Pepper Purée can be made ahead and refrigerated or frozen. Garnish with slivers of red peppers.

SCALLOPS

2 tablespoons butter
2 1/2 pounds tiny scallops
Salt
Pepper
1 cup dry white wine

1/3 cup dry sherry
1 cup heavy cream
Red Pepper Purée (recipe
   follows)

Melt butter in a large skillet. Add scallops and sauté over high heat until opaque, approximately 3 to 5 minutes. Add salt and pepper to taste. Using a slotted spoon, transfer to a bowl and keep warm. Add the wine and sherry to the liquid remaining in the skillet. Boil, stirring frequently, until reduced to the consistency of a thick syrup. Whisk in the heavy cream. Continue cooking until thickened to a saucelike consistency. Stir in Red Pepper Purée, mixing well. Add the scallops and heat gently. Taste and correct for seasonings. Serve immediately.

RED PEPPER PURÉE

2 tablespoons butter
1 pound red bell peppers,
   seeded, and cut into pieces
1 tablespoon sugar

1 tablespoon vinegar
1/2 teaspoon Hungarian sweet
   paprika

Melt the butter in a saucepan. Stir in the peppers, sugar, vinegar, and paprika. Cover and cook slowly until peppers are soft, approximately 45 minutes. Uncover pan, increase heat, and stir until all liquid evaporates. Purée peppers through a food mill or process in a food processor and then strain to remove the skins.

TROPICAL SCALLOPS

SERVES 4
PREPARATION TIME 5 MINUTES
COOKING TIME 20 MINUTES

Serve in puff pastry shells or over rice.

5 tablespoons butter
1/2 cup finely chopped onion
1 teaspoon curry powder
1/4 cup sherry
1 cup heavy cream
2 teaspoons chili sauce
2 teaspoons mango chutney

Salt
1 pound small scallops
Flour for dredging
1 banana
Chopped pistachio nuts
Sliced pimento

Melt 2 tablespoons of the butter in a small skillet. Add the onion and cook until soft. Stir in the curry powder. Add the sherry and bring to a boil. Reduce to a tablespoon. Stir in cream, chili sauce, chutney, and salt to taste. Reduce sauce until thickened.

Wash and dry scallops. If using large scallops, cut into quarters. Dredge lightly with a little flour. Sauté in 2 tablespoons of the butter until the scallops turn opaque. Remove from the pan with a slotted spoon and add to the sauce.

Peel and slice the banana. Coat the slices in flour. Brown in the remaining tablespoon of butter. Fold into the scallop mixture. Reheat gently. Serve over rice or in pastry shells garnished with the chopped pistachio nuts and pimento slices.

SHRIMP À LA FRANÇAISE

SERVES 6 TO 8
PREPARATION TIME 10 MINUTES
COOKING TIME 10 MINUTES

Be sure to serve this dish with crusty French bread to dip into the extra sauce. It tastes so good you won't want to waste it.

3 pounds large shrimp, peeled and deveined
¹/₃ cup olive oil
6 garlic cloves
3/4 cup dry white wine
2 tablespoons fresh lemon juice
6 ounces (1 ¹/₂ sticks) unsalted butter, cut into pieces

2 tablespoons chopped fresh parsley
1 tablespoon snipped fresh chives
2 teaspoons chopped fresh tarragon
Freshly ground pepper
Salt

Pat shrimp dry. Heat oil in large skillet. Add shrimp and sauté until they turn pink, about 3 minutes. Remove from the pan with a slotted spoon and drain on paper towels.

Blanch the garlic in boiling water for 2 minutes. Drain and mince. Remove all but 1 tablespoon of oil from the pan. Place over a medium heat and add the garlic. Cook for 30 seconds. Pour in the wine, increase the heat, and reduce the mixture by half. Add the lemon juice and return to a boil. Remove from the heat. Whisk in the butter, a piece at a time, until thick and creamy. Stir in parsley, chives, and tarragon. Season with pepper. Taste and season with salt and additional lemon juice, if necessary. Arrange shrimp on individual plates. Spoon the sauce over the top and serve immediately.

CAJUN SHRIMP

SERVES 4
PREPARATION TIME 20 MINUTES
REFRIGERATION TIME 2 HOURS
COOKING TIME 20 MINUTES

2 pounds large shrimp
4 ounces (1 stick) butter
1/2 cup olive oil
1/2 cup chili sauce
1 lemon, sliced
2 cloves garlic, chopped
2 tablespoons lemon juice
1 1/2 tablespoons
 Worcestershire sauce

1 1/2 tablespoons liquid smoke
1/2 tablespoon fresh chopped
 parsley
1 teaspoon paprika
1 teaspoon oregano
1 teaspoon red pepper
1/2 teaspoon Tabasco sauce
Salt
Freshly ground pepper

Wash the shrimp. Shell and devein, leaving tail intact. Spread out in a shallow pan. Combine the remaining ingredients in a saucepan. Heat over a low heat until warm. Pour over the shrimp. Refrigerate for several hours, basting and turning every 30 minutes.

Preheat the oven to 300 degrees. Bake in the pan for 20 minutes. Turn the shrimp after 10 minutes of baking. Serve in soup bowls with French bread to dip in the sauce.

SHRIMP À LA CREOLE

SERVES 6
PREPARATION TIME 15 MINUTES
COOKING TIME 40 MINUTES

CREOLE SAUCE
4 tablespoons butter
1 cup chopped green pepper
1 cup chopped onion
1/2 cup chopped celery
3 cups chopped tomatoes,
 peeled and seeded, or a
 28-ounce can, undrained
1/2 teaspoon dry thyme
2 bay leaves

4 cloves minced garlic
2 tablespoons minced parsley
1 teaspoon paprika
1/4 teaspoon salt
1/8 to 1/4 teaspoon cayenne
1 tablespoon tomato paste
1 tablespoon cornstarch
2 tablespoons cold water

Melt the butter in a saucepan and sauté the green pepper and onion until soft. Add all the remaining ingredients for the sauce, except the cornstarch and water. Simmer for 20 minutes. Adjust salt and cayenne to taste. Mix the cornstarch and water and blend into the sauce. Cook for a few more minutes to thicken.

SHRIMP

2 pounds shrimp, peeled and deveined	Cayenne
Salt	**6 tablespoons butter**

Sprinkle the shrimp with salt and cayenne. Heat the butter and sauté the shrimp until slightly cooked, 3 to 4 minutes. With a slotted spoon, transfer the shrimp to Creole Sauce. Simmer together for 10 minutes.

SHRIMP À LA MOUTARDE

SERVES 4
PREPARATION TIME 20 MINUTES
COOKING TIME 10 MINUTES

5 tablespoons butter	**2 tablespoons chopped parsley**
2 tablespoons flour	**1/4 cup dry white wine**
1 cup warm milk	**2 tablespoons Dijon mustard**
Grating of fresh nutmeg	**1 egg yolk**
Pinch of cayenne	**1 pound shrimp, shelled and**
Salt	**deveined**
Freshly ground black pepper	**2 tablespoons freshly grated**
2 tablespoons chopped shallots	**Parmesan cheese**

Preheat the oven to 450 degrees. Melt 2 tablespoons of the butter in a saucepan. Stir in the flour and cook for 2 minutes without browning. Whisk in the warm milk slowly until blended and thickened. Stir in nutmeg, cayenne, salt, and pepper. Cook an additional 2 minutes, stirring constantly.

Melt another tablespoon of the butter in another pan and sauté the shallots for 1 minute. Add the parsley and white wine. Cook until almost all of the wine evaporates. Add to the sauce and cook for an additional 5 minutes. Remove from the heat and stir in 1 1/2 tablespoons of the mustard and the egg yolk.

Melt the remaining 2 tablespoons of butter in a skillet. Add the shrimp and cook until pink, about 3 to 4 minutes. Remove from the heat and stir in the remaining mustard and 1/3 of the sauce.

Divide the shrimp among 4 ramekins. Spoon the sauce over each and sprinkle with the cheese. Bake for 5 minutes, or until bubbly. Let rest for 5 minutes before serving.

SHARK AMANDINE

SERVES 4
PREPARATION TIME 15 MINUTES
COOKING TIME 15 MINUTES

Swordfish or mahi-mahi may be substituted if shark is unavailable.

1/2 **cup slivered almonds**	**4 shark fillets**
2 **tablespoons butter**	**4 tablespoons sherry**
2 **tablespoons chopped parsley**	**Freshly ground pepper**
6 **tablespoons melted butter**	1/2 **pound bacon, fried and**
1 **tablespoon grated lemon rind**	**crumbled**
2 **tablespoons freshly squeezed**	**4 green onions, chopped**
lemon juice	**Lemon wedges**

Lightly brown the almonds in the butter and set aside. Combine the parsley, butter, lemon rind, and juice. Rub both sides of the fillets with the sherry and place on a broiler pan. Sprinkle with pepper. Spoon some of the butter mixture over each fillet.

Broil for 5 to 10 minutes, depending on the thickness of the fillets. Turn over, spoon on more butter sauce and continue broiling until done. Do not overcook or the fish will be dry.

Remove to a serving platter. Sprinkle with the almonds, bacon, and green onions. Garnish with lemon wedges.

RED SNAPPER OLÉ

SERVES 6
PREPARATION TIME 10 MINUTES
COOKING TIME 10 MINUTES

Be sure to use a mild green chili salsa so as not to overpower the taste of the fish.

6 red snapper fillets
1/2 cup flour seasoned with salt
   and pepper
4 tablespoons butter
6 ounces mild green chili salsa

6 ounces Jack cheese, grated
6 ounces sharp Cheddar
   cheese, grated
3 tablespoons chopped fresh
   parsley

Preheat the oven to 350 degrees. Coat the fish with the flour. Melt the butter in a skillet. Lightly sauté the fillets. Transfer to a shallow baking dish. Cover with the salsa. Sprinkle with the cheeses. Bake approximately 8 to 10 minutes, or until cheeses have melted. Remove from oven. Sprinkle the parsley over the melted cheese and serve immediately.

MUSTARD SHALLOT SNAPPER

SERVES 6
PREPARATION TIME 10 MINUTES
COOKING TIME 6 MINUTES

6 red snapper fillets
4 ounces (1 stick) butter
4 tablespoons Meaux (whole
   seed) mustard
2 tablespoons finely chopped
   shallots

1 tablespoon lemon juice
1 teaspoon paprika
Pinch of cayenne
Salt

Preheat the broiler. Place fillets on greased broiler pan. Melt the butter in a small saucepan. Add the mustard, shallots, lemon juice, paprika, cayenne, and salt to taste. Mix until well blended and creamy. Spoon the sauce evenly over the fillets. Broil for 5 to 6 minutes or until fillets are firm and the top is nicely browned.

BLACKENED RED SNAPPER

SERVES 8
PREPARATION TIME 5 MINUTES
COOKING TIME 5 MINUTES

This is not a dish for timid palates. You should also have a powerful fan over your stove or your house will be filled with smoke.

4 teaspoons salt
6 teaspoons paprika
2 teaspoons cayenne pepper
1 1/2 teaspoons white pepper
3/4 teaspoon black pepper
3/4 teaspoon dried thyme

1/2 teaspoon dried oregano
8 skinless snapper fillets, each
   weighing 8 to 10 ounces
8 ounces (2 sticks) melted
   butter
8 lemon wedges

Combine all of the spices. Have the fish very cold. Dip both sides of the fish in the spice mixture and rub over fillets to cover well.

Heat a *heavy* skillet over a high heat until extremely hot. Have the kitchen fan running on high speed. Dip the fish into the melted butter and place directly into the hot skillet. Drizzle with an additional teaspoon of butter. Cook for 2 minutes and turn. Drizzle with more butter and cook an additional minute. Serve with the lemon wedges.

SNAPPER WITH WALNUT MAYONNAISE

SERVES 4
PREPARATION TIME 10 MINUTES
COOKING TIME 20 MINUTES

2 egg yolks
2 tablespoons white wine
   vinegar
1 tablespoon lemon juice
2 cloves crushed garlic
1/2 teaspoon salt
1/2 cup olive oil
1/4 cup vegetable oil

1/4 cup walnut oil
1/2 cup ground walnuts
1/2 cup chopped fresh parsley
4 red snapper fillets, 8 ounces
   each
Oil for brushing
Salt
Lemon wedges

In a food processor or blender, blend egg yolks, vinegar, lemon juice, garlic, and salt until smooth. With machine running, gradually add the oils in a steady stream. Transfer to a bowl and stir in the walnuts and parsley.

Preheat the broiler. Brush the fillets on both sides with a little oil. Broil for about 5 minutes per side, or until fish separates easily with a fork. Remove from heat and salt lightly.

Transfer to a plate and spoon some of the sauce over each fillet. Garnish with the lemon wedges and pass the remaining sauce. Serve immediately.

STUFFED PETRALE SOLE EN CROÛTE

SERVES 8
PREPARATION TIME 45 MINUTES
COOKING TIME 35 MINUTES

4 petrale sole fillets, 8 ounces each

1 pound puff pastry

3 tablespoons butter

1/2 pound fresh mushrooms, finely chopped

2 tablespoons chopped shallots

1 teaspoon chopped fresh tarragon

1 teaspoon chopped fresh parsley

1/2 teaspoon salt

1/2 teaspoon freshly ground pepper

1 beaten egg white

Choron Sauce†

Pat fish fillets dry with paper towels. Divide the pastry into 2 halves and roll out as thin as possible. Place 1 fillet on top of each pastry sheet. Transfer to a baking tray and refrigerate while making the filling.

Preheat the oven to 425 degrees. Melt the butter in a skillet. Sauté the mushrooms over high heat for 2 minutes, stirring constantly. Add the shallots, tarragon, and parsley and cook for an additional minute. Salt and pepper to taste. Let cool slightly.

Spread herb filling equally over the two fillets. Place the remaining fillets over the fillings, in effect, making a sandwich. Bring pastry up over the fish fillets. Seal around the edges and cut off and discard any excess pastry. Refrigerate for 30 minutes before baking.

Brush the top with the egg white, being careful not to let any drip onto the baking tray. Make several diagonal slits across the top to let out the steam. Bake for 15 to 20 minutes. Turn the heat down to 375 degrees and continue baking until crust is golden brown. Transfer to a serving platter. Slice and serve with Choron Sauce.

SAUTÉED SOLE WITH CHARDONNAY SAUCE

SERVES 4
PREPARATION TIME 10 MINUTES
COOKING TIME 15 TO 20 MINUTES

This lovely dish deserves a good bottle of California Chardonnay.

1 1/2 pounds sole fillets
1/2 cup flour
4 to 6 tablespoons butter
1 cup Chardonnay wine
2 tablespoons chopped shallots
1 clove finely chopped garlic

1/4 cup heavy cream
1/2 teaspoon sugar
1/8 teaspoon salt
Pinch of cayenne
3 to 4 tablespoons butter

Dredge the fish fillets in flour and shake off the excess. Sauté lightly in the butter. Transfer to a plate and keep warm.

Deglaze the skillet with the Chardonnay. Add the shallots and garlic and cook until reduced by half. Add the cream, sugar, salt, and cayenne. Simmer the sauce over low heat, stirring often, until thickened. Whisk in the remaining butter, one tablespoon at a time. Spoon sauce over fish and serve immediately.

POISSON AVEC ARTICHAUTS

SERVES 6
PREPARATION TIME 20 MINUTES
COOKING TIME 15 MINUTES

This dish works equally well with any firm-fleshed white fish. Tiny shrimp may also be substituted for the crab meat. Serve with steamed vegetables which will be enhanced by the sauce from the fish.

1/2 cup chopped green onions
4 cloves garlic
2 tablespoons olive oil
1 1/2 cups sliced artichoke
    hearts, fresh or frozen
1/3 cup dry white wine
2 cups heavy cream
3/4 pound crab meat

1/4 cup Dijon mustard
Dash of hot pepper sauce
6 sole fillets, 8 ounces each
Flour for coating
4 ounces (1 stick) butter
Paprika
Chopped fresh parsley

Sauté the onions and garlic in the olive oil for 2 to 3 minutes. Stir in the artichoke hearts and cook for an additional minute. Add the wine and cook until reduced to 2 tablespoons. Add the cream and cook until slightly thickened. Stir in the crab meat, mustard, and hot pepper sauce. Remove the cloves of garlic. Reduce the heat and simmer very gently while preparing the fish.

Lightly coat the fish with flour. Heat the butter in a skillet large enough to hold the fish in a single layer. Add the fish and cook about 3 to 4 minutes per side or until just opaque. Transfer to warmed plates. Spoon the sauce over the fillets, covering the entire surface. Sprinkle with the paprika. Garnish with the parsley and serve immediately.

BAKED SOLE WITH CREAMY LEEK SAUCE

SERVES 4 TO 6
PREPARATION TIME 15 MINUTES
COOKING TIME 45 MINUTES

The leek sauce can be prepared several days in advance and refrigerated. Reheat gently before adding the fish.

3 1/2 cups sliced leeks	Salt
3 tablespoons butter	Freshly ground pepper
2 tablespoons flour	Freshly grated nutmeg
1 cup dry white wine	2 pounds sole fillets
1 cup heavy cream	4 tablespoons butter
2 tablespoons lemon juice	

Wash the leeks well. Slice into thin disks, using only the white part. Pat dry. Sauté in the butter for 5 minutes. Remove from pan with a slotted spoon and set aside. Whisk the flour into the pan, stirring constantly. Cook for 3 minutes, without browning. Whisk in wine, cream, and leeks, stirring until the sauce comes to a boil. Reduce heat and simmer, uncovered, for 10 minutes. Cover and simmer an additional 15 minutes, stirring occasionally. Season with the lemon juice, salt, pepper, and nutmeg.

Preheat oven to 350 degrees. Spoon half of the leeks into an ovenproof baking dish. Place the fillets on top of the leeks. Sprinkle with salt and pepper. Dot with butter. Cover with the remaining leeks. Place a piece of buttered parchment paper directly over the fish. Bake about 15 minutes or until opaque.

FILLET OF SOLE WITH TOMATO CREAM SAUCE

SERVES 4
PREPARATION TIME 15 MINUTES
COOKING TIME 35 MINUTES

This fish dish can be prepared earlier in the day and baked just before serving.

4 sole fillets, 8 ounces each
1/4 pound tiny cooked shrimp
1/3 cup finely chopped shallot
2 tablespoons butter
Salt
White pepper
1/3 cup dry white wine

2 large tomatoes, peeled,
  seeded, and chopped
1 cup heavy cream
2 egg yolks, lightly beaten
Fresh lemon juice
Chopped fresh parsley

Preheat oven to 350 degrees. Pat fillets dry. Place 1 ounce of shrimp in the center of each fillet. Roll up and place, seam side down, in an ovenproof baking dish. Set aside.

Sauté the shallot in the butter until soft. Season with salt and pepper. Add the wine and bring to a boil. Cook until the wine is reduced by half. Add the tomatoes and continue cooking, stirring occasionally, until thickened. Stir in the heavy cream and cook an additional 5 minutes. Whip a large spoonful of the hot sauce into the egg yolks. Whisk briskly and return to the rest of the sauce. Cook over a low heat until thickened but do not allow to boil.

Pour the sauce over the rolled fillets and bake for 20 to 25 minutes or until sole flakes easily with a fork. Sprinkle with the lemon juice and parsley. Serve immediately.

GRILLED SWORDFISH
WITH LIME BEURRE BLANC

SERVES 6
PREPARATION TIME 10 MINUTES
COOKING TIME 15 MINUTES

6 tablespoons white wine
  vinegar
1/4 cup minced shallots
2 tablespoons fresh lime juice
1/4 cup heavy cream

8 ounces (2 sticks) butter, cut
  into small pieces
Grated peel of 1 lime
6 swordfish steaks
Lime slices

Combine the vinegar, shallots and lime juice in a saucepan. Cook until reduced to 2 tablespoons. Add the heavy cream and continue cooking until again reduced to 2 tablespoons. Remove the pan from the heat. Whisk in a few pieces of the butter. Return the pan to the heat and whisk in the remaining butter, being careful not to overheat. The sauce should have the consistency of a light mayonnaise. Stir in the lime peel.

Brush the grate of the hot grill with a little oil. Cook the fish for 6 to 8 minutes per side, depending on thickness. Do not overcook. Transfer to a plate and let rest for a few minutes. Place a little of the lime sauce in the middle of each steak. Garnish with the lime slices and serve the additional sauce on the side.

SWORDFISH STEAKS WITH LEMON AND CAPERS

SERVES 6
PREPARATION TIME 10 MINUTES
COOKING TIME 10 MINUTES

3 medium lemons	Flour
6 swordfish steaks, 8 ounces each	4 tablespoons oil
Salt	8 tablespoons butter
White pepper	1/4 cup drained capers
Milk for dipping	Chopped fresh parsley

Peel the lemons, removing all of the white part. Cut out the membrane from between the lemon sections and remove the segments. Cut the segments into tiny pieces and set aside until needed.

Season the steaks with salt and pepper. Dip in milk. Coat with the flour. Heat the oil and 4 tablespoons of the butter in a skillet large enough to hold the fish in a single layer. Add the steaks and sauté until lightly browned on both sides. Continue cooking over low heat until fish turns opaque. Remove from the pan and keep warm.

Pour off any oil remaining in the skillet. Add the remaining butter and cook until lightly browned. Stir in the lemon pieces and capers. Spoon the sauce over the steaks and sprinkle with the parsley.

SWORDFISH WITH CREAMY MUSTARD SAUCE

SERVES 4
PREPARATION TIME 10 MINUTES
COOKING TIME 16 MINUTES

Pommery mustard is a very thick, grainy specialty food. Since 1632, French kings have enjoyed this exquisite "mustard for gourmets," so-called by the honored gastronome Brillat-Savarin. It adds complexity to this creamy sauce.

1 tablespoon chopped shallots	Salt
3 tablespoons white wine	Pepper
1 cup heavy cream	4 swordfish steaks
1/2 teaspoon Dijon mustard	Oil
1 tablespoon Pommery or Meaux mustard	

Combine the shallots and wine in a pan. Bring to a boil. Reduce heat and simmer until wine evaporates. Add the heavy cream and cook until reduced to 1/3 of a cup. Add the mustards, salt and pepper to taste.

Preheat the broiler. Place fillets on a broiling pan and rub with oil. Broil for 4 to 8 minutes per side, depending upon the thickness of the steaks. Remove to warmed plates and spoon a little of the sauce over each steak.

SAUTÉED SQUID STEAKS

SERVES 6
PREPARATION TIME 25 MINUTES
COOKING TIME 10 MINUTES

6 squid steaks	4 tablespoons vegetable oil
Flour for dredging	Chopped fresh parsley
1 beaten egg	Lemon wedges
4 tablespoons butter	

Dredge the steaks in flour, shaking off the excess. Dip into the egg. Place on a rack and refrigerate for 20 minutes. Melt the butter and oil in a skillet. Add the steaks and sauté quickly, 2 to 3 minutes per side, over a fairly high heat. Do not overcook or the squid will become tough. Sprinkle with the parsley. Serve with the lemon wedges.

TROUT WITH SHRIMP AND CHIVE SAUCE

SERVES 4
PREPARATION TIME 10 MINUTES
COOKING TIME 30 MINUTES

TROUT

4 boned trout, 12 ounces each

Salt

Freshly ground pepper

1/3 cup flour

2 tablespoons butter

2 tablespoons oil

Rinse the fish and pat dry. Sprinkle inside and out with the salt and pepper. Dredge lightly in flour, shaking off the excess. Melt the butter and oil in a large skillet. Sauté the fish for 4 to 5 minutes on each side, or until done. If skin starts to brown too quickly, reduce the heat. Transfer to a heated platter and cover with foil.

SHRIMP AND CHIVE SAUCE

2 tablespoons butter

1/4 cup minced onions

1/4 cup dry white wine

1 tablespoon white wine
   vinegar

1 cup heavy cream

1/4 pound tiny cooked shrimp

3 tablespoons chopped fresh
   chives

Scrape up any brown bits from the bottom of the skillet. Discard together with the cooking oil. Wipe out the skillet with a paper towel. Add the butter and melt over a low heat. Sauté the onions until soft, about 5 minutes. Add the wine and vinegar. Increase the heat and boil until reduced to 1 tablespoon. Stir in the cream. Season with salt and pepper. Reduce until the sauce thickens and coats the back of a wooden spoon. Stir in the shrimp. Simmer over low heat until heated through. Remove from heat and stir in chives.

Discard the skin from the top of the trout. Transfer to a serving platter. Spoon the sauce over the top of each trout. Serve immediately.

BAKED TROUT

SERVES 6
PREPARATION TIME 10 MINUTES
COOKING TIME 15 MINUTES

6 whole trout
4 ounces (1 stick) butter, melted
2 tablespoons lemon juice
1 teaspoon Worcestershire sauce

1/4 cup finely chopped green onion
1 tablespoon chopped fresh parsley
Salt
Freshly ground pepper

Preheat the oven to 400 degrees. Fillet the trout. Place skin side down on a foil-lined baking sheet. Combine the remaining ingredients and sprinkle evenly over the fish. Cover loosely with foil and bake for 15 minutes or until it flakes.

MARINATED GRILLED TUNA

SERVES 8
PREPARATION TIME 5 MINUTES
REFRIGERATION TIME 1 HOUR
COOKING TIME 10 TO 15 MINUTES

Shark or swordfish may be substituted for the tuna in this dish.

1/2 cup soy sauce
1/2 cup dry sherry
1 tablespoon lemon juice

1/4 cup vegetable oil
1 clove crushed garlic
8 tuna fillets, 1/2 inch thick

Combine all of the ingredients, except the tuna. Pour into a shallow pan that will hold the fish in a single layer. Coat the fish on both sides with the marinade. Refrigerate and marinate for 1 to 2 hours. Do not let marinate for longer than 2 hours or the flavor of the marinade will be too strong.

Preheat a grill or broiler. Grill or broil fillets 5 to 6 minutes per side.

SEAFOOD FONDUE

SERVES 8
PREPARATION TIME 20 MINUTES
COOKING TIME 30 MINUTES

4 cups clam juice
2 cups dry white wine
1 cup water
1 large onion, chopped
1 large carrot, chopped
1 celery stalk, chopped
4 peppercorns

1 bay leaf
1 pound sole fillets
1 pound medium shrimp
12 large scallops
4 lobster tails (or monkfish pieces)
Lettuce leaves

Combine all the ingredients, except the fish and the lettuce leaves, in a saucepan. Simmer for 30 minutes. Strain into a fondue pot. Set aside until ready to serve.

Cut the sole into 2-inch pieces. Shell and devein the shrimp. Cut the scallops in half. Cut the lobster tail or monkfish into bite-size pieces. Place a bed of lettuce leaves on 8 individual plates. Arrange the fish pieces on the plates. Heat the broth in the fondue pot. Dip the fish pieces into the hot broth. Serve with fondue sauces.

EMERALD MAYONNAISE

MAKES 3 CUPS
PREPARATION TIME 10 MINUTES

Try this versatile dressing as a dip for vegetables or as a mayonnaise for poached fish or chicken.

1 egg
2 egg yolks
1 teaspoon vinegar
2 teaspoons Dijon mustard
1 to 2 cloves chopped garlic
3/4 cup vegetable oil
2 tablespoons minced green onion

2 tablespoons minced fresh parsley
1 cup cooked spinach leaves
Salt
Freshly ground pepper

In a food processor or blender, combine the whole egg, egg yolks, vinegar, mustard, and garlic. Process for 1 minute. With the machine running, slowly add the oil until mixture has thickened. Add the green onion and parsley. With your hands, squeeze as much water as possible from the spinach. Add to the other ingredients. Process until smooth. Season to taste with salt and pepper. Chill.

POULTRY

Valley of the Moon

Valley of the Moon, also known as Sonoma Valley, derives its name from the word "Sonoma," which means "Vale of Many Moons" in the Suisun Indian language. This valley, which lies at the western edge of the Mayacamas Mountains, has its southern border at the town of Sonoma. Scenic Highway 12 runs through the length of the valley and is a popular ride for bicyclists, who can stop and quench their thirst with a wine-tasting tour at one of the valley's scenic wineries. The famous writer of adventure stories Jack London was a resident of the quaint village of Glen Ellen, whose houses are little changed since his time. Jack London romanticized Sonoma in his novel, *The Valley of the Moon.*

The valley is also renowned for its hot springs, featuring picturesque names such as Boyes Hot Springs, Kenwood, Agua Caliente, and Fetters Hot Springs. Even the original Spanish land grant notes the geological phenomena of this valley, for the grant was entitled "Rancho Agua Caliente," which means "Hot Water Ranch."

Valley of the Moon is a sub-section of the wine-grape region known as Sonoma Valley, which extends north to Santa Rosa, south to the town of Sonoma, and west to Petaluma. Petaluma, famous for its production of poultry, is located on the Petaluma River, navigable by boat from San Francisco Bay. It is a graceful old town, renowned for its "iron front" Victorians, which were made in San Francisco. The iron fronts were usually manufactured in foundaries out of cast iron or sheet iron, then shipped in small sections and used only for the street side of a building. Few of these historic buildings survived the famous San Francisco earthquake of 1906, and as a result, Petaluma probably has the greatest number of "iron front" Victorians anywhere. Petaluma is also the site of General Vallejo's historic Petaluma Adobe, a 1,000-acre vineyard.

The savory recipes that follow, such as Chicken Petaluma and Marinated Turkey Breasts, bring to mind exciting adventures of Jack London and vignettes of California history for which this region is renowned.

CHICKEN PETALUMA

SERVES 3 TO 4
PREPARATION TIME 10 MINUTES
COOKING TIME 20 MINUTES

2 whole chicken breasts, split,
 skinned, and boned
Salt
Freshly ground pepper
Flour
4 tablespoons butter
1/2 cup white wine
3/4 cup heavy cream or Crème
 Fraîche†

1 10-ounce package frozen
 artichoke hearts, thawed and
 drained
1 cup pitted black olives,
 halved
Lemon wedges

Pound the breasts between sheets of wax paper to a 1/4-inch thickness. Slice each breast into 3 pieces. Sprinkle with salt and pepper. Coat lightly with flour. Sauté the chicken in the butter over medium-high heat, turning once, until golden brown. Remove to heated platter and keep warm.

Pour off the butter remaining in the skillet. Add the wine and bring to a boil. Cook for a few minutes and add the cream. Simmer over moderate heat until the sauce thickens. Stir in the artichokes and olives.

Place 3 chicken slices on each plate. Spoon some of the sauce over each fillet. Garnish with the lemon wedges to squeeze over each serving.

CHICKEN PARMIGIANA

SERVES 6
PREPARATION TIME 10 MINUTES
COOKING TIME 45 minutes

6 split chicken breasts, skinned
 and boned
2 eggs, lightly beaten
1/4 teaspoon salt
1/8 teaspoon pepper
1/2 cup dry plain bread crumbs
1 cup Parmesan cheese

1/4 to 1/2 cup vegetable oil
1 clove garlic, minced
2 cups tomato sauce
1/4 teaspoon dried basil
1 tablespoon butter
8 ounces mozzarella cheese,
 sliced

Preheat the oven to 325 degrees. Pound the chicken breasts to a thickness of 1/4 inch. Combine the eggs, salt, and pepper. Mix the bread crumbs with 1/2 cup of the Parmesan cheese. Dip the chicken into the eggs and then into the bread crumbs. Heat the oil in a heavy skillet. Quickly brown the chicken on both sides. Remove to a shallow baking dish.

Pour off any oil remaining in the pan. Add the garlic and sauté briefly. Stir in the tomato sauce, basil, salt and pepper to taste. Bring to a boil, reduce heat, and simmer for 10 minutes. Stir in the butter. Spoon the sauce over the chicken. Sprinkle with the remaining Parmesan cheese. Cover and bake for 30 minutes. Uncover and arrange the mozzarella slices over the chicken. Return to the oven and continue baking until the cheese melts.

MUSTARD CHICKEN IN PHYLLO

SERVES 6 TO 8
PREPARATION TIME 1 HOUR
COOKING TIME 15 MINUTES

Thick slices of spicy chicken under a blanket of flaky phyllo create an elegant main course.

4 tablespoons butter
3 whole chicken breasts, skinned, boned, and cut into pieces
Salt
Freshly ground pepper
1/2 cup Dijon mustard

2 cups heavy cream
6 phyllo pastry sheets
4 ounces (1 stick) unsalted butter, melted
1/4 cup toasted bread crumbs
1 egg yolk mixed with 1 tablespoon water

Preheat oven to 425 degrees. Melt the butter in a large skillet. Sprinkle chicken with salt and pepper. Sauté chicken pieces until no longer pink, about 4 to 5 minutes. Do not overcook. Transfer to a platter.

Pour off the butter remaining in the pan. Add the mustard, scraping up any brown bits remaining on the bottom of the pan. Whisk in the heavy cream and bring to a boil. Reduce heat and simmer until reduced to about one cup. Pass sauce through a strainer. Add to the chicken pieces and toss to coat completely.

Lay 1 sheet of phyllo on a baking tray. Brush with a little of the butter and sprinkle with some of the bread crumbs. Repeat with 4 more sheets of phyllo. Place the last sheet of phyllo on top. Place the chicken on the bottom of the long side of dough, leaving a slight edge. Turn up the bottom edge and fold in the sides. Roll up jelly-roll fashion. Have seam side down on the baking sheet.

Brush the dough with the egg wash. Bake until crisp and golden brown, about 15 minutes. Cut into 2-inch slices and serve immediately.

CHICKEN COUNTRY CAPTAIN

SERVES 4 TO 6
PREPARATION TIME 10 MINUTES
COOKING TIME 45 MINUTES

A simple adaptation of a traditional American specialty.

3 whole chicken breasts, split and boned
1/4 cup flour
1 teaspoon salt
1/4 teaspoon freshly ground pepper
4 tablespoons butter
1/2 cup diced onion
1/2 cup diced green pepper

1 clove garlic, crushed
1 1/2 teaspoon curry powder
1/2 teaspoon thyme
1 pound canned stewed tomatoes
3 tablespoons raisins
Toasted almonds
Chutney
Coconut

Dredge the chicken breasts in the flour seasoned with salt and pepper. Heat the butter in a skillet and brown the chicken. Remove the chicken from the skillet and add the onion, green pepper, garlic, curry powder, and thyme. Cook briefly, stirring constantly. Add the canned tomatoes with their liquid. Cut the chicken into strips and return to the skillet. Cover and simmer for 30 minutes.

Just before serving, stir the raisins into the sauce. Serve over white rice with the toasted almonds, chutney, and coconut.

BRANDIED CHICKEN BREASTS

SERVES 6
PREPARATION TIME 10 MINUTES
COOKING TIME 30 MINUTES

6 split chicken breasts, boned and skinned
1/4 cup brandy
Salt
White pepper
Marjoram
6 tablespoons butter

1/2 cup sherry
3 egg yolks, beaten
1 cup heavy cream
Freshly ground pepper
Fresh nutmeg
1 cup grated Swiss cheese
1/3 cup buttered bread crumbs

Rub the chicken breasts with the brandy. Let stand for 15 minutes. Remove from the marinade and sprinkle with salt, pepper, and marjoram.

Melt the butter in a skillet. Sauté the chicken breasts over medium heat for 5 to 6 minutes on each side. Remove to an ovenproof dish and keep warm. To the butter remaining in the pan, add the sherry and the brandy from the chicken marinade and cook until reduced by half. Beat the egg yolks with the heavy cream. Gradually whisk into the pan, stirring constantly, until the sauce thickens. Season to taste with salt, pepper, and a few grindings of fresh nutmeg.

Preheat the broiler. Spoon the sauce over the chicken breasts. Mix the Swiss cheese and bread crumbs together. Sprinkle over the sauce. Place under the broiler just long enough to melt the cheese.

CHICKEN BREASTS IN
GREEN PEPPERCORN SAUCE

SERVES 4
PREPARATION TIME 15 MINUTES
COOKING TIME 15 MINUTES

The chefs of nouvelle cuisine *have renewed our interest in various peppercorns. Pink and green peppercorns are usually available packed in water or vinegar; white and black will be found dried. The flavor of the chicken and green peppercorns creates an ideal marriage of coloring and taste.*

4 large split chicken breasts, skinned and boned
4 tablespoons butter
3 tablespoons minced onion
1/3 cup dry white wine
1/2 cup heavy cream
2 teaspoons green peppercorns, drained and chopped

1 teaspoon whole peppercorns, drained
1 teaspoon fresh tarragon, or 1/4 teaspoon dried
Salt

Pound and flatten the chicken breasts. Sauté in the butter until nicely browned on both sides. Transfer to a heated platter and keep warm.

Add the onion to the skillet and sauté until soft. Add the wine and bring to a boil. Reduce to 2 tablespoons, scraping up any bits on the bottom of the pan. Stir in the heavy cream, peppercorns, and tarragon. Continue cooking until reduced and thickened. Remove from heat and correct seasonings. Spoon the sauce over the chicken breasts and serve immediately.

CHICKEN WELLINGTON

SERVES 4
PREPARATION TIME 1 HOUR
COOKING TIME 30 MINUTES

With the addition of cheese, this is a jaunty departure from the stately beef Wellington. Substituting chicken for the tenderloin en croûte *makes this decorative dish affordable, less tricky—but just as impressive.*

2 cups chicken stock	4 slices ham
1/2 cup dry white wine	4 slices Gruyère cheese
4 split chicken breasts, boneless and skinned	Salt
	Freshly ground pepper
1 sheet frozen puff pastry	4 thin slices truffle pâté

Heat stock and wine to boiling. Add the chicken breasts and simmer, covered, until tender. Remove the chicken and cool.

Divide the sheet of puff pastry into 4 pieces. Roll out on a floured board until large enough to wrap each chicken breast. In the center of each rolled-out square, place a piece of ham. Slice a piece of cheese in half and lay it over the ham. Place the chicken breast on top of the cheese. Season with salt and pepper. Cover the breast with the second half of the cheese. Place a slice of the pâté on top. Brush the edges of the dough with water. Fold each side over and wrap like an envelope. Place seam side down on a baking tray. Refrigerate for at least 15 minutes.

Preheat the oven to 400 degrees. Bake for approximately 30 minutes or until nicely browned and puffed.

CHICKEN WITH TARRAGON

SERVES 4
PREPARATION TIME 5 MINUTES
COOKING TIME 25 MINUTES

4 split chicken breasts, boned and skinned	1 cup chicken stock
2 tablespoons butter	1 teaspoon dried tarragon
1/4 cup chopped shallots	3/4 cup heavy cream

Sauté the chicken breasts in the butter until browned on both sides, about 5 minutes. Add the shallots, stock, and tarragon. Cover and simmer for 6 to 8 more minutes. Remove chicken from the pan and keep warm.

Boil the juices remaining in the pan until reduced to 1/2 cup. Add the heavy cream and again bring to a boil. Reduce to 3/4 cup or until thick enough to coat the chicken nicely. Return the chicken to the pan and coat both sides with the sauce. Serve immediately.

CHICKEN CACCIATORE

SERVES 6 TO 8
PREPARATION TIME 50 MINUTES
COOKING TIME 45 MINUTES

Since dried red chilies range in potency from mild to very hot, choose one to suit your taste. Regardless of your choice, these peppers will add a snappy flavor to this inimitable chicken stew. An old favorite you'll return to again and again.

4 whole chicken breasts, halved and boned
Flour
3 tablespoons oil
2 3-ounce jars marinated artichoke hearts
1 tablespoon olive oil
3 cloves garlic, minced
2 large onions, chopped
6 carrots, chopped
6 stalks celery, chopped
2 green bell peppers, chopped

1/2 pound fresh mushrooms, sliced
1 28-ounce can crushed plum tomatoes
1/2 teaspoon dried oregano
1 tablespoon dried basil
1/2 teaspoon salt
Freshly ground black pepper
2 dried red chilies
1 bay leaf
Freshly grated Parmesan cheese

Preheat the oven to 350 degrees. Dredge the chicken breasts in flour and shake off the excess. Heat the oil in a skillet and fry chicken until browned. Remove from the pan. Drain and reserve the marinade from the artichokes.

Heat the olive oil and artichoke marinade in a 4-quart Dutch oven. Sauté the garlic, onions, carrots, celery, bell peppers, and mushrooms until limp. Add the tomatoes, artichokes, oregano, basil, salt, pepper, chilies, and bay leaf. Bring to a simmer. Add the chicken to the casserole and spoon the sauce over the chicken. Cover the casserole and bake for 30 minutes. Remove the cover and bake an additional 15 minutes. Remove the red chilies and bay leaf. Sprinkle with freshly grated Parmesan cheese.

CRISPY STUFFED AND ROLLED CHICKEN BREASTS

SERVES 8 TO 10
PREPARATION TIME 15 MINUTES
REFRIGERATION TIME 30 MINUTES
COOKING TIME 1 HOUR

The beauty of this dish is that most of it can be prepared ahead of your guests' arrival.

8 large whole chicken breasts,
    skinned and boned
1/2 pound Black Forest ham (8
    to 16 slices)
8 green onions, tops only
1 cup milk
4 eggs
1 1/2 cups flour seasoned with 1
    tablespoon dried tarragon, 2
    teaspoons salt, 1 1/4
    teaspoons freshly ground
    pepper, 1 1/4 teaspoons
    paprika, 1/4 teaspoon garlic
    powder, and 1/4 teaspoon dry
    mustard

1 2/3 cups bread crumbs
6 to 8 tablespoons butter
4 cups chicken stock
3 1/2 cups heavy cream
Salt
Freshly ground pepper

Pound the whole chicken breasts between wax paper until 1/4-inch thick. Divide the ham into 8 portions and place on top of each breast. Arrange 2 pieces of green onion tops over the ham and about 3 inches apart. Be careful not to let any ham or onion hang over the sides of the chicken breasts. With the shortest side toward you, roll up jelly-roll fashion. Secure with a toothpick, if necessary.

Beat the milk and eggs together. Coat the chicken with the seasoned flour, shaking off the excess. Dip in the milk-egg mixture. Coat with the bread crumbs, patting in place. Arrange on a rack in a baking dish. Refrigerate at least 30 minutes or overnight.

Preheat oven to 350 degrees. Melt approximately 5 tablespoons of the butter in a large skillet (adding more as necessary). Sauté the chicken pieces over medium-high heat until all four sides are browned. Return chicken to rack and remove toothpicks. Bake for 20 to 25 minutes.

While the chicken is baking, boil the stock until reduced to 1/2 cup. In a separate saucepan, boil the heavy cream until reduced to 1 1/2 cups. Add the reduced stock to the reduced cream and continue cooking until thickened to a saucelike consistency. Add salt and pepper to taste.

Arrange a spoonful of the sauce over the bottom of the plate. Slice the chicken on the diagonal into 1/2-inch pieces. Place some of the chicken slices over the sauce. Serve immediately. Pass extra sauce.

POULET À L'ORANGE

SERVES 4 TO 6
PREPARATION TIME 10 MINUTES
COOKING TIME 1 HOUR

Pull a sprig of rosemary or thyme through the center of an orange slice for a fanciful presentation.

8 boneless chicken breast
  halves
1/3 cup flour
1 teaspoon salt
1 teaspoon garlic powder
1/2 teaspoon paprika
1/2 cup sliced almonds
5 tablespoons butter
1 6-ounce can frozen orange-
  juice concentrate

1 1/2 cups water
1 teaspoon dried rosemary,
  crumbled
1/4 teaspoon dried thyme,
  crumbled
1 to 1 1/2 tablespoons
  cornstarch

Preheat the oven to 350 degrees. Coat the chicken with a mixture of the flour, salt, garlic powder, and paprika. In a large pan, sauté the almonds in the butter until golden. Remove with a slotted spoon and drain on paper towels. Add the chicken breasts to the pan and brown. Transfer to a baking dish and arrange in a single layer.

Pour off any remaining fat in the pan. Add the orange-juice concentrate, water, rosemary, and thyme; bring to a boil, scraping up any bits remaining on the bottom of the pan. Pour over the chicken.

Cover and bake for 1 hour, or until the chicken is tender. Remove chicken from pan and keep warm. Pour sauce into a pan and bring to a boil. Mix the cornstarch with a tablespoon of the sauce. Whisk back into the pan and continue cooking until thick enough to coat a spoon. Arrange the chicken breasts on a platter. Mask with the sauce and sprinkle with the toasted almonds.

PRINCESS CHICKEN

SERVES 2
PREPARATION TIME 20 MINUTES
COOKING TIME 5 MINUTES

2/3 pound boneless chicken
breast
2 tablespoons soy sauce
2 tablespoons dry sherry or
white wine
3 tablespoons water
2 teaspoons cornstarch
2 tablespoons peanut oil

1 to 1 1/2 teaspoons dried
red pepper flakes
1 teaspoon sugar
1 teaspoon sesame oil
1 teaspoon rice wine vinegar
1 teaspoon water
1 teaspoon cornstarch

Lightly flatten chicken breasts. Cut into bite-size pieces. Mix 1 tablespoon of
the soy sauce, 1 tablespoon of the sherry, the 3 tablespoons of water and 2
teaspoons of cornstarch together. Toss over the chicken pieces and let marinate for 20 minutes.

Heat the peanut oil in a wok or skillet. Stir-fry the pepper flakes for 30
seconds. Add the chicken pieces and stir-fry until the chicken changes color.
Mix the remaining tablespoon of soy sauce, the remaining tablespoon of
sherry, the sugar, sesame oil, rice vinegar, and remaining water and cornstarch. Add to the chicken and stir-fry until all ingredients are mixed and the
sauce thickens. Remove to a serving platter and serve immediately.

STUFFED CURRIED CHICKEN BREASTS

SERVES 4
PREPARATION TIME 15 MINUTES
COOKING TIME 35 MINUTES

4 whole chicken breasts, boned
and skinned
3 tablespoons raisins
4 tablespoons butter
1/2 cup finely chopped onion
1/2 cup finely chopped celery
1 clove minced garlic
1 bay leaf

1 cup peeled, cored, and cubed
apple
3 tablespoons chopped chutney
Salt
Freshly ground pepper
1/2 cup heavy cream
1 tablespoon curry powder

Preheat oven to 425 degrees. Flatten the chicken breasts between sheets of wax paper. Soak the raisins in water until plump.

Heat 2 tablespoons of the butter in a skillet. Add the onion, celery, garlic, and bay leaf. Cook until soft, about 10 minutes. Stir in apple and cook for 1 minute. Drain the raisins and add to mixture together with the chutney. Stir and remove from heat. Let cool slightly. Remove the bay leaf.

Season the chicken breasts with salt and pepper. Divide the filling among the chicken breasts. Fold over and secure with a toothpick.

Sauté the breasts in the remaining 2 tablespoons of butter until lightly browned. Place in a shallow baking dish. Bake for 10 minutes. Blend the cream and curry powder. Pour over the chicken breasts. Bake for an additional 10 minutes.

SLICED CHICKEN WITH MUSHROOMS

SERVES 4
PREPARATION TIME 30 MINUTES
COOKING TIME 10 MINUTES

As with all chicken, do not overcook. For a dressy look, serve this easy-to-prepare dish in an oval copper skillet or shallow pan.

3/4 pound boneless chicken breast, sliced
1 egg white
Pinch of salt
Pinch of pepper
1 teaspoon cornstarch
1 tablespoon dry sherry
5 tablespoons oil
1/2 teaspoon salt

1/4 pound fresh mushrooms, sliced
2 celery stalks, sliced
10 water chestnuts, sliced
2 cloves garlic, minced
3 green onions, sliced
2 teaspoons soy sauce
1/2 teaspoon sugar

Lightly flatten the chicken breast and slice into pieces. Mix the egg white, salt, pepper, cornstarch, and sherry. Toss with the chicken pieces and let marinate for 10 minutes.

Heat 2 tablespoons of the oil and the salt in a wok or skillet. Sauté the mushrooms, celery, and water chestnuts for 2 minutes. Remove from the pan.

Heat the remaining 3 tablespoons of oil in the same pan. Stir-fry the garlic, green onions, and chicken for a few minutes over high heat. Add the soy sauce and sugar; toss. Add the cooked vegetables and stir-fry for 1 minute. Transfer to a platter. Serve immediately.

GRILLED HERBED CHICKEN

SERVES 8
PREPARATION TIME 15 MINUTES
MARINATING TIME 2 HOURS
COOKING TIME 15 TO 20 MINUTES

This chicken is perfect summer fare when your garden is full of fresh herbs.

8 large whole chicken breasts
1/2 cup olive oil
1/2 cup freshly squeezed
  lemon juice
1 teaspoon Dijon mustard
4 cloves crushed garlic

1/4 cup chopped fresh parsley
1 tablespoon each of chopped
  fresh rosemary, tarragon,
  sage, oregano, and chives
1/2 teaspoon salt
Freshly ground pepper

Split the chicken breasts and place in a marinating pan. Combine the remaining ingredients. Pour over the chicken and allow to marinate at least 2 hours.

Preheat the grill. Drain the chicken, reserving the marinade. Grill the breasts approximately 10 minutes each side, depending on the size of the breasts. Brush frequently with the marinade while cooking.

PECAN-CRUSTED CHICKEN BREASTS

SERVES 4 TO 6
PREPARATION TIME 15 MINUTES
COOKING TIME 30 MINUTES

The pecan crust adds a delectable texture to the delicate chicken without overpowering it. Because of this subtle taste, use the lively mustard sauce to moisten, not saturate, the chicken.

6 split chicken breasts, skinned
  and boned
Salt and pepper
4 ounces (1 stick) butter
3 tablespoons Dijon mustard
8 ounces finely chopped pecans
4 tablespoons butter

1 tablespoon vegetable oil
2/3 cup sour cream
1 tablespoon Dijon mustard
1/8 teaspoon salt
1/8 teaspoon freshly ground
  pepper
Whole pecans, toasted

Preheat oven to 350 degrees. Flatten the chicken breasts between two pieces of wax paper. Season lightly with salt and pepper. Melt the butter and whisk in the 3 tablespoons of mustard. Dip each piece of chicken into the butter-mustard mixture. Coat with the pecans.

Melt 3 tablespoons of the butter and the oil in a skillet over medium heat. Sauté half of the chicken breasts until lightly browned on both sides. Repeat with the remaining breasts. Transfer to a baking dish and bake for 15 to 20 minutes, depending on the size of the breasts.

Melt the remaining tablespoon of butter in a saucepan. Add the sour cream, the remaining tablespoon of mustard, the salt and pepper. Whisk together and remove from heat. Taste and correct seasonings.

Place a spoonful of the mustard sauce on a dinner plate. Cover it with the chicken breast. Garnish with the whole pecans.

MEXICAN CHICKEN KIEV

SERVES 8
PREPARATION TIME 1 HOUR
REFRIGERATION TIME 4 HOURS
COOKING TIME 30 MINUTES

8 split chicken breasts, boned and skinned
1 7-ounce can diced green chilies
8 slices Jack cheese, 1 ounce each
3/4 cup dry bread crumbs
1/3 cup Parmesan cheese

1 1/2 tablespoons chili powder
3/4 teaspoon salt
1/4 teaspoon cumin
1/4 teaspoon freshly ground pepper
6 tablespoons melted butter
Spicy Tomato Sauce†

Pound each breast to 1/4-inch thickness between wax paper. Put 2 tablespoons of chilies and 1 slice of cheese on each breast, leaving a slight edge. Roll up the breasts tightly and tuck in the ends. Secure with a toothpick, if necessary. Combine the bread crumbs, Parmesan cheese, chili powder, salt, cumin, and pepper. Roll the breasts in the butter and dip in the crumb mixture. Gently pat the crumbs into the breasts. Place in a baking dish and refrigerate at least 4 hours or overnight.

Preheat the oven to 400 degrees. Remove the toothpicks if used. Bake the breasts for 20 minutes. Place some of Tomato Sauce on the bottom of a dinner plate. Place the baked breast in the center. Sprinkle with chopped fresh parsley, if desired.

CHICKEN BREASTS WITH SPINACH-RICOTTA TOPPING

SERVES 6 TO 8
PREPARATION TIME 1 HOUR
COOKING TIME 35 MINUTES

SAUCE

4 tablespoons butter
4 tablespoons flour
1 to 1 1/2 cups warm chicken
   stock

3 tablespoons tomato paste
1/4 cup dry white wine

Melt the butter in a saucepan over a low heat. Stir in flour and cook without browning for 2 minutes. Gradually whisk in the warm stock. Continue cooking over low heat, stirring constantly. Whisk in the tomato paste and wine and boil for 1 minute. Reduce heat and simmer for 20 to 30 minutes. Keep warm over very low heat.

CHICKEN

1 tablespoon olive oil
1 clove garlic, crushed
6 ounces cooked fresh spinach,
   finely chopped
Salt
Freshly ground pepper
2/3 cup ricotta cheese

1/2 cup grated Parmesan cheese
8 split chicken breasts, skinned
   and boned
Flour for dredging
3 tablespoons butter
3 tablespoons olive oil
1 cup grated mozzarella cheese

Heat the olive oil and sauté the crushed garlic until brown. Remove garlic and discard. Add the cooked spinach and toss gently in the oil. Season with salt and pepper. With a slotted spoon, transfer to a bowl and let cool. Mix in the ricotta and Parmesan cheeses. Taste and adjust seasonings.

Preheat oven to 375 degrees. Flatten chicken breasts slightly. Sprinkle with a little salt and pepper. Coat lightly in flour, shaking off the excess. Heat the butter and oil in a heavy skillet. Brown the chicken breasts on both sides.

ASSEMBLY

Spoon a thin layer of sauce into a baking dish large enough to hold the chicken in a single layer. Arrange the breasts over the sauce. Spread some of the spinach topping over each breast. Cover with the remaining sauce. Sprinkle with the grated mozzarella cheese. Bake 10 minutes or until heated through.

Preheat the broiler. Place the dish under the broiler until the topping is golden brown, about 5 minutes. Serve immediately.

ENCHILADAS WITH TOMATILLO SAUCE

SERVES 6
PREPARATION TIME 30 MINUTES
COOKING TIME 45 MINUTES

Tomatillos are small, firm green tomatoes. Their notable acid flavor makes them ideal for sauces.

TOMATILLO SAUCE

6 tablespoons oil
2 medium onions, chopped
1 7-ounce can diced green
  chilies
2 13-ounce cans tomatillos,
  drained

1 cup chicken stock
3 tablespoons fresh lime juice
2 teaspoons dried oregano
2 teaspoons sugar
1 teaspoon ground cumin
1/2 teaspoon salt

Heat the oil in a saucepan. Add the onions and cook until soft, about 5 minutes. Stir in the remaining ingredients. Simmer 25 minutes over low heat. Taste and correct seasonings. Purée in food processor or blender until smooth.

ENCHILADAS

Oil for frying
12 corn tortillas
4 cups cooked shredded
  chicken
2 cups shredded Jack cheese
1 7-ounce can diced green
  chilies

1 1/2 teaspoons dried oregano
Salt
Freshly ground pepper
8 ounces shredded Jack cheese
2 cups finely shredded lettuce
1/2 cup sour cream
Lime slices

Preheat oven to 350 degrees. Heat 1/2 inch of oil in a frying pan. Fry the tortillas just until soft, about 5 seconds on each side. Lay flat and drain on paper towels.

Combine the chicken, Jack cheese, green chilies, oregano, and salt to taste. Spoon 1/2 cup of filling down the center of each tortilla. Cover with 2 tablespoons of Tomatillo Sauce. Roll up the tortilla to enclose.

Lay tortillas, seam side down, in a 10 × 15-inch baking pan. Bake, covered, approximately 15 minutes or until hot. Uncover and sprinkle with the remaining Jack cheese. Bake, uncovered, until cheese has melted.

To serve: Spoon 3/4 cup of Tomatillo Sauce onto dinner plates. Set 2 enchiladas on each plate. Top with some of the shredded lettuce and a dollop of sour cream. Garnish with the lime slices.

CAPER CHICKEN

SERVES 4 TO 6
PREPARATION TIME 10 MINUTES
COOKING TIME 45 MINUTES

Used by Egyptians, Greeks, and Romans, capers are one of the oldest known seasonings.

2 tablespoons butter
1 broiling chicken, cut up, or 6
  breasts
1 cup heavy cream
3 tablespoons capers

3 tablespoons caper juice
3/4 teaspoon dried oregano
1 bay leaf (optional)
Freshly ground pepper

Preheat oven to 350 degrees. Melt the butter in a large skillet. Add the chicken pieces and brown well on all sides. Transfer chicken pieces to a baking dish. Pour off any fat remaining in the skillet. Add the remaining ingredients to the pan. Bring to a boil, reduce heat, and simmer for 2 minutes, stirring occasionally. Remove the bay leaf.

Pour the sauce over the chicken. Bake for 45 minutes to an hour, depending on the size of the chicken pieces. Baste occasionally while baking. Transfer to a heated serving platter. Serve immediately.

CHEESE-STUFFED CHICKEN BREASTS

SERVES 4 TO 6
PREPARATION TIME 45 MINUTES
COOKING TIME 30 MINUTES

6 split chicken breasts, skinned
  and boned
3 teaspoons butter
6 tablespoons grated Fontina
  cheese
6 tablespoons grated
  Parmesan cheese
6 slices of prosciutto
6 teaspoons chopped
  fresh parsley

Dried ground sage
Flour for dredging
4 tablespoons butter
2 tablespoons oil
8 large mushrooms, thinly
  sliced
3/4 cup dry white wine

Flatten the chicken breasts to 1/2-inch thickness between sheets of wax paper. Spread the top of each breast with a ½ teaspoon softened butter. Sprinkle with 1 tablespoon each of Fontina and Parmesan cheese. Arrange a slice of prosciutto over the cheese. Sprinkle with 1 teaspoon parsley and a pinch of sage. Beginning at the short end, roll up each breast. Secure with a toothpick. Dust with flour.

Heat 2 tablespoons of the butter and the oil in a skillet large enough to hold the chicken breasts. Sauté the breasts over low heat for 10 to 15 minutes, or until nicely browned and cooked through. While the chicken is cooking, sauté the mushrooms in the remaining butter in another skillet.

When the breasts have cooked, pour off any remaining cooking fat. Add the sautéed mushrooms and the wine to the skillet containing the chicken. Bring to a boil and simmer for 10 minutes. Transfer the chicken to a heated serving platter. Remove the picks. Boil the sauce to reduce slightly. Spoon over the chicken and serve immediately.

POCKET CHICKEN BREASTS

SERVES 6 TO 8
PREPARATION TIME 15 MINUTES
COOKING TIME 12 MINUTES

This versatile dish is perfect fare for a summer party. Hot or cold, it can be served on a bed of spinach leaves or sliced crosswise and arranged on a platter.

8 slices bacon
2 tablespoons bacon drippings
1 large onion, finely chopped
1 10-ounce package frozen
   spinach, thawed and
   squeezed dry
1 egg, beaten
½ cup bread stuffing crumbs

¼ cup Parmesan cheese
1 tablespoon chopped pimentos
8 split chicken breasts, boned
   and skinned
Salt
Freshly ground pepper
3 to 4 tablespoons butter
2 tablespoons oil

Fry the bacon until crisp, and drain on paper towels. Crumble fine. Fry the onion in the bacon drippings until soft. Remove from the heat and stir in the spinach, egg, crumbs, cheese, pimentos, and crumbled bacon. Mix together well.

Cut a pocket in the thick side of each chicken breast, making it as large as possible. Stuff with the spinach mixture and close with a toothpick. Sprinkle with salt and pepper. In a large skillet, melt the butter and oil. Brown the breasts over medium heat for 12 to 15 minutes, turning frequently. Remove and drain on paper towels. Serve hot or cold.

CHICKEN IN ORANGE-GINGER SAUCE

SERVES 6
PREPARATION TIME 20 MINUTES
COOKING TIME 30 MINUTES

This easy-to-prepare and tasty dish is low in calories.

2 tablespoons vegetable oil
A 3-pound chicken, cut into
   pieces
1/2 cup chicken stock
1/2 cup orange juice
1 cup fresh tomato, peeled,
   seeded, and chopped

1 tablespoon finely sliced fresh
   ginger root
Salt
Freshly ground pepper
2 tablespoons chopped fresh
   cilantro

Heat the oil in a casserole and sauté the chicken until browned, about 15 minutes. Pour off all the cooking fat. Add the stock, orange juice, tomato, and ginger root to the pan. Season with the salt and pepper. Cover and simmer until the chicken is tender, about 15 to 20 minutes. Sprinkle with the cilantro. Serve with rice, if desired.

MINTED CHICKEN

SERVES 4
PREPARATION TIME 20 MINUTES
COOKING TIME 20 MINUTES

3 tablespoons butter
2 tablespoons oil
4 large split chicken breasts,
   boned and skinned
Flour for dredging
1 tablespoon butter
1/4 cup minced shallots
1 cup dry white wine
1 cup chicken stock
1/4 cup freshly squeezed orange
   juice

Grated zest of 2 oranges
1/2 cup chopped fresh mint
   leaves
1 cup heavy cream
Salt
White pepper
1 orange, peeled and thinly
   sliced
Fresh mint leaves

Heat butter and oil in a large skillet. Dredge the chicken breasts in flour, shaking off the excess. Sauté until nicely browned on both sides, about 6 minutes per side. Transfer to a platter and keep warm.

Pour off any fat remaining in the pan. Add 1 tablespoon butter and cook the shallots until soft. Stir in the wine and stock. Bring to a boil, scraping up any bits clinging to the bottom of the pan. Continue cooking until reduced to 1/2 cup. Add the remaining ingredients, except the sliced orange, and bring to a boil. Continue cooking over a high heat until reduced by half. Season to taste with salt and pepper. Arrange the chicken breasts on individual plates. Spoon some sauce over each breast. Garnish the plate with 2 slices of the orange and fresh mint leaves.

PAPAYA CHICKEN

SERVES 4
PREPARATION TIME 30 MINUTES
COOKING TIME 45 MINUTES

1/3 cup flour
3 tablespoons curry powder
Salt
Freshly ground pepper
A 3 1/2-pound chicken, cut into pieces
Oil
1 tablespoon cornstarch

2 1/2 cups papaya nectar
1/4 cup chopped crystallized ginger
2 tablespoons brown sugar
3 tablespoons lemon juice
2 papayas, peeled, seeded, and sliced

Preheat oven to 375 degrees. Combine the flour, curry powder, salt, and pepper. Coat chicken pieces in mixture. Brown the chicken pieces in a little oil over medium-high heat. Drain and arrange in a shallow baking dish large enough to hold the pieces in a single layer. Bake for 40 minutes or until tender.

While chicken is baking, pour off any oil remaining in the pan. Dissolve the cornstarch in 3 tablespoons of the nectar and set aside. Pour the remaining nectar into the skillet. Add the ginger and sugar. Simmer over moderate heat, stirring to scrape up any pieces on the bottom of the pan. Stir in the cornstarch mixture. Continue stirring and cook until thickened. Stir in the lemon juice.

Drain off any fat from the baked chicken. Arrange the papaya slices over the chicken pieces. Cover with the sauce. Return to the oven and cook for an additional 5 minutes, or until heated. Serve with steamed rice, if desired.

COQ AU VIN

SERVES 6
PREPARATION TIME 30 MINUTES
MARINATING TIME 12 HOURS
COOKING TIME 1 HOUR 15 MINUTES

A variation of an old favorite; the changes are worthwhile. Our version adds a bevy of carrots and other flavors to the pool of red wine sauce. For deeper flavor prepare a day ahead.

A 4-pound chicken, cut into
    pieces
3 1/4 cups red wine
1/2 cup dry white wine
3/4 cup brandy
1/2 cup olive oil
4 carrots, sliced
2 onions, peeled and quartered
4 cloves garlic
2 sprigs parsley
2 bay leaves
1/2 teaspoon dried thyme

9 tablespoons butter
5 tablespoons flour
Salt
Freshly ground pepper
1 cup chicken stock
2 ounces blanched diced
    salt pork
12 medium mushrooms,
    quartered
2 dozen small white onions,
    peeled and parboiled

In a large bowl, combine the chicken, 2 cups of the red wine, white wine, 1/2 cup of the brandy, olive oil, carrots, onions, garlic, parsley, bay leaves, and thyme. Mix well. Cover and marinate overnight at room temperature.

Remove the chicken and vegetables from the marinade. Discard the garlic and bay leaves and reserve the rest of the vegetables. Strain the marinade. Heat 4 tablespoons of the butter and sauté the chicken pieces until they begin to brown, about 10 minutes. Sprinkle with the flour, salt, and pepper. Add the remaining 1/4 cup brandy and cook until it evaporates. Add the marinade, chicken stock, and remaining red wine. In another pan, sauté the vegetables and herbs from the marinade in 1 tablespoon of the butter. Add to the chicken. Cover the pot and cook slowly until done, about 45 to 60 minutes.

Transfer the chicken pieces to a plate and keep warm. Strain the liquid from the chicken into a clean bowl. Melt 3 tablespoons of the butter in a saucepan. Add 3 tablespoons of flour and cook until slightly browned. Slowly add the strained liquid and cook until smooth and thickened. Sauté the salt pork, mushrooms, and onions in the remaining tablespoon of butter. Add to the sauce together with the chicken. Cover and cook until thoroughly heated.

KUNG PO CHICKEN

SERVES 4
PREPARATION TIME 20 MINUTES
MARINATING TIME 30 MINUTES
COOKING TIME 10 MINUTES

Hoisin, a type of bean sauce, is almost always sweet as well as a bit spicy. Often used as part of a marinade on grilled or roasted meats, it is an integral part of many sauces in a variety of Chinese dishes.

1/2 pound boneless chicken, cut into bite-size pieces
2 tablespoons soy sauce
1 teaspoon cornstarch
1/2 teaspoon sugar
1/2 teaspoon white pepper
2 to 3 tablespoons peanut oil
1 hot chili pepper, seeded and chopped
2 green onions, chopped
1 teaspoon minced fresh ginger root

1/2 cup diced bamboo shoots
1/2 cup sliced water chestnuts
1 tablespoon soy sauce
1 tablespoon rice wine
1 tablespoon sugar
1 tablespoon cornstarch
2 teaspoons hoisin sauce
1/4 teaspoon sesame oil
2 tablespoons roasted unsalted peanuts
Red pepper flakes (optional)

In a bowl, combine the chicken with the soy sauce, cornstarch, sugar, and pepper. Marinate for 30 minutes.

Heat the oil in a wok or heavy skillet. Add the chicken and stir-fry until it turns white. Remove the chicken with a slotted spoon. Add the chili pepper, green onions, and ginger. Stir-fry for 30 seconds. Add the bamboo shoots and water chestnuts. Stir-fry for 30 seconds. Combine the soy sauce, rice wine, sugar, cornstarch, and hoisin sauce. Add to the wok, together with the chicken. Stir-fry until heated through. Stir in the sesame oil and peanuts. For a hotter dish, add red pepper flakes. Serve immediately.

FRENCH COUNTRY CHICKEN

SERVES 8 TO 10
PREPARATION TIME 1 HOUR
COOKING TIME 1 1/2 HOURS

A much tastier version of chicken pot pie.

2 whole chickens, about 4
  pounds each
4 ounces (1 stick) butter or
  chicken drippings
1/2 cup flour
2 cups chicken stock
1 cup dry white wine
1/2 cup dry sherry
1 cup heavy cream
Garlic salt
White pepper

1/2 cup chopped parsley
1 1/2 cups sliced carrots,
  blanched
16 small pearl onions, peeled
  and parboiled
1 cup peas, fresh or frozen
1 pound fresh, tiny mushrooms
  (or large ones, quartered)
2 cups drained artichoke hearts
1/2 pound puff pastry

Roast or poach the chicken until tender. Cool, bone, and cut into 2-inch pieces. Heat the butter or chicken drippings in a large saucepan. Stir in the flour and cook for 1 minute without browning. Add the stock, white wine, and sherry. Cook, stirring constantly, until smooth. Bring to a boil and add heavy cream. Reduce heat and simmer for 20 minutes. Season to taste with garlic salt and pepper. Stir in the parsley.

Preheat oven to 375 degrees. Arrange chicken and remaining vegetables in a deep casserole. Pour the sauce over the chicken and vegetables and mix gently. Let cool. Roll out puff pastry and fit over top of casserole. Bake for 1 hour or until nicely browned.

ROAST LEMON CHICKEN

SERVES 6
PREPARATION TIME 15 MINUTES
COOKING TIME 1 1/2 HOURS

6 ounces (1 1/2 sticks) softened
  butter
3 teaspoons grated lemon rind
2 tablespoons lemon juice
Salt

White pepper
A 6-pound chicken
2 tablespoons lemon juice
1 lemon, thinly sliced

Preheat oven to 425 degrees. Cream together the butter and the lemon rind. Beat in the first 2 tablespoons of lemon juice slowly. Add salt and white pepper to taste. Loosen the skin of the chicken by carefully slipping the fingers between the skin and meat. Start at the neck and work down to the drumsticks, being careful not to pierce the skin. Spread half of the butter mixture under the skin and pat to smooth the butter into a uniform layer. Truss the chicken and rub with the remaining butter.

Arrange, breast side down, on a rack in a baking pan. Bake for 20 minutes. Turn breast side up, and sprinkle with the remaining lemon juice. Roast the chicken, basting with the pan juices, for 1 hour, or until juices run clear when pricked. Remove from oven and let rest for 10 minutes. Transfer to a heated serving platter. Garnish with the lemon slices.

GALLIANO GAME HENS

SERVES 4
PREPARATION TIME 25 MINUTES
COOKING TIME 1 hour 10 MINUTES

HENS

6 ounces orange marmalade	**1/4 cup chopped walnuts**
2 tablespoons Galliano liqueur	**1 teaspoon grated orange peel**
1/4 teaspoon whole cloves	**Salt**
1 6-ounce package white and wild rice	**Freshly ground pepper**
	4 Cornish game hens

Preheat oven to 375 degrees. In a small saucepan, heat the marmalade, Galliano, and cloves. Cook rice according to instructions on package. Combine 1 1/2 cups of the cooked rice, walnuts, orange peel, salt, and pepper to taste. Fill the hens with the rice mixture. Place the stuffed hens in a baking dish. Generously brush with the orange glaze. Place any remaining stuffing in foil. Place in the oven with the hens. Roast hens for 20 to 30 minutes or until tender and well browned. Baste frequently with the glaze while cooking.

SAUCE

3/4 cup orange juice	**1 bay leaf**
1/2 cup chicken broth	**1 tablespoon cornstarch**
1 tablespoon Galliano	**dissolved in 1 tablespoon**
1/2 teaspoon thyme	**cold water**

While the hens are cooking, prepare the sauce. Combine the orange juice, chicken broth, Galliano, thyme, and bay leaf. Bring to a boil. Whisk in the cornstarch and water mixture, stirring constantly until smooth and slightly thickened. Boil 1 minute. Remove bay leaf.

To serve: remove the cooked hens from the oven. Place on a warmed plate and cover with the sauce. Garnish with watercress sprigs, if desired.

STUFFED CORNISH HENS WITH ROAST POTATOES

SERVES 4
PREPARATION TIME 20 MINUTES
COOKING TIME 45 TO 60 MINUTES

The stuffing is placed under the skin of the hens, creating a wonderful aroma and resulting in a delicate flavor.

4 tablespoons butter
1/4 cup chopped shallots
3/4 pound fresh spinach, washed, cooked and drained
1/2 pound mushrooms, chopped
1/2 cup ricotta cheese
4 tablespoons grated Parmesan cheese
1/2 teaspoon dried thyme

Salt
Freshly ground pepper
2 Rock Cornish hens, 1 1/2 pounds each, or 4 small hens
4 large cloves garlic, crushed
Few sprigs fresh parsley
8 to 12 tiny red potatoes
3 tablespoons melted butter

Preheat oven to 425 degrees. Heat the butter in a skillet over moderate heat. Sauté the shallots for 2 minutes. Squeeze the spinach as dry as possible. Chop fine. Add to shallots along with the mushrooms. Cook over high heat, stirring frequently, until the mushrooms are browned and the pan is dry. Let cool slightly and stir in the ricotta cheese, Parmesan cheese and thyme. Season to taste with salt and pepper.

Place the hens on a work surface. Season the inside of the cavities with salt and pepper and stuff with the garlic cloves and parsley sprigs. With skin side up and drumsticks facing you, gently open up the skin from the breast meat by loosening it with your hands. Divide the stuffing mixture evenly under the skin of each hen. Tie legs and wings close to the body with string. Place the hens in a shallow roasting pan with the potatoes. Sprinkle with salt and pepper. Brush with the melted butter. Roast, basting frequently with the pan drippings, until hens are nicely browned and potatoes are tender, about 40 minutes to an hour (depending on size). Let rest for a few minutes. Remove string and garlic and parsley from cavities. If the hens are large, split and serve ½ hen per person. Spoon some of the pan drippings over hens and potatoes. Serve immediately.

TARRAGON GAME HENS

SERVES 6
PREPARATION TIME 15 MINUTES
MARINATING TIME 2 HOURS
COOKING TIME 30 TO 45 MINUTES

⅓ cup tarragon vinegar
4 cloves garlic
4 green onions
1 tablespoon sugar
2 tcaspoons Dijon mustard
2 teaspoons salt

1 ½ teaspoons freshly
  ground pepper
1 teaspoon fresh tarragon
  (optional)
2 cups vegetable oil
6 Cornish game hens

Combine all ingredients, except oil and hens, in a food processor. Blend until smooth. With machine running, gradually add oil until mixture is thick.

Cut the hens in half and remove the backbone. Rub the mixture into the hens and marinate at least 2 hours or overnight in the refrigerator.

Preheat the oven to 400 degrees. Place the hens in a shallow roasting pan. Brush with the marinade. Roast the hens for approximately 45 minutes, basting occasionally with the marinade and pan drippings. Arrange on a serving platter and spoon over some of the marinade.

DUCK BREASTS WITH ORANGES AND GRAPES

SERVES 4 TO 6
PREPARATION TIME 15 MINUTES
COOKING TIME 20 MINUTES

4 oranges
Breasts and thighs of 2 ducks
2 tablespoons butter
1/4 cup orange juice
1/2 cup Madeira wine

1/2 cup beef stock concentrate
3/4 cup seedless grapes
2 tablespoons butter
Salt
Freshly ground pepper

Remove the zest from the oranges. Peel and section the oranges. Sauté the duck breasts and thighs in the butter, turning frequently, until brown. For nice pink meat, the cooking time should be no more than 10 to 12 minutes total. Remove the duck pieces to a platter and keep warm. Pour off the fat from the pan.

Add the orange juice, orange zest, and Madeira. Bring to a boil and reduce to 1/4 cup. Add the beef concentrate and deglaze the pan. Reduce sauce until slightly thickened.

Remove the skin and fat from the duck meat and carve into thin slices across the grain. Briefly sauté the grapes in the butter. Add to the sauce with the orange sections. Season with salt and pepper. Place a piece of thigh and breast meat in the center of a warmed plate. Spoon some of the sauce and fruit over the meat.

CANARD AU POIVRE VERT

SERVES 2 TO 3
PREPARATION TIME 30 MINUTES
COOKING TIME 1 HOUR 10 MINUTES

1 duckling, about 5 pounds
Salt
Freshly ground pepper
1/2 cup Madeira wine
2 tablespoons butter
2 teaspoons Cognac

1 teaspoon green peppercorn
  juice
2 tablespoons drained green
  peppercorns
1/2 cup heavy cream

Preheat the oven to 425 degrees. Trim the duck of all loose fat. Dry it thoroughly and sprinkle inside and out with salt and pepper. Truss the duck and prick the fatty parts with a skewer. Place on a rack in a roasting pan. Roast in the oven 1 hour, or until juices run out slightly pink when pricked with a fork. Remove duck from oven. Cut off the wings and remove skin from the breast. Separate drumstick. Keep the duck meat warm while preparing the sauce.

Pour off all the fat from the roasting pan. Stir in the Madeira and butter. Heat over high heat until reduced to 1/4 cup, scraping up all the brown bits clinging to the bottom and sides of the pan. Add the Cognac, green peppercorn juice, and green peppercorns and boil for 1 minute. Add the heavy cream and salt to taste. Cook over moderate heat until heated through.

Cut the breast meat into long strips. Put a wing or drumstick on each plate, along with several strips of the duck breast. Spoon some of the sauce over the duck.

LE CANARD À LA CRÈME DE CASSIS

SERVES 8
PREPARATION TIME 40 MINUTES
COOKING TIME 1 TO 1 1/2 HOURS

4 ducks, about 4 pounds each
Salt
Freshly ground pepper
4 ounces (1 stick) butter
3 shallots, minced
10 ounces currant jelly
1 cup crème de cassis

2 cups strong chicken or duck
   stock
1 8-ounce can Bing cherries,
   pitted and drained

Wild rice (optional)

Preheat oven to 425 degrees. Place the ducks in a shallow roasting pan on a rack. Roast for 1 to 1 1/2 hours, turning halfway through baking time. Melt the butter in a skillet and sauté the shallots until soft, about 5 minutes. Add the jelly and crème de cassis and boil until reduced by half. Whisk in the stock and return to a boil. Continue boiling until reduced and thickened.

Cut the ducks into serving pieces and arrange on a platter. Stir the cherries into the sauce and heat thoroughly. Spoon the sauce over the ducks. Serve immediately with wild rice, if desired.

CANARD AUX FRAMBOISES

SERVES 4
PREPARATION TIME 40 MINUTES
COOKING TIME 1 HOUR 40 MINUTES

The unusual trio of raspberries, tomato, and peppercorns adds a piquant contrast to the rich duck meat in this dazzling centerpiece. Perfect for any special occasion.

A 5-pound duck, cut into 8 pieces, breast boned
1 carrot, chopped
1 onion, chopped
1 1/2 cups dry white wine
1 1/2 cups water
4 whole peppercorns
4 tablespoons butter
1 teaspoon sugar
2 cloves garlic
1/2 cup raspberry vinegar

2 teaspoons tomato purée
1 ripe tomato, peeled, seeded, and chopped
1/2 teaspoon each dried thyme and tarragon
1 bay leaf
2 sprigs fresh parsley
Salt
Freshly ground pepper
1 cup fresh raspberries

Make a stock with the bones, wing, and neck of the duck. Place in a pot with the carrot, onion, white wine, water, and peppercorns. Bring to a boil, reduce heat, and simmer for 1 hour. Strain through a fine mesh strainer.

Heat the butter in a heavy casserole. Brown the duck pieces well on both sides. Add the sugar and garlic. Cover and cook for 15 minutes, stirring occasionally.

Remove as much fat as possible from the casserole. Deglaze the remaining pan juice by adding the raspberry vinegar and scraping any bits off the bottom of the pot. Stir in the tomato purée and tomato. Combine the herbs and wrap in a piece of cheesecloth. Add to the casserole. Cover and cook 10 minutes longer.

Preheat oven to 375 degrees. Transfer the duck pieces to a serving platter and keep warm. Add the stock to the casserole. Bring to a boil and cook until reduced by half. Salt and pepper to taste. Strain the sauce over the duck with a fine mesh strainer, pressing down to force some of the solids through the strainer. Sprinkle with the raspberries and place in the oven for 5 minutes before serving.

CREAMED TURKEY CROUSTADES

SERVES 4
PREPARATION TIME 30 MINUTES
COOKING TIME 30 MINUTES

This is the tastiest way we found to prepare leftover turkey. It may well become your traditional "day after Thanksgiving" dinner, too.

1 unsliced loaf white bread
4 tablespoons melted butter
2 cups water
3/4 pounds sliced mushrooms
2 tablespoons butter
3 tablespoons lemon juice
3/4 cup dry white wine
1/4 cup minced green onion
1 tablespoon dried tarragon
1 tablespoon dried chervil

1 cup chicken stock
2 cups heavy cream
2 cups bite-size turkey pieces
1/4 cup sour cream
1/4 cup minced fresh parsley
1/4 cup minced fresh green
    onion tops
Salt
White pepper

Preheat the oven to 350 degrees. Cut the bread into four 2-inch slices. Remove the crusts and trim the corners. With a small knife, hollow out each square halfway down, leaving the sides 1/4 inch thick. Brush inside and out with the butter. Place on a baking sheet and bake for 20 to 25 minutes or until golden.

In a saucepan, combine the water, mushrooms, butter, and lemon juice. Bring to a boil and simmer for 5 minutes. Transfer to a bowl. In the same saucepan, combine the wine, green onion, tarragon, and chervil. Reduce over high heat to 2 tablespoons. Strain the liquid from the mushrooms into the pan, reserving the mushrooms. Add the chicken stock and reduce, over high heat, to 1/2 cup.

Strain the liquid and return to the pan. Add the heavy cream and reduce the sauce to 2 cups. Add the mushrooms and turkey. Cook until heated through. Stir in sour cream, parsley, and onion tops and bring to a simmer. Season to taste with salt and pepper. Arrange the croustades on a platter or individual plates. Spoon the creamed turkey into the center. Serve immediately.

TURKEY SPANAKOPITA

SERVES 8
PREPARATION TIME 25 MINUTES
COOKING TIME 45 MINUTES

2 tablespoons butter
1 1/2 pounds ground turkey
2 pounds fresh spinach, cooked
and drained
4 ounces feta cheese, crumbled
1/2 teaspoon salt

1/2 teaspoon pepper
1/2 teaspoon allspice
1 egg
15 sheets phyllo dough
1/3 cup melted butter

Preheat the oven to 350 degrees. Melt the butter in a frying pan and brown
the turkey in it. Remove from the heat and pour off any of the fat remaining
in the pan. Stir in the spinach, feta cheese, seasonings, and egg.

Lightly grease a 10-inch deep-dish pie plate. Fold a sheet of phyllo and
place across the plate, extending both ends of the dough over the edge of the
plate. Brush with some of the melted butter. Fold 10 more sheets of phyllo in
half. Fan out around the plate, covering the bottom completely. Brush with a
little butter. Spoon the filling into the phyllo. Fold the edges over the top.
Place the remaining phyllo sheets over the top. Brush with butter. Bake for
40 to 45 minutes, or until golden.

MARINATED TURKEY BREAST
WITH CAPER SAUCE

SERVES 8
PREPARATION TIME 10 MINUTES
MARINATING TIME 4 HOURS
COOKING TIME 1 HOUR 30 MINUTES

*The turkey breast can be marinated overnight in the refrigerator. Bring to room temperature before
cooking.*

1 cup chopped fresh parsley
5 cloves garlic, minced
1 1/2 cups fresh lemon juice
1 cup olive oil
4 teaspoons dried rosemary,
crumbled

1 teaspoon salt
1 6-pound turkey breast, bone
in
Freshly ground pepper
6 tablespoons butter
1/4 cup drained capers

Combine parsley, garlic, lemon juice, oil, rosemary, and salt. Whisk together until well blended and thickened. (You can combine everything in a processor and blend.) Pour the marinade into a heavy plastic bag. Add the turkey breast and seal airtight. Marinate 4 hours at room temperature.

Preheat oven to 400 degrees. Drain the turkey, reserving the marinade. Pat the turkey dry and sprinkle with salt and pepper. Place in a roasting pan. Pour out 2/3 cup of the reserved marinade and set aside to be used later for the sauce. Cook turkey approximately 1 to 1 1/2 hours, or until a thermometer inserted into the thickest part registers 165 degrees. Baste occasionally with the remaining marinade while baking. Let the turkey stand at room temperature while preparing the sauce.

In a saucepan, bring the 2/3 cup reserved marinade to a boil. Remove from the heat and whisk in 2 tablespoons of the butter. Place the pan over very low heat and whisk in the remaining butter, piece by piece. If the sauce breaks down at any time, remove the pan from the heat and whisk in 2 tablespoons of cold butter. Stir in the capers. Taste and adjust seasonings. Cut the turkey breast into slices. Serve with the sauce.

CHESTNUT DRESSING

MAKES 12 TO 14 CUPS
PREPARATION TIME 25 MINUTES
COOKING TIME 10 MINUTES

This dressing makes enough to stuff a fourteen-pound turkey.

1 pound chestnuts, fresh or canned
Boiling water
8 ounces (2 sticks) butter
1 1/2 cups chicken stock
1/2 cup dry white wine
1 cup minced celery
1 small onion, peeled and chopped
1/2 cup dried apricots
2 8-ounce packages herb-seasoned stuffing
1/2 teaspoon ground sage
4 tablespoons fresh chopped parsley
1 teaspoon salt
1/2 teaspoon freshly ground pepper
2 eggs, beaten

If using fresh chestnuts, place in a large saucepan. Cover with boiling water. Cook for 15 minutes, or until tender. Cool; remove outside shell and inner skin. Chop chestnuts. Melt half of the butter in the chicken stock and wine.

Melt the remaining butter in a saucepan. Sauté celery and onion until soft.

Cover the apricots with boiling water. Cook until soft and drain. Finely chop apricots. Place the stuffing in a large bowl. Add the chestnuts, sautéed vegetables, apricots, herbs, and seasonings. Add the stock mixture and toss lightly to blend. Mix in eggs, adding additional liquid if necessary.

MEATS

Alexander Valley

Alexander Valley and its neighbors, Knights Valley and Dry Creek Valley, lie at the northern and eastern end of Sonoma County. Vineyards extend as far as the eye can see in all directions, and the prevailing microclimate produces some of the best premium red grapes in California. Cabernet Sauvignon is a notable example.

Geyserville, reached by following Highway 128 through the length of Knights and Alexander Valleys, is a pleasant country town set amid vineyards, with several restored Victorian mansions offering bed-and-breakfast accommodations. An interesting geologic feature of this area, for which the town was named, is its geysers, located in the mountains just east of Alexander Valley. These geysers are now being commercially exploited as a source of electrical power for Northern California. Calistoga, in Napa Valley, is also the home of a geyser, California's "Old Faithful" which is a smaller version of Yellowstone National Park's famous geyser and erupts at regular intervals.

Notable sights in Alexander Valley are the beautiful white Victorians, some dating back almost to General Vallejo's time. Many are shaded by magnificent spreading California oak trees and surrounded by magnificent lawns.

One can envision the Grilled Lamb Chops Niçoise or Mesquite Grilled Pork Tenderloin served under the shade of the old oaks or the Filet de Boeuf Périgourdine in an ornately appointed dining room, accompanied by a lusty, full-bodied Alexander Valley Cabernet Sauvignon.

FILET DE BOEUF SAUCE CHORON

SERVES 6 TO 8
PREPARATION TIME 15 MINUTES
COOKING TIME 40 MINUTES

This Sauce Choron is a béarnaise with tomato purée added. For an elegant presentation, spoon the sauce into artichoke bottoms and arrange around the beef.

TENDERLOIN

1 **whole beef fillet**	**Salt**
2 **tablespoons butter**	**Freshly ground pepper**

Preheat oven to 425 degrees. Remove all fat and membrane from the fillet. Tuck under the tail and tie with string to give it a nicer shape. Melt the butter in a skillet over high heat. Sprinkle with salt and pepper. Sear the meat on all sides. Place in the oven for approximately 20 to 25 minutes. A meat thermometer should register approximately 120 to 125 degrees for a nice rare roast. Place on a heated serving platter and allow to rest for 10 minutes.

SAUCE CHORON

4 **tablespoons white vinegar**	1/3 **cup tomato purée**
2 **tablespoons dried tarragon,** **or** 4 **tablespoons fresh**	**Salt**
1/4 **cup chopped shallots**	**Freshly ground pepper**
1/4 **cup water**	2 **tablespoons chopped fresh** **parsley**
4 **egg yolks**	2 **tablespoons chopped fresh**
8 **ounces (2 sticks) softened** **butter**	**tarragon**

Place the vinegar, tarragon, and shallots in a small saucepan. Boil the vinegar down to almost nothing. Remove the pan from the heat and let cool slightly. Add the water and egg yolks, whisking constantly. Over low heat, whisk in the butter a little at a time until thick and creamy. Stir in the tomato purée. Season to taste with salt and pepper. Keep warm in a water bath. Stir in the parsley and tarragon just before serving.

To serve: carve the beef into thin slices and arrange on a warmed serving platter. Cover the center of the slices with some of the sauce. Pass additional sauce on the side.

GRILLED TENDERLOIN WITH
MUSTARD CAPER SAUCE

SERVES 6 TO 8
PREPARATION TIME 15 MINUTES
COOKING TIME 25 MINUTES

Perfect for a summer buffet, this dish can be prepared well in advance. The sauce can be prepared two days early and refrigerated. The tenderloin can be cooked in the oven. Everything should be served at room temperature.

TENDERLOIN
1 **beef tenderloin**
3 **tablespoons olive oil**

Heat the coals on the barbecue until gray. Let burn for 15 minutes so that the coals will be very hot. Have the tenderloin at room temperature. Rub with the oil and let stand while the coals are heating.

Place the beef on a hot grill 3 inches from the coals. Cook about 10 minutes. Turn and cook another 8 to 10 minutes, or until a meat thermometer registers 125 to 130 degrees for rare. Transfer to a platter and let cool.

MUSTARD CAPER SAUCE

3 **tablespoons coarse-grained Dijon mustard**
2 **egg yolks, room temperature**
1 **green onion, chopped**
1/4 **teaspoon fresh marjoram**
2 **to 3 tablespoons fresh lemon juice**

3/4 **cup olive oil**
1/4 **cup vegetable oil**
1/4 **to 1/2 cup heavy cream, lightly whipped**
2 **tablespoons drained capers**

Combine the mustard, egg yolks, onion, marjoram, and lemon juice in a food processor or blender. Mix until pale and creamy. With machine running, gradually add the oils in a steady stream until thickened. Transfer to a bowl. Gently fold in the whipped cream and capers. (If preparing the sauce a day or two in advance, do not fold in cream and capers until ready to use.)

To serve: thinly slice the beef. Arrange on a serving platter with the pieces overlapping slightly. Spoon some of the sauce down the center. Pass the remainder of the sauce separately.

WHOLE FILLET OF BEEF WITH HORSERADISH

SERVES 8 TO 10
PREPARATION TIME 5 MINUTES
COOKING TIME 35 TO 45 MINUTES

This tastes great cold for a tailgate party or a do-ahead buffet. Thinly slice the beef and serve on sliced baguettes.

1 **whole beef tenderloin**	**Salt**
1 **to 2 bottles prepared**	**Freshly ground pepper**
horseradish	

Preheat oven to 400 degrees. Remove all fat, muscles, and tendons from the tenderloin. Place the fillet in a roasting pan. Cover entire top surface with a generous layer of horseradish. Sprinkle with salt and pepper to taste. Roast for 35 to 45 minutes for medium rare.

Horseradish loses its "bite" when cooked. The surface will turn nicely brown. It will keep the fillet moist and impart a garlicky flavor to the meat. Allow meat to rest 10 minutes before slicing. Slice thinly and serve with freshly grated horseradish root or a horseradish sauce.

FILET DE BOEUF PÉRIGOURDINE

SERVES 8
PREPARATION TIME 20 MINUTES
COOKING TIME 30 MINUTES

The classic rendition of this dish always contains truffles in the sauce. You can substitute fresh sautéed mushrooms if truffles are too expensive.

TENDERLOIN

1 **whole beef fillet**	**3 tablespoons butter**
1 **teaspoon salt**	**Freshly ground pepper**

Preheat oven to 425 degrees. Trim the fillet of all fat and sinews. Tuck the tail under and tie. Sprinkle the meat with the salt and pepper. Melt the butter in a roasting pan. Brown the meat on all sides over high heat. This should take about 5 minutes. Place in the oven for approximately 20 minutes, basting frequently with the pan juices. A meat thermometer should register 125 degrees for rare. Place on a heated platter and let rest for 10 minutes while preparing the sauce.

PÉRIGUEUX SAUCE

1/2 cup Madeira wine	Salt
2 cups Brown Sauce†	Freshly ground pepper
1/4 cup chopped black truffles	2 tablespoons unsalted butter
Juice from the truffles	
1 tablespoon arrowroot diluted	
with 1/4 cup cold water	

Pour off all the fat from the roasting pan. Add the Madeira and bring to a boil, scraping up all the brown bits on the bottom of the pan. Stir in Brown Sauce and return to a boil. Strain into a saucepan. Add the truffles and their juices. Slowly add a little of the arrowroot and water to thicken the sauce. Add only enough to thicken slightly. Simmer for 10 minutes. Salt and pepper to taste. Whip in the butter, piece by piece.

If carving the whole fillet at the table, cover with the sauce, reserving some to pass separately. If serving on individual plates, pour the sauce around the slices of beef.

GRILLED CHUCK STEAK

SERVES 4
PREPARATION TIME 10 MINUTES
MARINATING TIME 4 HOURS
COOKING TIME 15 TO 20 MINUTES

A 3-pound chuck steak	1 clove garlic, crushed
1/2 cup olive oil	2 teaspoons sweet pickle relish
1/2 cup ketchup	1 teaspoon sugar
1/4 cup vinegar	1 teaspoon chili powder
1/4 cup chopped onion	1/2 teaspoon Tabasco

Pierce both sides of the steak with a fork. Combine the remaining ingredients. Pour over steak. Let stand at least 4 hours at room temperature or overnight in the refrigerator. Turn every half hour while marinating.

Heat the coals in the barbecue until a white ash forms. Remove the steak from the marinade and place on a hot grill over the coals. Cook on both sides to desired degree of doneness, depending on the thickness of the steak. Brush with the marinade occasionally while cooking.

BEEF CURRY

SERVES 6 TO 8
PREPARATION TIME 10 MINUTES
COOKING TIME 1 HOUR

1 1/2 pounds ground beef
1 onion, chopped
1 teaspoon chopped garlic
2 tablespoons oil
1 teaspoon cumin
3/4 teaspoon coriander
1/2 teaspoon ginger
1/2 teaspoon cinnamon

1/2 teaspoon cayenne
1/4 teaspoon ground cloves
Dash of turmeric
2 medium tomatoes, cut into
  chunks
1/2 pound mushrooms, sliced
Salt

Fry the beef in a skillet just until it loses its red color. Transfer from pan with slotted spoon and set aside. Sauté the onion and garlic in the oil with the cumin, coriander, ginger, cinnamon, cayenne, cloves, and turmeric. Simmer for 15 minutes. Add the tomatoes and cook an additional 5 minutes. Add the ground beef and mushrooms. Simmer for 30 minutes, stirring occasionally. Salt to taste. Serve with rice.

BEEF FILLETS IN FLAKY PASTRY

SERVES 6
PREPARATION TIME 15 MINUTES
COOKING TIME 40 MINUTES

Both easy and special. Serve with a fresh steamed seasonal vegetable to accommodate the Béarnaise Sauce.

2 tablespoons butter
6 beef fillets, 6 ounces each,
  trimmed of all fat
6 tablespoons Madeira or
  sherry wine
3/4 pound fresh mushrooms,
  minced

1 package of 6 patty shells (or
  frozen puff pastry sheets)
Salt
Freshly ground pepper

Béarnaise Sauce†

Melt the butter in a heavy skillet. Sear steaks on both sides until nicely browned. Pour in 2 tablespoons of the wine and evaporate off. Transfer steaks to a platter and chill.

To the pan, add the remaining wine and mushrooms. Cook over medium heat, stirring, until all of the liquid evaporates. Chill mixture.

Roll out each shell on a lightly floured board to make a circle 8 inches in diameter. Place some of the mushroom mixture in the center of each circle. Place a fillet on top. Salt and pepper lightly. Fold pastry over steak and enclose tightly. Place on a baking tray seam side down. Cover and refrigerate at least 15 minutes or as long as overnight.

Preheat oven to 425 degrees. Bake for 18 to 20 minutes or until pastry is nicely browned. For the first 10 minutes, place baking sheet on lowest oven rack. After 10 minutes move to the highest rack. The meat will be rare. If you want a more well-done piece of meat, cook longer in the pan before placing in the pastry. Serve with Béarnaise Sauce.

ROPA VIEJA

MAKES 12 TO 16
PREPARATION TIME 20 MINUTES
COOKING TIME 2 HOURS

This shredded beef dish means literally "old clothes." It can be made several days in advance and reheated.

2 cups beef stock	1/4 cup oil
1 cup water	1 large onion, thinly sliced
12 whole peppercorns	2 cloves garlic, crushed
4 cloves garlic, crushed	1 16-ounce can whole tomatoes
2 bay leaves	Salt
3-pound flank steak or chuck roast	Freshly ground pepper
	Flour tortillas
6 fresh California chili peppers	Chopped fresh cilantro leaves

In a pot large enough to hold the beef, bring the stock, water, peppercorns, garlic, and bay leaves to a boil. Add the beef and return to a boil. Cover, reduce heat to low, and simmer for 1 1/2 to 2 hours, or until tender. When meat is tender, remove from heat and cool in the broth. When cool enough to handle, pull into shreds with fingers.

Char the skins of the chili peppers until black. Under running water, peel off the charred skin. Remove seeds and cut into strips. Heat the oil in a skillet. Sauté the onion and garlic until softened but not brown, about 5 minutes. Add the chili strips and sauté for 2 minutes. Add the meat and tomatoes and cook, uncovered, stirring occasionally, until the flavors are blended, about 10 minutes. Season to taste with salt and pepper.

Warm the flour tortillas on a griddle or in the oven. Spoon a bit of the shredded beef mixture on a flour tortilla. Sprinkle with some of the fresh cilantro. Fold the tortilla over and roll up. Serve immediately.

SHREDDED BEEF ENCHILADAS

SERVES 6

PREPARATION TIME 35 MINUTES

COOKING TIME 2 1/2 HOURS

These enchiladas team Ropas Viejas with green chilies and sour cream. They can be assembled in advance.

2 pounds beef chuck	2 7-ounce cans diced green
1/4 cup water	chilies
3 tablespoons vinegar	1 tablespoon flour
1 cup beef stock	2 cups sour cream
2 tablespoons chili powder	3/4 pound shredded Jack cheese
1 1/2 teaspoons ground cumin	Salt
2 tablespoons oil	Freshly ground pepper
1 onion, chopped	12 corn or flour tortillas

Place the meat in a large pan with the water. Cover and cook over medium heat for 30 minutes. Uncover and cook until liquid boils away and meat is browned. Remove the meat from the pan. Add the vinegar, scraping up any brown bits on the bottom of the pan. Stir in the beef stock, chili powder, and 1 teaspoon of the cumin. Return the meat to the pan and bring to a boil. Cover and simmer over low heat until meat is tender, about 2 hours. Let meat cool. Tear into shreds and mix with the juices remaining in the pan.

Heat the oil in a pan. Sauté the onion, chilies, and remaining cumin. Cook, stirring occasionally, until onion is soft, about 10 minutes. Mix in the flour and cook for a few minutes. Stir in the sour cream and cook until simmering. Remove from heat and blend in 1 cup of the cheese. Salt and pepper to taste.

Heat a small amount of oil in a frying pan. Cook the tortillas about 5 seconds on each side, until just limp. Drain on paper towels.

Spoon about 1/3 cup chili mixture and 1/4 cup shredded beef down the center of each tortilla. Roll to enclose. Set the enchiladas, seam side down, in a shallow baking dish. (The dish can be prepared in advance and refrigerated overnight at this point. Bring to room temperature before baking.)

Preheat oven to 375. Bake, covered, for 15 minutes. Uncover and sprinkle with the remaining cheese. Return to the oven and continue baking until the cheese melts.

ROAST BEEF WELLINGTON WITH HORSERADISH SAUCE

SERVES 6
PREPARATION TIME 20 MINUTES
COOKING TIME 35 MINUTES

2 tablespoons butter
1/2 pound fresh mushrooms, cut into slices
1 tablespoon minced shallot
1/2 teaspoon chopped fresh parsley
12 ounces Swiss cheese, coarsely grated
8 ounces rare roast beef, thinly sliced and julienned

3 tablespoons prepared horseradish
6 6×6-inch squares puff pastry
1 egg beaten with 1 teaspoon water

Horseradish Sauce (recipe follows)

Preheat oven to 425 degrees. Melt the butter in a large skillet. Add the mushrooms, shallot, and parsley. Sauté 3 to 4 minutes. Remove from the heat and let cool. Drain well.

Lightly grease a baking tray. Toss cheese, beef, horseradish and mushroom mixture in a large bowl. Place the puff pastry squares on a work surface. Divide the mixture among the six squares, placing in the center of each square. Fold up the corners and pinch to seal. Do not compress the filling. Place on the prepared tray, seam side down. Brush with the beaten egg mixture; do not allow to drip onto the tray. Bake until puffed and golden, approximately 25 to 30 minutes. Serve hot accompanied by Horseradish Sauce.

HORSERADISH SAUCE
1 1/2 cups sour cream
1/4 cup prepared horseradish
1/4 teaspoon minced garlic

Combine all ingredients and blend.

PICADILLO

SERVES 6
PREPARATION TIME 10 MINUTES
COOKING TIME 25 MINUTES

This Cuban dish was served at one of Ernest Hemingway's favorite restaurants.

2 pounds ground round
1 tablespoon oil
3 cloves of garlic, minced
2 large onions, chopped
1 cup tomato sauce
1 1/4 cups red wine
1/8 teaspoon oregano
Salt

Freshly ground pepper
1 1/2 cups golden raisins,
   soaked until plump
1/2 cup sliced pimento-stuffed
   olives
2 green peppers, seeded and
   chopped

Brown the beef in oil for 3 to 5 minutes. Add the garlic, onions, tomato sauce, wine, oregano, salt, and pepper. Simmer for 15 minutes. Drain the raisins. Add the raisins, olives, and green pepper to the beef. Simmer an additional 5 minutes. Serve on a bed of rice.

CHINESE BEEF AND CABBAGE

SERVES 4
PREPARATION TIME 45 MINUTES
COOKING TIME 10 MINUTES

1/2 pound flank steak
1/3 cup soy sauce
1/3 cup rice wine or sherry
1 tablespoon sesame oil
1 clove garlic, minced
1 teaspoon bean sauce
   (optional)
1/2 teaspoon sugar
1/2 teaspoon freshly ground
   pepper
6 water chestnuts, sliced

6 fresh mushrooms, sliced
1/2 pound Chinese cabbage,
   sliced into strips
2 green onions, sliced
1 green pepper, sliced into
   strips
1/4 cup toasted sesame seeds
1 tablespoon cornstarch
   dissolved in 2 tablespoons
   sherry

Slice the flank steak into strips. Combine the soy sauce, wine, oil, garlic, bean sauce if desired, sugar and pepper. Pour over the meat and let marinate for 30 minutes.

Heat wok or skillet. Add the meat and braise until brown, turning constantly. Add the vegetables and sauté for 5 minutes. Stir in cornstarch mixture and cook until thickened. Serve immediately with steamed rice.

GRILLADES

SERVES 6 TO 8
PREPARATION TIME 45 MINUTES
COOKING TIME 2 HOURS

4 pounds beef top round,
  1/2 inch thick
1/2 cup bacon drippings
1/2 cup flour
1 1/2 cups chopped green
  pepper
2 cups chopped green onion
1 cup chopped onion
3/4 cup chopped celery
2 cloves garlic, minced
2 cups chopped tomatoes
1/2 teaspoon dried tarragon

2/3 teaspoon dried thyme
1 cup water
1 cup red wine
3 teaspoons salt
1 teaspoon freshly ground
  pepper
2 bay leaves
1/2 teaspoon Tabasco
2 tablespoons Worcestershire
  sauce
3 tablespoons chopped fresh
  parsley

Remove all fat from the meat and cut into serving-size pieces. Pound to 1/4-inch thickness. Heat 4 tablespoons bacon grease in a Dutch oven. Brown meat well on all sides, a few pieces at a time. As meat browns, transfer to a plate. Add the remaining bacon grease. Stir in the flour and cook until browned. Add the green pepper, onions, celery, and garlic. Sauté until soft. Add tomatoes, tarragon, and thyme. Cook for 5 minutes. Add water, wine, salt, pepper, bay leaves, Tabasco, and Worcestershire. Stir well and return meat to the pan. Lower the heat and simmer, covered, approximately 2 hours. Remove bay leaves and stir in parsley. Let the grillades sit for several hours or overnight in the refrigerator before serving. Reheat and serve over grits or rice.

PEPPERED TOP ROUND

SERVES 4
PREPARATION TIME 10 MINUTES
COOKING TIME 5 TO 10 MINUTES

A 2-pound beef top round
  steak
1 tablespoon black
  peppercorns, crushed
1 tablespoon green
  peppercorns, crushed
1 tablespoon butter
1/2 teaspoon minced garlic

1 tablespoon oil
1/2 cup red wine
1/4 cup brandy
1 cup heavy cream
1 1/2 teaspoons Dijon mustard
Salt
2 tablespoons chopped fresh
  parsley

Remove all fat from the top round steak. Combine peppercorns, butter, and garlic. Spread evenly on both sides of the steak. Heat the oil in a heavy skillet over medium-high heat. Add the steak and brown on both sides to desired degree of doneness. Allow 5 minutes for rare and 7 to 8 minutes total for medium rare. Place on a serving platter and keep warm.

Add the wine and brandy to the pan. Cook over high heat, scraping all the juices off the bottom, until reduced to 1/4 of a cup. Add the heavy cream and mustard and continue cooking until further reduced and thickened. Season to taste with salt. Just before serving, stir in the parsley.

Carve the steak diagonally across the grain into thin slices. Cover with the sauce. Serve immediately.

MARINATED FLANK STEAK

SERVES 4 TO 6
PREPARATION TIME 5 MINUTES
MARINATING TIME 6 HOURS
COOKING TIME 10 TO 12 MINUTES

1/4 cup soy sauce
1/4 cup honey
1/4 cup dry white wine
1/4 cup thinly sliced green
  onions
2 tablespoons grated onion

2 tablespoons balsamic vinegar
2 tablespoons sesame oil
2 cloves garlic, crushed
2 teaspoons sesame seeds
1 teaspoon ginger
A 2- to 3-pound flank steak

Combine all the ingredients, except the flank steak, for the marinade. Pour over the steak and marinate at least 6 hours at room temperature or overnight in the refrigerator.

Heat a barbecue or grill until coals are white. Place the steak on the hot grill and cook 4 to 5 minutes per side, basting with the marinade. Slice thinly on the diagonal and serve.

FLAUTA TART

SERVES 6
PREPARATION TIME 15 MINUTES
COOKING TIME 2 HOURS

Serve this unique tart with Orange and Jícama Salad. Accompany with an imported Mexican beer.

2 teaspoons oil	3/4 cup chopped green onion
1 pound boneless beef	1/2 cup chopped green chilies
2 teaspoons paprika	3 eggs, beaten
1/4 teaspoon chili powder	Salt
1 large onion, chopped	Pepper
1 clove garlic, minced	1 12-inch flour tortilla
1 1/2 cups grated Jack cheese	1/2 to 1 cup sour cream
1 cup sour cream	Sliced avocado

Heat the oil in a skillet. Pat the meat with the paprika and chili powder. Add meat, onion, and garlic to the pan and brown. Reduce the heat to low and cook, covered, until tender, about 1 1/2 to 2 hours. (If meat starts to stick during cooking, add a little water to the pan.) When meat is tender, remove lid and evaporate off any liquid in the pan. Let meat cool, then shred it.

Preheat oven to 375 degrees. Combine meat mixture with cheese, the 1 cup of the sour cream, green onion, chilies, and eggs. Mix well. Season to taste with the salt and pepper. Place the tortilla into a greased 9-inch pie plate. Brush with a little oil and bake for 5 minutes, or until nicely browned. Pour the filling onto the prepared tortilla, spreading the top evenly. Bake 55 to 65 minutes or until the filling is set. Cool slightly. Spread the top with the sour cream and decorate with the avocado slices. Serve with a Mexican salsa if desired.

FLANK STEAK PINWHEELS

SERVES 6
PREPARATION TIME 10 MINUTES
MARINATING TIME 8 HOURS
COOKING TIME 8 MINUTES

2 pounds flank steak, cut into
   1/2-inch strips
3/4 cup vegetable oil
1/2 cup soy sauce
2 tablespoons honey

2 tablespoons vinegar
1 1/2 teaspoons ground ginger
1 teaspoon chopped garlic
1 green onion with top,
   chopped

Roll the flank-steak strips tightly and secure with a toothpick. Place in a shallow roasting pan. Combine the remaining ingredients in a food processor or blender. Mix until blended. Pour the marinade over the pinwheels. Marinate at least 8 hours, turning occasionally. Barbecue or broil 4 minutes per side for medium rare.

GOLDEN GATE SLOPPY JOES

SERVES 6
PREPARATION TIME 30 MINUTES
COOKING TIME 30 MINUTES

It is always nice to have a few easy ground-beef entrees for the family. Serve with toasted French buns and a green salad.

2 tablespoons oil
1 onion, finely chopped
2 cloves garlic, minced
3/4 cup grated carrots
3/4 cup chopped mushrooms
1 pound lean ground beef
1 cup tomato sauce
2 tablespoons red wine vinegar
2 tablespoons ketchup

1 tablespoon molasses
1 teaspoon Worcestershire
   sauce
1 teaspoon each paprika and
   chili powder
Salt
Freshly ground pepper
Shredded Cheddar cheese
   (optional)

Heat the oil in a frying pan. Sauté the onion, garlic, carrots, and mushrooms until soft. Add the meat and cook until it loses its red color. Stir in tomato sauce, vinegar, ketchup, molasses, Worcestershire, paprika, and chili powder. Cover and simmer for 15 minutes. Salt and pepper to taste. Serve over toasted buns. If desired, top with shredded cheese and run under the broiler briefly.

MARIN MIXED GRILL

SERVES 8
PREPARATION TIME 30 MINUTES
MARINATING TIME 24 HOURS
COOKING TIME 15 MINUTES

Three different meats, fruit, and vegetables are combined to make an unusual and tantalizing dish.

MARINADE

3/4 cup vegetable oil
3/4 cup red wine
1/3 cup soy sauce
2 tablespoons ketchup
3 teaspoons chopped fresh
  ginger

3 cloves garlic, crushed
2 teaspoons curry powder
1/2 teaspoon freshly ground
  pepper
1/4 teaspoon Tabasco sauce

Blend all the ingredients for the marinade in a food processor or blender until smooth.

KABOBS

1 pound sirloin steak, cut into
  2-inch cubes
1 pound boneless lamb, cut
  into 2-inch cubes
1 pound pork tenderloin, cut
  into 2-inch cubes

12 mushrooms
1 eggplant
4 firm green apples
2 large green bell peppers

Place meat in a bowl and cover with the marinade. Cover and refrigerate at least 24 hours.

Two hours prior to serving, prepare the vegetables. Wash and dry the mushrooms. Peel and slice eggplant. Sprinkle with salt and let sit for 30 minutes. Rinse and pat dry with paper towels. Cut into 2-inch squares. Peel the apples and cut into wedges. Seed peppers and cut into 2-inch squares. Place all of the vegetables in a bowl. Remove some of the marinade from the meat and add to the vegetables. Toss to coat well.

Preheat the barbecue or broiler. On large skewers, alternate the meats and vegetables, placing the apples in the middle of the skewers. Barbecue or broil 5 to 7 minutes on each side.

BRAISED CORNED BEEF IN BEER

SERVES 8
PREPARATION TIME 10 MINUTES
COOKING TIME 3 HOURS

3 to 4 pounds corned beef
1/2 cup Dijon mustard
2/3 cup brown sugar
4 whole cloves
2 tablespoons oil

2 cans beer
1 large onion, quartered
1/2 cup celery leaves
10 peppercorns

Preheat oven to 375 degrees. Rub the beef with the mustard and roll in the brown sugar. Press the whole cloves into meat. Heat the oil in a large ovenproof pan or Dutch oven. Brown the meat, taking care not to burn the sugar. Add the beer, onion, celery leaves and peppercorns. Cover the pot with foil. Roast in the oven for 2 1/2 to 3 hours.

STRIP STEAK IN LEMON SAUCE

SERVES 4
PREPARATION TIME 10 MINUTES
COOKING TIME 5 TO 10 MINUTES

4 sirloin strip steaks, 1/2-inch
   thick
Salt
Freshly ground pepper
4 teaspoons dry mustard
4 tablespoons butter
2 to 3 tablespoons fresh lemon
   juice

2 teaspoons chopped fresh
   chives
1 teaspoon Worcestershire
   sauce
2 tablespoons chopped fresh
   parsley
Thinly sliced lemon

Pound steaks to 1/3-inch thickness. Sprinkle both sides with the salt, pepper, and mustard. Pound into the meat. Heat the butter in a skillet. Cook the steaks for 2 minutes on each side. Transfer to a serving platter and keep warm.

Add the lemon juice, chives, and Worcestershire sauce to the skillet and bring to a boil. Stir in the parsley. Spoon over the steaks. Garnish with the lemon slices. Serve immediately.

SCALLOPINI À LA NORTH BEACH

SERVES 4
PREPARATION TIME 15 MINUTES
COOKING TIME 15 MINUTES

The creamy bordelaise-type sauce makes this dish unusual.

SAUCE

1 tablespoon chopped onion	1 tablespoon flour
1 tablespoon butter	1/2 cup beef stock
1/4 cup chopped celery	1 tablespoon tomato paste
1/4 cup chopped carrot	Dash of Worcestershire sauce
1 teaspoon chopped fresh parsley	1 tablespoon dry red wine
	Salt
1/2 teaspoon crushed bay leaf	Freshly ground pepper

Sauté the onion in the butter until soft. Add the celery, carrot, parsley, and bay leaf. Stir in the flour and cook for 2 minutes, browning slightly. Stir in stock and cook until smooth and thickened. Add tomato paste, Worcestershire sauce, and wine. Cook over low heat, stirring constantly, until smooth. Season to taste with salt and pepper. Strain and set aside.

VEAL

4 large slices of veal scallops (1/4 to 1/3 pound each)	1/4 cup butter
	4 thin slices prosciutto
	4 slices Jack cheese
1/4 cup flour	1/2 cup heavy cream

Preheat oven to 375 degrees. Dredge the pieces of veal in flour. Heat the butter in a skillet. Sauté the veal until nicely browned on both sides. Remove to an ovenproof dish. Cover each slice of veal with a slice of the prosciutto and the cheese.

ASSEMBLY

Add the heavy cream to the strained sauce. Pour over the veal in the dish. Bake until the cheese has melted and the sauce bubbles.

LEMONY VEAL PICCATA

SERVES 4
PREPARATION TIME 15 MINUTES
COOKING TIME 5 MINUTES

Sautéed veal scallops in a rich wine sauce combine for a delicate rendition of a popular Italian entree. Accompany with wild rice and a Pinot Noir or Cabernet Sauvignon.

1 pound veal scallops, pounded thin
Flour
Salt
Freshly ground pepper
3 tablespoons olive oil
1 large clove garlic, minced
$1/2$ cup dry white wine

$1/2$ cup strong chicken stock
3 tablespoons capers
1 small lemon, peeled with all white removed, seeded, and diced
2 tablespoons butter
2 tablespoons chopped fresh parsley

Dredge the veal in flour, shaking off the excess. Season lightly with salt and pepper. Sauté in the oil until lightly browned, about 2 to 3 minutes. Remove from pan and keep warm.

Pour off any oil remaining in pan. Add the garlic and sauté briefly. Add the wine and stock and bring to a boil. Reduce to $1/3$ cup. Stir in capers and lemon. Return to a boil. Swirl in butter and parsley, and continue cooking until sauce thickens slightly and turns creamy. Dip veal slices in sauce to coat. Arrange on a platter and spoon the remaining sauce over the scallops.

VEAL SCALLOPS WITH LIME

SERVES 4
PREPARATION TIME 30 MINUTES
COOKING TIME 5 TO 10 MINUTES

$1/4$ cup flour
$1 1/2$ teaspoons grated lime zest
1 teaspoon dried tarragon, crumbled
Salt
White pepper
8 veal scallops, weighing $1 1/4$ pounds total, and $1/8$ inch thick

3 tablespoons butter
2 tablespoons oil
$3/4$ cup dry white wine
2 tablespoons fresh lime juice
2 tablespoons minced parsley
1 tablespoon minced pine nuts
$1/2$ teaspoon minced garlic
1 lime, thinly sliced

Preheat oven to 200 degrees. Mix the flour, 1 teaspoon of the lime zest, tarragon, and a pinch of salt and pepper. Dust the veal pieces in the seasoned flour, shaking off the excess. Heat the butter and oil in a large skillet. Sauté the veal scallops, a few at a time, until lightly browned, about 30 seconds on each side. Transfer to an ovenproof dish. Cover and keep warm in the oven.

Pour off any fat remaining in the pan. Add the wine and cook, scraping up any bits remaining on the bottom, until reduced to 1/2 cup. Stir in the lime juice, parsley, pine nuts, garlic, and the remaining lime zest. Remove the veal from the oven and dip each piece into the sauce. Arrange on a serving platter. Spoon the remaining sauce over the veal slices. Garnish with the lime slices. Serve immediately.

VEAL STROGANOFF

SERVES 4 TO 6
PREPARATION TIME 15 MINUTES
COOKING TIME 1 HOUR

A special blend of flavors in this delicious variation of a traditional stroganoff. It tastes even better if made ahead.

1 1/2 pounds boneless veal stew
2 tablespoons butter
1 clove garlic, crushed
4 mild Italian sausages, cut
   into 1-inch slices
2 onions, chopped
1/2 pound mushrooms, halved
   or quartered
1 red bell pepper, seeded, and
   cut into cubes

1 cup beef stock
1/2 cup dry sherry
1 cup sour cream
2 tablespoons flour
1/2 teaspoon salt
Freshly ground pepper
Freshly grated nutmeg
Chopped fresh parsley

Cut the veal into 1/2-inch cubes. Heat the butter in a large skillet. Brown the veal with the garlic clove. Add the sausage and brown well. Stir in the onions and mushrooms and cook until soft, about 10 minutes. Remove the garlic clove and add the red pepper, beef stock, and sherry. Bring to a boil. Reduce heat and simmer partially covered for 1 hour, stirring occasionally. If preparing in advance, cook up to this point and refrigerate.

While the veal is cooking, mix sour cream, flour, salt, pepper, and a few grindings of fresh nutmeg. Whisk into the veal mixture and heat slowly for 5 minutes. Sprinkle with the parsley and serve immediately.

MARINATED VEAL CHOPS

SERVES 4
PREPARATION TIME 5 MINUTES
MARINATING TIME 24 HOURS
COOKING TIME 8 TO 15 MINUTES

4 12-ounce center-cut veal
  chops
1/2 cup olive oil
1/2 of a small onion, chopped
1/4 cup tarragon vinegar

2 tablespoons chopped garlic
1 teaspoon oregano
Salt
Freshly ground pepper

Combine all of the ingredients, except the veal chops, and mix well. Add the veal chops; cover and marinate for 24 hours in the refrigerator. Remove from marinade and grill to desired doneness.

HUNGARIAN VEAL GOULASH

SERVES 6 TO 8
PREPARATION TIME 20 MINUTES
COOKING TIME 2 HOURS

A true Hungarian goulash is a spicy, rather thin stew to which potatoes and other vegetables are added before serving. Traditionally it is cooked in a caldron over an open fire. A good goulash is a meal in itself. This is a variation, using veal instead of beef.

3 tablespoons butter
3 cups thinly sliced onion
3 pounds veal stew, cut into
  2-inch cubes
1 1/2 tablespoons Hungarian
  paprika
1 tablespoon flour
1 1/2 teaspoons salt

1 cup hot beef stock
1 cup julienne-cut green bell
  pepper
1 cup peeled and chopped
  tomato
1/4 to 1/2 teaspoon caraway
  seeds
1/2 cup sour cream

Melt the butter in a Dutch oven or heavy pot. Brown the onion and veal over medium heat, stirring to brown all sides of the veal. Add the paprika, flour, and salt. Cook for 2 minutes. Stir in the stock. Cover and simmer over low heat for 1 hour.

Add the green pepper, tomato, and caraway seeds. Cover and cook an additional 30 minutes, or until tender. Stir occasionally and add a little more stock or white wine if more liquid is needed. Blend in the sour cream. Taste and adjust seasonings. Serve with egg noodles, if desired.

VEAU À L'ALSACE

SERVES 4
PREPARATION TIME 10 MINUTES
COOKING TIME 25 MINUTES

The sauce in this entree is so versatile it can be used over tournedos, veal chops, or even chopped sirloin.

1 cup heavy cream
1 tablespoon dried tarragon
1 tablespoon Dijon mustard
1 to 1 1/2 pounds veal scallops
  (large slices if possible)
Salt
Freshly ground pepper

Flour
5 tablespoons butter
1 tablespoon oil
2 cups very thinly sliced onions
1 small clove garlic, pressed
1/4 cup tarragon vinegar

Combine cream, tarragon, and mustard and set aside. Season the veal with salt and pepper. Dredge lightly in flour, shaking off the excess. Heat 3 tablespoons of the butter and oil in a skillet until hot. Add the veal and sauté until nicely browned on both sides, about 2 to 3 minutes per side. Remove from pan and keep warm.

Pour off any fat remaining in the skillet. Add the remaining butter. Sauté the onions and garlic until soft but not brown, about 5 minutes. Season to taste with salt and pepper. Add the vinegar and reduce by half. Add the cream mixture and cook until sauce has reduced and coats a spoon. Taste and correct seasonings. Spoon over the veal and serve immediately.

VEAL PORTOFINO

SERVES 6   .
PREPARATION TIME 15 MINUTES
COOKING TIME 15 MINUTES

An easy, savory main course with a Mediterranean character.

2 pounds veal cutlets,
  sliced thin
2 tablespoons butter
1 tablespoon oil
1/2 cup chopped onion
2 cloves garlic, minced
1/2 cup dry white wine
4 large tomatoes, peeled,
  seeded, and chopped

12 black olives, cut in half
3 teaspoons capers
1/2 teaspoon dried oregano
Salt
Freshly ground pepper
2 tablespoons chopped fresh
  parsley

Sauté the veal in the butter and oil until lightly browned, a minute or two on each side. Remove the veal and add the onion and garlic to the pan. Sauté for a few minutes without browning. Add the wine and boil for 1 minute. Stir in the tomatoes, olives, capers, oregano, salt and pepper to taste. Cover and simmer for 15 minutes. Return veal to pan and heat through. Transfer to a serving platter and sprinkle with the parsley.

VEAL IN GRAINY-MUSTARD SAUCE

SERVES 8
PREPARATION TIME 20 MINUTES
COOKING TIME 30 MINUTES

Grainy mustard can actually crunch in your mouth; the texture comes from mustard seed hulls. The combination of Dijon and grainy mustard gives this recipe a new dimension.

2 1/2 pounds veal scallops
3 tablespoons butter
1/2 onion, chopped
1 1/2 cups white wine

1 cup chicken or veal stock
3 cups heavy cream
1/2 cup Dijon mustard
1/2 cup grainy mustard

Sauté the veal in the butter until lightly browned. Remove the veal from the pan. Add the onion and sauté until soft. Add wine and stock and bring to a boil. Return veal to pan and simmer, covered, for 20 minutes. Remove veal and keep warm. Reduce stock until syrupy. Add the heavy cream and reduce further until it has a saucelike consistency. Whisk in the mustards. Return veal to pan until just heated through.

VITELLO TONNATO

SERVES 6 TO 8
PREPARATION TIME 40 MINUTES
COOKING TIME 2 1/2 HOURS
REFRIGERATION TIME 24 HOURS

Although this dish does require time, it is made at least 24 hours in advance so you won't feel rushed. Homemade mayonnaise is essential.

4 cups water
1 carrot
1 medium onion
1 stalk celery
3 sprigs fresh parsley
1 bay leaf
A 2 1/2- to 3-pound boneless veal roast, tied
1 7-ounce can tuna fish, drained

1 small can anchovy fillets, drained
1/4 cup fresh lemon juice
3/4 cup olive oil
3 tablespoons capers
1/2 cup Mayonnaise†
Lemon slices
Capers

In a deep pot, place the water, the carrot, onion, celery, parsley, and bay leaf. Bring to a boil and add the veal roast. Return to a boil, reduce heat, cover, and simmer for 2 hours or until tender. Remove the pot from the heat and allow meat to cool in the broth.

In a processor, purée the tuna with the anchovies and lemon juice. Add the oil, a drop at a time, until the mixture has the consistency of a mayonnaise. Transfer to a bowl. Fold in the capers and mayonnaise. Taste and correct for seasonings.

When the meat is cold, remove from the broth. Slice the roast thinly and arrange on a serving platter. Cover with the sauce. Cover with plastic wrap and refrigerate at least 24 hours. (It will keep nicely up to a week.) When ready to serve, garnish with lemon slices and capers.

VEAL MEDALLIONS IN CREAMY CHIVE SAUCE

SERVES 6
PREPARATION TIME 10 MINUTES
COOKING TIME 15 MINUTES

A deliciously delicate sauce.

6 veal medallions, 6 ounces
  each, taken from the loin
2 tablespoons flour
4 tablespoons unsalted butter
2 shallots, chopped
1/2 cup chicken stock

1/2 cup dry vermouth
1 cup heavy cream
4 ounces (1 stick) unsalted
  butter
3/4 cup chopped chives

Dredge the veal in the flour, shaking off the excess. Heat the butter in a heavy skillet until hot. Add the veal pieces and brown on both sides. Lower heat and cook a few minutes more. Transfer veal to a platter and keep warm.

Add the shallots to the pan and sauté until soft. Pour in the chicken stock and vermouth. Cook until reduced to a thick glaze. Whisk in the cream and cook until reduced and thickened, about 10 minutes. Remove from heat and whisk in the butter. Stir the chopped chives into the sauce. Taste and correct seasonings. Arrange the medallions on plates. Spoon some of the sauce over each medallion. If desired, garnish with a tablespoon of Uncooked Tomato Sauce.†

VEAL SHANKS WITH LEMON

SERVES 4
PREPARATION TIME 15 MINUTES
COOKING TIME 1 HOUR 15 MINUTES

Wonderful family fare. Serve with plain noodles or rice; there is plenty of sauce to cover.

4 pieces of veal shank, with
  bone, and weighing about
  3 1/2 pounds
Flour
Salt
Pepper
1/4 cup olive oil
1 cup finely chopped onion

1 teaspoon finely minced garlic
1/2 cup dry white wine
1/2 cup chicken stock
Juice of 1 small lemon
2 sprigs fresh parsley
1/2 teaspoon dried thyme
1 teaspoon grated lemon rind

Dredge the veal shanks in flour, shaking off the excess. Season with salt and pepper. Heat the oil in a heavy skillet. Brown the veal well on both sides. Pour off the fat from the skillet. Stir in onion and garlic and cook until vegetables are soft. Add the wine and cook, scraping up the pieces clinging to the bottom of the pan. Stir in chicken stock, lemon juice, parsley, and thyme. Cover and bring to a boil. Reduce heat and continue cooking over a low heat for 1 hour and 15 minutes, or until tender. Stir in lemon rind just before serving.

GYROS

SERVES 4 TO 6
PREPARATION TIME 20 MINUTES
COOKING TIME 10 MINUTES

Gyros are sandwiches made in pita-bread pockets. This version, made with a ground lamb mixture, is popular with children and adults alike.

GYROS

1 pound ground lamb	1/2 teaspoon dried thyme
1 large clove garlic, pressed	1/2 teaspoon dried rosemary
2 teaspoons lemon juice	1/2 teaspoon pepper
1/2 teaspoon dried basil	1/4 teaspoon salt
1/4 teaspoon ground dried marjoram	2 tablespoons chopped fresh parsley

Combine all the ingredients for the gyros in a large bowl and blend well. Heat a skillet and cook the mixture, over medium heat, stirring constantly until the meat is nicely browned. Drain off any fat.

SAUCE

2 cups sour cream	1/2 teaspoon salt
1 medium cucumber, peeled, seeded, and puréed	3 pita breads, cut in half and warmed
1 clove garlic, pressed	2 tomatoes, chopped
2 tablespoons sugar	1 onion, chopped

Combine the ingredients for the sauce and blend well. Spoon the meat mixture into the pita pockets and top with the tomatoes and onions. Spoon some of the sauce over each sandwich and serve immediately.

GRILLED LAMB CHOPS NIÇOISE

SERVES 4
PREPARATION TIME 15 MINUTES
COOKING TIME 10 MINUTES

1/4 cup olive oil
2 large onions, thinly sliced
4 cloves garlic, minced
4 tomatoes, peeled, seeded, and
  chopped
1 cup pitted black olives,
  halved
2 tablespoons capers
1/2 cup strong beef stock

1 teaspoon dried basil
1/4 teaspoon dried oregano
Pinch of sugar
1/2 cup chopped fresh parsley
Salt
Freshly ground pepper
8 loin lamb chops
Olive oil

Heat oil in a large skillet. Add onions and garlic and cook until soft, about 10 minutes. Add the tomatoes, olives, and capers and sauté for 5 minutes. Turn heat to high and stir in stock, basil, oregano, and sugar. Cook for a few minutes. Taste and correct seasonings. Stir in parsley. Keep warm.

Preheat the grill or broiler. Brush the chops with a little olive oil. Salt and pepper lightly. Grill to desired degree of doneness. Place the chops on a serving platter. Cover with some of the sauce. Serve immediately.

AGNEAU À LA PROVENÇALE

SERVES 4 TO 6
PREPARATION TIME 20 MINUTES
COOKING TIME 2 1/2 HOURS

Prepare this traditional French lamb stew on a chilly winter's night.

4 to 5 pounds lamb shoulder
5 tablespoons olive oil
Salt
Freshly ground pepper
2 teaspoons dried thyme
2 teaspoons dried oregano
2 teaspoons dried marjoram
1 teaspoon dried savory

1 bay leaf
2 heads garlic, unpeeled
  and cloves separated
1 1/2 cups dry white wine
2 cups veal or chicken stock
4 tablespoons (1/2 stick) butter
2 tablespoons chopped fresh
  parsley

Preheat oven to 350 degrees. Remove all the fat from the lamb. Cut into serving pieces. Heat the oil in a heavy pan. Add the pieces of lamb, a few at a time, and brown well. Sprinkle with salt and pepper. Stir in the herbs and garlic cloves. Stir in the white wine and 3/4 cup of the stock. Cover tightly and cook slowly in the oven, adding small amounts of the stock as needed to keep the lamb moist. Cook until tender, about 2 hours.

Remove the meat from the sauce and strain the sauce through a sieve, using a wooden spoon to press the garlic through the sieve. Skim off any excess fat and reduce sauce to thicken, if necessary. Taste and correct seasonings. Whisk in the butter. Arrange the lamb on a serving platter and coat with the sauce. Sprinkle with the parsley.

BUTTERFLIED LEG OF LAMB

SERVES 6 TO 8
PREPARATION TIME 10 MINUTES
MARINATING TIME 24 HOURS
COOKING TIME 40 TO 60 MINUTES

1 tablespoon black peppercorns, crushed
1 tablespoon green peppercorns, crushed
1 tablespoon white peppercorns, crushed
4 large cloves garlic, crushed
4 tablespoons fresh rosemary

3 sprigs fresh mint
1/2 cup red wine vinegar
1/2 cup dry red wine
1/4 cup soy sauce
A 4- to 6-pound leg of lamb, boned and butterflied
3 tablespoons Dijon mustard

Combine all of the peppercorns and blend well. Set half of the peppercorns aside. Combine the remaining peppercorns with the garlic, rosemary, mint, vinegar, wine, and soy sauce. Mix well and pour over the lamb. Marinate under refrigeration for 24 hours.

Preheat oven to 450 degrees. Remove lamb from the marinade and pat dry. Reserve the marinade. Spread the mustard and the other half of the peppercorns over the lamb, skin side up. Place in a shallow roasting pan. Spoon some of the marinade around the meat. Roast in the oven approximately 10 to 12 minutes per pound for medium rare. Baste with the marinade every 15 minutes while roasting. Remove from the oven and let rest 10 minutes before carving. Slice into thin strips and serve with the pan juices.

LAMB SHISH KABOBS

SERVES 6 TO 8
PREPARATION TIME 10 MINUTES
MARINATING TIME 2 HOURS
COOKING TIME 20 MINUTES

This dish is excellent for summer entertaining because everything is done well in advance. The kabobs should always be marinated for several hours—the longer, the better. If you chill the vegetables before putting on the skewers, they will not overcook.

MARINADE

1 1/2 cups salad oil	2 tablespoons dry mustard
3/4 cup soy sauce	2 tablespoons chopped fresh
1/2 cup wine vinegar	parsley
1/3 cup fresh lemon juice	1 tablespoon freshly ground
1/4 cup Worcestershire sauce	pepper
1 clove garlic	2 1/2 teaspoons salt

Blend all ingredients for marinade in processor or blender for 1 minute. Store tightly covered in the refrigerator until ready to use. (This recipe makes 3 1/2 cups of marinade.) Soak the meat in the marinade at least for several hours.

KABOBS

2 1/2 pounds lamb, cut in 2-inch squares	Cherry tomatoes
	Large mushrooms
Green peppers, cut into 2-inch squares	Tiny onions
	Bacon squares (optional)

Start the charcoal fire. Arrange the meat on the skewers, alternating green peppers, tomatoes, mushrooms, onions, and bacon (if desired). Have skewers 3 to 4 inches above the fire. Broil for 15 to 20 minutes, brushing occasionally with some of the marinade. Turn the skewers frequently so that the meat will cook evenly. Serve with rice pilaf or lemon pasta.

LAMB IN PHYLLO

SERVES 2 TO 4
PREPARATION TIME 45 MINUTES
COOKING TIME 30 MINUTES

A 3- to 3 1/2-pound rack of
  lamb, boned and trimmed of
  fat
2 teaspoons vegetable oil,
  heated
Salt
Freshly ground pepper
4 tablespoons butter

1/2 pound fresh mushrooms,
  finely chopped
3 shallots, finely chopped
3 sheets of phyllo dough
1 egg lightly beaten

Madeira Sauce†

Sauté the lamb in the hot oil, over high heat, until nicely browned on all sides, about 3 to 4 minutes. The meat should remain very rare. Sprinkle with salt and pepper. Wrap and refrigerate until cold.

Preheat the oven to 400 degrees. To the skillet the meat was cooked in add 1 tablespoon of the butter. Sauté the mushrooms and shallots over high heat, stirring frequently, until the moisture from the mushrooms evaporates. Let cool to room temperature. Season with salt and pepper.

Melt the remaining butter. Lay 1 sheet of phyllo on a flat surface, short side toward you. Brush with some of the butter. Place another sheet of phyllo on top. Brush with butter. Repeat with the third sheet. Spoon half of the mushroom mixture across the phyllo, leaving a 2-inch margin on all sides. Place the lamb on top and cover with the remaining mushroom mixture. Fold the bottom of the phyllo up and over the lamb. Fold in the long edges. Starting at the bottom, roll up about three quarters of the phyllo to enclose the lamb. Brush a strip across the top with some of the beaten egg. Finish rolling up the lamb and press the top edge of the phyllo to seal. Transfer to a baking sheet, seam side down. Brush the top of the dough with the remaining egg.

Bake for 20 minutes for medium rare. Let rest for 10 minutes. Carve into 4 thick slices. Serve immediately accompanied by the Madeira Sauce.

PERSIAN LAMB

SERVES 6 TO 8
PREPARATION TIME 30 MINUTES
COOKING TIME 1 HOUR 30 MINUTES

This dish looks lovely served on a large oval platter. Place the lamb in the center and spoon a ring of couscous around the outside. Sprinkle paprika and chopped parsley over lamb for a vibrant color.

LAMB

3 pounds lean lamb, cut into 1/2-inch cubes

2 medium onions, finely chopped

2 teaspoons coriander

2 teaspoons cumin

1 teaspoon cinnamon

1/2 teaspoon saffron powder

1/2 teaspoon ground ginger

1/2 to 1 teaspoon salt

1/2 teaspoon freshly ground pepper

2 dashes cayenne

4 tablespoons butter

2 to 3 cups water

3/4 pound dried apricots, soaked, drained, and chopped

1/2 cup raisins, soaked until plump, then drained

2 ounces ground almonds

1 teaspoon rose water

Couscous (recipe follows)

Mix the lamb with the onions, spices, and seasonings. Melt the butter in a large skillet that can be covered. Brown the lamb-and-onion mixture over a medium heat, stirring frequently. Add just enough water to cover the lamb. Cover pan and simmer over low heat for 1 hour.

Stir in apricots, raisins, and almonds. Simmer an additional 30 minutes, adding water if necessary. Stir in rose water just prior to serving. Mix thoroughly. Serve with couscous.

COUSCOUS

3 cups water

2 chicken bouillon cubes

2 dashes of Tabasco (optional)

1 1/2 to 1 3/4 cups couscous

4 tablespoons butter

Bring the water and bouillon cubes to a boil in a large saucepan. Add the Tabasco and slowly stir in the couscous. Cover and simmer for 20 minutes. Toss in the butter and serve.

MEDALLION OF LAMB WITH JAPANESE EGGPLANT

SERVES 4
PREPARATION TIME 45 MINUTES
COOKING TIME 10 MINUTES

Serve this unique combination at your next dinner party and revel in the glory.

2 small Japanese eggplants
Salt
2 tablespoons minced shallot
1 clove garlic, minced
2 tablespoons unsalted butter
1/2 cup Madeira wine
1 cup veal or beef stock
1 tablespoon olive oil
1 large tomato, peeled, seeded, and chopped
2 teaspoons coarse-grained mustard

3 tablespoons unsalted butter
1 teaspoon snipped fresh chives
1 teaspoon minced fresh tarragon leaves
3/4 teaspoon chopped fresh thyme leaves
1 teaspoon fresh lemon juice
Drop of Tabasco sauce
4 tablespoons olive oil
2 pounds lamb medallions, trimmed of all fat and carved into 1/4-inch slices

Beginning at the stem end, slice the eggplant crosswise into 1/4-inch slices, leaving 1 1/2 inches on the blossom end intact. Peel the 1 1/2-inch pieces and chop fine. You should have approximately 4 tablespoons. Sprinkle the eggplant slices and the chopped eggplant with salt. Let stand for 30 minutes. Rinse the slices and pat dry with paper towels. Rinse the chopped eggplant and squeeze dry.

In a small saucepan, sauté the shallot and garlic in the butter over moderate heat until golden. Stir in the Madeira and stock. Bring to a boil and cook until reduced by half. Strain. Heat the olive oil in a skillet. Sauté the chopped eggplant until golden. Stir in the tomato and cook for 5 minutes. Stir in the strained sauce and reduce to 2/3 cup. Remove from heat and whisk in mustard, butter, chives, tarragon, thyme, lemon juice, and Tabasco sauce. Keep warm.

Sauté the eggplant slices in 2 tablespoons of the olive oil until golden. Drain on paper towels. Add the remaining oil to the pan and quickly sauté the lamb slices, 2 to 3 minutes per side.

Arrange the lamb slices and the eggplant slices on each plate in an alternating pattern. Spoon the sauce over all. Serve immediately.

SONOMA STUFFED LEG OF LAMB

SERVES 8 TO 10
PREPARATION TIME 1 HOUR
MARINATING TIME 4 HOURS
COOKING TIME 1 HOUR 10 MINUTES

LAMB

A 4- to 4 1/2-pound leg of lamb, boned, with most of the fat removed

Juice of 1 large lemon

2 tablespoons olive oil

1 clove garlic, crushed

1 tablespoon dried crushed rosemary

2 pounds fresh spinach, stemmed and cooked

1 onion, finely chopped

1 clove garlic, minced

2 tablespoons butter

2 tablespoons olive oil

1 cup chopped mushrooms

1 egg, beaten

Salt

Freshly ground pepper

Place the lamb in a shallow baking dish. Combine the lemon juice, olive oil, garlic, and rosemary. Pour over the lamb. Marinate for several hours or overnight in the refrigerator.

Preheat oven to 450 degrees. Squeeze out the moisture from the spinach. Finely chop. Sauté the onion and garlic in the butter and oil until softened, about 10 minutes. Add the spinach and mushrooms. Sauté over high heat until all the moisture evaporates. Let cool slightly. Stir in the egg. Season to taste with salt and pepper. Fill the cavity of the lamb with the spinach mixture. Sew the lamb closed. Place, seam side down, in a shallow roasting pan. Roast for 10 minutes. Turn oven down to 375 and continue roasting for 30 to 45 minutes for pink lamb.

SAUCE

4 cups beef consommé

1 cup red wine

1/2 cup tomato purée

1 bay leaf

1/4 cup Madeira wine

2 tablespoons lemon juice

2 tablespoons butter

3 tablespoons chopped fresh parsley

While the lamb is cooking, prepare the sauce. In a saucepan, combine the beef consommé, red wine, tomato purée, and bay leaf. Bring to a boil. Reduce the heat and cook until reduced to 2 cups. Remove the bay leaf. Stir in the Madeira and lemon juice. Boil for 3 minutes. Just prior to serving, swirl in the butter and parsley.

To serve: carve the leg of lamb into thin slices and arrange on a serving platter. Spoon over some of the sauce. Serve with additional sauce in a gravy boat.

LAMB MEDALLIONS WITH MADEIRA SAUCE

SERVES 4 TO 6
PREPARATION TIME 30 MINUTES
COOKING TIME 30 MINUTES

These medallions are presented on artichoke bottoms stuffed with a delicate onion sauce.

2 large onions, finely chopped	White pepper
6 tablespoons butter	6 cooked artichoke bottoms
2 tablespoons flour	12 French-cut lamb chops
3/4 cup milk	6 tablespoons butter
Bay leaf	1/2 cup Madeira wine
Salt	1/2 cup beef stock

Cover the onions with water, bring to a boil, and simmer for 5 minutes. Drain in a sieve. Melt 4 tablespoons of the butter in a saucepan. Add the onions and cook slowly, without browning, for 10 minutes. In another saucepan, melt the remaining butter. Stir in the flour and cook for 2 minutes, without browning. Slowly whisk in the milk. Add the bay leaf and bring to a boil, stirring constantly. Add salt and pepper to taste. Remove the bay leaf and add the sauce to the onions. Cover and simmer for 5 minutes. Purée in a processor or food mill. Set aside. Heat the artichoke bottoms in simmering water.

Remove the bone and all fat from the lamb chops. Sauté the medallions in 2 tablespoons of the butter over a high heat until nicely browned, about 3 to 4 minutes on each side. Remove from the pan and keep warm.

Pour off any fat remaining in the pan. Add the Madeira and stock. Cook over high heat until reduced by half. Swirl in the remaining butter. Season with salt and pepper.

Slice the warm artichoke bottoms in half horizontally. Arrange on a serving platter. Fill each bottom with the onion sauce. Place a lamb medallion on top. Drizzle the Madeira sauce over all. Serve immediately.

SWISS CROWN ROAST OF LAMB

SERVES 8
PREPARATION TIME 1 HOUR
COOKING TIME 1 1/2 HOURS

3 rib rack of lamb, made into a
   crown roast, trimmed of all
   fat and tied
Juice of 1 small lemon
1 tablespoon olive oil
2 large cloves garlic
2 tablespoons rosemary
8 medium baking potatoes,
   coarsely grated

1 pound bacon, diced
1 large onion, diced
1 teaspoon garlic salt
Freshly ground black pepper
1/2 cup chopped fresh parsley
1 cup grated Swiss cheese
Salt

Preheat the oven to 400 degrees. In a food processor or blender, mix the lemon juice, olive oil, garlic, and rosemary until well blended. Rub the inside and outside of the roast with the mixture. Roast in the oven for 20 minutes. Remove from the oven, drain off any fat, and cool.

While the lamb is cooking, prepare the potatoes. Soak in a bowl of cold water for 15 minutes. Drain and pat dry. Fry the bacon until crisp. Remove with a slotted spoon and drain on paper towels. Pour off all but 4 tablespoons of the bacon grease. Add the onion and sauté until transparent. Stir in the potatoes, garlic salt, and pepper. Fry for 20 to 25 minutes, or until the potatoes are cooked. Stir in the cheese, parsley, and salt to taste.

Fill the center of the roast with the potatoes. Bake for 20 minutes. Serve with a Madeira sauce.

SHREDDED PORK WITH GARLIC SAUCE

SERVES 4
PREPARATION TIME 20 MINUTES
COOKING TIME 5 MINUTES

For a hotter dish, add 1 teaspoon black bean sauce with chili.

3/4 pound lean pork, cut into shreds
1 tablespoon soy sauce
1 teaspoon rice wine or sherry
2 teaspoons cornstarch mixed with 3 tablespoons water
2 to 3 tablespoons oil
2 green onions, chopped
2 small cloves garlic, chopped
1 tablespoon bean paste
1 tablespoon chopped ginger root

4 ounces water chestnuts, sliced
1/2 cup carrot strips
1 tablespoon rice wine or sherry
2 teaspoons soy sauce
2 teaspoons sugar
1 teaspoon sesame oil
1 teaspoon plum sauce
1 teaspoon cornstarch mixed in 2 tablespoons water
Black bean sauce with chili (optional)

Mix pork with soy sauce, wine, or sherry, and cornstarch mixture. Let sit for 30 minutes.

Heat the oil in a wok or skillet. Stir-fry meat over medium heat until it loses its pink color. Remove from the pan and set aside. Add the green onions, garlic, bean paste, and ginger root and stir-fry for one minute. Stir in the water chestnuts and carrots. Return pork to pan. Mix the remaining ingredients together and add to the pan. Toss together lightly. Transfer to a serving platter and serve immediately.

CHERRY ALMOND GLAZED PORK

SERVES 6
PREPARATION TIME 30 MINUTES
COOKING TIME 1 1/2 HOURS

Buy whole nutmeg to grate as you need it; commercially ground nutmeg quickly loses its flavor.

A 3-pound boneless pork loin
  roast
Salt
Freshly ground pepper
1 10-ounce jar cherry preserves
1/4 cup red wine

2 tablespoons light corn syrup
1/4 teaspoon each ground
  cinnamon, nutmeg, and
  cloves
1/4 cup toasted slivered
  almonds

Preheat oven to 375 degrees. Trim excess fat from the roast. Rub with a little salt and pepper. Place fat side up on a rack in a shallow roasting pan.

In a saucepan, combine the preserves, wine, corn syrup, and spices. Bring to a boil, stirring constantly. Reduce the heat and simmer for 5 minutes. Add the almonds.

Brush the roast with some of the glaze. Bake for approximately 1 to 1 1/2 hours or until a meat thermometer registers 170 degrees. Brush with the glaze frequently while baking. Remove from the oven and let rest for 5 minutes before carving. Serve with the remaining glaze on the side.

PORK BRAISED WITH WHISKEY

SERVES 6
PREPARATION TIME 30 MINUTES
COOKING TIME 2 HOURS

18 prunes
1 1/2 cups warm beef stock
A 3-pound boneless pork loin
  roast
1/3 pound smoked ham, thickly
  sliced and cut into strips
1/3 cup Dijon mustard

2/3 cup dark brown sugar
2 tablespoons oil
2/3 cup bourbon
Salt
Freshly ground pepper
Bouquet garni of thyme, sage,
  and parsley

Preheat the oven to 375 degrees. Soak the prunes in 1 cup of the stock. Trim all fat off the pork roast and tie. Insert the ham strips into the pork loin with the tip of a sharp knife. Brush with the mustard and roll in the brown sugar. Heat the oil in a heavy casserole. Brown the roast on all sides for about 10 minutes, taking care not to burn the sugar. Pour half of the bourbon over the roast and flame it. Add the remaining half cup of stock and salt and pepper. Cook, covered, for 1 1/2 hours. Halfway through cooking, turn the meat and add the bouquet garni. Add the prunes and stock the last 10 minutes of cooking.

Remove the roast from the pan and keep warm. Skim off and discard the fat remaining in the pan. Bring the pan juices to a boil and add the remaining bourbon. Scrape to loosen any brown bits clinging to the bottom of the pan. Simmer for 5 to 7 minutes or until nicely thickened. Season to taste with salt and pepper. Slice the roast and arrange in overlapping slices on a warmed platter. Spoon on some sauce and garnish with the prunes. Serve immediately.

WINTER PORK AND SQUASH BAKE

SERVES 6
PREPARATION TIME 20 MINUTES
COOKING TIME 1 HOUR

Colorful with a light, subtle flavor.

2 pounds boneless pork, trimmed and cut into 3/4-inch pieces	1 tablespoon oil
	1 1/2 cups chicken stock
2 tablespoons mustard	1/2 to 1 teaspoon salt
1/4 cup brown sugar	1/4 teaspoon pepper
3 tablespoons flour	1/2 teaspoon dried thyme
2 tablespoons butter	2 pounds winter squash, peeled and cut into 1-inch cubes

Preheat oven to 350 degrees. Brush the pork pieces with the mustard. Combine the brown sugar and flour. Roll the pork pieces in the mixture and coat well. Heat the butter and oil in a skillet. Brown the pork well and transfer to a casserole. Pour off the fat remaining in the skillet. Add stock, salt, pepper, and thyme to the skillet and bring to a boil, stirring to scrape off all the brown bits clinging to the bottom. Pour into the casserole. Drop the squash into boiling water and cook for 5 minutes. Drain and add to the pork.

Cover the casserole and bake for 30 minutes, stirring once. Uncover and bake for an additional 30 minutes, stirring often, until sauce thickens and the meat is tender.

PORK TENDERLOIN WITH ENOKI MUSHROOMS

SERVES 6
PREPARATION TIME 15 MINUTES
COOKING TIME 20 MINUTES

Enoki are Japanese mushrooms found fresh in the produce department of many grocery stores. They usually come packaged. Cut off just above the root end to separate.

2 1-pound pork tenderloins
5 tablespoons butter
2 tablespoons oil
8 large mushrooms, thinly
   sliced

3 large shallots, finely chopped
3/4 cup dry Marsala wine
1/2 cup strong beef stock
3/4 cup heavy cream
2 packages enoki mushrooms

Preheat oven to 400 degrees. Dry the tenderloins and tuck under the small tail end. Melt 2 tablespoons of the butter and oil over high heat in a heavy pan. Sauté the tenderloins until nicely browned, about 3 minutes per side. Transfer to a shallow baking dish. Roast in the oven for approximately 10 minutes while preparing the sauce.

Pour off all the fat remaining in the pan. Add the remaining butter and sauté mushrooms and shallots over high heat until golden. Pour in the Marsala and stock, scraping the bottom of the pan. Bring to a boil and reduce to 1/2 cup. Stir in the heavy cream and continue to boil until thickened. Stir in the enoki mushrooms. Season to taste with salt and pepper.

Slice the tenderloins. Arrange in overlapping slices on a serving platter. Spoon the sauce down the center of the slices. Serve immediately.

PORK TENDERLOIN CHINESE STYLE

SERVES 6
PREPARATION TIME 10 MINUTES
MARINATING TIME 3 HOURS
COOKING TIME 45 TO 60 MINUTES

MARINADE
1 cup chicken stock
2 tablespoons brown sugar
2 tablespoons soy sauce
2 tablespoons ketchup

2 green onions, chopped
1 clove garlic
1 walnut-size piece fresh ginger

Place all ingredients together in food processor or blender. Blend until mixed.

TENDERLOIN

2 1-pound pork tenderloins
2 tablespoons soy sauce
2 tablespoons ketchup

2 tablespoons toasted sesame
seeds

Marinate the tenderloins for 3 hours. Preheat oven to 350 degrees. Bake for approximately 30 minutes, basting often with the marinade. Turn once during cooking.

Combine the soy sauce and ketchup. Roll the cooked roast in the mixture. Sprinkle with the sesame seeds. Serve with a hot mustard or a sweet-and-sour sauce.

PORK CHOPS WITH RASPBERRY VINEGAR SAUCE

SERVES 4
PREPARATION TIME 10 MINUTES
COOKING TIME 30 MINUTES

4 large boneless pork chops
2 tablespoons flour
Salt
1/4 teaspoon white pepper
1/2 teaspoon dried rosemary
1 clove garlic, pressed

2 tablespoons oil
1/2 cup beef stock
1/2 cup dry vermouth
1/4 cup raspberry vinegar
1/4 cup heavy cream

Dredge the pork chops in the flour, shaking off the excess. Season both sides with the salt, pepper, and rosemary. Sauté the garlic in the oil for 1 minute. Add the pork chops and brown. Pour off the fat in the pan. Stir in the stock and vermouth. Cover and simmer for 20 to 30 minutes. Remove the chops from the pan and keep warm.

Turn up heat to high and reduce sauce in pan until thick. Add the raspberry vinegar and continue cooking until thickened. Add the heavy cream and simmer until sauce is thick enough to coat the chops. Taste and adjust seasonings. Arrange the pork chops on a platter. Spoon over the sauce. Serve immediately.

PORK MEDALLIONS WITH MARSALA SAUCE

SERVES 4
PREPARATION TIME 10 MINUTES
COOKING TIME 15 TO 20 MINUTES

1 1/2 pounds pork tenderloin,
   cut into 1/2-inch slices
Flour
8 tablespoons butter
2 shallots, minced
6 large mushrooms, very thinly
   sliced

2/3 cup dry Marsala wine
1/3 cup chicken stock
Salt
Freshly ground pepper

Preheat oven to 200 degrees. Place the pork pieces between 2 sheets of wax paper. Flatten to 1/4-inch thickness. Dredge in flour, shaking off the excess. Melt 4 tablespoons of the butter in a skillet over medium-high heat. Add the pork medallions, a few at a time, and sauté until golden, about 2 to 3 minutes per side. Transfer to a platter and keep warm in the oven.

Pour off all the fat remaining in the skillet. Add 2 tablespoons butter and sauté the shallots for 2 minutes. Add the mushrooms and continue sautéing over high heat until lightly colored. Stir in the Marsala and stock. Boil over high heat until reduced by a third. Remove from heat and swirl in the remaining butter. Season to taste with salt and pepper. Spoon over the pork medallions. Serve immediately.

MESQUITE-GRILLED PORK TENDERLOIN

SERVES 4 TO 6
PREPARATION TIME 20 MINUTES
COOKING TIME 40 MINUTES

The fresh plum sauce nicely complements the delicious flavor of the mesquite-grilled pork. Serve with a Chenin Blanc.

2 cups chicken stock
1 cup fruity white wine
1 1/4 pounds fresh red plums,
   pitted and finely chopped
1 to 2 tablespoons sugar
1/2 to 1 teaspoon lemon juice

Salt
Freshly ground pepper
1 cup mesquite wood chips
2 1-pound pork tenderloins
4 red plums, sliced into thin
   wedges

Bring the chicken stock and wine to a boil in a large saucepan. Continue boiling until reduced to 1/2 cup, about 20 to 30 minutes. Stir in the plums, sugar, lemon juice, salt and pepper to taste. Heat to boiling and cook an additional 5 minutes. Remove from heat. Taste for seasonings. Adjust sugar and lemon juice as necessary. Purée in a food processor. Pass through a food mill or strainer. The sauce should be fairly thick. If it is not thick enough to hold its shape, cook longer.

Prepare a charcoal fire or grill. Scatter about 1 cup mesquite wood chips over the hot coals. Let the wood start to smoke. Fold ends of each tenderloin under middle to make a uniform thickness. Grill pork directly on hot grill, turning frequently, for about 20 minutes, or until a meat thermometer registers 150 degrees. Remove to a warmed platter and let rest 5 minutes.

Stir the sliced plums into the sauce and heat gently. Slice the tenderloins into 1/4-inch slices. Spoon a few tablespoons of the sauce on warmed dinner plates. Arrange the pork slices on top of the sauce. Garnish with the sliced plums. Serve immediately.

THIRTEEN-SPICE TENDERLOIN

SERVES 8
PREPARATION TIME 30 MINUTES
MARINATING TIME 24 HOURS
COOKING TIME 1 HOUR

3 pork tenderloins
1 teaspoon oil
5 bay leaves, finely chopped
1 1/2 teaspoons each of paprika, ground cloves, grated nutmeg, ground peppercorns, and ground thyme
1 teaspoon ground mace
3/4 teaspoon each of ground basil, ground oregano, and cinnamon

1/4 teaspoon allspice
1 tablespoon oil
1 clove garlic, pressed
1/2 teaspoon dried rosemary
1 cup beef stock
1/2 cup dry white wine
2 green onions, chopped
1/2 cup water
1 teaspoon Dijon mustard mixed with 1/2 teaspoon cornstarch

Rub the pork tenderloins with the oil. Combine the bay leaves with the remaining spices (to the allspice). Rub into the pork. Cover and refrigerate 24 hours. You can marinate the pork for as little as 1 hour, but the flavor is better if you allow it to marinate the entire 24 hours.

Preheat oven to 375 degrees. Heat the oil in a pan. Brown the tenderloins on all sides. Transfer to a roasting pan. Combine the garlic and rosemary and spread over the tenderloin. Bake for approximately 30 minutes or until a meat thermometer registers 150 to 160 degrees.

In a saucepan, combine stock, wine, and onions. Cook until reduced to 1/2 cup. Transfer the tenderloins to a platter and keep warm. Place the roasting pan over medium heat and add the water. Bring to a boil, scraping up any juices on the bottom of the pan. Add the pan juices to the reduced stock. Whisk in the mustard mixture. Simmer until thickened.

Carve the tenderloins into 1/3-inch slices. Arrange on a serving platter. Spoon on some of the sauce. Serve surrounded by assorted steamed and buttered vegetables.

CROWN OF PORK WITH SAFFRON RICE STUFFING

SERVES 6 TO 8
PREPARATION TIME 30 MINUTES
COOKING TIME 1 HOUR

A crown roast must be ordered in advance from your butcher. Make sure he ties it securely. A spectacular entree ideal for a New Year's party.

A 9-rib prepared pork loin crown roast
1 onion, chopped
1 carrot, chopped
1 celery stalk, chopped

3 sprigs fresh rosemary
3 sprigs fresh parsley
Saffron Rice Stuffing (recipe follows)

Preheat oven to 450 degrees. Cover the pork bones with foil to keep from browning. Place the onion, carrot, celery, rosemary, and parsley in a shallow roasting pan. Place the crown roast on top and bake for 10 minutes. Reduce the temperature to 400 degrees and continue baking for 20 to 25 minutes per pound. Remove the roast from the oven 40 minutes before it is done and fill the center with the saffron rice stuffing. Return to the oven and finish roasting.

SAFFRON RICE STUFFING
3 cups chicken stock
4 tablespoons butter
1/4 teaspoon saffron powder
1 1/2 cups long-grain rice

5 ounces dried apricots, sliced
1 cup sliced celery
2/3 cup pecan pieces

In a saucepan, combine the stock, 2 tablespoons of the butter, and the saffron. Bring to a boil and stir in the rice. Lower heat, cover, and cook for 15 minutes. Add the apricots and continue cooking, covered, until all the liquid is absorbed and the rice is tender, about 10 to 15 minutes.

Sauté the celery and pecans in the remaining butter until the celery is tender and the pecans are browned. Remove the rice from the heat and stir in the celery and nuts. Fill the center cavity of the roast. Spoon any remaining rice stuffing in a baking pan and cover with foil. Heat in the oven with the roast.

MAUI RIBS

SERVES 6 TO 8
PREPARATION TIME 15 MINUTES
MARINATING TIME 4 HOURS
COOKING TIME 1 HOUR

These ribs can either be baked in the oven or grilled outdoors. If you have the time, marinate overnight.

4 to 6 pounds lean, well-trimmed baby back ribs	**3 tablespoons grated fresh ginger root**
Boiling water	**1 cup orange marmalade**
1 cup dry sherry	**1/4 cup lemon juice**
1/2 cup soy sauce	**2 tablespoons soy sauce**
2 cloves garlic, crushed	**2 tablespoons drained horseradish**
2 tablespoons dry mustard	

Place the ribs in a large pot and cover with boiling water. Let sit for 5 minutes and drain. This will remove the excess fat. Combine the sherry, soy sauce, garlic, mustard, and ginger root and mix well. Pour over the ribs and marinate at least 4 hours (preferably overnight), turning and brushing with the marinade occasionally.

Preheat the oven to 400 degrees. Place in a shallow roasting pan and brush with the marinade. Bake for 30 to 40 minutes, basting with the marinade or more sherry or turning occasionally.

Prepare a sauce by combining the orange marmalade, lemon juice, soy sauce and horseradish. Place in a saucepan and bring to a boil. Reduce heat and simmer for 5 minutes. Spoon sauce over ribs and return to the oven for 5 minutes to glaze. Pass additional sauce on the side.

To barbecue: Heat the coals until hot. Grill the ribs, basting with the marinade, until tender, about 20 to 30 minutes. Baste with the sauce the last 5 minutes of cooking.

SKEWERED PORK

SERVES 8 TO 10
PREPARATION TIME 10 MINUTES
MARINATING TIME 24 HOURS
COOKING TIME 8 TO 10 MINUTES

For easy summer entertaining, have your guests prepare their own skewers for barbecuing. If you prepare these under the broiler, do not overcook, or they will be very dry.

4 pounds lean pork
2 cloves garlic, minced
1 tablespoon ground coriander
1 tablespoon chili powder
1 teaspoon salt
1/4 cup oil
1 medium onion, chopped

1/4 cup lemon juice
1/4 cup dry sherry
4 tablespoons soy sauce
2 tablespoons brown sugar
1/2 teaspoon freshly ground
    pepper

Trim all the fat from the pork and cut into 1-inch pieces. Combine garlic, coriander, chili powder, salt, and oil. Let stand for 5 minutes. Add remaining ingredients. Toss with pork and let marinate 24 to 48 hours.

Preheat the barbecue coals. Soak bamboo sticks in water for 15 minutes. Skewer the pork pieces on the bamboo sticks. Grill over hot coals for 6 to 7 minutes per side, basting with the marinade while cooking.

FRUITED PORK LOIN

SERVES 6
PREPARATION TIME 20 MINUTES
COOKING TIME 2 1/2 HOURS

1 center-cut loin of pork
    (6 chops)
4 tablespoons olive oil
4 tablespoons soy sauce
4 tablespoons vinegar
4 tablespoons sugar
2 cloves garlic, minced
1/4 teaspoon dried mustard

1/4 teaspoon ground coriander
1/4 teaspoon ground cloves
1/4 teaspoon freshly ground
    pepper
1 fresh pineapple
2 pears, peeled, cored, and
    sliced
Seedless grapes

Preheat the oven to 375 degrees. Have the butcher remove the backbone from the ribs. In a saucepan, mix oil, soy sauce, vinegar, sugar, garlic, mustard, coriander, cloves, and pepper. Bring to a boil. Lower heat and simmer for 30 minutes.

Preheat oven to 375 degrees. Cut pineapple in half. Remove the flesh, keeping the skin intact, and reserve. Place the pork loin in a 9 × 9 baking pan. Brush with the sauce. Cover with the pineapple skin. Roast for about 1 1/2 hours, basting frequently with the sauce, or until done.

Cut the reserved pineapple flesh into wedges. Place in a baking dish together with the pear slices. Brush with the sauce. Bake in the oven with the pork, basting frequently, until just heated through, 10 to 12 minutes. Serve the sliced pork garnished with the pineapple, pear slices, and grapes.

BARBECUED BURRITOS

INDIVIDUAL SERVINGS
PREPARATION TIME 5 TO 10 MINUTES
COOKING TIME 4 TO 6 MINUTES

If you don't have an indoor grill, you can prepare these tasty burritos in the oven. The proportions given are for individual servings, so you can make as many as you like.

FOR EACH BURRITO

1 12-inch flour tortilla, warmed in oven

1/2 cup shredded Cheddar or Jack cheese

1 teaspoon chopped green chili

1/4 cup Polish sausage, cut into bite-size pieces, or cooked, crumbled Italian sausage

2 to 3 thin slices of tomato

3 to 4 red onion rings

Heat grill until hot or heat oven to 375 degrees. Distribute the cheese down the center of the tortilla to within 1 to 2 inches of each edge. Top with the remaining ingredients. Fold the narrow edges over the filling. Fold one side over the filling and then fold the filled section over onto opposite edge of the tortilla.

Let the burrito cook, folded side down, until tortilla is toasted and crisp. Turn smooth side down and let cook until toasted. This will take 2 to 3 minutes per side on a hot grill. Done in the oven, it will take approximately 10 minutes.

DRUNKEN AUNT'S BEAN CURD

SERVES 4
PREPARATION TIME 10 MINUTES
COOKING TIME 10 MINUTES

This quick and easy stir fry combines lean ground pork and firm tofu. Serve with steamed rice.

4 tablespoons vegetable oil
3 small cloves garlic, minced
7 green onions, chopped
1 tablespoon chopped ginger
   root
1/2 pound lean ground pork
2 squares firm tofu (bean curd),
   diced

1 cup water
2 tablespoons hot bean paste
1 1/2 tablespoons soy sauce
1 tablespoon rice wine or
   sherry
1 1/2 teaspoons cornstarch
   mixed with 1 tablespoon
   water

Heat the oil in a wok or large skillet. Stir-fry the garlic, green onions, and ginger until fragrant, about one minute. Add the pork and cook, separating into small pieces, until pork changes color. Add the tofu, water, bean paste, soy sauce, and wine or sherry. Cover and steam for 3 minutes. Stir in cornstarch mixture and cook until thickened. Transfer to a serving platter. Serve immediately.

POLISH SAUSAGE AND LENTIL CASSEROLE

SERVES 6
PREPARATION TIME 20 MINUTES
COOKING TIME 1 HOUR

1 cup lentils, well rinsed
2 tablespoons oil
2 medium onions, chopped
3 cloves garlic, crushed
1 1/2 cups canned tomatoes,
   drained and chopped

2 pounds Polish sausage
   (kielbasa)
1 bay leaf
1 teaspoon sugar
1/2 teaspoon freshly ground
   pepper

Put the rinsed lentils in a large saucepan with salted water to cover. Bring lentils to a boil, cover and cook over low heat for about 20 minutes, or until tender but will still hold their shape. Drain and reserve the cooking liquid.

Preheat oven to 350 degrees. Heat the oil in a large casserole. Sauté the onions and garlic until soft, 5 minutes. Stir in the tomatoes and cook until all the liquid evaporates. Peel the casing from the sausages and cut the meat into 1/2-inch slices. Stir into the tomatoes and cook for a few minutes. Add the lentils, bay leaf, sugar, pepper, and a little of the reserved lentil liquid to moisten. Cover and bake for 30 minutes, adding more lentil liquid if the casserole looks dry during baking.

CREAMY MARJORAM-LEMON SAUCE

MAKES 1 1/2 CUPS
PREPARATION TIME 10 MINUTES

Good on steak and other grilled meats.

2 egg yolks, room temperature
Juice of 1/2 large lemon
3 tablespoons grainy mustard
1 green onion, chopped

1/4 teaspoon fresh marjoram
1 cup light olive oil
1/4 to 1/2 cup heavy cream
2 tablespoons drained capers

In a food processor or blender, combine the egg yolks, lemon juice, mustard, onion, and marjoram. Beat until creamy. With the machine running, gradually pour in the olive oil. Add the heavy cream and capers. Mix until blended. Serve at room temperature.

LAMB MARINADE

MAKES 4 CUPS
PREPARATION TIME 5 MINUTES

Especially good on butterflied leg of lamb to be barbecued. Marinate overnight in the refrigerator.

2 cups soy sauce
2 cups peanut oil

1 cup Dijon mustard
2 cloves garlic, crushed

Combine all of the ingredients and stir until blended.

BARBECUE SAUCE

MAKES APPROXIMATELY 2 CUPS
PREPARATION TIME 5 MINUTES
COOKING TIME 10 MINUTES

1/2 can beer
1/2 cup molasses
1/2 cup chili sauce
1/4 cup prepared mustard

1 small onion, chopped
Dash of Worcestershire sauce
Salt
Freshly ground pepper

In a saucepan, combine all ingredients and blend. Bring to a boil. Reduce heat and simmer for 10 minutes. If the sauce gets too thick, add more beer. The non-used portion can be stored in the refrigerator for several weeks.

ORANGE-HONEY MARINADE

MAKES 1 CUP
PREPARATION TIME 5 MINUTES

Use to marinate pork or chicken in the refrigerator overnight. Baste with the marinade as it is grilled.

3/4 cup fresh orange juice
3 tablespoons honey
3 tablespoons red wine vinegar
1 onion, thinly sliced
1 tablespoon grated orange rind
6 cloves

1 bay leaf, crumbled
1/2 teaspoon dried thyme
1/2 teaspoon salt
1/4 teaspoon ground allspice
1/4 teaspoon ground ginger
1/4 teaspoon freshly ground pepper

In a non-metallic bowl, combine all the ingredients. Stir until blended.

TANGY MUSTARD

MAKES ABOUT 2 CUPS
PREPARATION TIME 5 MINUTES
COOKING TIME 5 MINUTES

Good over grilled meats.

1/2 cup milk
1/2 cup sugar
4 teaspoons dry mustard
1 teaspoon salt

2 eggs, beaten
3 tablespoons butter, melted
1/4 cup red wine vinegar

Heat the milk in a double boiler set over simmering water. Mix together the sugar, mustard, and salt and blend into the eggs. Stir this mixture into the warm milk. Stir in the butter. Slowly add the vinegar. Serve warm or cold.

HOISIN MARINADE

MAKES 3/4 CUP
PREPARATION TIME 5 MINUTES

Hoisin sauce is available at oriental markets. Use to marinate pork or beef in the refrigerator overnight.

1/4 cup hoisin sauce
3 tablespoons rice wine
2 tablespoons soy sauce
2 tablespoons minced green
onion

2 cloves garlic, minced
1 teaspoon fresh minced ginger
root
1 teaspoon sugar
1 teaspoon salt

Combine all ingredients. Stir to blend.

BREADS

Russian River District

The Russian River District, a wine-growing sub-region of Sonoma County, lies predominately west of the other major wine-growing Sonoma County regions. Because the Russian River District lies closer to the ocean, it is a cooler region than Sonoma's interior valleys. Varietals that prefer cooler temperatures thrive here because of the coastal breezes and coastal fogs, which sometimes creep inland before burning off in midmorning. This district also receives more rainfall because of its proximity to the Pacific Ocean.

The Russian River, which meanders through this region flanked by the many vineyards thriving along its banks, was once called the Slavianka River, and Russians from Fort Ross trapped furs nearby. Spring and early summer rainwater runoff makes the Russian River a popular spot for canoeing and picnicking, especially around Guerneyville and Healdsburg. Sebastopol, also in the Russian River District, is known for its Gravenstein Apple Fair, held every August. Gravensteins can be utilized in producing hard ciders and apple wines, which provide tantalizing flavors when used in cooking.

The early history of the Russian River District dates to the establishment of Fort Ross on the Sonoma coast in 1812. Those first Russians planted vegetables, orchards, and vineyards, although their chief interest was in the rich fur-trapping potential of the area: the sea otters. The combination of the decline in the sea otter population, plus the northern advance of Mexican dominion over California, caused the Russians ultimately to withdraw their claims to Northern California. Still standing, Fort Ross provides an interesting side trip from wine-tasting excursions.

Those coastal wine-country towns feature wonderful bakeries, providing local sourdough breads and other delights to accompany the premium wines and produce of this rich region. Enjoy a Russian River District wine with the Apple Cinnamon, Strawberry Pecan, or Blue Cheese breads.

STREUSEL NUT MUFFINS

MAKES 16 TO 18
PREPARATION TIME 15 MINUTES
COOKING TIME 20 TO 25 MINUTES

3 cups flour
1 1/2 cups packed brown sugar
6 ounces (1 1/2 sticks) unsalted butter
1 cup chopped walnuts
2 teaspoons baking powder

1 teaspoon ground ginger
1 teaspoon ground nutmeg
1/2 teaspoon baking soda
1/2 teaspoon salt
1 cup buttermilk
2 eggs, beaten

Preheat oven to 350 degrees. Grease the muffin cups or line with papers. Combine 2 cups of the flour with the brown sugar. Cut in the butter until crumbly. Measure out 3/4 cup of the mixture and stir in 1/4 cup of the walnuts. Set aside.

To the remaining crumbly mixture, add the remaining 1 cup of flour, baking powder, ginger, nutmeg, baking soda, and salt. Stir in the remaining 3/4 cup of walnuts. Combine buttermilk and eggs. Stir into the dry ingredients just to moisten. Spoon into the prepared muffin cups, filling 2/3 full. Spoon some of the crumb-nut topping over each muffin.

Bake for 20 to 25 minutes, or until a tester inserted in the center comes out clean. Cool for 10 minutes before removing from the pan.

BERRY CRUNCHY OATMEAL MUFFINS

MAKES 12 MUFFINS
PREPARATION TIME 20 MINUTES
COOKING TIME 15 TO 20 MINUTES

Very light wheat muffins. Cranberries, blueberries, raspberries, or pitted cherries can be used in the filling.

3/4 cup flour
3/4 cup whole wheat flour
1/2 cup quick-cooking oats
1/2 cup packed brown sugar
2 teaspoons baking powder
1 teaspoon baking soda
1 cup fresh or partially frozen berries

2 eggs
1/2 cup buttermilk
4 ounces (1 stick) butter, melted
Crunchy Crust (recipe follows)

Preheat oven to 400 degrees. In a large bowl, mix the flours, oats, sugar, baking powder and baking soda. Add the berries. Gently toss to coat. In another bowl, whip the eggs with a fork. Beat in buttermilk and butter. Add to flour mixture, stirring just until blended. Fill greased muffin tins 2/3 full. Top with Crunchy Crust. Bake for 15 to 20 minutes, or until a tester inserted in the center comes out clean.

CRUNCHY CRUST

4 tablespoons butter
1/4 cup packed brown sugar
1/4 cup rolled oats

1/4 cup flour
1 1/4 teaspoons cinnamon

Mix all ingredients together until crumbly.

BLUEBERRY CREAM CHEESE MUFFINS

MAKES 12 TO 14
PREPARATION TIME 10 MINUTES
COOKING TIME 30 MINUTES

If you are lucky enough to go berry picking, store as many blueberries as possible. They freeze perfectly for a long time.

4 ounces cream cheese
1 tablespoon lemon juice
2 teaspoons vanilla extract
2 eggs
1/2 cup milk
4 tablespoons unsalted butter, melted
2 cups cake flour

3/4 cup sugar
1 1/2 teaspoons baking powder
1/2 teaspoon baking soda
Pinch of salt
1 1/4 cups blueberries
1 1/2 tablespoons sugar mixed with 1 teaspoon cinnamon

Preheat oven to 350 degrees. Fill the cups of a muffin tin with cupcake liners. Set aside. In a mixer or processor, whip cream cheese with lemon juice and vanilla extract until smooth. Beat in eggs. Add milk and butter and mix until well blended.

Combine flour, sugar, baking powder, baking soda, and salt in a bowl. Beat into the cream-cheese mixture until well mixed. Gently fold in blueberries. Pour into the prepared muffin tins, filling each one 3/4 full. Sprinkle the tops with the sugar mixture. Bake for approximately 30 minutes, or until a tester inserted in the middle comes out clean.

PUMPKIN MUFFINS

MAKES 12
PREPARATION TIME 10 MINUTES
COOKING TIME 20 MINUTES

Quick and easy muffins, not overly sweet, and not too spicy.

2 cups buttermilk baking mix
  (Bisquick)
1/2 cup sugar
1/2 teaspoon cinnamon
1/4 teaspoon nutmeg
1/4 teaspoon ground cloves

1 egg, slightly beaten
3/4 cup milk
2 tablespoons vegetable oil
2/3 cup pumpkin purée
1/2 cup chopped walnuts
  (optional)

Preheat oven to 400 degrees. Grease and flour muffin tins. Combine baking mix, sugar, cinnamon, nutmeg, and cloves. Mix the egg with the milk and oil. Add the pumpkin and nuts (if desired). Stir into the dry ingredients until blended. Fill the tins 3/4 full with batter. Bake for 20 minutes, or until tester inserted in center comes out clean. Serve immediately.

BANANA LEMON MUFFINS

MAKES 18
PREPARATION TIME 10 MINUTES
COOKING TIME 20 MINUTES

Serve these light-textured muffins piping hot with a crock of sweet butter.

4 ounces (1 stick) unsalted
  butter
1 1/4 cups sugar
2 large eggs
1 cup mashed bananas
2 tablespoons lemon juice

1 teaspoon vanilla
2 cups flour
1 teaspoon baking soda
Pinch of salt
3/4 cup buttermilk

Preheat oven to 350 degrees. Grease 18 muffin cups. Cream the butter and sugar until light and fluffy. Beat in the eggs, one at a time. Whip in bananas, lemon juice, and vanilla. Sift flour, baking soda, and salt together. Stir into banana mixture alternately with the buttermilk. Bake for 20 minutes, or until tester inserted in center comes out clean.

APPLE MUFFINS

MAKES 2 DOZEN
PREPARATION TIME 15 MINUTES
COOKING TIME 30 MINUTES

3 1/2 cups flour
3 cups peeled, finely chopped apples
2 cups sugar
1 teaspoon salt
1 teaspoon baking soda

1 teaspoon cinnamon
1 1/2 cups vegetable oil
2 eggs, lightly beaten
1/2 cup chopped toasted nuts
1 teaspoon vanilla

Preheat oven to 350 degrees. Grease and flour muffin tins or fill with cupcake liners. In a large bowl, thoroughly combine flour, apples, sugar, salt, baking soda, and cinnamon. Stir in the oil, eggs, nuts, and vanilla. The batter will probably be stiff but may vary according to the type of apples used.

Fill the muffin tins 1/2 to 2/3 full. Bake approximately 30 minutes, or until a tester inserted in the center comes out clean. Serve immediately.

ORANGE RAISIN MUFFINS

MAKES 14 TO 16
PREPARATION TIME 20 MINUTES
COOKING TIME 15 MINUTES

1 cup raisins
Zest of 1 orange
4 ounces (1 stick) unsalted butter
1/2 cup brown sugar
2 eggs

1/2 teaspoon salt
1 teaspoon baking soda
1 cup buttermilk
2 cups flour, sifted
Juice of 1 orange

Preheat oven to 400 degrees. Grind the raisins with the orange zest in a food processor. Set aside until needed. Cream the butter and sugar until smooth. Add the eggs and salt and beat until fluffy. Stir the baking soda into the buttermilk. Add the buttermilk alternately with the flour to the egg mixture. Stir until mixed. Fold in the raisin-and-orange mixture.

Line muffin tins with papers. Spoon the batter into the lined tins. Bake approximately 15 minutes or until golden brown, and a tester inserted in the center comes out clean. While still warm, paint with the orange juice and sprinkle with superfine sugar to taste. Let cool in baking tins.

BRAN MUFFINS

MAKES ABOUT 18
PREPARATION TIME 20 MINUTES
COOKING TIME 20 TO 25 MINUTES

These light bran muffins can be baked either in the tiny muffin tins or in the larger ones. The batter will keep for weeks in covered quart jars.

1 cup boiling water
1 cup 40% Bran Flakes
1 cup sugar
1/2 cup vegetable oil
2 eggs
1 cup buttermilk
2 1/2 cups sifted flour
2 teaspoons baking soda
1 teaspoon salt

1 teaspoon cinnamon
1/4 teaspoon ground cloves
1/4 teaspoon allspice
1/4 cup All-Bran
2 teaspoons grated orange rind
1/2 cup chopped nuts (optional)
2 tablespoons sugar mixed with
    1 teaspoon cinnamon

Preheat oven to 400 degrees. Pour the boiling water over the Bran Flakes. Mix and cool. Cream the sugar and oil. Beat in the eggs. Stir the buttermilk into the bran mixture and add to the egg mixture.

In another bowl, sift together the flour, baking soda, salt, cinnamon, cloves, and allspice. Add the All-Bran, orange rind, and nuts. Combine well with the other bran mixture. Pour into well-greased muffin tins. Sprinkle with the sugar and cinnamon. Bake for 15 to 20 minutes, or until a tester inserted in the center comes out clean. Serve immediately.

CHOCOLATE CHIP COFFEE CAKE

SERVES 8
PREPARATION TIME 15 MINUTES
COOKING TIME 45 MINUTES

TOPPING
1/4 cup granulated sugar
1/3 cup brown sugar
1 teaspoon cinnamon

1 cup chopped nuts
1 cup chocolate chips

Combine all the ingredients. Mix well and set aside.

CAKE

4 ounces (1 stick) unsalted butter, softened	2 teaspoons vanilla
1 cup sugar	1 teaspoon baking powder
2 eggs	1 teaspoon soda
1 cup sour cream	1 teaspoon salt
	2 cups sifted flour

Preheat oven to 350 degrees. Cream the butter and sugar until smooth. Add the eggs, sour cream, vanilla, baking powder, baking soda, and salt. Mix well. Stir in flour and mix until just blended. Generously butter a tube pan. Sprinkle with half of Topping. Spoon half of the batter over Topping. With a knife, gently swirl Topping and batter together. Spread with the remaining Topping. Cover with the remaining batter. Bake for 45 to 50 minutes, or until a tester inserted in the center comes out clean.

TOSCA CAKE

SERVES 6 TO 8
PREPARATION TIME 10 MINUTES
COOKING TIME 30 MINUTES

A delicious coffee cake with a sliced-almond topping.

CAKE

2 eggs	4 ounces (1 stick) unsalted butter, melted
3/4 cup sugar	
1 cup flour	Topping (recipe follows)
2 teaspoons vanilla	

Preheat oven to 375 degrees. Beat eggs and sugar together. Stir in flour, vanilla, and melted butter. Pour into a greased and floured 9-inch square pan. Bake for 20 minutes. Spread Topping across the top of the cake. Continue baking for 10 minutes, or until a tester inserted in the center comes out clean.

TOPPING

6 tablespoons unsalted butter	3 tablespoons flour
1/2 cup sliced almonds	2 tablespoons half-and-half
1/2 cup sugar	

In a small saucepan, combine all the above ingredients. Heat but do not allow to come to a boil.

CARROT BREAD

MAKES 1 LOAF
PREPARATION TIME 20 MINUTES
COOKING TIME 40 TO 45 MINUTES

Excellent for holiday-gift giving. Prepare in small bundt pans. Unmold and, when cooled thoroughly, wrap in brightly colored plastic foil and pretty gold ribbon.

2 eggs
1 cup sugar
2/3 cup oil
1 1/2 cups flour
1 teaspoon baking soda
1 teaspoon cinnamon

1 teaspoon nutmeg
1/2 teaspoon salt
1 1/2 cups finely grated carrots
1 cup chopped walnuts
3/4 cup raisins

Preheat oven to 350 degrees. Beat eggs with sugar and oil. Sift together the flour, baking soda, cinnamon, nutmeg, and salt. Add to the egg mixture and beat well. Stir in the carrots, walnuts and raisins. Grease a 9 × 5-inch loaf pan. Bake for approximately 40 minutes, or until a tester inserted in the center comes out clean. Cool several hours before serving.

STRAWBERRY PECAN BREAD

MAKES 1 LOAF
PREPARATION TIME 40 MINUTES
COOKING TIME 70 MINUTES

1 10-ounce package frozen
   sweetened strawberries, or 2
   cups frozen unsweetened
   strawberries and 1 cup sugar
2 eggs
3/4 cup oil

1 1/2 cups flour
1 cup sugar
1 teaspoon cinnamon
1/2 teaspoon baking soda
3/4 cup chopped pecans

Preheat the oven to 325 degrees. Thaw the frozen strawberries but do not drain. Purée the strawberries. Combine the purée with the eggs and oil. Sift the dry ingredients into a bowl. Stir in the strawberry mixture and the nuts; blend well. Pour into a lightly greased 9 × 5-inch loaf pan. Bake for 1 hour and 10 minutes, or until a tester inserted in the middle comes out clean. Let cool in the pans.

CRANBERRY BREAD

MAKES 1 LOAF
PREPARATION TIME 15 MINUTES
COOKING TIME 1 HOUR

2 cups sifted flour
1 cup sugar
1 1/2 teaspoons baking powder
1/2 teaspoon baking soda
1 teaspoon salt
1/2 cup fresh orange juice
Grated rind of 1 large orange

2 tablespoons vegetable oil and
   enough boiling water to
   measure 1 cup
1 egg, well beaten
1 cup raw cranberries, each
   berry cut in half

Preheat oven to 350 degrees. Sift together the flour, sugar, baking powder, baking soda, and salt. In another bowl, combine the orange juice and rind, oil and water, and egg; blend well. Stir the liquid into the dry ingredients blending only until the flour mixture is dampened. Fold in cranberries. Pour into a greased 9 × 5-inch loaf pan. Spread the batter into the corners of the pan, leaving the center slightly hollowed out for a well-rounded loaf. Let the batter stand in the pan for 20 minutes before baking. Bake for 1 hour, or until a tester inserted in the center comes out clean. Cool thoroughly before slicing.

APPLE CAKE

SERVES 8
PREPARATION TIME 20 MINUTES
COOKING TIME 40 TO 50 MINUTES

2 cups tart green apples, peeled
   and diced
1 egg
1/4 cup vegetable oil
1 cup sugar
1/2 teaspoon cinnamon

1 cup flour
1 cup chopped nuts
3/4 cup raisins
1 teaspoon baking soda
1/4 teaspoon salt

Preheat oven to 350 degrees. Grease an 8 × 8-inch pan. Place the apples in a large bowl and stir in the egg. Pour the oil over the apples. Mix in the sugar and cinnamon. Stir in the remaining ingredients. Pour into the prepared pan. Bake for 40 to 50 minutes, or until a tester inserted in the center comes out clean.

FLAKY CINNAMON TWISTS

MAKES 36
PREPARATION TIME 30 MINUTES
REFRIGERATION TIME 2 HOURS
COOKING TIME 20 MINUTES

1 package dry yeast
1/4 cup warm water
1 teaspoon sugar
4 cups flour
1 cup vegetable shortening
1/2 teaspoon salt

3 eggs
1 cup sour cream
1 teaspoon vanilla
Sugar (about 2 cups)
Cinnamon

Dissolve yeast in the warm water and sugar. Let stand until bubbly. Combine flour, shortening, and salt until crumbly.

Whip the eggs. Beat in the sour cream, vanilla, and yeast mixture. Add to the dry ingredients and blend. Refrigerate for 2 hours.

Preheat the oven to 375 degrees. Sprinkle the sugar onto a board. Turn out the dough onto the sugar. Sprinkle more sugar over the dough and roll to a 12-inch square. Fold dough to center from either side. Roll again, sprinkling with sugar. Repeat this folding and rolling process 4 times, adding as much sugar as necessary to prevent sticking. Cut dough into 1-inch × 4-inch strips. Sprinkle with more sugar and some cinnamon. Twist loosely. Place on an ungreased baking sheet. Bake for 20 minutes, or until nicely browned.

OLD-FASHIONED CRUMB CAKE

SERVES 8
PREPARATION TIME 20 MINUTES
COOKING TIME 30 TO 35 MINUTES

2 1/4 cups sifted flour
1 3/4 teaspoons cinnamon
1/4 teaspoon salt
1 cup packed brown sugar
3/4 cup granulated sugar
3/4 cup vegetable oil

1/2 cup chopped nuts
1/2 teaspoon nutmeg
1 teaspoon baking powder
1/2 teaspoon baking soda
1 egg, lightly beaten
1 cup buttermilk

Preheat oven to 350 degrees. Sift together the flour, 3/4 teaspoon of the cinnamon, and salt. Add both sugars and the oil. Mix until fluffy. Measure out 3/4 cup of this mix for the topping. To this topping add the nuts, the remaining 1 teaspoon of cinnamon, and nutmeg. Add the baking powder, baking soda, egg, and buttermilk to the remaining flour mixture. Stir until smooth. Spoon into a well-greased 9 × 13-inch pan and smooth the top. Sprinkle with the topping mixture and press in lightly with the back of a spoon. Bake for 30 to 35 minutes, or until a tester inserted in the center comes out clean.

POPPY SEED CAKE

SERVES 8 TO 10
PREPARATION TIME 20 MINUTES
COOKING TIME 50 MINUTES

If you want to serve this homey American classic as a dessert, use your favorite topping on it—a vanilla or orange glaze or chocolate buttercream.

1/2 cup poppy seeds
1 cup buttermilk
8 ounces (2 sticks) unsalted
  butter
1 cup sugar
4 eggs
2 1/2 cups sifted flour
2 teaspoons baking powder

1 teaspoon baking soda
1/2 teaspoon salt
1 teaspoon vanilla extract
1 1/2 tablespoons grated orange
  rind
2 tablespoons sugar
1 teaspoon cinnamon

Preheat oven to 350 degrees. Combine poppy seeds and buttermilk. Cream butter and the 1 cup of sugar until light. Beat in eggs, one at a time. Sift the flour with the baking powder, baking soda, and salt. Blend into the egg mixture and add vanilla extract and orange rind. Stir in poppy seeds and buttermilk.

Pour half of the batter into a buttered 6- or 8-cup bundt pan. Sprinkle with the sugar and cinnamon. Cover with the remaining batter. Bake for approximately 50 to 55 minutes, or until a tester inserted in the center comes out clean. Let rest for 15 minutes. Invert and cool on a rack.

APPLE CINNAMON BREAD

MAKES 2 LOAVES
PREPARATION TIME 15 MINUTES
COOKING TIME 55 MINUTES

Almonds, pecans, and walnuts go especially well with the apples in this loaf. For a breakfast or brunch treat, serve with a warm compote of berries and other fruits.

2 eggs
2 cups sugar
1 teaspoon vanilla
1/2 cup plus 2 tablespoons
    vegetable oil
2 tablespoons water
2 cups flour

3 teaspoons cinnamon
2 teaspoons baking soda
1/2 teaspoon salt
1 cup chopped nuts
4 cups peeled and chopped tart
    green apples (about 3 large)

Preheat oven to 350 degrees. Combine eggs, sugar, and vanilla until light and fluffy. Add the oil and water and beat until smooth. Sift flour, cinnamon, baking soda, and salt together; stir into egg mixture. Fold in the nuts and apples. Spoon into two greased and floured 9 × 5-inch loaf pans. Bake for 1 hour, or until a tester inserted in the center comes out clean.

NORWEGIAN CHRISTMAS BREAD

MAKES 2 LOAVES
PREPARATION TIME 2 HOURS
COOKING TIME 1 HOUR

An easy fail-proof bread for those hesitant about working with yeast doughs.

2 cups milk
1 cup sugar
8 ounces (2 sticks) unsalted
    butter
1 teaspoon salt
3 packages dry yeast dissolved
    in 1/2 cup warm water
3 cups flour
2 teaspoons ground cardamom
    or 2 teaspoons vanilla

3 eggs, beaten
1 cup coarsely chopped
    candied cherries and
    pineapple
1 1/2 cups golden raisins
4 to 5 cups flour (enough to
    make a soft dough)
1 1/2 cups sifted powdered
    sugar
1 1/2 tablespoons milk

Heat the milk almost to boiling. Stir in the sugar, butter, and salt. Let cool to lukewarm. Add the yeast mixture. Stir in the 3 cups of flour. Cover and let rise for 1 hour.

Add the cardamom or vanilla and the eggs to the yeast mixture. Mix the candied fruit and raisins with 1/4 cup of the remaining flour. Add to the dough. Add just enough flour to make the dough soft but not sticky (about 4 cups). Knead on a well-floured board for 5 to 10 minutes. Let rise until light, about 30 minutes.

Preheat oven to 450 degrees. Generously grease two 9 × 5-inch loaf pans. Punch down dough. Divide the dough in half and fill the loaf pans half full. Let rise until doubled in size. Bake for 10 minutes. Reduce heat to 325 degrees and bake an additional 50 minutes, or until nicely browned.

In a small bowl, combine sugar and milk. Mix well. Drizzle icing over bread after it has cooled.

PUMPKIN APPLESAUCE BREAD

MAKES 2 LOAVES
PREPARATION TIME 15 MINUTES
COOKING TIME 1 HOUR

2/3 cup shortening
2 1/2 cups sugar
4 eggs
1 cup applesauce
1 cup canned mashed pumpkin
3 1/3 cups flour, sifted
2 teaspoons baking soda
1/2 teaspoon baking powder

1 teaspoon salt
1 teaspoon cinnamon
1/2 teaspoon mace
1/2 teaspoon nutmeg
2/3 cup apple juice
1 cup chopped walnuts or
  pecans

Preheat the oven to 350 degrees. Grease two 9-inch loaf pans. Cream the shortening and the sugar. Add the eggs, one at a time, beating well after each addition. Stir in the applesauce and pumpkin. Sift the dry ingredients. Add to the egg mixture alternately with the apple juice. Stir in the nuts. Pour into the prepared pans. Bake for 1 hour, or until a tester inserted in the center comes out clean.

KAHLÚA CINNAMON RAISIN ROLLS

MAKES 12 ROLLS
PREPARATION TIME 2 HOURS
COOKING TIME 25 MINUTES

Refrigerate overnight before the second rising and bake fresh in the morning.

ROLLS

1 package dry yeast	1/4 cup sugar
1/4 cup warm water	1/2 teaspoon salt
1/2 cup boiling milk	2 1/2 to 2 3/4 cups flour
1/4 cup shortening	1 egg, beaten

Soften the yeast in the water. Combine the hot milk, shortening, sugar, and salt. Add 1 cup of the flour and beat well. Add the egg, yeast mixture, and remaining flour, mixing to form a moderately stiff dough. Turn out onto a lightly floured surface and knead gently for 7 minutes. Cover and let rise for 1 hour.

FILLING

1/2 cup brown sugar	1 tablespoon Kahlúa
4 tablespoons butter	1/2 cup chopped raisins
1 tablespoon cinnamon	

Combine the brown sugar, butter, cinnamon, Kahlúa, and raisins. Roll the dough into a 12 × 16-inch rectangle. Spread with the filling. Roll up jelly-roll fashion. Cut into 12 slices.

SYRUP

1/3 cup brown sugar	4 tablespoons butter
1/4 cup Kahlúa	1 tablespoon light corn syrup

Place the remaining brown sugar, Kahlúa, butter, and corn syrup in a small saucepan. Bring to a simmer.

ASSEMBLY

Place all but 1/3 cup of the syrup in a 9-inch round cake pan. Place the slices on top of the syrup, cut side down. Press slices to flatten slightly. Let rise until double in bulk, about 25 minutes.

Preheat oven to 375 degrees. Bake for 20 to 25 minutes. Remove from the oven and let stand in the pan for 5 minutes. Turn out upside down onto a serving plate. Spoon the reserved syrup over the top.

BASIC PIZZA DOUGH

MAKES ENOUGH FOR ONE 12-INCH
REGULAR PIZZA
PREPARATION TIME 4 HOURS

1 package dry yeast
2/3 cup warm water
3 tablespoons olive oil
1 teaspoon salt

1 1/2 to 1 3/4 cups all-purpose
flour
Extra flour for kneading

Dissolve the yeast in the warm water. Let stand until bubbly. Stir the oil, salt, and 1 1/2 cups of the flour into the yeast mixture. Form into a ball. Turn out onto a lightly floured surface. Knead for 5 minutes, adding flour as necessary to make a soft, slightly sticky dough. Place in a large, lightly oiled bowl. Cover and let rise in a warm place until tripled in bulk, 3 to 4 hours.

Punch dough down. Roll out on a lightly floured surface to a 12-inch circle.

FOCACCIO (FLATBREAD)

MAKES 2 12-INCH ROUNDS
PREPARATION TIME 2 1/2 HOURS
COOKING TIME 20 MINUTES

2 packages dry yeast
1/2 cup warm water
8 cups all-purpose flour
2 tablespoons olive oil

4 teaspoons salt
2 1/2 cups warm water
Olive oil
Coarse kosher salt

Dissolve the yeast in the 1/2 cup of water. Set aside until bubbly. Mix the flour, the 2 tablespoons olive oil, and salt. Add the yeast mixture and remaining water. Either by machine or hand, knead the dough until smooth and elastic. Place in a large greased bowl. Cover and place in a warm place until doubled in bulk, about 1 to 2 hours.

Preheat oven to 400 degrees. Punch down. Place on a large baking sheet and flatten to 1/2 inch. Make indentations in the dough with your thumb. Brush evenly with olive oil. Sprinkle with the kosher salt. Bake for 20 to 25 minutes or until golden brown.

PESTO PIZZA

MAKES 1 12-INCH PIZZA
PREPARATION TIME 45 MINUTES
COOKING TIME 30 MINUTES

A lighter, more refined filling.

1 cup tightly packed fresh basil
  leaves
1/4 cup olive oil
3 tablespoons pine nuts
1 clove garlic
1/2 teaspoon salt
1/4 teaspoon freshly grated
  black pepper

1/4 cup freshly grated Parmesan
  cheese
Basic Pizza Dough†
8 slices Italian Fontina or
  mozzarella cheese

Combine the basil, oil, pine nuts, garlic, salt, and pepper in a processor or blender and purée. Transfer to a bowl and stir in the grated cheese. Refrigerate until needed.

Grease a 12-inch pizza pan. Roll out or pat Pizza Dough into a 12-inch circle. Place on the prepared pan. Pinch up the edges of the dough to form a rim. Spread Pesto Sauce evenly over the dough. Let stand in a warm place for 30 minutes.

Preheat the oven to 400 degrees. Place the cheese slices on top of the Pesto Sauce. Bake until the crust is golden brown, about 20 to 30 minutes. Let stand 5 minutes. Cut into wedges.

QUICK WHOLE WHEAT BREAD

MAKES 2 LOAVES
PREPARATION TIME 45 MINUTES
COOKING TIME 50 TO 55 MINUTES

3 packages dry yeast
3 cups warm water
1/3 cup honey
3 tablespoons oil
1 cup powdered milk

1 tablespoon salt
6 to 6 1/2 cups whole wheat
  flour
Melted butter for brushing the
  tops of the loaves

Mix the yeast, water, honey, and oil. Combine the dry ingredients. Add ¹/₂ of the dry ingredients to the yeast mixture. Mix until the batter is smooth. Add the remaining half to make a soft dough. Knead until well mixed, about 5 minutes. Place in a large bowl, cover and let rise in a warm spot for 15 minutes.

Turn out and knead for 10 minutes. Shape into two loaves and place in two well-greased loaf pans. Cover and let rise in a warm place for 15 minutes.

Preheat oven to 350 degrees. Bake for 50 to 55 minutes or until done. Brush the tops with butter when done. Cool slightly before slicing.

SWEET ONION-MUSTARD BREAD

MAKES 1 LOAF
PREPARATION TIME 2 ¹/₄ HOURS
COOKING TIME 40 TO 45 MINUTES

1 package dry yeast
¹/₄ cup warm water
2 teaspoons sugar
1 cup finely chopped sweet
   red onion
¹/₂ cup water
¹/₂ cup Dijon mustard
4 tablespoons unsalted butter,
   melted

1 teaspoon salt
2 ¹/₂ to 3 ¹/₂ cups all-purpose
   white flour
1 cup whole wheat flour
1 egg white mixed with 2
   tablespoons water

Dissolve yeast in the warm water. Stir in the sugar and set aside for 10 minutes. Combine the yeast mixture with the onion, water, mustard, butter, and salt. Beat in 1 cup of the white flour. Mix in the remaining flours, adding enough to make a soft dough. The dough will feel slightly sticky. Knead by hand for 15 minutes or in a machine for 5 minutes. Place the dough in a greased bowl. Cover and let rise until doubled in bulk, about 1 hour.

Turn dough out onto a lightly floured surface. Punch down and knead for a few minutes. Divide into 2 long ropes. Twist ropes together to form a tight braid. Place on a greased baking sheet. Cover and let rise until doubled, about 45 minutes.

Preheat oven to 375 degrees. Brush with the egg wash. Bake for 40 to 45 minutes or until golden brown. Cool before slicing.

ITALIAN PARMESAN BATTER ROLLS

MAKES 24
PREPARATION TIME 2 HOURS
COOKING TIME 20 TO 30 MINUTES

3 1/4 cups all-purpose flour
2 packages dry yeast
1/2 cup milk
1/2 cup water
4 ounces (1 stick) butter

3 tablespoons sugar
2 teaspoons salt
1 egg
1 cup grated Parmesan cheese
Butter or oil for brushing

Sift 1 cup of the flour with the yeast. Heat the milk, water, butter, sugar, and salt over low heat until warm (not over 120 degrees). Add the liquid, all at once, to the flour mixture. Beat for 3 minutes. Blend in the egg and cheese. Beat for 2 minutes. Stir in the remaining flour to make a thick batter. Cover and let rise in a warm place for 1 hour.

Preheat oven to 350 degrees. Stir down batter. Drop by rounded table-spoons onto a greased baking sheet. Brush with butter or oil. Let rise until double in bulk. Bake for 20 to 25 minutes or until golden.

FRENCH BAGUETTE

MAKES 4 BAGUETTES
PREPARATION TIME 3 HOURS
COOKING TIME 30 MINUTES

Sure to become a favorite, this versatile bread can be made in baguette molds or shaped into round country loaves. For a harder crust, toss 1/4 of a cup of water directly into the oven twice during the first ten minutes of baking.

3 packages dry yeast
3 1/2 cups warm water

9 cups all-purpose flour
1 tablespoon salt

Mix the yeast and water together. Let sit until bubbly, about 10 minutes. Place 6 cups of the flour in a large bowl of an electric mixer. Add the yeast mixture to the flour. Using a dough hook, beat on medium speed for 5 minutes. Add 2 more cups of the flour and the salt. Continue beating on medium for 3 minutes. Turn the machine to low and slowly knead in the remaining flour. More or less flour may be needed, depending on the weather and other variables. Continue kneading for 5 to 6 minutes. The dough should be smooth and shiny. Sprinkle with flour. Place in a large bowl. Cover and place in a warm area, to rise, for 2 hours. The dough will more than double in volume. This dough can have two risings if you prefer a lighter bread. Punch down after 2 hours and let rise again.

Turn out onto a lightly floured work surface. Knead the dough for 1 to 2 minutes to release all of the air bubbles. Cut the dough into strips, approximately 3/4 to 1 pound each. Place into baguette trays. Let the baguettes rise until doubled in size, about 1 hour.

Preheat oven to 425 degrees. Wash with a beaten egg or brush with flour. Slash the tops with a knife. Bake for 30 minutes, or until nicely browned and hollow-sounding when tapped.

BLUE CHEESE BREAD

2 LOAVES
PREPARATION TIME 2 HOURS
COOKING TIME 35 TO 45 MINUTES

2 packages dry yeast
1 1/2 cups warm water
2 tablespoons sugar
1 1/2 cups white flour
1 cup milk
3 tablespoons butter

2 teaspoons salt
3 ounces crumbled blue cheese
1 teaspoon Worcestershire
    Sauce
6 cups all-purpose flour
3 tablespoons milk

Dissolve the yeast in the warm water. Stir in the sugar and the 1 1/2 cups of flour. Mix until smooth. Let rest for 30 minutes. By this time, the mixture will have started to bubble.

Heat the milk, butter, and salt until the butter melts. Let cool. Add to the yeast mixture. Stir in the blue cheese and Worcestershire sauce. Add the remaining 6 cups of flour to form a soft dough. Knead until smooth, 5 minutes in a machine or 15 minutes by hand. Place in a greased bowl. Cover and let rise in a warm dry place for 1 hour.

Turn out onto a lightly floured surface and punch down. Divide in half and place in 2 greased loaf pans. Cover and let rise for 45 minutes.

Preheat oven to 350 degrees. Slash the top of the loaves. Brush with the milk. Bake for 35 to 45 minutes, or until nicely browned and hollow-sounding when tapped.

BRIOCHE DOUGH

MAKES ABOUT 1 POUND
PREPARATION TIME 3 HOURS
REFRIGERATION TIME 8 HOURS
COOKING TIME 20 TO 40 MINUTES

Baked brioches freeze well. You must, however, place them in a sealed plastic bag while still warm to prevent drying out.

1 tablespoon dry yeast
2 tablespoons sugar
1/4 cup warm water
1/4 cup warm milk
3 1/2 cups all-purpose flour
6 eggs

1 teaspoon salt
8 ounces (2 sticks) unsalted
  butter, softened
1 egg beaten with 1 tablespoon
  of water

In a large mixing bowl, dissolve the yeast and the sugar in the water and milk. Add 2/3 cup of the flour and 2 of the eggs. Beat until well mixed. Sprinkle the remaining flour over the mixture. Cover and let stand in a warm place for 1 hour.

Beat in the remaining eggs, one at a time. Add the salt and butter. Mix until smooth, about 2 minutes in a machine. Tightly cover the bowl and allow the dough to rise until doubled in bulk, about 2 hours.

Deflate the dough by gently pushing and lifting with your fingers. Turn the dough out onto a lightly floured surface. Gently lift dough up from the table and flip over. Repeat this procedure. Sprinkle the dough with flour. Place in a large plastic bag and refrigerate at least 8 hours.

To make small brioches, generously butter individual brioche molds (3/4-cup size). Cut the dough into 3-ounce pieces. Roll on a lightly floured table in a circular motion. Place in the prepared mold. Cut a cross on the top of the dough. Form a ball with another smaller piece of dough. Press the smaller piece down into the cross. Brush with the egg wash. Repeat with the remaining dough. Let the brioches rise in a warm place for 1 1/2 to 2 hours. A large brioche is done similarly.

Preheat the oven to 400 degrees. Bake the small brioches for approximately 20 to 25 minutes or until golden. Bake the larger ones for approximately 40 minutes or until golden. Store in plastic bags.

CHEESE BREAD

MAKES 1 LOAF
PREPARATION TIME 2 HOURS
COOKING TIME 30 TO 40 MINUTES

Especially good warm or toasted.

1 package dry yeast
1 teaspoon sugar
1 cup warm water
2 cups flour
1/2 cup cake flour
1 teaspoon salt

1/2 cup shredded Cheddar
cheese
2 teaspoons poppy seeds
2 teaspoons onion flakes
(optional)
1 egg beaten with a little salt

Stir yeast and sugar into the water. Let set until bubbly. Place both flours and salt in a mixing bowl or in a food processor. With dough hook in place and on, gradually pour in the yeast mixture. Knead for 3 minutes. Add cheese, poppy seeds, and onion flakes. Knead for an additional minute. The dough will be sticky. Place in a greased bowl. Cover with a damp towel and let rise in a warm dry place until double in bulk, about 1 hour.

Turn out onto a lightly floured surface. Pat down and shape into a loaf. Slash the top with a knife. Place on a cookie sheet. Cover with a cloth and let rise for 45 minutes.

Preheat the oven to 400 degrees. Brush with the egg wash. Bake for 30 to 35 minutes, or until nicely browned and hollow-sounding when tapped.

CHIVE BISCUITS

MAKES ABOUT 18
PREPARATION TIME 10 MINUTES
COOKING TIME 15 MINUTES

2 cups flour
2 teaspoons baking powder
1/2 teaspoon salt
4 tablespoons butter

1/2 cup chopped fresh chives
3/4 cup milk
Melted butter for brushing

Preheat the oven to 450 degrees. Sift the flour with the baking powder and salt. Cut in the butter and chives until the mixture resembles coarse meal. Stir in the milk with a fork. Form into a soft ball. Turn out onto a lightly floured surface. Knead briefly. Roll out to a thickness of 1/2 inch. Cut into small rounds. Place on a buttered baking sheet. Brush with melted butter. Bake for 12 to 15 minutes or until nicely browned.

SEASONED FRENCH BREAD

SERVES 6 TO 8
PREPARATION TIME 5 MINUTES
COOKING TIME 15 MINUTES

1 baguette loaf
4 ounces (1 stick) butter
1/4 cup grated Parmesan cheese
1/4 cup chopped fresh parsley
1/4 teaspoon garlic salt

1/4 teaspoon dried basil or
    oregano
1/4 teaspoon thyme
1/8 teaspoon cayenne

Preheat oven to 350 degrees. Slice the baguette loaf in half lengthwise. Combine all of the remaining ingredients. Beat until blended. Spread on the baguette halves. Place the two halves together. Wrap in foil. Bake for 15 minutes.

GARLIC AND HERB FRENCH BREAD

SERVES 8 TO 10
PREPARATION TIME 5 MINUTES
COOKING TIME 15 MINUTES

1 1-pound loaf French bread
8 ounces (2 sticks) butter, softened
4 tablespoons olive oil
2 to 4 cloves garlic, pressed

1/2 cup grated Parmesan cheese
1/2 teaspoon Italian herb seasoning or oregano
Paprika

Preheat oven to 400 degrees. Slice French bread in half lengthwise. Combine all the remaining ingredients, except the paprika. Blend thoroughly. Spread half of the butter mixture on each half of the bread. Generously sprinkle with the paprika. Cut slices into the bread about 2/3 of the way through. Wrap each half loaf in foil. Bake for 15 minutes.

DESSERTS

Lake County

Lake County is situated north of Napa County and inland from the coastal counties of Sonoma and Mendocino. Its dominant geographical feature is Clear Lake, easily a hundred miles long, which glitters like a jewel rimmed by mountains on all sides. A picturesque string of towns skirts its shores and the lake features boating, fishing, water-skiing, and other recreation year round.

The visitor reaches Lake County by driving north on Highway 29 and leaving Napa Valley behind. This route ascends the slopes of Mount St. Helena, which also serves as the southern boundary of Lake County.

A relative newcomer as a California wine-growing area, Lake County now boasts five wineries in different parts of the county. Lake County's inland location provides warm days, but the higher altitude brings the cooler nights that the grapevines need to produce premium wines. The microclimate of this area provides ideal conditions for premium red varietals: Cabernet Sauvignon, Merlot, and Cabernet Franc.

The Guenoc Valley at the southern end of Lake County was first developed as a wine-growing region in 1888 by the famous British actress Lillie Langtry, called the Jersey Lily. Today her portrait is featured on the label of a local winery. She called this valley a "piece of Paradise," an apt description.

Lake County wineries produce velvety rich wines of smoothness and complexity. If one has never tried a premium red wine, such as Cabernet Sauvignon, with a dessert—particularly the Delectable Bittersweet Chocolate Cake—these winemakers suggest you try this alternative for a pleasant surprise.

ILONA TORTE

SERVES 12 TO 14
PREPARATION TIME 1 HOUR
COOKING TIME 35 TO 45 MINUTES
COOLING TIME 2 HOURS

Guests will ask for this again and again. A chocolate lover's dream.

CAKE

1 cup sugar
1/4 cup water
5 ounces semisweet chocolate, cut into pieces
6 tablespoons unsalted butter, softened

8 eggs, separated
8 ounces walnuts, coarsely ground
2 tablespoons soft bread crumbs
Pinch of salt

Preheat oven to 375 degrees. Generously butter a round 10-inch cake pan. Place a circle of wax paper or parchment paper on the bottom. Butter it. Flour the pan, shaking out any excess.

To prepare the cake, combine the sugar and water in a saucepan. Cook over moderate heat for 5 minutes, or until the sugar dissolves and the syrup is clear. Add the chocolate and remove the pan from the heat. Stir until the chocolate melts. Set aside to cool.

Beat the butter until fluffy. Beat in the yolks, one at a time, beating until each is incorporated before adding another. Slowly beat in half of the chocolate mixture and the walnuts. Add the remaining chocolate and the bread crumbs. Mix until just blended.

Whip the egg whites with a pinch of salt until firm. Carefully fold into the chocolate mixture until thoroughly blended. Pour into the prepared pan. Bake in the center of the oven for 35 to 40 minutes, or until the center feels set when pressed.

Cool the torte in the pan for 15 minutes. Run a knife around the outside edges and invert on a rack covered with a paper towel. Cool completely before frosting.

BUTTERCREAM FROSTING

6 ounces semisweet chocolate, cut into pieces
1/3 cup water
2 teaspoons instant coffee espresso powder

9 ounces (2 sticks plus 2 tablespoons) unsalted butter
3 egg yolks
2/3 cup powdered sugar
1/3 cup ground walnuts

While the cake is cooling, prepare frosting. In a saucepan, combine the chocolate, water, and coffee powder. Stir over low heat until the chocolate melts. Transfer to a bowl and let cool.

With a mixer, cream the butter until light. Beat in the egg yolks, one at a time, beating until each is incorporated before adding another one. Gradually add the powdered sugar. Stir in the chocolate mixture and mix until thoroughly blended.

ASSEMBLY

Reserve 3/4 cup of the frosting for decoration. Slice the torte in half horizontally. Place the top half cut side up. Spread evenly with 3/4 cup of the frosting. Place the other layer on top of the filling, the bottom side upward. Spread the remaining frosting on the top and sides of the cake. Press the nuts evenly onto the sides of the cake. Using a pastry bag fitted with a star tip, make a star design around the top of the cake with the reserved frosting. Transfer the torte to a serving dish. Refrigerate until ready to serve.

BUTTER-ALMOND CAKE

SERVES 8
PREPARATION TIME 15 MINUTES
COOKING TIME 35 MINUTES

5 ounces (1 1/4 sticks) unsalted butter, room temperature	Grated zest of 1 orange
1 cup almond paste, room temperature	2/3 cup flour
	1/2 teaspoon baking powder
2/3 cup sugar	1/8 teaspoon salt
4 eggs	3/4 cup sliced almonds

Preheat the oven to 350 degrees. Generously grease and flour a 9-inch square pan. Cream the butter until light. Slowly add the almond paste; mix well. Add the sugar and continue beating until light and fluffy. Add the eggs, one at a time, beating until each is incorporated before adding another. Stir in the orange zest.

Sift together the flour, baking powder, and salt; stir into the butter mixture. Top with the almonds. Bake for 35 minutes, or until a tester inserted in the center comes out clean. Cool in the pan for 5 minutes. Turn out onto a rack and continue cooling.

SACHER TORTE

SERVES 8
PREPARATION TIME 30 MINUTES
COOKING TIME 40 MINUTES
REFRIGERATION TIME 3 HOURS

A classic that is still a favorite. It is usually presented with the name "Sacher" piped across the top.

7 ounces semisweet chocolate
4 ounces (1 stick) unsalted
  butter, melted
8 egg yolks
1 teaspoon vanilla extract
10 egg whites

Pinch of salt
3/4 cup sugar
1 cup sifted flour
1/2 cup strained apricot jam
Glaze (recipe follows)

Preheat the oven to 350 degrees. Butter two 9-inch round cake pans. Line the bottoms with circles of wax paper or parchment paper. Butter the paper circles. Sprinkle the pans with flour, shaking off the excess.

Melt the chocolate with the butter over low heat. Let the mixture cool. Beat the egg yolks and vanilla into the chocolate mixture. Beat the egg whites with the salt until foamy. Add the sugar, 1 tablespoon at a time, continuing to beat until the egg whites form firm peaks. Fold 1/3 of the egg whites into the chocolate. Take this mixture and pour it over the remaining egg whites. Sift the flour on top. Carefully fold the mixtures together until no trace of the whites remain. Do not overfold.

Pour the batter into the prepared pans. Bake for 25 to 30 minutes, or until a tester inserted in the middle comes out clean. Run a knife around the sides of the cakes to loosen. Turn out on a cake rack and remove the wax paper. Let cool while preparing Glaze.

GLAZE

4 ounces semisweet chocolate
1 cup heavy cream
1/4 cup sugar

1 teaspoon corn syrup
2 egg yolks
1 teaspoon vanilla

In a small saucepan, combine the chocolate, cream, sugar, and corn syrup. Cook over low heat, stirring constantly, until the chocolate and sugar melt. Cook over medium heat for 5 minutes without stirring. Let cool slightly.

Beat the egg yolks until light. Stir 4 tablespoons of the chocolate into the yolks. Pour this into the remaining chocolate. Cook over low heat for 3 to 4 minutes. Remove from the heat and add the vanilla. Cool Glaze to room temperature.

Spread one of the cake layers with the apricot jam. Place the other layer on top. Pour Glaze over the top. Smooth around the sides and on the top of the cake with a spatula. Refrigerate for 3 hours, or until Glaze sets. Remove from the refrigerator 1/2 hour before serving.

GINGER PEAR CAKE

SERVES 8
PREPARATION TIME 30 MINUTES
COOKING TIME 55 MINUTES

For a different flavor, try substituting 1 1/2 teaspoons vanilla and 1/4 teaspoon almond extract for the ginger.

3 cups water
3/4 cup sugar
1 tablespoon lemon juice
3 large, uniform pears, peeled,
   halved, and cored
1/2 cup blanched almonds
1/4 cup flour
1 teaspoon baking powder

1 teaspoon ground ginger
2 large eggs
3/4 cup sugar
5 tablespoons unsalted butter,
   melted
1/2 cup heavy cream
2 tablespoons powdered sugar

In a pan large enough to hold the pear halves in a single layer, combine the water, sugar, and lemon juice. Bring to a boil, stirring until the sugar dissolves. Add the pear halves. Simmer, uncovered, for 8 to 10 minutes or until tender. Using a slotted spoon, remove the pears from the pan. Place cut side down on paper towels to drain.

Preheat oven to 325 degrees. Generously butter a 9-inch round glass or ceramic baking dish. Place the pears in the dish with their cut sides down and stem ends pointing toward the center. Set aside.

In a food processor, chop the almonds with the flour, baking powder, and ginger until finely ground, about 1 to 2 minutes. Remove from the processor and set aside. Put the eggs and sugar in the bowl. Mix for 1 minute. With the machine running, add the butter and process for 10 seconds. Scrape down the sides of the bowl. Add the flour mixture. Process just until the flour disappears. Pour the batter evenly over the pears. Bake for 40 to 45 minutes, or until a tester inserted in the center comes out clean.

Whip the cream with the powdered sugar. Serve the cake warm, accompanied by the cream.

CHOCOLATE-CHESTNUT CAKE

SERVES 8
PREPARATION TIME 15 MINUTES
COOKING TIME 45 MINUTES

A lovely holiday dessert.

CAKE
4 ounces semisweet chocolate
3 tablespoons unsalted butter
4 large eggs, separated

1/2 cup sugar
8 ounces canned chestnut
  purée

Preheat the oven to 350 degrees. Generously grease and flour a 9- or 10-inch cake pan. Melt the chocolate with the butter. Let cool. Beat the egg yolks with the sugar until thick. Beat in the chocolate and the chestnut purée. Whisk the egg whites until firm. Fold into the chocolate mixture. Pour into the prepared pan. Bake for 40 minutes, or until a tester inserted in the center comes out clean. Cool in the pan for 10 minutes. Transfer to a cake rack.

CHOCOLATE CREAM FROSTING
4 ounces semisweet chocolate
4 tablespoons heavy cream
2 tablespoons powdered sugar

1 tablespoon Marsala wine
1/2 cup heavy cream, whipped

Prepare Chocolate Cream Frosting while the cake is cooling. Melt the chocolate with the 4 tablespoons of heavy cream, powdered sugar, and Marsala. Let cool. Fold the whipped cream into the chocolate mixture. Spread over the top and sides of the cake. Refrigerate until ready to serve.

CARAMEL CRUNCH CAKE

SERVES 8 TO 10
PREPARATION TIME 30 MINUTES
COOKING TIME 70 MINUTES

CAKE
1 1/4 cups sifted cake flour
1 1/2 cups sugar
6 egg yolks
1/4 cup water
1 tablespoon lemon juice

1 teaspoon vanilla
7 egg whites
1 teaspoon cream of tartar
1 teaspoon salt

Preheat oven to 350 degrees. Mix together the flour, 3/4 cup of the sugar, egg yolks, water, lemon juice, and vanilla. Beat until a smooth batter is formed.

Whip the egg whites with the cream of tartar and salt until soft peaks form. Beat in the remaining 3/4 cup of sugar, a tablespoon at a time, until the egg whites are stiff. Gently fold the batter into the whites until just blended. Spoon into an ungreased tube pan. Bake for 50 to 55 minutes, or until the top springs back when touched. Remove from the oven and immediately invert over the neck of a bottle. Let the cake hang until cool. Loosen with a knife and remove from the pan.

TOPPING

1 1/2 cups sugar
1/4 cup strong coffee
1/4 cup white corn syrup
3 teaspoons sifted baking soda

1 cup heavy cream
2 tablespoons powdered sugar
1 teaspoon vanilla

Combine the sugar, coffee, and syrup in a saucepan. Stir and bring to a boil. Cook until it reaches 310 degrees on a candy thermometer. Remove from the heat and immediately add the soda. Stir vigorously just until the topping thickens and pulls away from the sides of the pan. Immediately pour into an ungreased shallow metal pan. Do not stir or spread. Let cool. When cool, knock out of pan. Crush into coarse crumbs.

Slice the cake into 4 layers. Whip the heavy cream with the powdered sugar and vanilla until firm. Spread half of the whipped cream between the layers. Spread the remainder on the top and sides of the cake. Refrigerate until ready to serve. Just prior to serving, cover the cake generously with the crushed caramel topping.

MOCHA TRUFFLE CAKE

SERVES 10 TO 12
PREPARATION TIME 15 MINUTES
COOKING TIME 50 MINUTES
REFRIGERATION TIME 12 HOURS

A chocoholic's dream.

CAKE

1 pound (4 sticks) unsalted
   butter, cut into pieces
1 pound semisweet chocolate

1 cup strong coffee
2 cups sugar
8 large eggs, room temperature

Preheat oven to 350 degrees. Completely line the bottom and sides of a 10-inch cake pan with foil, allowing some of the foil to extend beyond the top of the pan. Smooth out the foil as much as possible. Generously coat with some of the butter.

Melt the chocolate with the remaining butter, coffee, and sugar over low heat. Simmer over low heat until the sugar dissolves.

Beat the eggs until thick, about 5 minutes. Stir into the chocolate mixture. Pour into the prepared pan. Bake for approximately 50 minutes, or until the center is just set. Cool completely in the pan. Cover and refrigerate in the pan until firm, at least 8 hours or overnight.

FROSTING

1 cup heavy cream	1/4 teaspoon vanilla
1/4 cup powdered sugar	Chocolate Flakes

A few hours prior to serving, whip the cream with the sugar and vanilla. Invert cake onto a serving platter. Carefully remove the foil. Frost the cake with the whipped cream. Garnish with the Chocolate Flakes. To make Chocolate Flakes, melt semisweet chocolate and spread on a marble slab or large flat plate. Let the chocolate harden. Scrape against it with a knife and it will flake into thin pieces.

RUM-NUT TORTE

SERVES 10 TO 12
PREPARATION TIME 20 MINUTES
COOKING TIME 20 MINUTES
REFRIGERATION TIME 24 HOURS

2 cups hazelnuts, finely ground and chilled	1 teaspoon baking powder
1/3 cup flour, chilled	2 1/2 cups walnuts, chopped
1/4 cup granulated sugar, chilled	1 1/2 cups shredded coconut
4 ounces (1 stick) butter, cut into small pieces and chilled	2/3 cup flour
1 3/4 cups packed brown sugar	1/3 cup dark rum
4 eggs	1/2 cup strained raspberry preserves
1 egg yolk	Powdered sugar
	Hazelnuts
	Whipped cream

Preheat oven to 375 degrees. Butter and flour two 10-inch springform pans.

In a bowl, combine the hazelnuts, the chilled flour, and the granulated sugar. Cut in the butter. Mix until well blended. Press the mixture evenly into the bottoms of the pans.

Beat together the brown sugar, eggs, egg yolk, and baking powder until thickened and foamy. Fold in the walnuts, coconut, and remaining flour. Divide the batter evenly between the pans. Bake until just set, about 20 minutes. Let cool for 15 minutes. Brush with the rum. Remove the springform pans and let cool.

Spread the raspberry preserves on top of one layer. Top with the second layer, bottom side up. Cover with plastic wrap and refrigerate overnight.

Place a decorative doily on top of the cake. Using a sifter, sprinkle with powdered sugar. Carefully remove the doily. Garnish with the hazelnuts and whipped cream.

DELECTABLE BITTERSWEET CHOCOLATE CAKE

SERVES 10
PREPARATION TIME 25 MINUTES
COOKING TIME 35 MINUTES
REFRIGERATION TIME 3 HOURS

An incredibly rich cake only for the "diet-unconscious."

Cocoa
**11 ounces unsweetened
 chocolate**
**11 ounces (2 3/4 sticks) unsalted
 butter**
1 tablespoon brandy
11 egg yolks

1 2/3 cups sugar
8 egg whites, room temperature
Pinch of cream of tartar
Pinch of salt

Crème Fraiche† (optional)

Preheat the oven to 350 degrees. Butter a 9-inch springform pan. Dust with cocoa, shaking out the excess. Melt the chocolate and butter over low heat. Let cool. Stir in the brandy.

Beat the egg yolks and 1 1/3 cups of the sugar until thick and creamy. Fold into the chocolate mixture.

In another bowl, beat the egg whites with the cream of tartar and salt until soft peaks form. Beat in the remaining 1/3 cup of sugar, a tablespoon at a time, until the egg whites are stiff. Carefully fold 1/3 of the whites into the chocolate mixture. Reverse the process and pour the chocolate mixture over the remaining whites. Carefully fold together until no white remains.

Spoon 2/3 of the mixture into the prepared pan, reserving the remaining 1/3 at room temperature. Bake for 25 minutes, or until a tester inserted in the center comes out clean. Let the cake cool in the pan for 10 minutes. Remove from the pan and finish cooling. Spread the reserved filling on top. Using a sifter, dust lightly with cocoa. Refrigerate at least 3 hours or overnight. Serve with Crème Fraîche, if desired.

DOUBLE INDULGENCE

SERVES 8 TO 10
PREPARATION TIME 15 MINUTES
COOKING TIME 20 MINUTES
REFRIGERATION TIME 12 HOURS

When port or Cognac isn't enough to top off a fine meal, try this stunning finale. Cut into wedges and placed on a pool of raspberry sauce, this luscious cake is then encircled with delicate fresh raspberries and topped with a cloud of whipped cream.

CAKE
1 pound sweet chocolate
6 ounces (1 1/2 sticks) unsalted
  butter

4 eggs
1 tablespoon sugar
1 tablespoon flour

Preheat oven to 400 degrees. Line an 8-inch cake pan with parchment paper.

In a saucepan, melt the chocolate and butter over low heat. Place un-cracked eggs in a bowl of hot water for 5 minutes. Crack and combine the eggs and sugar in the bowl of an electric mixer. Beat on high speed for 8 to 10 minutes, or until tripled in volume. Sift the flour on top. Fold into the eggs. Stir 1/4 of the egg mixture into the chocolate. Carefully fold the chocolate into the remaining eggs until thoroughly combined.

Pour into the prepared pan. Bake for 20 minutes. The cake will still be slightly soft in the middle. Cool completely in the pan. Cover and refrigerate in the pan overnight. The cake can be frozen for two weeks at this point.

RASPBERRY SAUCE
8 ounces raspberries, fresh or
  frozen
Superfine sugar to taste

1 cup heavy cream
1 teaspoon vanilla
Fresh raspberries

Purée the raspberries and strain. Add enough sugar to sweeten. Whip the heavy cream with the vanilla until firm. Invert the cake onto a platter and cut into wedges. Spoon some of the raspberry sauce onto the bottom of a dessert plate. Place a wedge of the cake in the center of the sauce. Spoon a dollop of whipped cream on top of the cake. Form a circle with the raspberries around the wedge.

ALMOND APRICOT ROLL

SERVES 8 TO 10
PREPARATION TIME 45 MINUTES
COOKING TIME 20 MINUTES

CAKE

4 ounces almonds, finely
   chopped
1/2 teaspoon cinnamon
1/4 teaspoon salt
Grated zest of 1 lemon

6 eggs, warmed in a bowl of
   hot water
3/4 cup sugar
2 teaspoons vanilla
Powdered sugar

Preheat the oven to 350 degrees. Butter a 10 × 15-inch jelly-roll pan. Line it with parchment paper. Generously butter and flour the paper, shaking out the excess.

Combine the almonds, cinnamon, salt, and lemon. Mix well and set aside. Beat the eggs, sugar, and vanilla on high speed of an electric mixer until tripled in volume, 5 to 7 minutes. Fold 1/3 of the egg mixture into the nuts. Add the remaining nut mixture to the eggs and carefully fold until blended. Pour the batter into the prepared pan. Bake for 20 to 30 minutes, or until golden and spongy to the touch. Spread a clean dish towel on a work surface. Liberally sprinkle with powdered sugar. Invert the warm cake on top. Peel off the paper. Starting with the long end facing you, roll up the cake tightly with the towel inside, jelly-roll style. Let cool.

FILLING

1 cup heavy cream
2 tablespoons powdered sugar
1 teaspoon vanilla

3/4 cup warm apricot preserves,
   strained
1/3 cup sliced almonds, toasted

Beat the heavy cream with the powdered sugar and vanilla until firm. Unroll the cooled cake. Brush with some of the apricot preserves. Spread a layer of the whipped cream over the roll, coming to within 1/4-inch of the sides.

Reroll the cake. Brush the outside with the remaining apricot preserves. Refrigerate until ready to serve.

Just prior to serving, sprinkle the toasted almonds over the outside of the roll. Dust with powdered sugar.

FROZEN CHOCOLATE ROLL

SERVES 8 TO 10
PREPARATION TIME 30 MINUTES
COOKING TIME 25 MINUTES
FREEZING TIME 3 HOURS

6 egg whites, room temperature
1/2 teaspoon cream of tartar
1 cup sugar
6 egg yolks, room temperature
4 tablespoons cocoa
4 teaspoons sifted flour
1/4 teaspoon salt

1 teaspoon vanilla
Cocoa for rolling
1 quart vanilla ice cream,
  softened
Fudge Sauce†
Whipped cream (optional)

Preheat oven to 325 degrees. Grease a 15 1/2 × 12 1/2-inch jelly-roll pan. Line with greased wax paper or parchment paper. Beat the egg whites with the cream of tartar until soft peaks form. Beat in 1/2 cup of the sugar, 2 tablespoons at a time, until stiff and glossy.

In another bowl, beat the egg yolks until thick. Add the remaining 1/2 cup of sugar and continue beating until cream-colored. Sift together the cocoa, flour, and salt. Beat into the yolk mixture together with the vanilla. Carefully fold the yolk mixture into the whites. Pour into the prepared pan and spread evenly. Bake for 20 to 25 minutes, or until a tester inserted in the center comes out clean.

Dust a sheet of wax paper liberally with cocoa. Invert the cake out onto the sheet and remove the wax paper. Roll up lengthwise. After 5 minutes, unroll and cover with the ice cream. Reroll and place in the freezer until firm, for at least 3 hours.

Spoon some of the Fudge Sauce in the center of each dessert plate. Place a slice of the chocolate roll on the sauce. If desired, pipe rosettes of whipped cream around the rim of the sauce. Serve accompanied by additional sauce.

AMARETTO CHEESECAKE

SERVES 10 TO 12
PREPARATION TIME 45 MINUTES
COOKING TIME 45 MINUTES
REFRIGERATION TIME 4 HOURS

A good cup of espresso is a nice complement to this Italian cheesecake.

3/4 cup very finely crushed
   imported amaretti biscuits
   (18 to 20 biscuits)
2 tablespoons butter, softened
1 1/2 pounds cream cheese,
   room temperature
3/4 cup plus 2 tablespoons
   sugar

1 tablespoon flour
4 eggs, room temperature
6 tablespoons Amaretto liqueur
1/2 teaspoon vanilla
1 cup sour cream, room
   temperature

Preheat oven to 350 degrees. Combine the amaretti crumbs and butter. Crumble until well blended. Reserve 1 tablespoon of the crumb mixture. Press the remaining mixture onto the bottom and sides of a greased 10-inch springform pan. Refrigerate until ready to use.

Beat the cream cheese until light and fluffy, scraping down the bowl as necessary. Beat in the 3/4 cup of sugar, 2 tablespoons at a time, beating thoroughly after each addition. Beat in the flour. Add the eggs, one at a time, beating well after each addition. Stir in the Amaretto and vanilla. Pour into the prepared pan. Bake until the cheesecake begins to pull away from the sides of the pan and the center is not quite set, about 30 to 35 minutes. Carefully remove from the oven. Cool on a rack for 20 minutes.

Combine the sour cream and remaining 2 tablespoons of sugar. Let stand until the sugar dissolves completely; stir to blend. Carefully spread the sour-cream mixture in a smooth layer over the top of the cake, up to but not touching the sides of the pan. Return to the oven. Bake for an additional 15 minutes.

Cool, in the pan, to room temperature. Sprinkle the reserved crumbs around the outside rim of the cake to form a border. Loosely cover the pan with plastic wrap. Refrigerate until thoroughly chilled and set, for at least 4 hours. Remove the sides of the pan. Let cake stand at room temperature for 10 minutes prior to serving.

CAPPUCCINO CHEESECAKE

SERVES 10 TO 12
PREPARATION TIME 20 MINUTES
COOKING TIME 1 HOUR 15 MINUTES
REFRIGERATION TIME 6 HOURS

Don't despair if the top of the cheesecake cracks. Just frost with sweetened whipped cream and garnish with candy coffee beans.

CRUST

3 1/2 tablespoons melted
   butter
3/4 cup chocolate wafer
   cookie crumbs
1 1/2 tablespoons sugar

Preheat oven to 350 degrees. Coat a 9-inch springform pan with butter. Combine the melted butter, cookie crumbs, and sugar. Press the crumb mixture onto the bottom and sides of the pan. Refrigerate for 10 minutes. Bake for 8 minutes. Cool on a cake rack.

FILLING

2 1/4 pounds cream cheese, room temperature
1 cup sugar
1/4 cup heavy cream
1 1/2 teaspoons vanilla
5 eggs

1 ounce ground semisweet chocolate
1/4 cup strong hot espresso coffee
3 tablespoons coffee liqueur
1/2 teaspoon lemon juice

In a large bowl, beat the cream cheese until smooth and fluffy. Beat in the sugar, heavy cream, and vanilla. Add the eggs, one at a time, beating well after each addition. Scrape down the sides of the bowl as necessary.

Set aside 2 1/4 cups of the filling. Mix the chocolate with the hot coffee and stir until dissolved. Stir in the coffee liqueur. Add to the remaining batter; blend well. Pour into the prepared crust. Bake for 40 minutes, or until the rim of the cake is set. The center should still be soft. Carefully remove from the oven.

Turn the oven down to 325 degrees. Stir the lemon juice into the reserved filling. Carefully pour around the inside rim of the pan where the cake is set. Allow the filling to flow into the center. Do not pour directly onto the center or it will collapse. Return to the oven. Continue baking until the sides rise and the center is just set, about 35 minutes.

Cool on a rack. When the bottom and sides are completely cool, remove the rim. Continue to cool at room temperature. Cover loosely with plastic wrap and refrigerate until firm, preferably overnight.

CHEDDAR BEER CHEESECAKE

SERVES 10 TO 12
PREPARATION TIME 30 MINUTES
COOKING TIME 1 HOUR 45 MINUTES

Serve this unusual cheesecake with fresh fruit slices.

CRUST

1 cup sifted flour
1/4 cup sugar
1 teaspoon grated lemon rind
4 ounces (1 stick) butter,
  softened

1 egg yolk
1/4 teaspoon vanilla

Preheat the oven to 500 degrees. To prepare the crust, mix the flour, sugar, and lemon rind. Cream with the butter. Add the egg yolk and vanilla. Stir until a soft dough is formed. Press 1/3 of the dough onto the bottom of an 8-inch springform pan. Bake for 8 to 10 minutes or until lightly browned. Watch carefully, as it burns quickly. Let cool. Press the remaining dough around the sides of the pan, coming to within 1 inch of the top.

FILLING

2 pounds cream cheese
1 cup finely grated sharp
  Cheddar cheese
1 3/4 cups sugar
1/4 teaspoon vanilla
1/2 teaspoon each lemon and
  orange rind

4 eggs
2 eggs yolks
1/4 cup beer or ale
1/4 cup heavy cream

Beat the cream cheese until light and fluffy. Beat in the Cheddar cheese until well blended. Add the sugar, vanilla, and lemon and orange rinds. Beat until smooth. Add the eggs and yolks, one at a time, beating well after each addition. Stir in beer and heavy cream. Pour into the prepared crust. Return to the 500 degree oven and bake for 8 to 10 minutes or until lightly browned.

Reduce the oven temperature to 250 degrees. Bake for 1 to 1 1/2 hours, or until a tester inserted in the center comes out fairly clean. Cool to room temperature. Serve warm or chilled.

MOCHA CHIP CHEESECAKE

SERVES 10 TO 12
PREPARATION TIME 30 MINUTES
COOKING TIME 2 HOURS
REFRIGERATION TIME 6 HOURS

6 tablespoons unsalted butter, melted
1 1/2 cups chocolate wafer crumbs
2 tablespoons sugar
1 1/2 pounds cream cheese, room temperature
1 cup sugar

4 eggs, room temperature
1/3 cup heavy cream
1 tablespoon instant coffee powder
1 teaspoon vanilla
6 ounces mini semisweet chocolate chips

Preheat oven to 350 degrees. Butter a 10-inch springform pan. Combine the butter, cookie crumbs, and the 2 tablespoons of sugar. Press onto the bottom and partially up the sides of the pan. Chill for 5 minutes. Bake for 10 minutes. Set aside to cool.

Reduce the oven temperature to 200 degrees. In an electric mixer, beat the cream cheese until light and fluffy. Beat in the sugar. Add the eggs, one at a time, beating well after each addition. Stir in the cream, instant coffee, and vanilla. Beat for 2 minutes.

Pour half of the filling into the prepared pan. Fold the chocolate chips into the remaining filling and carefully pour over the filling in the pan. Bake for 2 hours, or until a tester inserted in the center comes out clean. Cool completely at room temperature. Refrigerate until set, at least 6 hours, but preferably overnight.

HAZELNUT CHEESECAKE

SERVES 8 TO 10
PREPARATION TIME 15 MINUTES
COOKING TIME 1 1/2 HOURS
REFRIGERATION TIME 4 HOURS

A fresh raspberry sauce nicely complements the richness of this cake.

1/3 cup graham cracker crumbs
1 1/2 cups (8 ounces) shelled
  hazelnuts
2 pounds cream cheese, room
  temperature
1 1/4 cups sugar

1/2 cup heavy cream
1 teaspoon vanilla
4 eggs, room temperature

Raspberry Sauce†

Preheat the oven to 350 degrees. Coat the bottom of an 8-inch springform pan with butter. Press the crumbs onto the bottom of the pan. Toast the hazelnuts in the oven until nicely browned, about 10 to 15 minutes. Remove from the oven and while still warm briskly rub the nuts together inside a dish towel to remove most of the skins. Finely chop in a food processor. Transfer to a bowl and set aside.

In a food processor, beat the cream cheese, sugar, cream, and vanilla until smooth. Add the eggs, one at a time, beating well after each addition. Stir in the nuts. Pour into the prepared crust. Place the pan in a shallow baking dish. Add enough water to come halfway up the sides of the pan. Bake for 1 1/2 hours. Let cool to room temperature. Refrigerate for at least 4 hours. Serve accompanied by Raspberry Sauce.

SWEET PASTRY

MAKES ONE 8- TO 9-INCH CRUST
PREPARATION TIME 35 MINUTES

A sweet pastry that is not quite as flaky as the All-Purpose Pastry. Good for all tarts.

1 cup all-purpose flour
2 tablespoons sugar
1/4 teaspoon salt
4 ounces (1 stick) unsalted
  butter, cut into pieces

1 egg yolk
1 teaspoon vinegar or lemon
  juice

Combine the flour, sugar, and salt. Work the butter into the flour until crumbly. Add the egg yolk and vinegar. Gather the dough into a ball. Flatten out slightly. Wrap in plastic. Refrigerate for 30 minutes before rolling.

This pastry can be prepared in a food processor. With the metal blade in place, mix the flour, sugar, and salt. Add the butter and process until crumbly. With the machine running, add the egg and vinegar. Let the dough spin until it forms a ball. Remove from the machine, flatten slightly and wrap in plastic. Refrigerate for 30 minutes before rolling.

SHORTBREAD PASTRY

MAKES ONE 8- TO 9-INCH CRUST
PREPARATION TIME 35 MINUTES

A sweet, cookielike pastry that can be used interchangeably with Sweet Pastry.

1 1/2 cups all-purpose flour
1/4 cup sugar
1/4 teaspoon salt
5 ounces (1 1/4 sticks) unsalted
  butter, cut into pieces

2 egg yolks
2 teaspoons lemon juice

Combine the flour, sugar, and salt. Work the butter into the flour until the mixture is crumbly. Add the eggs and lemon juice. Gather into a ball. Wrap in plastic. Refrigerate for 30 minutes before rolling.

To prepare this pastry in a food processor, follow the directions for Sweet Pastry.

ALL-PURPOSE PASTRY

MAKES ONE 8- TO 9-INCH CRUST
PREPARATION TIME 35 MINUTES

This is a basic, all-purpose unsweetened pastry.

1 cup all-purpose flour
1/4 teaspoon salt
5 ounces (1 1/4 sticks) unsalted
   butter, cut into pieces

1 teaspoon vinegar
3 to 4 tablespoons ice water

Combine the flour and salt. Work the butter into the flour until the mixture is crumbly. Add the vinegar and enough water to form the dough into a ball. Gather into a ball and flatten slightly. Wrap in plastic. Refrigerate for 30 minutes before rolling out.

This pastry can also be made in a food processor. With the metal blade in place, mix the flour and salt. Add the butter and process until crumbly. With the machine running, add the vinegar and water. Let the dough spin until it forms a ball. Remove from the machine, flatten slightly and cover with plastic. Refrigerate for 30 minutes before rolling.

CHOCOLATE PASTRY

MAKES ONE 10-INCH CRUST
PREPARATION TIME 5 MINUTES
REFRIGERATION TIME 2 1/2 HOURS

This crust will enhance the taste of any fruit or cream pie.

1 1/3 cups all-purpose flour
4 ounces (1 stick) unsalted
   butter, cut into pieces
1 teaspoon sugar
1/8 teaspoon salt

2 tablespoons warm water
3 ounces bittersweet chocolate,
   melted and cooled to room
   temperature

Place the flour in a medium bowl. Work in the butter until the mixture is crumbly. Dissolve the sugar and salt in the water. Stir into the chocolate. Drizzle the chocolate mixture over the flour while tossing with a fork. Gently knead on a lightly floured board. Shape into a ball and flatten slightly. Wrap in plastic. Refrigerate for 2 hours.

Preheat oven to 375 degrees. Working quickly, roll out the dough between 2 sheets of wax paper to a 12-inch circle. Ease into a 9- to 10-inch tart pan. Press against the bottom and sides of the pan. Patch any holes. Refrigerate for 20 minutes.

Prick the bottom and sides of the shell with a fork. Bake on the lowest shelf of the oven until pastry is set and the edges are crisp, about 15 to 20 minutes. Cool on a wire rack.

CHOCOLATE ANGEL MOUSSE PIE

SERVES 8 TO 10
PREPARATION TIME 1 HOUR
COOKING TIME 70 MINUTES
REFRIGERATION TIME 6 HOURS

In color, texture and flavor, a crisp meringue shell forms a unique contrast to ubiquitous chocolate mousse. For a tastier meringue, add some ground nuts. Almonds and hazelnuts would work beautifully.

MERINGUE SHELL
4 egg whites
1/4 teaspoon cream of tartar
1 cup sugar

Preheat the oven to 300 degrees. Beat the egg whites with the cream of tartar until firm. Add the sugar, 2 tablespoons at a time, and beat until glossy. Spread in a 10-inch pie plate, making a deep rim around the edge. Bake for 1 hour. Let cool on a wire rack.

FILLING

8 ounces semisweet chocolate	**1 1/2 cups heavy cream,**
4 egg yolks	**whipped**
1 teaspoon vanilla	**Shaved sweet chocolate**
2 egg whites	

Melt the chocolate in the top of a double boiler over simmering water. Let cool. Beat the yolks until thick. With the vanilla, beat them into the chocolate. Beat the egg whites until firm. Fold into the chocolate mixture together with half of the whipped cream. Pour into the meringue shell. Spread the remaining whipped cream over the top. Chill until firm, for at least 6 hours. Just prior to serving, sprinkle with the shaved chocolate.

COCONUT ALMOND TART

SERVES 10 TO 12
PREPARATION TIME 15 MINUTES
REFRIGERATION TIME 40 MINUTES
COOKING TIME 40 MINUTES

PASTRY

1 cup flour

5 ounces (1 1/4 sticks) unsalted butter, room temperature

1/2 cup firmly packed brown sugar

Cream the flour, butter, and sugar until smooth. Gather into a ball. Wrap in plastic. Refrigerate for 30 minutes.

Roll the dough between two sheets of wax paper to a circle 1/8-inch thick. Carefully remove the top sheet of paper. Invert the dough into an 11-inch tart pan with a removable bottom. Remove the remaining sheet of paper. Gently press the dough into the pan. Trim and form edges. Refrigerate for 10 minutes.

Preheat the oven to 350 degrees. Place a piece of wax paper over the dough. Fill with beans or rice. Bake for 12 to 15 minutes, or until the shell begins to brown. Remove the beans and paper from the shell.

COCONUT ALMOND FILLING

1 cup firmly packed brown sugar

3 large eggs

1 tablespoon Amaretto liqueur

1 1/2 cups sweetened flaked coconut

1 1/2 cups chopped toasted almonds

2 teaspoons flour

1/2 teaspoon baking powder

Whisk the sugar, eggs, and Amaretto until blended. Stir in the coconut, almonds, flour, and baking powder. Pour into the prepared tart shell. Bake until nicely browned, about 18 to 20 minutes. Cool to room temperature before serving.

ALMOND TART WITH GRAND MARNIER

SERVES 6 TO 8
PREPARATION TIME 25 MINUTES
COOKING TIME 1 HOUR

CRUST

1 cup flour
4 ounces (1 stick) unsalted
   butter, room temperature
1 tablespoon sugar

Pinch of salt
1 tablespoon vanilla
1 1/2 teaspoons water

Preheat oven to 400 degrees. In a small bowl of an electric mixer, combine the flour, butter, sugar, and salt. Beat on low speed until the mixture is crumbly. Mix the vanilla with the water. Pour into the bowl, mixing until just blended. Do not overmix. Gather the dough into a ball. Press into a 9-inch tart pan. Bake for 10 to 15 minutes or until set.

FILLING

3/4 cup sugar
3/4 cup heavy cream
1 teaspoon Grand Marnier

1/8 teaspoon almond extract
Pinch of salt
1 cup sliced almonds

Reduce the oven temperature to 350 degrees. Combine sugar, heavy cream, Grand Marnier, almond extract, and salt. Beat with a fork until slightly thickened. Stir in the almonds, mixing well. Pour into the prepared crust. Bake until golden brown, about 40 to 45 minutes. Let cool at room temperature.

FRESH LEMON TART

SERVES 6 TO 8
PREPARATION TIME 20 MINUTES
COOKING TIME 35 MINUTES

A refreshing dessert with a subtle tart taste.

1 recipe Shortbread Pastry†
2 large lemons
4 egg yolks
3/4 cup sugar

2 teaspoons cornstarch
1 tablespoon heavy cream

Sweetened whipped cream

Prepare the Shortbread Pastry and chill. Preheat the oven to 400 degrees. Roll out the dough to fit a 9-inch shallow fluted tart pan.

Grate the rind of 1 lemon and squeeze its juice (about 1/3 of a cup). Mix the lemon rind, juice, yolks, sugar, cornstarch, and heavy cream. Whip for 5 minutes until slightly thickened. Pour onto the dough, spreading it evenly. Press the edges of the crust down so that they just come to the top of the lemon filling. From the remaining lemon, remove all skin and white so that only the flesh remains. Cut the lemon into very thin slices and discard the seeds. Arrange the slices on top of the filling in a decorative pattern. Bake for 30 to 35 minutes or until the filling is lightly browned and set. If the filling starts to get too brown before the crust is done, place a piece of foil over the top of the tart pan. Let cool to room temperature. Serve accompanied by the sweetened whipped cream.

DATE TART

SERVES 8 TO 10
PREPARATION TIME 20 MINUTES
COOKING TIME 30 MINUTES

Serve with a scoop of vanilla ice cream.

PASTRY

2 cups flour	1 egg yolk
6 ounces (1 1/2 sticks) butter, room temperature	1 to 2 tablespoons cold water

FILLING

1 pound pitted dates, sliced or chopped	1 1/2 cups heavy cream
2 tablespoons kirsch	1 1/2 teaspoons cornstarch
	2 tablespoons sugar

Preheat the oven to 400 degrees. Work the flour and butter together until crumbly. Stir in the egg yolk and enough water to gather the dough into a ball. Divide the dough in half. Roll out half of the dough on a heavily floured surface. Use it to line a 10-inch tart pan. Spread the dates over the dough. Sprinkle with the kirsch. Mix together the heavy cream and cornstarch. Pour mixture over the dates. Roll out the remaining dough. Cover the tart. Seal and flute the edges. Brush the top with cold water. Prick in a few places with the tines of a fork. Sprinkle with the sugar. Bake for 30 minutes or until nicely browned. Cool to room temperature before serving.

DEEP-DISH NECTARINE PIE

SERVES 6 TO 8
PREPARATION TIME 20 MINUTES
COOKING TIME 45 MINUTES

6 large fresh nectarines	1 teaspoon grated lemon peel
1/3 cup flour	Pastry for two-crust 9-inch pie
1/2 cup sugar	2 tablespoons unsalted butter
1/2 teaspoon cinnamon	2 tablespoons sugar
1/4 teaspoon salt	

Preheat the oven to 400 degrees. Slice the nectarines (about 6 cups). Combine the flour, sugar, cinnamon, salt, and lemon peel. Mix lightly with the nectarines. Roll half the pastry to fit into a deep 9-inch pie plate. Spoon the nectarine mixture into the crust. Dot with the butter. Roll the remaining pastry. Place over the fruit. Crimp the edges to seal well. Cut slits in the top to allow the steam to escape. Sprinkle with the sugar. Bake for 45 minutes or until nicely browned.

GLAZED BERRY TARTS

MAKES 12 TARTS
PREPARATION TIME 30 MINUTES
COOKING TIME 20 MINUTES

One rich bite of this berry-crowned cream cheese tart will be pleasing to the palate. Bake and fill the tarts ahead for relaxed entertaining.

PASTRY

1 cup flour	6 tablespoons unsalted butter
2 tablespoons sugar	1 egg yolk

Preheat the oven to 325 degrees. Mix the flour and sugar. Cut in the butter until the mixture is crumbly. With a fork, stir in the egg yolk until blended. With your hands, form the dough into a smooth, non-crumbly ball.

For each tart, place a tablespoon of the dough into a 2-inch muffin cup or tart pan. Press into the bottom and sides. Bake until nicely browned, about 20 minutes. Let cool in pans. Invert and tap lightly to remove the shells.

CREAM CHEESE FILLING

6 ounces cream cheese
2 tablespoons powdered sugar
1/2 teaspoon grated lemon peel
1 tablespoon lemon juice

2 1/2 cups fresh blueberries,
   blackberries, Olallieberries,
   or raspberries.
1/2 cup currant jelly, warmed

Beat the cream cheese with the powdered sugar until creamy. Beat in the lemon peel and juice. Spread 1 tablespoon of the mixture on the bottom of each cooled shell. Top with the berries. Generously brush the berries with the warm jelly to glaze. Refrigerate, loosely covered, until ready to serve.

LINZER TORTE

SERVES 8
PREPARATION TIME 30 MINUTES
REFRIGERATION TIME 2 HOURS
COOKING TIME 1 HOUR

A rich, crunchy cake of Austrian fame. Splendid, too, cut up into squares or fanciful shapes and served as a holiday cookie.

8 ounces (2 sticks) unsalted
   butter, softened and cut into
   pieces
1/2 cup sugar
2 egg yolks
Grated rind of 1 lemon
1 cup sifted flour

1 teaspoon cinnamon
1/2 teaspoon ground cloves
Pinch of salt
2 cups toasted ground almonds
   or hazelnuts
1 cup raspberry jam
Powdered sugar

Cream butter and sugar until light and fluffy. Beat in the egg yolks and lemon rind. Combine the flour, cinnamon, cloves, and salt. Sift into the butter mixture. Add nuts and mix thoroughly. Gather dough into a smooth ball. Wrap in plastic. Refrigerate for 2 hours.

Preheat the oven to 350 degrees. Butter and flour an 8-inch springform pan. Roll out 2/3 of the dough to a thickness of 1/4 inch. Press gently into the prepared pan. The sides should be slightly higher than the center. Spread with the jam. Roll the remaining dough and cut into 8-inch strips. Arrange in a crisscross pattern over the jam. Bake for 1 hour, or until nicely browned and pulling away from the sides of the pan. Cool and remove from the pan. Dust with powdered sugar. Serve at room temperature.

PEACH-BLUEBERRY TART

SERVES 8
PREPARATION TIME 2 HOURS
REFRIGERATION TIME 1 1/2 HOURS
COOKING TIME 30 MINUTES

Try any combination of fresh fruits in this refreshing tart. A glaze brushed on the bottom of the crust prevents it from becoming soggy, and a kirsch-scented glaze makes a handsome topping for the poached fruit.

TART SHELL

2 cups flour
2 tablespoons sugar
Pinch of salt
6 ounces (1 1/2 sticks) unsalted
  butter, cut into pieces

3 tablespoons shortening
3 to 4 tablespoons cold water
1/2 cup strained apricot jam

In a food processor fitted with a metal blade, combine the flour, sugar, and salt. Add the butter and shortening; mix until crumbly. Add the water. Process until the dough forms a ball. Wrap in plastic. Refrigerate for 1 hour.

On a floured surface, roll the dough to fit a 14 × 4-inch rectangular tart pan. Line the pan with the crust. Cover with a piece of parchment paper. Fill with beans or rice to weight down while baking. Refrigerate for 30 minutes.

Preheat the oven to 375 degrees. Bake the crust just until the edges begin to brown, about 15 minutes. Remove the paper and weights. Continue to bake until the crust is nicely browned on the bottom, about 15 to 20 minutes. Spread the apricot jam over the bottom of the crust while still warm.

FRUIT FILLING AND GLAZE

1 cup water
1/2 cup sugar
2 tablespoons crème de cassis
8 large ripe peaches, sliced

1/2 cup blueberries
1/2 cup red currant jelly
1 teaspoon kirsch

In a large saucepan, bring the water, sugar, and cassis to a boil. Add the peach slices. Simmer for 5 minutes or until just tender. Remove from the syrup with a slotted spoon. Set aside to cool. Pour the hot syrup over the blueberries. Let stand for 4 minutes; drain.

Arrange the peach slices in overlapping rows down the sides of the tart. Arrange the blueberries down the middle. Heat the currant jelly with the kirsch. Brush over the fruit to glaze. Serve at room temperature.

LEMON MERINGUE PIE

SERVES 8
PREPARATION TIME 40 MINUTES
COOKING TIME 40 MINUTES

1 recipe Shortbread Pastry†
1 cup milk
1 teaspoon vanilla
3 egg yolks
2 tablespoons sugar
3 tablespoons cornstarch

Rind of 2 small lemons, finely
   grated
3/4 cup fresh lemon juice
3 egg whites, room temperature
3/4 cup sugar
1/4 cup water

Preheat the oven to 425 degrees. Roll out and line an 8- or 9-inch pie pan with Shortbread Pastry. Cover the dough with parchment paper. Fill the paper with beans or rice. Bake for 20 to 25 minutes or until dough is nicely browned. Cool and remove the beans and paper.

In a saucepan, bring the milk and vanilla to a boil. Beat the egg yolks and sugar until thick and cream-colored. With a whisk, stir in the cornstarch. Pour some of the hot milk into the egg-and-sugar mixture, whisking constantly. Pour this mixture back into the saucepan. Add the lemon rind and juice. Bring almost to a boil, stirring constantly so that the mixture does not stick to the bottom of the pan. Cook until nicely thickened. Rub the surface of the lemon cream with a little butter so that a skin does not form. Set aside and let cool.

Beat the egg whites until soft peaks form. Add 2 tablespoons of the sugar. Continue to beat until very firm. Place the remaining sugar and water in a saucepan. Bring to a boil and cook for 3 to 4 minutes. Begin beating the egg whites again. Pour the cooked sugar into them, adding quickly. Continue beating at low speed until the mixture cools, about 5 minutes.

Fold 1/3 of the meringue into the lemon cream. Spread this mixture into the prepared crust. Place the remaining meringue into a pastry bag fitted with a star tip. Pipe little peaks around the top of the tart, covering it entirely. Place under the broiler until golden brown, 2 to 3 minutes. Refrigerate until ready to serve.

BLACK RUSSIAN PIE

SERVES 8
PREPARATION TIME 30 MINUTES
COOKING TIME 5 MINUTES
REFRIGERATION TIME 4 HOURS

This luscious dessert, laced with liqueur, will warm you on a cold winter's night.

KAHLÚA CRUMB CRUST
- 1 **cup graham crackers or chocolate wafer crumbs**
- 2 **tablespoons unsalted butter, melted**
- 2 **tablespoons Kahlúa**

Combine the graham crackers or wafer crumbs, butter and Kahlúa. Mix well. Press onto the bottom and sides of a 9-inch pie plate. Chill for 10 minutes.

BLACK RUSSIAN FILLING
- 1/2 **cup milk**
- 2 **envelopes unflavored gelatin**
- 1/2 **cup Kahlúa**
- 2 **eggs**
- 1/2 **cup sugar**
- 1/3 **cup vodka**
- 1 1/2 **cups heavy cream, whipped**
- **Shaved chocolate**

Heat the milk to boiling. Add the gelatin and Kahlúa; stir until dissolved. In a food processor or blender, mix the eggs, sugar, and vodka. With the machine running, pour in the milk mixture and blend well. Transfer to a bowl. Chill for 15 to 30 minutes or until slightly thickened, stirring occasionally. Fold the gelatin mixture into the whipped cream. Pour into the prepared crust. Chill until set, about 3 hours. Sprinkle shaved chocolate on top just before serving.

FROZEN DELIGHT WITH CHOCOLATE SAUCE

SERVES 6 TO 8
PREPARATION TIME 15 MINUTES
COOKING TIME 10 MINUTES
FREEZING TIME 2 HOURS

Tiny chunks of melted chocolate and toasted slivers of almond are gently whipped into an icy meringue of liqueur-flavored cream. Top with a warm chocolate sauce for a heavenly dessert.

MERINGUE

4 egg whites, room temperature
1/8 teaspoon cream of tartar
1/8 teaspoon salt
1/4 cup sugar
2 cups heavy cream
2 tablespoons Galliano

1 tablespoon vanilla
2 teaspoons powdered sugar
1 cup chocolate chips
1/2 cup toasted slivered
 almonds

Beat the egg whites until foamy. Add the cream of tartar and salt; beat until soft peaks form. Add the 1/4 cup of sugar, 2 tablespoons at a time, and continue beating until stiff and glossy. Beat the cream until soft. Stir in the Galliano, vanilla, and powdered sugar; beat until firm. Fold into the whites, blending completely. Transfer to a shallow bowl and freeze just until ice crystals form, about 1 hour.

Melt the chocolate chips over low heat. Stir in the almonds. Thoroughly fold into the icy meringue mixture. Small chunks of chocolate will form. Cover and return to the freezer for at least 1 hour.

CHOCOLATE SAUCE

8 ounces dark or milk chocolate
4 to 8 tablespoons heavy cream

Before serving, melt the chocolate with 4 tablespoons of the cream over low heat. Thin with the additional cream, if desired. Spoon the frozen meringue into dessert dishes. Spoon some of the warm Chocolate Sauce over each serving. Pass the remaining sauce separately.

PEPPERMINT FRANGO

MAKES 36
PREPARATION TIME 15 MINUTES
COOKING TIME 5 MINUTES

This is a dessert that freezes well. Keep a bunch on hand in a tightly sealed container for those unexpected guests.

4 ounces unsweetened
   chocolate
8 ounces (2 sticks) unsalted
   butter, softened
2 cups superfine sugar

4 eggs
2 teaspoons vanilla
2 teaspoons peppermint extract
1 cup vanilla wafers, finely
   ground

Melt the chocolate in a double boiler over low heat. Set aside to cool. Cream the butter and sugar until light and fluffy. Whip in the cooled chocolate. Beat in the eggs, one at a time. Continue mixing until the sugar and eggs are well blended and the sugar dissolves. Stir in the vanilla and peppermint extract.

Sprinkle half of the ground cookie crumbs in cupcake liners. Spoon in the filling. Sprinkle the remainder of the crumbs over the top. Freeze until set. Serve frozen.

PUMPKIN ICE CREAM PIE

SERVES 8
PREPARATION TIME 20 MINUTES
COOKING TIME 10 MINUTES
FREEZING TIME 3 HOURS

Nice light texture—an alternative to traditional holiday pumpkin pie.

CRUST
2 cups gingersnap cookie
   crumbs
4 tablespoons melted butter

Preheat oven to 325 degrees. Stir together the cookie crumbs and butter. Press into an 8- or 9-inch pie pan. Bake for 8 to 10 minutes. Let cool.

FILLING

1 quart vanilla ice cream,
  softened
1 cup canned pumpkin
1/4 cup light brown sugar
1 teaspoon pumpkin pie spice

1/4 teaspoon allspice
1/4 teaspoon powdered ginger
1/4 teaspoon ground cloves
1/4 teaspoon nutmeg

In a food processor, combine all the filling ingredients. Mix until well blended. Pour into the prepared crust. Cover and freeze until firm, 3 to 4 hours. Remove from the freezer 5 minutes before serving. Slice with a very sharp knife as the crust may be difficult to cut.

MOCHA SUNDAE PIE

SERVES 8 TO 10
PREPARATION TIME 20 MINUTES
COOKING TIME 10 MINUTES
FREEZING TIME 4 HOURS

A crowd pleaser. Simple to prepare, delightful to see.

18 Oreo cookies
1/3 cup melted unsalted butter
2 ounces unsweetened
  chocolate
2 tablespoons unsalted butter
1/2 cup sugar
1 small can (7 oz) evaporated
  milk

1 quart coffee or Mocha
  Almond Fudge ice cream,
  softened
1 cup heavy cream
2 tablespoons powdered sugar
2 tablespoons Kahlúa
1/2 cup chopped nuts

Lightly butter a 9-inch springform pan. Crush the cookies. Stir in the melted butter and mix well. Press into the prepared pan. Chill until firm.

In a heavy saucepan, melt the chocolate with the butter over low heat. Stir in the sugar. Slowly pour in the evaporated milk. Cook over high heat for 5 to 10 minutes, or until thickened. Transfer to a bowl and chill.

Fill the shell with the ice cream, smoothing evenly. Chill in the freezer until the ice cream is firm. Spread with the chocolate sauce. Return to the freezer. Whip the cream with the sugar and Kahlúa until firm. Spread over the pie. Sprinkle with the chopped nuts. Freeze until firm, about 4 hours. Let stand for 5 minutes before serving.

SONOMA MELBA TORTE

SERVES 10 TO 12
PREPARATION TIME 30 MINUTES
COOKING TIME 10 MINUTES
FREEZING TIME 6 HOURS

CRUST
2 cups finely crushed vanilla
    wafers or gingersnaps
4 tablespoons melted butter

Stir together the crumbs and butter until well mixed. Set aside 2 tablespoons. Press the remainder evenly over the bottom and about 2 inches up the sides of a 9-inch springform pan. Set aside.

PEACH SAUCE

2 1/2 cups peeled and sliced fresh peaches	**4 tablespoons light corn syrup**
3/4 cup sugar	**2 tablespoons cornstarch**
	2 tablespoons water

In a food processor or blender, purée the peaches. In a saucepan, combine the peach purée, sugar, and light corn syrup. Mix the cornstarch with the water; blend until smooth. Stir into the purée. Cook over medium heat, stirring, until it boils. Cook for 2 minutes. Remove from the heat. Transfer to a bowl; cover and chill.

RASPBERRY SAUCE

3 cups raspberries, fresh or frozen	**1/3 cup water**
2/3 cup sugar	**1/2 gallon vanilla ice cream, softened**
1/3 cup light corn syrup	
1/4 cup cornstarch	

In a saucepan, combine the raspberries, sugar, and corn syrup. Mix the cornstarch with the water; blend until smooth. Stir into the berries. Cook over medium heat, stirring and mashing the berries with a spoon until the mixture boils. Cook for 2 minutes. Strain into a bowl. Cover and chill.

ASSEMBLY

Spoon a third of the ice cream into the crust. Spread 1/4 of the Peach Sauce and 1/2 of the Raspberry Sauce over the ice cream. Repeat, ending with the ice cream. You should have half of the Peach Sauce left. Sprinkle the top with the remaining crumbs. Cover and freeze until firm, at least 6 hours or for as long as 3 days.

Unwrap torte and let stand at room temperature for 10 minutes prior to serving. Cut into wedges with a sharp knife. Top with the remaining Peach Sauce.

WHITE CHOCOLATE MOUSSE

SERVES 6 TO 8
PREPARATION TIME 30 MINUTES
COOKING TIME 10 MINUTES
REFRIGERATION TIME 2 HOURS

6 ounces white chocolate
1/2 cup warm milk
1 package unflavored gelatin
1 teaspoon vanilla
2 egg whites

Pinch of salt
1 cup heavy cream, chilled
Dash of lemon juice
Bittersweet Fudge Sauce† or
  Raspberry Sauce†

Chop the chocolate into small pieces. Melt with 6 tablespoons of the milk in the top of a double boiler over hot water. Stir until smooth. Remove from the heat and set aside. Soften the gelatin in the remaining 2 tablespoons of warm milk. Stir until dissolved. Stir the gelatin mixture and vanilla into the chocolate mixture until smooth. Cool to room temperature.

Beat the egg whites with the salt until stiff peaks form. Fold a third of the whites into the chocolate mixture. Gently fold in the remainder, a little at a time. Whip the cream until firm. Fold the whipped cream and lemon juice into the chocolate mixture. Pour into a serving bowl. Chill until firm for at least 2 hours.

Serve the mousse in a pool of Fudge Sauce or Raspberry Sauce. Garnish with chocolate leaves or fresh raspberries, if desired.

COLD LEMON CUSTARD SOUFFLÉS

SERVES 8
PREPARATION TIME 30 MINUTES
COOKING TIME 45 MINUTES
REFRIGERATION TIME 4 HOURS

1 cup sugar
1/4 cup flour
1/8 teaspoon salt
2 tablespoons melted butter
5 tablespoons lemon juice

Grated rind of 1 lemon
3 egg yolks, well beaten
1 1/2 cups milk, scalded
3 egg whites

Preheat the oven to 325 degrees. Generously butter 8 custard cups. Combine the sugar, flour, salt, and butter. Stir in the lemon juice and rind. Whisk the beaten yolks into the hot milk. Whisk the yolk mixture into the lemon mixture until well blended.

Beat the egg whites until firm but not dry. Fold the lemon mixture into the egg whites. Spoon into the prepared custard cups. Place the filled cups in a baking pan. Fill with enough hot water to come halfway up the sides of the cups. Bake for 45 minutes. Cool to room temperature. Refrigerate until chilled, about 4 hours. Serve cold.

ORANGE CARAMEL CUSTARD

SERVES 6
PREPARATION TIME 20 MINUTES
COOKING TIME 40 MINUTES

Light and luscious.

1 cup sugar
1/4 cup water
2 cups milk
A 1-inch cinnamon stick
Rind of 1 orange
3 whole eggs

2 egg yolks
1 teaspoon orange-flavored
liqueur
1 orange, peeled with all white
removed, and sliced

Preheat the oven to 350 degrees. In a heavy saucepan, combine 1/2 cup of the sugar and the water. Bring to a boil. Cook, without stirring, until the mixture is a dark amber color. Quickly pour the syrup into 6 custard cups. Set aside to cool.

In a saucepan, slowly bring the milk, cinnamon stick, and orange rind to a boil. Remove from the heat and let stand for 10 minutes. When cool, remove the cinnamon stick and orange rind.

Beat together the eggs, egg yolks, remaining 1/2 cup of sugar, and the liqueur. Whisk into the milk and mix well; strain.

Spoon into the caramel-coated cups. Cover each with a piece of foil. Place the cups in a baking pan and add enough hot water to come halfway up the sides of the cups. Bake for 30 minutes, or until a tester inserted in the center comes out clean. Cool on a rack. To serve, unmold onto dessert plates and allow the caramel to run over the top. Garnish with the orange slices.

GRAND MARNIER SOUFFLÉ

SERVES 6 TO 8
PREPARATION TIME 20 MINUTES
COOKING TIME 25 MINUTES

You don't have to feel pressured about making a last-minute dessert. The base can be prepared well in advance. Have the egg whites ready at room temperature. Just the whipping and folding are left.

1 tablespoon unsalted butter	3 ounces orange-juice
2 tablespoons sugar	concentrate
8 egg yolks at room	3 ounces Grand Marnier
temperature	8 egg whites, room temperature
2/3 cup superfine sugar	Pinch of salt
Grated rind of 1 large orange	Powdered sugar

Grease a 2-quart soufflé dish with the butter. Sprinkle with the 2 tablespoons of sugar. Place the egg yolks in the top of a double boiler. Add the superfine sugar and the orange rind. Beat the egg-yolk mixture over hot water on medium heat until thickened. (It will have the consistency of hollandaise sauce.) Remove from the hot water and stir in the orange-juice concentrate and Grand Marnier. Place in the refrigerator to cool.

Preheat the oven to 375 degrees. In a copper bowl, beat the egg whites with the salt until firm but not dry. Fold in the egg-yolk mixture. Pour into the prepared soufflé dish. Bake for 20 to 25 minutes, or until lightly browned. The soufflé should be soft and runny in the center. Sprinkle the top with powdered sugar. Serve immediately.

PUFFED PEACH SOUFFLÉ

SERVES 6
PREPARATION TIME 30 MINUTES
COOKING TIME 50 MINUTES

A variation of the English trifle.

2 large peaches
3 tablespoons sugar
4 ladyfingers, split
4 tablespoons strained
  raspberry jam, warmed
1 tablespoon butter
1 tablespoon cornstarch
1 teaspoon lemon juice

1/4 teaspoon almond extract
Pinch of mace
2 egg yolks
3 egg whites
1/2 teaspoon cream of tartar
Pinch of salt
Custard Sauce (recipe follows)

Preheat oven to 375 degrees. Peel, halve, and pit the peaches. Slice 1 peach thickly and place on the bottom of a 6-cup soufflé dish. Sprinkle with 1 tablespoon of the sugar. Cover with the split ladyfingers. Spoon the jam over the ladyfingers. Set the dish in a baking pan. Add enough boiling water to come 1 inch up the sides of the dish. Place in the oven while preparing the soufflé.

In a food processor or blender, purée the remaining peach. You should have 2/3 cup of purée. In a saucepan, melt the butter. Stir in the cornstarch. Add the peach purée and cook, stirring constantly, until the mixture comes to a boil. Remove from the heat and stir in the lemon juice, almond extract, and mace.

Beat the egg yolks until thick. Whisk the hot mixture into them. Set aside. Beat the whites with the cream of tartar and salt until soft peaks form. Add the remaining sugar, a tablespoon at a time, and continue beating until the whites are stiff. Fold 1/4 of the egg whites into the peach mixture. Gently fold in the remaining whites.

Remove the soufflé dish from the oven. Spoon the soufflé mixture into the dish. Bake for 45 to 50 minutes, or until puffed and lightly browned on top. Pass the Custard Sauce to spoon over each serving.

CUSTARD SAUCE
1 tablespoon cornstarch
1 1/4 cups half-and-half
3 egg yolks

2 tablespoons sugar
1 teaspoon vanilla

Combine the cornstarch and half-and-half in a small pan. Bring to a boil, stirring constantly. Remove from the heat. Beat the egg yolks with the sugar until thick. Stir the hot mixture into the yolks. Return the mixture to the saucepan. Cook over very low heat for 3 to 4 minutes, stirring constantly. Do not allow the mixture to boil. Remove from the heat and stir in the vanilla. Transfer to a bowl and set in a pan of cold water to cool quickly.

CHOCOLATE SOUFFLÉ

SERVES 8
PREPARATION TIME 35 MINUTES
COOKING TIME 1 HOUR

A light, spectacular dessert. Since soufflés fall as quickly as it takes to admire them, timing is very important in the mastery of this delicious dazzler.

2 tablespoons unsalted butter
2 tablespoons sugar
1 1/2 cups flour
3/4 cup Dutch cocoa
1 cup sugar
1/4 teaspoon salt
2 cups milk
6 egg yolks, at room
    temperature for 1 hour

2 tablespoons unsalted butter,
    softened
1 teaspoon vanilla
8 egg whites, at room
    temperature for 1 hour
1/4 teaspoon cream of tartar
Powdered sugar

Sweetened whipped cream

Preheat the oven to 350 degrees. Grease a 2-quart soufflé dish with 1 table-spoon of the butter. Fold a piece of wax paper large enough to reach around the soufflé dish into thirds. Grease with the other tablespoon of butter. Form a 2-inch collar around the dish; tie with kitchen twine. Sprinkle the dish and paper with the 2 tablespoons of sugar.

In a heavy saucepan, blend together the flour, cocoa, 3/4 cup of the sugar, and the salt. Gradually whisk in the milk. Cook over medium heat, stirring constantly, until the mixture comes to a boil. Whip the egg yolks until thick. Beat in some of the cocoa mixture. Slowly whisk the yolk mixture into the saucepan. Stir in the 2 tablespoons of butter and the vanilla. Let cool slightly.

Beat the egg whites with the cream of tartar until soft peaks form. Add the remaining 1/4 cup sugar, 2 tablespoons at a time, beating well after each addition. Continue beating until smooth and shiny. Fold a third of the cocoa mixture into the egg whites. Fold in the remaining cocoa mixture. Gently pour into the prepared dish.

Set the soufflé dish in a large baking pan. Into the pan, pour in enough hot water to measure 1 inch. Bake for 1 to 1 1/4 hours. Remove the collar from the dish. Sprinkle the top with sifted powdered sugar. Serve accompanied by the sweetened whipped cream.

APPLE-RAISIN CRISP

SERVES 8
PREPARATION TIME 20 MINUTES
COOKING TIME 40 MINUTES

This delightful crumb pie will lose its crispness if reheated. Delicious with ice cream.

1/3 cup packed raisins
4 tablespoons unsalted butter
2 1/2 pounds tart green apples,
　peeled, cored, and sliced
3 tablespoons lemon juice
2 tablespoons sugar

1 tablespoon vanilla
1 cup flour
3/4 to 1 cup dark brown sugar
4 ounces (1 stick) butter
3/4 teaspoon cinnamon
1/4 teaspoon nutmeg

Preheat oven to 400 degrees. Cover the raisins with warm water. Let stand until plump. Generously coat a 9 × 13-inch baking dish with 1 tablespoon of the butter. Melt the remaining first 3 tablespoons of butter in a large skillet. Stir in the apples and coat with the butter. Add the lemon juice, sugar, and vanilla; toss to coat. Cook over low heat, stirring frequently, until the apples absorb most of the liquid. Drain the raisins; stir into the apples. Spoon into the prepared dish and smooth to an even layer.

In a food processor or mixer, combine the remaining ingredients. Mix until crumbly. Sprinkle evenly over the apples. Bake until the top is well browned and crisp, about 35 to 40 minutes. Serve warm.

ALMOND PUFF PASTRY

SERVES 6
PREPARATION TIME 20 MINUTES
REFRIGERATION TIME 1 HOUR
COOKING TIME 25 MINUTES

Flavor the whipped cream with your favorite liqueur.

12 ounces puff pastry,
　homemade or frozen
1 cup sliced almonds
1 cup granulated sugar
1 to 2 egg whites, lightly
　beaten

1 egg yolk beaten with 1
　tablespoon water
2 cups heavy cream, whipped
Powdered sugar

Preheat the oven to 375 degrees. Cut the pastry into 6 rectangles. On a lightly floured surface, roll each to a rectangle about 3 × 2 inches and about 1/4 inch thick. Place two inches apart on a baking sheet. Mix the almonds with the sugar. Stir just enough of the egg white to hold the mixture together. Brush the pastry tops with the egg-yolk mixture. Spread the nut mixture evenly on each pastry. Bake for 20 to 25 minutes or until well puffed and crisp. Remove to racks and cool completely.

Split the pastries in half lengthwise. Generously top with the whipped cream. Replace the top half. Refrigerate for 1 hour. Let stand at room temperature for 15 minutes. Dust with powdered sugar.

SAN FRANCISCO BREAD PUDDING

SERVES 6 TO 8
PREPARATION TIME 10 MINUTES
COOKING TIME 45 MINUTES

5 ounces stale French bread, broken into small pieces
1 cup milk
1 cup heavy cream
1 cup sugar
4 tablespoons unsalted butter, melted
1 whole egg
1 egg yolk

1/2 cup raisins
1/2 cup shredded coconut
1/2 cup chopped pecans
1 tablespoon vanilla
1/2 teaspoon cinnamon
1/4 teaspoon nutmeg
Lemon Rum Sauce (recipe follows)

Preheat oven to 350 degrees. In a large bowl, combine all the ingredients; blend well. The mixture should be very moist. Pour into a buttered 11 × 7-inch baking dish. Bake for 45 minutes, or until set. Serve warm with Lemon Rum Sauce.

LEMON RUM SAUCE
6 tablespoons unsalted butter
3 tablespoons sugar
1/4 cup lemon juice

Grated rind of 1 large lemon
2 egg yolks, beaten
3 to 6 tablespoons rum

In a saucepan, combine the butter and sugar. Cook over low heat until well blended. Stir in lemon juice and rind. Pour some of the butter mixture into the yolks and whisk to blend. Pour this mixture back into the pan. Whisk over low heat until slightly thickened. Stir in rum to taste.

APPLE FRITTERS

SERVES 6
PREPARATION TIME 15 MINUTES
COOKING TIME 5 MINUTES

2 cups flour
1 tablespoon baking powder
1/4 teaspoon salt
1 egg
1/4 cup sugar
1 cup milk
1 cup coarsely chopped, peeled,
  and seeded apple

3 tablespoons orange juice
1 teaspoon grated orange peel
1/2 teaspoon vanilla
Oil for frying
Powdered sugar

Sift together the flour, baking powder, and salt. Beat the egg with the sugar until thick. Add the remaining ingredients and mix well. Fold the dry ingredients into the egg mixture, just until the flour is moistened.

Heat the oil in a deep-fat fryer or large pan until it measures 350 degrees on a candy thermometer. Drop the fritters by rounded teaspoons into the hot oil. When the fritters rise to the surface, turn and brown on the other side. Drain well on paper towels. Roll in sifted powdered sugar. Serve hot.

APPLE STRUDEL

SERVES 18 TO 20
PREPARATION TIME 30 MINUTES
COOKING TIME 40 MINUTES

Serve accompanied by brandied whipped cream.

1 pound puff pastry, homemade
  or frozen
3 pounds tart cooking apples,
  peeled, seeded, and chopped
1/2 cup raisins
1/2 cup pecan pieces
1 cup sugar

1/4 teaspoon cinnamon
Juice of 1/2 lemon
Grated peel of 1/2 lemon
1/2 cup fine dry bread crumbs
1 egg beaten with 1 teaspoon
  water
Powdered sugar

Preheat the oven to 400 degrees. Moisten a jelly-roll pan with water, shaking off the excess. If using frozen pastry, thaw and keep chilled until ready to use.

In a bowl, combine apples, raisins, pecans, sugar, cinnamon, lemon juice, and lemon peel; lightly toss to mix. Roll the pastry to a rectangle 10 × 15 inches long and 1/8 inch thick. Sprinkle evenly with the bread crumbs. Place the apple mixture along one long side of the pastry, leaving a 2-inch border. Roll up and place seam side down on the pan. Brush the top of the pastry with the egg wash. Cut diagonal steam vents at 1/2-inch intervals.

Place in the oven and immediately reduce the oven temperature to 350 degrees. Bake approximately 40 minutes or until deep golden brown. Dust with powdered sugar. Serve warm.

POACHED PEARS WITH LINGONBERRY SAUCE

SERVES 4
PREPARATION TIME 20 MINUTES
COOKING TIME 55 MINUTES
REFRIGERATION TIME 1 HOUR

POACHED PEARS

1/2 cup water

2 cups dry white wine

1/2 cup sugar

1 tablespoon lemon juice

4 small pears, peeled

In a large saucepan, combine the water, wine, sugar, and lemon juice. Bring to a boil over high heat. Add pears. Lower heat to simmer and partially cover the pan. Poach for approximately 30 minutes, or until the pears are soft but not mushy. Remove from the poaching liquid. Cool and refrigerate.

LINGONBERRY SAUCE

1 cinnamon stick

2 cups port wine

1/4 cup sugar

2 14-ounce jars lingonberries

Fresh mint sprigs

Combine the cinnamon stick, port, and sugar. Cook until reduced to 3/4 cup. Add the lingonberries and simmer, uncovered, for 15 minutes. Cool and refrigerate.

ASSEMBLY

Slice pears in half and core. Cover the bottom of each dessert plate with Lingonberry Sauce. Cut each pear half into four slices. Arrange eight slices in a circular fashion over the sauce. Garnish with fresh mint sprigs.

BANANAS FOSTER

SERVES 4
PREPARATION TIME 10 MINUTES
COOKING TIME 5 MINUTES

Here's a refreshingly simple dessert of sweet and creamy fried bananas.

1/2 cup brown sugar
4 tablespoons unsalted butter
1/4 teaspoon cinnamon
Pinch of nutmeg
1/4 cup banana liqueur

4 bananas, peeled and sliced in
  half lengthwise
1/2 cup dark rum
Vanilla ice cream

In a large sauté pan or chafing dish, combine the sugar, butter, cinnamon, nutmeg, and liqueur. Heat until the butter melts, mixing well. Add the bananas and sauté until they begin to soften. Add the rum and heat well. Ignite sauce with a match.

Place 2 banana halves on each plate. Top with a scoop of ice cream. Spoon over some of the sauce. Serve immediately.

MINI CREAM CHEESE CRÊPES WITH STRAWBERRY SAUCE

MAKES 20 TO 24
PREPARATION TIME 10 MINUTES
REFRIGERATION TIME 1 HOUR
COOKING TIME 10 MINUTES

STRAWBERRY SAUCE
3 cups fresh or thawed frozen
  strawberries

1/2 to 3/4 cup sugar
1 tablespoon lemon juice

Purée and strain 2 1/3 cups of the strawberries. In a saucepan, combine the strawberry purée, sugar to taste, and the lemon juice. Bring to a boil. Cook until slightly thickened. Let cool. Stir in the reserved 2/3 cup whole berries. Let stand, covered, at room temperature.

CREAM CHEESE CRÊPES

8 ounces cream cheese, room temperature	1 tablespoon brandy
1 tablespoon sugar	1/4 teaspoon vanilla
1/4 teaspoon salt	1 cup flour
3 eggs, room temperature	Butter
1 tablespoon heavy cream	Powdered sugar

Beat the cream cheese, sugar, and salt until fluffy. Beat in the eggs, one at a time, until smooth. Beat in the cream, brandy, and vanilla. Gradually stir in the flour. Cover and refrigerate for 1 hour.

Brush a griddle or heavy skillet with melted butter. Spoon 2 tablespoons of batter onto the griddle. Cook until the batter sets and the edges begin to brown. Turn the crêpe and continue cooking until underside is nicely browned. Transfer to a plate and keep warm. Continue making crêpes until all the batter is used.

Spoon Strawberry Sauce around the crêpes on individual plates. Dust with powdered sugar. Serve immediately. Pass extra sauce.

PEARS IN CARAMEL SAUCE

SERVES 6 TO 8
PREPARATION TIME 10 MINUTES
COOKING TIME 15 MINUTES

4 large pears, peeled	3/4 cup sugar
4 ounces (1 stick) unsalted butter	1/2 cup Madeira wine
	1/2 cup heavy cream

Cut the pears in halves; remove the stems and cores. In a skillet large enough to hold the pears in a single layer, melt the butter. Stir in the sugar and Madeira. Cook, stirring constantly, until the sugar dissolves and the mixture is smooth. Add the pear halves. Cook, turning several times, until just tender, about 5 to 10 minutes. Transfer the pears to a plate and keep warm. Stir the heavy cream into the pan. Cook until nicely thickened. Return the pears to the pan and coat with the sauce.

Spoon some of the sauce onto a dessert plate. Place a pear half on top, cut side down. Make slices in the pear almost all the way to the stem end. Press gently to fan out. Cover with more of the sauce. Garnish the plate with a fresh mint sprig, if desired.

BANANA FLOAT

MAKES 6
PREPARATION TIME 5 MINUTES

Mash the bananas not more than 15 minutes before serving or they will turn dark. Garnish either with fresh raspberries, strawberries, or blueberries as available.

1 1/2 cups freshly squeezed
    orange juice
3 teaspoons fresh lemon juice
Sugar
2 ripe bananas

Almond extract
1/2 teaspoon vanilla
1/2 cup powdered sugar
1 1/2 cups heavy cream,
    whipped

Squeeze the juice from about 3 oranges to get 1 1/2 cups of juice. Pour into each of 6 sherbet glasses or wineglasses, 1/4 cup of the orange juice, 1/2 teaspoon of lemon juice, and sugar to taste. Stir until the sugar dissolves.

    In a bowl, mash the bananas. Add a dash of almond extract, the vanilla, and powdered sugar. Fold in the whipped cream. Spoon into the glasses. Garnish with fresh berries, if desired.

CRÊPES FILLED WITH LEMON SOUFFLÉ

SERVES 6 TO 8
PREPARATION TIME 1 HOUR 35 MINUTES
COOKING TIME 15 MINUTES

DESSERT CRÊPES
2 eggs
3/4 cup milk
1 tablespoon brandy
1/2 cup plus 1 tablespoon flour

1 tablespoon sugar
1 tablespoon unsalted butter,
    melted
Pinch of salt

In a food processor or blender, combine the eggs, milk, and brandy. Add the flour, sugar, butter, and pinch of salt and mix until blended. Allow the batter to stand for at least 40 minutes.

    Heat a crêpe pan. Grease with a little butter. Ladle in some of the batter. Cook over moderate heat until the bottom begins to brown and the top is dry. Turn over and brown the other side. Continue with the rest of the batter. Stack the cooked crêpes and cover. The crêpes may be refrigerated or frozen. This recipe makes about 12 to 14 dessert crêpes.

LEMON SOUFFLÉ FILLING

4 tablespoons (¹/₂ stick) butter	Grated rind and juice of 3
²/₃ cup sugar	lemons
Pinch of salt	5 eggs, separated
3 tablespoons cornstarch mixed with 1 ¹/₂ cups cold water	Sugar

Preheat oven to 400 degrees. In a saucepan, melt the butter. Add the sugar, salt, cornstarch mixture, and lemon rind and juice. Stir and bring to a boil. Cook, stirring constantly, until thickened. Remove from the heat and whisk in the egg yolks. Cook over low heat for 2 minutes. Let cool.

Beat the egg whites until firm. Fold the cooled lemon mixture into the beaten egg whites.

Generously butter a large casserole. Fill ¹/₂ of each crêpe with a large spoonful of the soufflé mixture and fold the other half over. Place in the casserole. Sprinkle with sugar. Bake for 15 minutes or until puffed and brown. Serve immediately, accompanied by a fresh raspberry sauce, if desired.

CHURROS

MAKES 2 DOZEN
PREPARATION TIME 30 MINUTES
COOKING TIME 15 MINUTES

A favorite Spanish sweet.

1 ¹/₄ cups water	1 cup flour
2 tablespoons unsalted butter	2 eggs
1 tablespoon sugar	Oil for frying
¹/₄ teaspoon salt	Powdered sugar

In a saucepan, combine the water, butter, sugar, and salt. Bring to a boil. Remove from the heat and add flour, all at once. Beat briskly with a wooden spoon until the mixture pulls away from the sides of the pan and is smooth. Stir in the eggs, one at a time, beating well after each addition.

Pour oil into a large skillet to a depth of 2 inches; heat to about 400 degrees on a thermometer. Spoon the batter into a pastry tube, funnel, or cookie press. Pipe the batter into the oil in strips 3 inches long. Fry until golden brown, turning once, about 3 to 4 minutes. Drain well on paper towels. Sprinkle with powdered sugar. Serve immediately.

MARIN DELUXE LEMON BARS

MAKES 24
PREPARATION TIME 15 MINUTES
COOKING TIME 45 MINUTES

PASTRY

1/2 cup powdered sugar
8 ounces (2 sticks) unsalted
  butter

2 cups flour
1/4 teaspoon salt

Preheat the oven to 350 degrees. Cream the butter and sugar until light and fluffy. Stir in the flour and salt. Mix well. Press the mixture into an ungreased 13 × 9-inch baking dish. Bake for 15 to 20 minutes or until light golden brown. Remove from oven and let cool slightly.

FILLING

4 eggs, beaten
2 cups sugar
1/4 cup fresh lemon juice

1/4 cup flour
1 teaspoon grated lemon rind
1/2 teaspoon baking powder

Blend all of the ingredients and pour over the baked crust. Bake for 25 minutes. Let cool. Sift additional powdered sugar over the top. Cut into squares.

MARBLED BROWNIES

MAKES 24
PREPARATION TIME 15 MINUTES
COOKING TIME 35 MINUTES

CHOCOLATE MIXTURE

1/2 cup flour
1/2 teaspoon baking powder
1/4 teaspoon salt
4 ounces semisweet chocolate
3 tablespoons unsalted butter

2 eggs
3/4 cup sugar
1 teaspoon vanilla
3/4 cup coarsely chopped
  walnuts

Butter a 9-inch square pan. Sift together the flour, baking powder, and salt. Set aside. Melt the chocolate with the butter. Remove from heat and let cool slightly.

Beat the eggs until foamy. Add the sugar and vanilla. Continue beating until light lemon-colored. Beat in the chocolate mixture and then the dry ingredients; mix well. Set aside 3/4 cup of the mixture. To the remainder, stir in 1/2 cup of the nuts. Spread this mixture into the prepared pan.

CHEESE MIXTURE

4 ounces cream cheese
2 tablespoons unsalted butter
1/2 teaspoon vanilla

1/4 cup sugar
1 egg

Preheat oven to 350 degrees. Beat the cream cheese with the butter until smooth. Add the vanilla and sugar and beat until fluffy. Beat in the egg. Spread cheese mixture over the chocolate layer. Place heaping tablespoons of the reserved 3/4 cup chocolate mixture over the cheese, forming 8 or 9 mounds. With a small spatula or knife, cut through the mounds in a zigzag layer, going almost but not quite through to the bottom. Sprinkle with the remaining 1/4 cup nuts. Bake for 35 minutes. Let stand at room temperature for a few hours before cutting.

CRÈME DE MENTHE BARS

MAKES 24
PREPARATION TIME 20 MINUTES
COOKING TIME 5 MINUTES
REFRIGERATION TIME 24 HOURS

10 ounces (2 1/2 sticks) unsalted butter
1/2 cup cocoa
3 1/2 cups sifted powdered sugar
1 egg, beaten

1 teaspoon vanilla
2 cups graham cracker crumbs
1/4 cup crème de menthe
1 1/2 cups semisweet chocolate chips

In a saucepan, combine 4 oz. of the butter and the cocoa. Heat and stir until smooth. Remove from the heat and add 1/2 cup of the powdered sugar, egg, and vanilla. Stir in the graham cracker crumbs. Press into an ungreased 13 × 9-inch pan.

Melt 4 oz. of the butter with the crème de menthe. With a mixer, whip in the remaining 3 cups of powdered sugar until smooth. Spread evenly over the graham cracker crust. Chill for 1 hour.

In a saucepan, melt the remaining 2 oz. of the butter and the chocolate chips. Spread over the other layers. Refrigerate for 24 hours. Allow to stand at room temperature for 10 minutes before slicing. Cut into squares.

KILLER CUPCAKES

MAKES 20 TO 22
PREPARATION TIME 15 MINUTES
COOKING TIME 30 MINUTES

Loved by all children from ages four to forty-four. The moist, fudgy cupcake holds a creamy cheesecake surprise.

CUPCAKES

4 ounces semisweet chocolate	4 eggs
1 teaspoon vanilla	1 1/2 cups sugar
8 ounces (2 sticks) butter	1 cup flour

Preheat the oven to 350 degrees. Fill 20 to 22 cupcake tins with liners. Melt together the chocolate, vanilla, and butter. Beat the eggs until thick and add the sugar. Beat in the flour. Fold in the butter-chocolate mixture. Spoon into the prepared tins, filling 2/3 full.

FILLING

8 ounces cream cheese, softened	Dash of salt
1/4 cup sugar	3/4 cup semisweet chocolate chips
1 egg, beaten	

Mix cream cheese, sugar, egg, and salt until just blended. Stir in the chocolate chips. Drop a rounded teaspoon of filling onto the top of each cupcake. Bake for 30 minutes.

APRICOT SWIRLS

MAKES 4 DOZEN
PREPARATION TIME 40 MINUTES
REFRIGERATION TIME 2 HOURS
COOKING TIME 20 MINUTES

SOUR CREAM PASTRY

8 ounces (2 sticks) unsalted butter	1 beaten egg yolk
2 cups sifted flour	1/2 cup sour cream

FILLING

3/4 cup apricot preserves

1/2 cup flaked coconut

1/4 cup finely chopped pecans

Sugar

Cut the butter into the flour until the mixture resembles fine crumbs. Combine the egg yolk and sour cream. Blend into the flour mixture and shape into a ball. Cover and refrigerate for several hours.

Preheat the oven to 350 degrees. Divide the dough into 4 equal portions. On a lightly floured surface, roll out each portion into a 10-inch circle. Spread each circle with 3 tablespoons of the preserves, 2 tablespoons of the coconut, and 1 tablespoon of the pecans. Cut each circle into 12 wedges. Roll each wedge into a crescent shape. Sprinkle with a little sugar. Place on ungreased cookie sheets. Bake for 20 minutes, or until lightly browned. If desired, sift powdered sugar on top of the cookies just prior to serving.

RASPBERRY DREAM JAM COOKIES

MAKES 2 DOZEN
PREPARATION TIME 1 HOUR
REFRIGERATION TIME 2 HOURS
COOKING TIME 15 MINUTES

1 1/2 cups flour

1 cup powdered sugar

1/4 teaspoon baking powder

1/4 teaspoon salt

5 1/2 ounces blanched, coarsely chopped almonds or hazelnuts

4 ounces (1 stick) unsalted butter, softened

1 egg

2 tablespoons heavy cream

1 teaspoon vanilla

Raspberry jam

Mix together the flour, powdered sugar, baking powder, and salt. Stir in the chopped nuts. Beat the butter with the egg, heavy cream, and vanilla. Add to the dry ingredients and mix until blended. Gather into a ball. Wrap and chill the dough for several hours.

Preheat oven to 350 degrees. Divide the dough in half. Roll out each piece to a thickness of 1/8 of an inch. Cut out 2-inch rounds with a cookie cutter. Cut a 1-inch hole in the center of half of the rounds. Bake for 12 to 15 minutes or until lightly browned. Cool completely on a wire rack. Spread a teaspoon of jam on the rounds without the cut-out centers. Sandwich the cut-out round on top. Place a little more filling in the hole, if necessary. If desired, sift powdered sugar on top just prior to serving.

BITTERSWEET CHOCOLATE CHUNK COOKIES

MAKES 4 DOZEN
PREPARATION TIME 15 MINUTES
COOKING TIME 10 MINUTES

Crunchy on the outside but delightfully chewy on the inside.

2 1/4 cups flour
1 teaspoon baking soda
1/4 teaspoon salt
1/4 teaspoon ground cinnamon
6 ounces (1 1/2 sticks) unsalted butter, room temperature
1/4 cup vegetable shortening
1 1/4 cups sugar

2 eggs
2 1/2 teaspoons vanilla
4 ounces bittersweet chocolate, melted and cooled
12 ounces bittersweet chocolate, chopped into 1/2-inch chunks
1 cup chopped pecans

Preheat oven to 375 degrees. Mix together the flour, baking soda, salt, and cinnamon. With an electric mixer, cream the butter and shortening until light. Beat in the sugar, 1/4 cup at a time. Beat in the eggs, one at a time. Stir in the vanilla and melted chocolate. Add the flour mixture, one third at a time, stirring until just blended. Fold in the chocolate chunks and pecans.

Drop rounded tablespoons of the dough, two inches apart, onto greased cookie sheets. Bake for 10 to 12 minutes or until firm to the touch. Cool for a few minutes on the cookie sheets. Transfer to a wire rack and cool completely.

PISTACHIO LACE COOKIES

MAKES 3 DOZEN
PREPARATION TIME 40 MINUTES
COOKING TIME 3 TO 5 MINUTES

Be creative in shaping these cookies; curl them around the end of a wooden spoon or form into cones.

1 cup shelled pistachios
4 ounces (1 stick) plus 1 tablespoon unsalted butter
2/3 cup packed brown sugar
1/3 cup light corn syrup

2 tablespoons orange-flavored liqueur
2 teaspoons grated orange rind
1 cup flour

Preheat oven to 375 degrees. If the nuts are salted, place in a sieve and rinse under cold running water. Pat dry with paper towels. Coarsely chop the nuts. Heat 1 tablespoon of the butter in a small skillet. Add the nuts and sauté, stirring constantly, until lightly browned. Drain on paper towels.

In a saucepan, combine the remaining butter, brown sugar, corn syrup, liqueur, and orange rind. Bring to a boil, stirring constantly. Remove from the heat and gradually beat in the flour. Stir in the nuts.

Drop the dough by teaspoonfuls on lightly buttered cookie sheets, leaving a lot of space between each. Bake for about 3 to 5 minutes or until the cookies spread to 3 to 4 inches and are golden brown. Cool on the sheets for 3 to 5 minutes. Transfer to a wire rack with a spatula.

CHOCOLATE WALNUT DROPS

MAKES 16 TO 20
PREPARATION TIME 30 MINUTES
REFRIGERATION TIME 1 HOUR
COOKING TIME 10 MINUTES

Almost a confection.

3 ounces semisweet chocolate
1 ounce unsweetened chocolate
1 tablespoon unsalted butter
1 egg
1/3 cup packed dark brown
   sugar
1 tablespoon water

1 teaspoon vanilla
2 tablespoons sifted flour
1/8 teaspoon baking powder
6 ounces semisweet chocolate
   chips
1 cup coarsely chopped walnuts

Melt the chocolates with the butter. Transfer to a bowl and let cool slightly. Add the egg, brown sugar, water, and vanilla; mix well. Stir in the flour and baking powder. Add the chocolate chips and walnuts. The dough will be sticky. Cover and refrigerate until firm, about 1 hour.

Preheat oven to 350 degrees. Shape the dough into 1-inch balls. Place on cookie sheets one inch apart. Bake until cookies are slightly firm to the touch, about 10 to 12 minutes. Let cool completely before removing from the cookie sheets. Store in a tightly covered container.

SESAME CRUNCH BUTTER COOKIES

MAKES 5 TO 6 DOZEN
PREPARATION TIME 15 MINUTES
REFRIGERATION TIME 1 HOUR
COOKING TIME 30 MINUTES

These sweet, buttery treats melt in your mouth.

1 pound (4 sticks) unsalted
    butter, room temperature
1 1/2 cups sugar
3 cups flour

1 cup sesame seeds
2 cups flaked coconut
3/4 cup finely chopped pecans

Cream the butter. Gradually add the sugar and continue beating until light and fluffy. Add the flour and mix until just combined. Stir in the sesame seeds, coconut, and pecans. Stir just until blended.

Divide the dough into fourths. Place one fourth on a long sheet of wax paper. Shape into a roll 1 1/2 inches in diameter. Repeat with the remaining dough. Wrap and refrigerate until firm, about 1 hour.

Preheat the oven to 300 degrees. Cut the rolls into 1/4-inch slices. Bake for 30 minutes or until lightly browned. Cool on wire racks.

CHOCOLATE-MINT ICE CREAM SANDWICHES

MAKES 10 SANDWICHES
PREPARATION TIME 20 MINUTES
REFRIGERATION TIME 1 HOUR
COOKING TIME 20 MINUTES
FREEZING TIME 3 HOURS

5 ounces semisweet chocolate
1/4 cup sugar
1/2 cup firmly packed light
    brown sugar
1 tablespoon cocoa powder
4 ounces (1 stick) unsalted
    butter, room temperature
1 egg

1 teaspoon vanilla
3/4 teaspoon peppermint
    extract
1 cup flour
1/2 teaspoon baking powder
Vanilla, chocolate, or chocolate
    chip ice cream, softened

Preheat oven to 375 degrees. In a food processor, combine the chocolate, sugars, and cocoa powder. Chop until the chocolate mixture is very fine, about 1 minute. Add the butter, egg, vanilla, and peppermint extract. Mix for 1 minute, scraping down the sides of the bowl once. Add the flour and baking powder to the bowl. Blend just until the flour is incorporated; do not over-process. Arrange the dough on a sheet of plastic wrap. Shape the dough into an 11-inch cylinder. Seal and refrigerate until firm, about 1 hour.

Preheat oven to 375 degrees. Cut the dough into 1/2-inch slices. Arrange on a baking sheet, 2 to 3 inches apart. Bake until the edges are lightly browned about 8 minutes. Let cool for 3 to 4 minutes. Transfer to a wire rack and cool completely. Spread some ice cream on one cookie. Cover with another cookie. Press together gently. Wrap in plastic wrap and freeze until firm.

CINNAMON SUGAR COOKIES

MAKES 3 DOZEN
PREPARATION TIME 20 MINUTES
COOKING TIME 10 MINUTES

The best cinnamon cookie we have ever tasted.

4 ounces (1 stick) unsalted
  butter
1 cup sugar
1 beaten egg
1 teaspoon vanilla
1 1/4 cups flour
2 teaspoons cinnamon

1 teaspoon baking powder
1/4 teaspoon salt
1/2 cup chopped walnuts or
  pecans
1/4 to 1/2 cup sugar for rolling
  cookies

Preheat oven to 375 degrees. Cream the butter with the 1 cup of sugar. Add the egg and vanilla; mix well. Sift together the flour, cinnamon, baking powder, and salt. Stir in the nuts and mix well. Stir into the butter mixture. Roll the dough into 1-inch balls. Roll in the remaining sugar. Flatten slightly with the bottom of a glass. Bake on ungreased cookie sheets for 10 to 12 minutes. Cool on wire racks. Store in tins.

CHOCOLATE MADELEINES

MAKES 18 TO 20 COOKIES
PREPARATION TIME 10 MINUTES
COOKING TIME 10 MINUTES

Butter for molds
2 ounces semisweet chocolate
4 ounces (1 stick) unsalted
   butter
2 eggs
4 tablespoons sugar
1 teaspoon vanilla

1 teaspoon hot water
1/2 teaspoon brandy
1/2 cup cake flour
2 teaspoons cocoa
1/2 teaspoon baking powder
Powdered sugar

Preheat oven to 325 degrees. Brush madeleine molds with the butter. Melt the chocolate with the butter. Beat the eggs with the sugar until thick. Beat in the chocolate mixture, vanilla, hot water, and brandy. Add the flour, cocoa, and baking powder. Mix just until the flour mixture disappears. Spoon the batter into the prepared molds, filling 2/3 full. Bake for 10 to 12 minutes or until a tester inserted in the center is clean. Loosen the madeleines and invert the pan over a cake rack. Cool to room temperature. Dust with powdered sugar before serving.

COCONUT GARDEN COOKIES

MAKES 3 DOZEN
PREPARATION TIME 15 MINUTES
REFRIGERATION TIME 1 HOUR
COOKING TIME 20 MINUTES

8 ounces (2 sticks) unsalted
   butter
1 cup sugar

2 cups flour
1 teaspoon salt
1 1/2 cups coconut

Preheat oven to 300 degrees. Cream the butter with the sugar. Sift together the flour and salt. Stir in the coconut. Mix into the butter mixture; blend well. Shape into rolls and wrap in wax paper. Refrigerate until firm. Cut into 1/4-inch slices. Bake for 20 minutes or until lightly browned.

APRICOT SQUARES

MAKES 24
PREPARATION TIME 30 MINUTES
COOKING TIME 40 MINUTES

3 ounces (3/4 stick) unsalted
  butter
1/2 cup sugar
Grated rind of 2 small lemons
2 egg yolks
1 cup sifted flour

1/2 teaspoon salt
1/4 teaspoon baking soda
1 cup strained apricot jam
2 egg whites
1/4 cup sugar
1/2 cup chopped nuts

Preheat oven to 350 degrees. Cream the butter, sugar, and lemon rind together. Beat in the yolks, one at a time, beating well after each addition. Sift the flour with the salt and baking soda. Stir into the egg-yolk mixture. Spread into a greased 9 × 13-inch baking pan. Cover with the jam. Beat the egg whites until soft. Add the sugar, one tablespoon at a time, and continue beating until stiff. Fold in the nuts. Spread evenly over the apricot jam. Bake for 40 minutes. Cool and cut into squares.

COCONUT-MACADAMIA TORTONI

MAKES 12
PREPARATION TIME 15 MINUTES
FREEZING TIME 3 HOURS

1 cup heavy cream
1/3 cup powdered sugar
1 tablespoon Curaçao
1 teaspoon vanilla

1 egg white
1 cup coconut
2/3 cup chopped macadamia
  nuts

Place cupcake liners in 12 cupcake tins. Whip the heavy cream with the powdered sugar, Curaçao, and vanilla until firm. Beat the egg white until firm. Fold the egg white into the cream along with the coconut and 1/3 cup of the macadamia nuts. Spoon into the cupcake liners. Sprinkle with the remaining nuts. Freeze until firm, about 3 hours.

GRAND MARNIER CREAM

SERVES 6
PREPARATION TIME 20 MINUTES
COOKING TIME 10 MINUTES
FREEZING TIME 2 HOURS

Softer than a conventional ice cream, this is particularly delicious served with fresh berries.

6 eggs	**Finely grated rind of 2 oranges**
1/3 cup water	**1/4 cup Grand Marnier**
1 cup sugar	**2 cups heavy cream**

Beat the eggs until thick. In a saucepan, combine the water, sugar, and orange rind. Cook, stirring constantly, until the sugar dissolves. Let boil, without stirring, until the mixture reaches 220 degrees on a candy thermometer. Pour the hot syrup into the eggs, beating constantly until the mixture cools. Stir in the Grand Marnier.

Whip the heavy cream until just slightly thickened. Fold into the egg mixture. Pour into an ice cream machine and process until firm. Freeze for at least 2 hours.

SORBET

SERVES 6
PREPARATION TIME 15 MINUTES
COOKING TIME 5 MINUTES
FREEZING TIME 2 HOURS

SUGAR SYRUP
2 1/2 cups sugar
2 cups water

In a saucepan, combine the sugar and water. Stir until sugar dissolves. Bring to a boil. Allow to boil for 1 minute. Remove from the heat and cool. The syrup can be kept in a covered jar in the refrigerator for up to 1 month.

STRAWBERRY SORBET
1 1/2 cups sugar syrup
3 1/4 cups strained strawberry
  purée
Lemon juice to taste

Mix the cold Sugar Syrup with the purée and lemon juice. Pour into an ice cream machine and process until frozen.

BLACKBERRY, RASPBERRY, OLALLIEBERRY, OR BLUEBERRY SORBET
1 2/3 cups sugar syrup
3 cups strained fruit purée

Mix the cold Sugar Syrup with the strained fruit purée. Pour into an ice cream machine and process until frozen.

PEACH, APRICOT OR NECTARINE SORBET
1 2/3 cups sugar syrup
2 1/2 cups unpeeled and
   strained fruit purée
Lemon juice to taste

Mix the cold Sugar Syrup with the strained fruit purée and lemon juice. Pour into an ice cream machine and process until frozen.

PEAR SORBET
1 1/2 cups sugar syrup
2 cups peeled and seeded
   pear purée

Mix the cold Sugar Syrup with the pear purée. Pour into an ice cream machine and process until frozen.

BLACK WALNUT ICE CREAM

SERVES 6 TO 8
PREPARATION TIME 15 MINUTES
COOKING TIME 5 MINUTES
FREEZING TIME 2 HOURS

3 cups heavy cream
1 tablespoon vanilla
Pinch of salt

8 egg yolks
1/2 cup honey
5 ounces shelled black walnuts

Bring the cream to a boil. Stir in the vanilla and salt. Beat the egg yolks with the honey until light and fluffy. Beat the hot cream into the yolks and continue beating until cooled. Stir in the walnuts. Pour into an ice cream machine and process until frozen.

IRRESISTIBLE GELATO

SERVES 6 TO 8
PREPARATION TIME 15 MINUTES
COOKING TIME 10 MINUTES
FREEZING TIME 2 HOURS

6 ounces semisweet chocolate
1/2 cup water
2 tablespoons instant espresso
   coffee
1/4 cup Grand Marnier

5 egg yolks
1/2 cup sugar
1/4 cup water
3 cups heavy cream

In a saucepan, melt the chocolate, water, and instant coffee. Stir in the Grand Marnier and set aside to cool. Beat the egg yolks until thick and cream-colored. In a saucepan, combine the sugar and water. Cook, stirring until the sugar dissolves. Let boil, without stirring, until the mixture reaches 230 degrees on a candy thermometer. Slowly, whisk the hot syrup into the egg yolks and beat until cool, about 5 minutes. Add the chocolate mixture to the egg yolks, beating until just blended. Whip the heavy cream just until slightly thickened. Fold the chocolate mixture into the cream. Pour into an ice cream machine and process until frozen.

ZABAGLIONE WITH CHAMPAGNE

SERVES 6 TO 8
PREPARATION TIME 5 MINUTES
COOKING TIME 8 MINUTES

4 egg yolks, room temperature
2/3 cup champagne
4 tablespoons sugar

2 baskets fresh strawberries,
   washed and stemmed

Place the egg yolks, champagne, and sugar in the top of a double boiler set over simmering water. Whisk over low heat until the sauce is thick and smooth, about 8 to 10 minutes. Do not overheat or the zabaglione will curdle. Remove from the heat. Place the strawberries in sorbet glasses. Spoon the warm sauce over the berries. Serve immediately.

NECTARINES WITH ORANGE
ZABAGLIONE SAUCE

SERVES 4
PREPARATION TIME 5 MINUTES
COOKING TIME 5 MINUTES

This sauce is also good cold.

2 medium nectarines or   2 tablespoons sugar
  peaches   1/3 cup orange juice
4 egg yolks   1/2 teaspoon vanilla

Slice the fruit into four dishes. Combine the yolks, sugar, orange juice, and vanilla in a saucepan. Cook over low heat, whisking constantly, for 5 minutes, or until thick. Do not boil. Remove from heat and continue beating for 2 to 3 minutes. Spoon over the fruit. Serve immediately.

HOT MOCHA SAUCE

MAKES 1 CUP
PREPARATION TIME 5 MINUTES
COOKING TIME 15 MINUTES

This sauce can be stored in a covered jar in the refrigerator.

3 tablespoons unsalted butter   1/4 cup light corn syrup
3 ounces unsweetened   1 cup sugar
  chocolate   Pinch of salt
1/2 cup strong coffee   1 teaspoon vanilla

In a saucepan, melt the butter and chocolate. Stir in the coffee, corn syrup, sugar, and salt. Bring the mixture to a boil. Boil the sauce gently, without stirring, until thick and smooth, about 10 minutes. Stir in the vanilla. Serve hot.

BITTERSWEET FUDGE SAUCE

MAKES 2 CUPS
PREPARATION TIME 5 MINUTES
COOKING TIME 5 MINUTES

An intense bittersweet sauce that thickens over ice cream.

1 cup Dutch cocoa
3/4 cup sugar
1/2 cup brown sugar
Pinch of salt

3/4 cup heavy cream
4 ounces (1 stick) unsalted
  butter
1 teaspoon vanilla

In a heavy saucepan, stir cocoa, sugars, and salt until blended. Mix in the cream and butter. Heat, stirring constantly, to boiling. Let stand for 5 minutes. Stir in the vanilla. Serve warm over ice cream.

BLUEBERRY SAUCE

MAKES 2 1/2 CUPS
PREPARATION TIME 5 MINUTES
COOKING TIME 15 MINUTES

Serve this sauce warm or cold.

3 cups blueberries
2/3 cup sugar

1/2 cup water
1/4 cup lemon juice

In a saucepan, combine all of the ingredients. Bring to a boil over moderate heat. Lower heat, cover, and simmer for 5 minutes. Purée the mixture and strain back into the pan. Bring to a boil over moderate heat. Simmer, uncovered, until reduced to 2 1/2 cups, about 10 minutes. Transfer to a serving bowl.

FRESH FRUIT SAUCE

MAKES 2 1/2 CUPS
PREPARATION TIME 5 MINUTES

This sauce can be made with any fruit you like. Some fruits, such as peaches and pears, have to be peeled and seeded.

1 pound fresh fruit
1 1/2 cups sugar

Place the fruit and sugar in a blender or food processor. Blend until well combined and smooth. The sauce can be stored in a tightly closed container in the refrigerator, for up to one week.

CRÈME ANGLAISE

MAKES 2 CUPS
PREPARATION TIME 5 MINUTES
COOKING TIME 5 MINUTES

A sauce well-suited to cake and fresh fruit desserts.

1 1/2 cups milk   **1/2 cup sugar**
4 egg yolks   **1 teaspoon vanilla**

In a saucepan, heat the milk almost to a boil. Let cool slightly. In a bowl, combine the yolks, sugar, and vanilla. Beat with a whisk until thick and pale. Add the yolk mixture to the warm milk. Cook on medium-low heat, stirring constantly, until the mixture coats a wooden spoon. Do not overcook. Strain through a fine sieve into a bowl. Refrigerate until ready to serve.

RASPBERRY SAUCE

MAKES 1 CUP
PREPARATION TIME 5 MINUTES
COOKING TIME 5 MINUTES

1 box frozen raspberries,
  defrosted
1 teaspoon cornstarch

2 tablespoons cold water
Juice of 1/2 lemon
2 tablespoons kirsch (optional)

Purée the raspberries and strain into a saucepan. Mix the cornstarch with the water. Stir into the purée. Cook over low heat until thickened slightly. Add the lemon juice and kirsch, if desired. Serve hot.

SWEET BRIE

SERVES 8 TO 10
PREPARATION TIME 5 MINUTES
COOKING TIME 4 MINUTES

An 8-inch round of Brie
1 cup chopped pecans
2 cups firmly packed brown
  sugar
Crackers

Preheat the broiler. Remove the top rind from the Brie. Place the Brie in a 10-inch baking dish. Sprinkle with the nuts. Cover the top and sides with the sugar, patting gently. Broil on the lowest oven rack until the sugar bubbles and melts, about 3 to 4 minutes. Serve immediately with the crackers.

APPENDIX

Menus

The recipe for each item marked with a dagger in the
menus that follow can be found in the Index.

BRUNCH

Super Bowl Brunch

† Candied walnuts
† Layered Mexican delight
† Mango chutney mold
† Aram sandwiches
† Spinach sausage frittata
† Orange-laced cauliflower salad
† Pumpkin applesauce bread
† Crème de menthe bars

May Day Brunch

  Sam's gin fizz
† Asparagus torte
† Eleven-layer salad
  Sliced cold ham
  Bowl of fresh fruit
† Banana lemon muffins
† Strawberry pecan bread

New Year's Day Brunch

  Irish coffee
† Canadian bacon puff
† Caprice spinach salad
† Poppy seed cake
† Berry crunchy oatmeal muffins
  Fruit and cheese board

LUNCHEON

Summer Tennis Luncheon

Fruited iced tea
† Insalata di mare
† Canlis' romaine salad
† Italian Parmesan batter rolls
† Sonoma melba torte

Fall Bridge Luncheon

† Autumn root soup
† Caraway cheese sticks
† Smoked turkey, apple, and walnut
  salad
† Lemon bars

Winter Birthday Luncheon

Fumé blanc
† Parmesan twists
† Szechuan sausage in pita pockets
† Tossed green salad with orange
  thyme vinaigrette
† Almond apricot roll

Spring Baby Shower

† Cream of asparagus soup
† Sandwich Niçoise
† Fire and ice tomatoes
† Coconut almond tart

DINNER

Winter Gala Buffet

† Parmesan cheese puff rounds
† Pâté de campagne
† Caviar soufflé roll
† Brie en croute
† Whole filet of beef and horseradish
† Fruity wild rice
† Spinach chutney salad
† Sweet onion and mustard bread
† Pistachio lace cookies
† Chocolate madeleines
† Chocolate walnut drops

Year of the Dragon Party

† Won tons
† Baked spring rolls
† Hot and sour soup
† Prawns in hot garlic sauce
† Kung Po chicken
† Snow peas and almonds
† Oriental rice
† Coconut garden cookies
  Sliced apples and oranges

Summer Cocktail Buffet

† Zucchini madeleines
† Open-faced biscuits
† Artichoke leaves with shrimp
† Chutneyed chicken liver pâté
† Vitello tonnato
† Poached salmon with raspberry
  beurre blanc
† Fruity wild rice
† Glazed berry tarts
† Apricot swirls
† Bittersweet chocolate chunk cookies

Black Tie Dinner Party

† Duck liver pâté with pistachios
† Three cheeses in puff pastry
† Pasta roll with tomato cream sauce
† Mustard shallot snapper
† Individual asparagus soufflés
† Tossed green salad with herbed
  vinaigrette
† Grand Marnier soufflé

Columbus Day Dinner

† Tapenade
† Rotolo al forno
† Fettucine capriccio
† Lemony veal piccata
† Genoa-style spinach
† Focaccio
† Frozen delight with chocolate sauce

Memorial Day Grill

† Spiced melon balls
† Parmesan pesto dip
† Grilled Bodega Bay oysters
† Mesquite-grilled pork tenderloin with
   plum sauce
† Green beans with pecans
† Three-way stuffed onions
† Peach blueberry tart

Cinco de Mayo Fiesta

† Quesadillas
† Tortilla soup
† Enchiladas and tomatillo sauce
† Orange and jícama salad
† Churros

December Holiday Dinner

† Caviar élégant
† Cream of chestnut soup
† Lamb in phyllo with Madeira sauce
† Garden fresh peas with toasted pine
   nuts
† Carrot purée
† Chocolate roll and fudge sauce

Moroccan Ali Baba Night Party

† Curried mushroom turnovers
† Stuffed Japanese eggplant
† Persian lamb
† Couscous
   Steamed vegetable platter
   Toasted pita bread
† Orange caramel custard

Teen Swim Party

† Spinach dip
† Potato skins
† Barbecued burritos
   Tossed green salad
† Killer cupcakes

INDEX

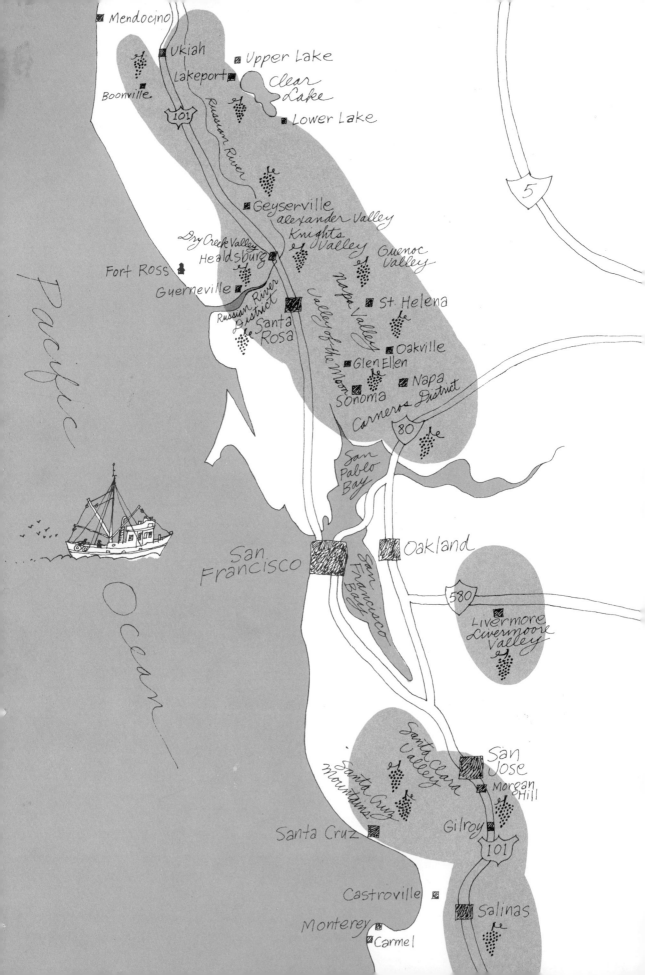